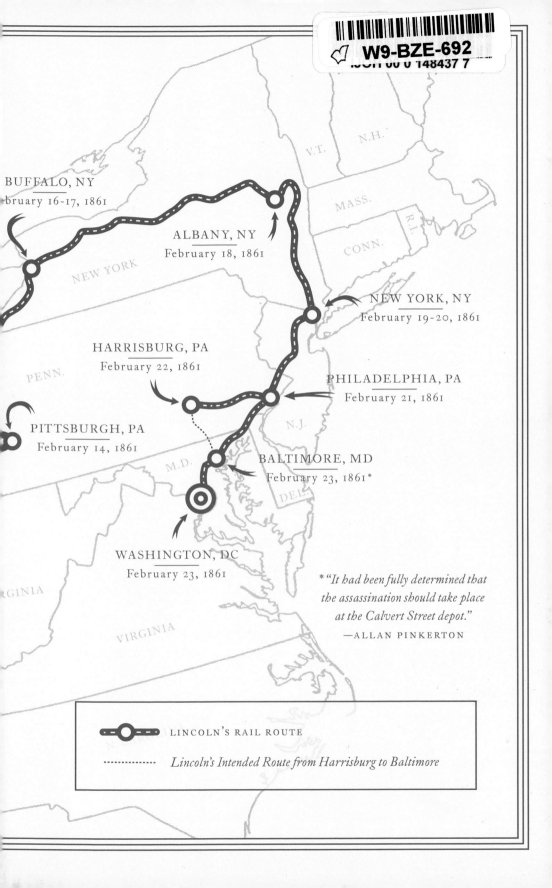

BUFFALO, NY
February 16-17, 1861

ALBANY, NY
February 18, 1861

NEW YORK, NY
February 19-20, 1861

HARRISBURG, PA
February 22, 1861

PHILADELPHIA, PA
February 21, 1861

PITTSBURGH, PA
February 14, 1861

BALTIMORE, MD
February 23, 1861*

WASHINGTON, DC
February 23, 1861

*"It had been fully determined that
the assassination should take place
at the Calvert Street depot."
—ALLAN PINKERTON

LINCOLN'S RAIL ROUTE

Lincoln's Intended Route from Harrisburg to Baltimore

THE HOUR OF PERIL

THE HOUR
OF PERIL

·

THE SECRET PLOT
TO MURDER LINCOLN
BEFORE THE CIVIL WAR

·

DANIEL STASHOWER

·

MINOTAUR BOOKS
NEW YORK

www.minotaurbooks.com

Library of Congress Cataloging-in-Publication Data

Stashower, Daniel.
    The hour of peril : the secret plot to murder Lincoln before the
Civil War / Daniel Stashower.—1st edition.
        p. cm.
    Includes bibliographical references.
    ISBN 978-0-312-60022-8 (hardcover)
    ISBN 978-1-250-02332-2 (e-book)
    1. Lincoln, Abraham, 1809–1865—Assassination attempt, 1861.
2. Presidents—Assassination attempts—United States.   3. Baltimore
(Md.)—History—Civil War, 1861–1865.   I. Title.
    E457.4.S85 2013
    973.7092—dc23

                                                            2012042103

First Edition: February 2013

10 9 8 7 6 5 4 3 2 1

For Sam and Jack,
Rebellious Sons of Maryland

CONTENTS

Author's Note   ix
Introduction: Long, Narrow Boxes   1

PART ONE: THE COOPER AND THE RAIL-SPLITTER   7
Prologue: His Hour Had Not Yet Come   9
  1. The Apprentice   17
  2. How I Became a Detective   25
  3. Ardent Spirits   37
  4. Pink Lady   47
  5. Let Us Dare to Do Our Duty   59
  6. It's Coming Yet   69

PART TWO: PLUMS AND NUTS   77
  7. A Pig-Tail Whistle   79
  8. Mobtown   95
  9. Suspicions of Danger   107
 10. Hostile Organizations   119
 11. The Man and the Hour   133
 12. If I Alone Must Do It   145
 13. A Postponed Rebellion   159
 14. A Rabid Rebel   169
 15. A Single Red Ballot   181
 16. Whitewash   195
 17. The Music Agent   211
 18. A Few Determined Men   221

19. An Assault of Some Kind 233
20. The Assassin's Knife 243

PART THREE: THE MARTYR AND THE SCAPEGOAT 257
21. The Flight of Abraham 259
22. The Hour of Peril 269
23. Some Very Tall Swearing 285
Epilogue: An Infamous Lie 303

Acknowledgments 333
Select Bibliography 335
Index 341

AUTHOR'S NOTE

In the following pages, I have standardized some of the eccentric spellings and capitalizations found in the source materials, and replaced the initials and code names used in Allan Pinkerton's records with the real names, when known, of the operatives concerned. Also, in that more genteel time, Pinkerton's operatives refrained from using profanity, employing discreet elliptical devices to obscure offending phrases. Recognizing that at least some contemporary readers will be familiar with these phrases and may find the device distracting, I have restored the original intent.

In the hour of the nation's peril, he conducted Abraham Lincoln safely through the ranks of treason to the scene of his first inauguration as President.

—Inscription on the grave of Allan Pinkerton

•

It is perfectly manifest that there was no conspiracy—no conspiracy of a hundred, of fifty, of twenty, of three; no definite purpose in the heart of even one man to murder Mr. Lincoln in Baltimore.

—WARD H. LAMON, *Lincoln's friend and self-appointed bodyguard*

INTRODUCTION
LONG, NARROW BOXES

•

"THIS TRIP OF OURS has been very laborious and exciting," the young poet wrote to a friend back home in Illinois. "I have had no time to think calmly since we left Springfield. There is one reason why I write tonight. Tomorrow we enter slave territory. Saturday evening, according to our arrangements, we will be in Washington. There may be trouble in Baltimore. If so, we will not go to Washington, unless in long, narrow boxes. The telegram will inform you of the result, long before this letter reaches you."

Twenty-two-year-old John Milton Hay had ample cause for worry as he set down these words in February 1861. He had signed on as a personal secretary to Abraham Lincoln just a few days earlier, on the eve of Lincoln's inauguration as president of

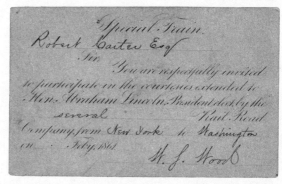

A special ticket issued for Abraham Lincoln's inaugural train. *Courtesy of the Alfred Whital Stern Collection, Rare Book and Special Collections Division, Library of Congress*

the United States. For several weeks, Lincoln had faced a mounting threat of assassination on his journey to the capital, culminating in a "clear and well-considered" murder plot to be carried out at a whistle-stop appearance in Baltimore. Over a period of thirteen days, as the president-elect traveled by train from Springfield to Washington, a makeshift, self-appointed security detail raced to uncover hard evidence of the looming peril, in the hope of persuading Lincoln to adopt "necessary and urgent measures" before placing himself in harm's way.

Leading the effort was the detective Allan Pinkerton, whose fame as a fierce and incorruptible lawman was sweeping through America's cities and out to the expanding edges of the frontier. Pinkerton and his agents were becoming legendary for their relentless, single-minded pursuit of lawbreakers, whose photographs were cataloged in a famous "rogue's gallery" at their Chicago headquarters. The dramatic Pinkerton logo—with the motto We Never Sleep coiled beneath the image of a stern, unblinking eye—became a potent emblem of vigilance, bringing the term *private eye* into the American lexicon.

In Baltimore, however, Pinkerton would be tested as never before. The detective had built his success on a slow, methodical style of investigation—"Our operations are necessarily tedious," he once declared—but the rapidly evolving situation in Baltimore required speed, improvisation, and no small measure of luck. Pinkerton, who had gone to the city to investigate a vague threat against railroad property and equipment, had not expected to uncover an assassination conspiracy. "From my reports you will see how accidentally I discovered the plot," he later admitted. "I was looking for nothing of the kind, and had certainly not the slightest idea of it." Once on the scent, however, he pursued it with feverish energy, and he soon became convinced that dramatic measures would be needed to spare the president-elect's life. By this time, however, the train had already left the station, in every sense of the phrase, as Lincoln made his slow, inexorable progress toward the capital, determined to make a public display of openness and goodwill in the days leading up to his inaugural. Pinkerton now found himself contending not only with the conspirators but also with the intractability of Lincoln and his advisers, who were reluctant to alter their careful plans—and invite public scorn—on the basis of vapory rumors. "All imagination," Lincoln declared at one stage. "What does anyone want to harm me for?"

The stakes were enormous. "Had Mr. Lincoln fallen at that time," wrote Pinkerton, "it is frightful to think what the consequences might have been." Lincoln's election three months earlier had thrown the country into crisis. By the time he set off for Washington, seven states had seceded from the Union. Lincoln hoped to "soothe the public mind" on his two-thousand-mile inaugural train journey, giving over a hundred speeches, in which he would offer calming words to the North and extend a hand of reconciliation to the South. Over half a million people flocked to see him at railroad depots and trackside watering stops, all of them anxious for a sign that the country would be safe in his hands. "The gradual disruption of the Union that dark winter lay like an agony of personal bereavement," wrote one well-wisher. "I longed to read in the face of our leader the indications of wisdom and strength that would compel the people to anchor in him and feel safe."

As the train rolled east, however, the warnings of danger grew more insistent. Newspapers throughout the South reported that a large cash bounty was on offer to "whomsoever" managed to assassinate Lincoln before he took office. There was also a real possibility that the state of Maryland, where Lincoln's train would cross below the Mason-Dixon line for the first time, would secede from the Union before he reached the border. If so, Washington would be entirely cut off from the North. As Maryland went, many believed, so went the nation.

In Baltimore, Pinkerton and his detectives were doggedly piecing together details of a "murderous compact" to be carried out at one of the city's train stations. "It had been fully determined that the assassination should take place at the Calvert Street depot," Pinkerton wrote. "When the train entered the depot, and Mr. Lincoln attempted to pass through the narrow passage leading to the streets, a party already delegated were to engage in a conflict on the outside, and then the policemen were to rush away to quell the disturbance. At this moment—the police being entirely withdrawn—Mr. Lincoln would find himself surrounded by a dense, excited and hostile crowd, all hustling and jamming against him, and then the fatal blow was to be struck." As the detective would explain to William Herndon, Lincoln's law partner turned biographer, the plot had been audaciously simple and efficient. "Excuse me for endeavoring to impress the plan upon you," he wrote. "It was a capital one, and much better conceived than the one which finally succeeded four years after in destroying Mr. Lincoln's life."

Others believed that an attack would be launched while Lincoln was still aboard his train, and that police and city officials were colluding in the plot. "Statesmen laid the plan, bankers endorsed it, and adventurers were to carry it into effect," ran an account in the *New York Times*. "[T]he idea was, if possible, to throw the cars from the road at some point where they would rush down a steep embankment and destroy in a moment the lives of all on board. In case of the failure of this project, their plan was to surround the carriage on the way from depot to depot in Baltimore, and assassinate him with dagger or pistol shot."

With time running out, Pinkerton hatched a desperate, perhaps fool-hardy plan: He would abandon the relative security of Lincoln's small cadre of escorts in favor of a surprise maneuver, catching the plotters unawares. The risks were enormous, as the detective readily admitted. If exposed by a careless word or intercepted message, the president-elect would be left almost entirely unprotected. In Pinkerton's view, however, this perilous feint offered the only chance that Lincoln would survive to become president. As the president-elect's train neared the "seat of danger," the only remaining difficulty was to convince Lincoln himself.

IN APPROACHING THE STORY of the Baltimore plot, a writer must make certain choices and assumptions. Most readers, it would seem, will know that Abraham Lincoln survived the crisis to become president of the United States, and that soon afterward the nation was plunged into the Civil War. The events of February 1861 continue to capture our attention, however, not only for the drama of the plot and its detection but also because Lincoln's handling of the crisis and its fallout would mark a fateful early test of his presidency, with many dark consequences. In charting the sweep of events that carried the nation into war, it is customary to focus on landmarks of policy and social change, such as the Missouri Compromise, the Kansas-Nebraska Act, and the Dred Scott decision. Set against these milestones, the drama in Baltimore is often overlooked, pushed aside by the more pressing urgencies that were to come, and obscured by its own uncertainties and contradictions. Seen in the light of what was to come, however, the Baltimore episode stands as a defining moment, marking a crucial transition from civilized debate to open hostilities, and presenting Lincoln with a grim preview of the challenges he would face as president. In many ways, it was the wrong story at the wrong time; Lincoln himself would be quick to diminish the importance of what had occurred, and its lessons were not learned.

Many dilemmas arise in exploring the facts of the Baltimore plot—sources conflict; historical agendas collide. There is also a certain mythologizing effect cast over the firsthand accounts, most of which were written in the heavy gloom that followed Lincoln's assassination, in 1865. As a result, the fallen president is portrayed as a saintly and resolute figure, preternaturally aware of his own destiny, and much given to gazing heroically into an uncertain future. In many cases, well-intentioned colleagues have placed dialogue in his mouth that might have been lifted from the hackneyed Beadle's Dime Novels of the day. At the same time, the sheer volume of

"Lincoln as I knew him" books presents its own challenge. It is quite possible that the two-thousand-mile route from Springfield to Washington could be paved over in volumes of reminiscence, and no two of them would agree on what Lincoln said or thought about the fateful trip through Baltimore, or even on the strangely controversial topic of what he wore on his head.

Allan Pinkerton presents an even greater set of contradictions. "Stormy, husky, brawling," as Carl Sandburg would say of Chicago, Pinkerton's adopted hometown, the detective and his legacy are riddled with paradoxes. A Scottish immigrant who made good in America, Pinkerton was proud of his rags-to-riches success, and collaborated on more than a dozen lively, self-promoting memoirs that detailed his most celebrated cases. Yet throughout his life, he remained guarded and difficult to read, as enigmatic as one of the cipher keys he used to send encrypted messages to agents in the field. He began his career as an idealistic social reformer, vowing never to investigate "trade-union officers or members in their lawful union activities," but he is remembered today as a strikebreaker, and a puppet of America's robber barons. Though he rose to fame as America's "Number One Lawman," he thought nothing of flouting the law in the service of a greater good, and spent years defying the Fugitive Slave Act, assisting runaways as a stationmaster on the Underground Railroad. Civil War historians castigate him for his work as General McClellan's chief of intelligence, during which he supposedly exaggerated his estimates of enemy troop strength, but during the Baltimore affair he came under fire for insisting that the conspiracy was far smaller than others had supposed, and that the danger was all the greater because of it. And finally, at the moment when he wished to collect laurels from the public for his service to President Lincoln, Pinkerton found himself branded a liar, and mired in a bitter feud that would cloud his legacy for generations to come.

As a result of these conflicts and ambiguities, the details of the Baltimore plot soon became a subject of controversy. Some critics questioned whether Pinkerton's actions were justified, while others were quick to point out the flaws in his investigation. Even Lincoln's personal secretaries, John Nicolay and John Hay—both of whom traveled with the president-elect on the train from Springfield—were decidedly cautious in stating that Pinkerton's case had "neither been proved nor disproved by the lapse of time."

There is no denying that at least some of Pinkerton's evidence was pure hearsay. Much of it was obtained in saloons and brothels, under circumstances where the telling of falsehoods is not unknown. But Pinkerton's detractors tend to overlook the fact that his conclusions were confirmed and amplified by Lincoln's most trusted advisers, including Lieutenant General Winfield Scott, the commanding general of the United States. There is no question that Pinkerton's methods were high-handed and at times unlawful, but many of the cavils that were heaped upon him in 1861 would not be expressed or even considered today. It is now understood that there are dangers to be apprehended when a president moves freely through a vast crowd or rides in an open conveyance. Those apprehensions did not yet exist at the start of the Lincoln presidency. As one New York newspaper noted at the time, "assassination is not congenial to the American character." Perhaps not, but it would soon become all too real.

"The events about to be related have been for a long time shrouded in a veil of mystery," Pinkerton wrote in a memoir published near the end of his life. "While many are aware that a plot existed at this time to assassinate the President-elect upon his contemplated journey to the capital, but few have any knowledge of the mode by which the conspiracy was detected, or the means employed to prevent the accomplishment of that murderous design."

Strangely, those words are as true today as they were in Pinkerton's time, and the detective was already swimming against a tide of criticism when he wrote them. The distinguished historian John Thomas Scharf, chronicling the history of his native Maryland in 1879, insisted that Pinkerton's actions had been an insult to the "fair fame of one of the chief cities of the country," and expressed a hope that the matter would "soon be settled once and for all."

I myself am a resident of Maryland, and I am as partial to blue crabs and black-eyed Susans as the next man. At a remove of 150 years, however, I believe it is possible to treat this episode without undue risk to the fair fame of Baltimore. It bears noting, however, that to this day our state song—"Maryland, My Maryland"—makes reference to "the despot's heel" and "tyrant's chain" of Lincoln and his kind, and builds to a final, spirited rallying cry: "Huzza! She spurns the Northern scum!"

Lincoln would likely have been amused. "Fellow citizens," he wisely declared in the early years of his presidency, "we cannot escape history."

PART ONE

•

THE COOPER and THE RAIL-SPLITTER

Allan Pinkerton in 1861. *Courtesy of the Library of Congress*

PROLOGUE
HIS HOUR HAD NOT YET COME

•

Lincoln's inaugural ceremonies, March 4, 1861. *Courtesy of the Library of Congress*

SECURITY THAT DAY was the tightest Washington had ever seen. Sharpshooters crouched on the rooftops along Pennsylvania Avenue and in the windows of the Capitol. Armed soldiers—many of them "in citizen's dress"—fanned out through the crowd, looking for agitators. Companies of uniformed volunteers swelled the ranks of the parade marchers, and a corps of West Point cadets readied themselves to form a sort of flying wedge around the presidential carriage. A cavalry officer riding nearby used his spurs to keep his mount—and those nearby—in an "uneasy state," making it difficult for a marksman to get off a shot "between the dancing horses." Inauguration Day—March 4, 1861—found the city tensed for a blow.

Just past noon, an elegant horse-drawn carriage rolled to a stop at the side entrance of Willard's Hotel on Fourteenth Street, two blocks east of the White House. Looking gray and doddery, President James Buchanan eased himself down from the open coach. The Old Public Functionary, as he was known, had just departed the Executive Mansion for the last time as president. In keeping with the solemnity of the occasion, he wore a formal but out-of-date swallowtail coat and an immense white cravat that spread over his chest "like a poultice." He appeared thoroughly worn-out, one observer noted, and had few political allies left to mourn his exit. "The sun, thank God, has risen upon the last day of the administration of James Buchanan," declared the *New York World*.

Willard's Hotel, the city's largest, was packed to capacity for the inaugural festivities, with proprietor Henry A. Willard booking an average of three people to a room. In the words of Nathaniel Hawthorne, the stately six-story building could be "much more justly called the centre of Washington and the Union than either the Capitol, the White House, or the State Department." This had been especially true since the arrival ten days earlier of President-elect Abraham Lincoln, whose presence in the hotel had sparked a "quadrennial revel" of visitors. "Everybody may be seen there," Hawthorne would write. "You exchange nods with governors of sovereign States; you elbow illustrious men, and tread on the toes of generals."

The arrival of President Buchanan would mark the end to the political scrum. Pausing for a moment outside the hotel, Buchanan removed his low-crowned silk hat and passed through the side entrance. Moments later, he reemerged, walking arm in arm with Abraham Lincoln. The president-elect wore a new black cashmere suit, which had been made for him in Chicago, and carried a gold-tipped ebony cane. As the two men stepped into the waiting carriage, a group of soldiers standing near the hotel entrance snapped to attention, and a Marine band struck up "Hail to the Chief." Lincoln smiled and tipped his stovepipe hat, but his face appeared drawn and even more heavily lined than usual. He had been up most of the night, laboring over a final draft of his inaugural address.

Moments earlier, while waiting for Buchanan to arrive, he had sat jotting notes as his son Robert read the speech aloud, giving him a better sense of how the words would strike the ears of his listeners. Distracted by this last-minute tinkering, Lincoln left Willard's Hotel without paying his tab. Several weeks later, when the lapse was brought to his attention, he sent the money over from the White House with a note of apology.

Lincoln and Buchanan sat side by side as their driver swung the carriage onto Pennsylvania Avenue, signaling the start of a "glad and sumptuous" parade that would carry them to the Capitol. The hour-long procession featured floats, marching bands, columns of veterans of the War of 1812, and a richly appointed "tableau car" carrying thirty-four "beauteous little girls," each representing a state of the Union. A throng of some 25,000 people crowded along both sides of the broad avenue. Many in the crowd had come from out of town to witness the proceedings, and a few had been obliged to spend the night sleeping on the pavement after being turned away at the city's overbooked hotels. Those who could not get a clear view scrambled for higher ground. "The trees upon the corners," reported a Philadelphia paper, were "as full of small boys as an apple tree in fruit-bearing season."

The temperature that afternoon had turned cool and bracing, and it is likely that the atmosphere in the presidential carriage was chillier still. During his campaign, Lincoln had criticized Buchanan sharply, though neither man escaped censure in the press as Inauguration Day approached, especially in the South: "An imbecile official is succeeded by a stupid Rail Splitter," declared an Atlanta newspaper. As the carriage neared the Capitol, however, Buchanan is said to have struck a conciliatory note. Anticipating his return to his estate in Pennsylvania, the outgoing president turned to his successor. "My

"The Inaugural Procession at Washington," from *Harper's Weekly,* March 1861.
Courtesy of the Library of Congress

dear sir," he said, "if you are as happy in entering the White House as I shall feel on returning to Wheatland, you are a happy man indeed."

Lincoln, by all accounts, gave a delicate reply: "Mr. President, I cannot say that I shall enter it with much pleasure, but I assure you that I shall do what I can to maintain the high standards set by my illustrious predecessors who have occupied it."

Barely two and a half years had elapsed since Lincoln had launched his campaign for the United States Senate—and the historic series of debates against Stephen A. Douglas—with his famous warning of the dangers of disunion over the issue of slavery: "A house divided against itself cannot stand." Now, as Lincoln prepared to take the oath to "preserve, protect and defend the Constitution" as president of the United States, many of the diplomats and politicians gathered at the Capitol believed that a civil war was inevitable and that Lincoln would take office only to preside over the disintegration of the Union. Almost at that very moment, some seven hundred miles away in Montgomery, Alabama, the "Stars and Bars" flag of the Confederacy was being raised at the state capitol, with seven stars to represent the seven states that had already seceded.

"A more enviable, but at the same time more delicate and more hazardous lot than that accorded to Abraham Lincoln never fell to any member of this nation," wrote journalist Henry Villard in the *New York Herald*. "The path he is about to walk on may lead to success, glory, immortality, but also to failure, humiliation and curses upon his memory. He may steer clear of the rock of disunion and the shoal of dissension among those that elevated him to the office he is about to assume, and safely conduct the Ship of State from amidst the turbulence of fanaticism and lawlessness to the port of peace and reunion. But he may, on the other hand, take his place at the helm of the craft only to sink with it."

In keeping with the gravity of the moment, Lincoln had spent weeks laboring over his inaugural address, which he saw as an opportunity to pull the divided nation back from crisis. The president-elect sought a great deal of advice about the speech, but even his closest advisers were at odds over whether he should extend an olive branch to the South or fire a warning shot. Lincoln himself initially favored a strong, even confrontational message, stating that the Union would be preserved at all costs, that secession was illegal, and that he, as commander in chief, intended to enforce the law of the land. Toward that end, he planned to close the address with a ringing, provocative challenge: "In *your* hands, my dissatisfied fellow countrymen, and not in *mine,* is the momentous issue of civil war . . . With *you,* and not with *me,* is the solemn question of 'Shall it be peace, or a sword?'"

As Inauguration Day approached, however, Lincoln moderated the warlike tone, acting on the counsel of advisers such as William H. Seward, his designated secretary of state, to display "the magnanimity of a victor." If the speech were delivered as originally drafted, Seward believed, both Virginia and Maryland would immediately secede, effectively cutting off Washington from the Northern states. "Every thought that we think ought to be conciliatory, forbearing and patient," he insisted.

Even as Lincoln revised and polished his address, however, there were many who felt that the moment for healing had passed. "Mr. Lincoln entered Washington the victim of a grave delusion," said Horace Greeley, the famed publisher of the *New-York Tribune*. "His faith in reason as a moral force was so implicit that he did not cherish a doubt that his Inaugural Address, whereon he had bestowed much thought and labor, would, when read throughout the South, dissolve the Confederacy as frost is dissipated by the vernal sun."

In order for Lincoln to deliver the address, however, he had to make it safely through the brief, final leg of his procession to the Capitol, a journey that had begun three weeks earlier in Springfield, Illinois. Many of Lincoln's most trusted advisers believed that his life had been in danger at every moment, especially during the thirteen days he had spent aboard the Lincoln Special, the private train that carried him on his winding, disjointed path to Washington. Even now, on the very doorstep of the presidency, many feared that there were sinister forces at work that would prevent Lincoln from taking the oath of office. The papers were filled with "persistent rumors" of an armed uprising, with a force of men numbering in the thousands poised to descend on Washington. Others spoke of groups of assassins hidden within the throngs at the Capitol grounds. "There is some apprehension felt concerning the possible action of a large gang of 'Plug-Uglies' who are here from Baltimore," reported the previous day's *New York Times*. "Strange to say, heavy bets are pending on the question of his safety through tomorrow's exercises, and great anxiety is felt at Head-quarters concerning certain unpublished designs." Lincoln himself had received anonymous threats of violent opposition to the inauguration. "Beware the Ides of March," warned one correspondent, "the Suthron people will not Stand your administration." Another spoke of a "sworn band of 10, who have resolved to shoot you in the inaugural procession." Lincoln waved such threats aside, the *Times* reported, and remained utterly unfazed: "He says, 'I am here to take what is my right, and I shall take it. I anticipate no trouble, but should it come I am prepared to meet it.'"

Though steps were taken to keep the security measures as inconspicuous as possible, some observers were appalled by the seemingly belligerent display of military force. "Nothing could have been more ill-advised or more ostentatious," declared an anonymous diarist of the day. "I never expected to experience such a sense of mortification and shame in my own country as I felt today, in entering the Capitol through hedges of Marines armed to the teeth." Not surprisingly, the Southern press seized on the unprecedented show of force to heap scorn on the incoming president. "I have seen today such a sight as I could never have believed possible at the capital of my country," wrote a journalist in the *Charleston Mercury*, "an inauguration of a President surrounded by armed soldiery, with loaded pieces and fixed bayonets." Lt. Gen. Winfield Scott, the seventy-four-year-old commanding general of the United States, offered no apologies. Convinced of the existence of a plot against Lincoln, the old soldier spent inauguration day commanding a battery of light artillery on Capitol Hill. "I shall plant cannon at both ends of Pennsylvania Avenue," he declared, "and if any of the Maryland or Virginia gentlemen who have become so threatening and troublesome of late show their heads, or even venture to raise a finger, I shall blow them to Hell!"

At a few minutes past 1:00 P.M., the inaugural procession arrived at the Capitol, with its new, half-finished steel dome obscured by scaffolding. Uniformed volunteers arrayed themselves in a double row along the length of the building, forming a human barrier between the crowd and a square-roofed wooden canopy that had been erected at the east portico. Lincoln and Buchanan, meanwhile, were escorted into the Senate Chamber along a makeshift covered walkway, which had been layered with planks to guard against the possibility of sniper fire. Once inside, Lincoln appeared "grave and impassive as an Indian martyr" during the swearing-in of his vice president, Hannibal Hamlin. The outgoing president, meanwhile, looked pale and distracted. "Mr. Buchanan sighed audibly, and frequently," noted a correspondent from the *New York Times*, "but whether from reflection upon the failure of his Administration, I can't say."

At about 1:30 P.M., a long line of politicians and dignitaries, including the justices of the Supreme Court, filed beneath the unfinished dome of the Capitol rotunda and passed through the doors leading outside to the east portico. As Lincoln emerged at the top of the Capitol steps, he received a "most glorious shout of welcome" from the crowd below.

At the bottom of the stairs, beneath the wooden canopy, stood a "miserable little rickety table" holding a pitcher of water and a glass. After introductory remarks by his friend Edward D. Baker, Lincoln—looking "pale, and wan, and anxious"—stepped forward to speak. For a moment, he hesitated, searching for a place to set down his hat. Stephen Douglas, the Illinois Democrat who had so vigorously contested Lincoln's bid for both the Senate and the White House, happened to be seated close by. Seeing Lincoln's predicament, he stepped forward to assist his former rival. "If I cannot be President," Douglas is supposed to have said, "I can at least be his hat-bearer." The *Times* correspondent, eager for one last dig at the outgoing president, noted that Buchanan, "who was probably sleepy and tired, sat looking as straight as he could at the toe of his right foot."

For some moments, the president-elect stood quietly and gathered himself, weighing down the loose pages of his speech with his ebony cane as he adjusted his eyeglasses. "The ten thousand threats that he should be assassinated before he should take the oath did not impel him to make a gesture implying fear or haste," observed the *New-York Tribune,* "and he stood forth a conspicuous mark for the villains who had threatened to shoot him as he read." When at last Lincoln began to speak, one listener recalled, his voice "rang out over the acres of people before him with surprising distinctness."

No incoming president had ever faced such a balancing act in trying to appease so bitterly divided a country, a dilemma that cartoonist Thomas Nast neatly captured in a double portrait called *The President's Inaugural.* In one panel, Lincoln appeared as an angel of peace, waving palm garlands over a caption that read: "This is the way the North receives it." But the facing panel showed Lincoln as a Roman centurion with his foot pressing down on a vanquished foe, brandishing a sword over the words "This is the way the South receives it."

Both sides found ample evidence in Lincoln's words to support their differing views. The speech contained many warnings to the South about the consequences of hostile action. "Physically speaking, we cannot separate," Lincoln declared, adding that the laws of the Union would be "faithfully executed in all the states." At the same time, however, he insisted that there was no need for "bloodshed or violence," a point he underscored as the address concluded with a ringing expression of hope for reconciliation:

> I am loth to close. We are not enemies, but friends. We must
> not be enemies. Though passion may have strained, it must
> not break our bonds of affection. The mystic cords of memory,
> stretching from every battle-field, and patriot grave, to every
> living heart and hearthstone, all over this broad land, will yet

swell the chorus of the Union, when again touched, as surely
they will be, by the better angels of our nature.

The address completed, Lincoln stepped back and bowed his head. Then,
in one of the day's many ironies, Chief Justice Roger B. Taney stepped forward to administer the oath of office. Taney, an eighty-three-year-old
Maryland slaveholder, had performed this service six times previously,
stretching back to the inauguration of Martin Van Buren, in 1837. More
recently, Taney had delivered the majority opinion in the notorious *Dred
Scott v. Sanford* case, declaring among other things that slaves were entitled
to no protections under the Constitution, and that Congress had no authority to prohibit slavery in federal territories. The decision had had a gal-
vanizing effect on the abolitionist movement and had helped to propel
Abraham Lincoln into the national spotlight. Now, as the slavery issue
pushed the country to the brink of war, Taney was obliged to swear in one
of his most outspoken critics as the sixteenth president of the United States.

For all the challenges that lay ahead, which Lincoln himself described as
greater than those faced by George Washington, he had already met the
first test of his presidency: He had survived his journey to the inaugural
ceremony. "No mean courage was required to face the probabilities of the
hour," wrote Frederick Douglass, the famed abolitionist. The new president
had "stood up before the pistol or dagger of the sworn assassin, to meet
death from an unknown hand, while upon the very threshold of the office
to which the suffrages of the nation had elected him." Horace Greeley concurred, recalling his own sense of foreboding as Lincoln delivered the inaugural address. "I sat just behind him as he read it," Greeley wrote, "expecting
to hear its delivery arrested by the crack of a rifle aimed at his heart."

For Greeley, at least, Lincoln's survival appeared to be a sign of providence. "It pleased God to postpone the deed," he concluded, "though
there was forty times the reason for shooting him in 1860 than there was
in '65, and at least forty times as many intent on killing or having him
killed. No shot was then fired, however; for his hour had not yet come."

Not even Greeley, who had followed Lincoln's fortunes closely for more
than a dozen years, knew what a near thing it had been, and the one person
who could have told him was nowhere to be seen. Allan Pinkerton, the
man who had done more than any other to ensure the peaceful transfer of
power that day, had long since returned to Baltimore to chase down rumors
of a fresh plot against the new administration.

"The Eye," as he was known, still had work to do.

CHAPTER ONE

THE APPRENTICE

•

Let none falter, who thinks he is right, and we may succeed.
—ABRAHAM LINCOLN, Springfield, Illinois, 1839

THE PECULIAR MARCH OF EVENTS that carried Allan Pinkerton to
Baltimore had begun twenty-two years earlier—on the night of November 3, 1839—on a rain-soaked field in South Wales. At that time, Abraham Lincoln was still a young legislator in Illinois, voicing early concern
over voting rights and the "injustice and bad policy" of slavery. An ocean
away, Pinkerton was also throwing himself at what he called "the higher
principles of liberty," even at the risk of his own freedom.

Pinkerton had traveled hundreds of miles from his home in Glasgow
to take his place amid a swelling band of protest marchers as they prepared to descend on the Welsh town of Newport. These "crazed and misguided zealots," as one newspaper called them, were the vanguard of the
Chartist agitation, a working-class labor movement struggling to make
its voice heard in Britain. Pinkerton, though barely twenty years old,
thought of himself as "the most ardent Chartist in Scotland."

Ragged and footsore, Pinkerton moved among the demonstrators as
they huddled beside campfires, listening to firebrand speeches and waiting for reinforcements that would never come. They were, as Pinkerton
himself would admit, a sorry-looking group. A few had tattered blankets
pulled tight around their shoulders for protection against a chilling rain;
others went barefoot in the squelching mud.

The Chartists' demands, as spelled out in the "People's Charter" of 1838,
included universal suffrage, equitable pay, and other democratic reforms for
Britain's "toiling class." Lately, the movement had been split by internal

conflict, with one faction espousing nonviolent "moral force" to achieve its goals, and another comprised of "physical force men," who were prepared—perhaps even eager—to take up arms. Matters came to a crisis in July 1839, when the House of Commons rejected a national petition bearing over a million signatures. The following month saw the charismatic Chartist leader Henry Vincent convicted on conspiracy charges, spurring the physical-force wing of the movement toward a large-scale uprising.

Henry Vincent had been imprisoned at Monmouth Castle, outside of Newport, and it was thought that several other Chartist leaders were being held in the town's Westgate Hotel. As thousands of marchers, many of them miners and mill workers, massed on the outskirts of town, it became clear that they intended to demonstrate their "fervid passions" to the country at large. Exactly how they intended to do so remains a subject of debate. Many believe that the marchers planned to storm the Westgate Hotel and free the prisoners they thought were inside. Others contend that a massive demonstration was planned to secure the release of Henry Vincent from his castle cell, perhaps signaling a nationwide uprising in support of the Chartist agenda. In any event, there were iron pikes and muskets in the hands of many of the marchers, suggesting that their intent could not have been entirely peaceful.

The original plan called for the marchers to advance on Newport under cover of darkness, but it was past nine o'clock in the morning before they finally descended on the town. The delay proved costly: Military forces from a nearby royal regiment had used the time to reinforce the hotel and surrounding buildings. As the rain-soaked, disorganized laborers massed in the village square, they found themselves facing off against a small but well-armed company of battle-trained soldiers.

The details of what followed are not entirely clear. According to some accounts, the Chartists surged forward and banged at the shuttered windows of the hotel to demand the release of the prisoners, only to be met with a withering volley of musket fire. Within minutes, the ranks broke and the marchers fell back in wild disorder, leaving their weapons scattered on the ground. The defending soldiers now turned their guns on a handful of Chartists who had managed to force their way inside the hotel. In moments, said a witness, "there was a scene dreadful beyond expression—the groans of the dying—the shrieks of the wounded, the pallid, ghostly countenances and the bloodshot eyes of the dead, in addition to the shattered windows, and the passages ankle-deep in gore."

When the smoke cleared, some twenty-two men lay dead, and many others were grievously injured. Most had scattered as the first shots rained down on their heads, fleeing back to their homes, as one witness recorded, like "so many yelping dogs gone to ground." In the aftermath, many of the Chartist marchers would be captured and their leaders condemned to be hung, drawn, and quartered.

"It was a bad day," recalled Allan Pinkerton. "We returned to Glasgow by the back streets and lanes, more like thieves than honest working men." The lessons of the Newport Rising, as the unhappy episode came to be known, would remain with Pinkerton to the end of his days. Within a few years, he would gain international fame as the leading figure of a new type of law enforcement, followed by no small measure of infamy as a strike-breaker, but Pinkerton never entirely fell out of step with the Newport marchers in his efforts for social justice. The tension between the ideals of his youth and the obligations of the career he created for himself—like the split between the moral-force and physical-force Chartists—created a strain in his character that he never entirely resolved. He understood the impulses of the poor and disenfranchised, whether they were criminals or enemy soldiers, but this only sharpened the edge of his ambition. Decades later, while commenting on labor unrest in America, Pinkerton offered a rare public glimpse of the beliefs he had forged in Scotland: "I believe that I of all others have earned the right to say plain things to the countless toilers who were engaged in these strikes. I say I have *earned* this right. I have been all my lifetime a working man." Life in America, he insisted, presented common workingmen with opportunities he had been denied in his homeland, with a chance to "rise above their previous conditions, and reach a nobler and happier condition of life."

If Pinkerton's words sound naïve and self-serving to the modern ear, it was a sentiment Abraham Lincoln would have recognized. "Twenty-five years ago I was a hired laborer," Lincoln once declared. "The hired laborer of yesterday labors on his own account today, and will hire others to labor for him tomorrow. Advancement—improvement in condition—is the order of things in a society of equals."

ALLAN PINKERTON WAS BORN in a two-room tenement flat on Muirhead Street in Glasgow, Scotland, in the summer of 1819. His family lived in the area on the south bank of the River Clyde known as the Gorbals, infamous at that time for its crime, brothels, and "persons in narrow circumstances." Named for his grandfather, a well-known blacksmith, Allan was one of eleven children, at least four of whom died in infancy.

His father, William, a hand-loom weaver, died when Allan was barely ten years old, forcing him to leave school and take a job as an errand boy. He worked "from dawn to dusk for pennies," as he later recalled, in the shop of a pattern maker named Neil Murphy, who had been a friend of his father. After work, the boy would stand on the street, waiting for his mother, Isabella, to return from her job at a spinning mill. A high point during this cheerless period—and a memory he would often recall in his old age—was the night she came home cradling a single fresh egg for their evening meal.

Pinkerton soon grew restless with what he called the "dreary existence" of an errand boy. At the age of twelve, he took the bold step of resigning in favor of an apprenticeship with a Glasgow cooper named William McAuley, learning the craft of making watertight casks, barrels, and kegs. By the age of eighteen, Pinkerton had earned his journeyman's card and joined the Coopers' Union, but by this time McAuley had no further work for him. Pinkerton took to the road and became a "tramp cooper," traveling the country to pick up piecemeal work at breweries and distilleries. He sent whatever money he could spare back to his mother in Glasgow, but he often found himself living so close to the bone that he slept outdoors and went without food.

Friends from this period described Pinkerton as quiet and rather serious, with penetrating blue eyes beneath a coarse thatch of reddish hair. Most accounts refer to him as a short or "diminutive" man, though his height is sometimes listed as five eight—by no means small for the time. A famous photograph taken many years later shows Pinkerton standing with Abraham Lincoln at the Antietam battlefield. The image gives an initial impression of Pinkerton as undersized and somewhat hunched, though in fact he appears to be only half a head shorter than Lincoln, who was six four. In a second image taken at the same time, however, Lincoln has shifted his stance and Pinkerton appears to have lost several inches in stature. Pinkerton would likely have been pleased by the disparity; in later years, he made a point of masking his appearance by frequently changing his style of dress and facial hair, making it easier to go undercover. At a time when Lincoln cultivated a beard to make his appearance more distinctive, Pinkerton sought to go unnoticed.

As a young barrel maker, Pinkerton earned a reputation as a hard worker, but he was also known for his quick temper and aggressive manner. An avid reader, he grew passionate about social reform, and it was known that he would not back down from a fight over the political issues of the day. His years of work with heavy tools, including a ten-pound cooper's hammer, gave him a thick torso and powerful arms. Friends sometimes remarked on his top-heavy gait; he tended to tilt forward, as if prepared at any moment to wade into a brawl.

After the Newport Rising, the youthful strain of radicalism in Pinkerton's character hardened into something dark and implacable. He knew that he had been lucky to escape Newport with his liberty. The death sentences handed out at the time were later commuted, but dozens of his fellow Chartists would be transported to Australia. Still, Pinkerton was undaunted, and he threw himself back into the fight with even greater vigor. Within weeks, after some "rather disagreeable talk" at a gathering of the Glasgow Universal Suffrage Association, Pinkerton stalked out of the meeting hall and launched a group of his own, the Northern Democratic Association, for the purpose of ratifying the People's Charter— "peaceably if we may, forcibly if we must."

Pinkerton soon fell under the sway of a controversial activist named Julian Harney, later a friend and supporter of Karl Marx and Friedrich Engels, who was often described as the Chartist movement's "enfant terrible." In January of 1840, when Pinkerton invited Harney to address an overflow crowd at Glasgow's Lyceum Theatre, there were loud jeers and catcalls from the rank and file, many of whom found the young firebrand's views too extreme. Outraged, Pinkerton sprang to his feet—his face scarlet and his fists clenched—ready to take on all comers. After a few tense moments, cooler heads prevailed and the lecture went ahead as scheduled.

Not all of Pinkerton's political meetings were so contentious. In the summer of 1841, he called on the choirmaster of a local Unitarian church to arrange a night of song at a neighborhood pub as a "whip round" fund-raiser for his Northern Democratic Association. Pinkerton attended the Thursday-night concert with his mother, and as the music began, he found himself unable to take his eyes off the choir's young soprano. Though only fourteen years old at the time, she had the bearing and polish of a seasoned performer, and she soon brought the crowd to its feet with a spirited rendition of a forbidden Chartist song. Hopelessly smitten, Pinkerton took his friend Robbie Fergus aside to learn all he could about the young singer. She was a bookbinder's apprentice from the nearby town of Paisley, Fergus told him, and her name was Joan Carfrae. At future concerts, Pinkerton made a point of sitting in the front row, wearing his best and perhaps only suit. He soon took it upon himself to escort

Miss Carfrae home after each appearance. "I got to sort of hanging around her, clinging to her, so to speak," Pinkerton later wrote, "and I knew I couldn't live without her."

Looking back on his courtship of Joan Carfrae in later years, Pinkerton recalled his distress, during the winter months of 1842, when a king's warrant was issued for his arrest as a prominent leader of the Chartist movement. "I had become an outlaw with a price on my head," he wrote. A number of his fellow Chartists were rounded up, but by the time the police sought out Pinkerton at his mother's flat, the young cooper had fled. For several months, Pinkerton's friends helped to hide him from the law, but he knew it was only a matter of time before he landed in jail, awaiting transportation to Australia. By this stage, many of his friends and Chartist colleagues had already decamped for America, including his friend Robbie Fergus, who had recently established himself in Chicago. Realizing that his options in Scotland were narrowing, Pinkerton resolved to follow Fergus and the others.

Joan Carfrae soon got wind of the plan. "When I had the price set on my head, she found me where I was hiding," Pinkerton recalled, "and when I told her I was all set up to making American barrels for the rest of my life and ventured it would be a pretty lonesome business without my bonnie singing bird around the shop, she just sang me a Scotch song that meant she'd go too, and God bless her she did."

In Pinkerton's memory of the event, he and Joan were married secretly and then—after a hasty good-bye to his mother—smuggled aboard a ship bound for America, under the wing of the kindly Neil Murphy, the family friend who had given Pinkerton his start as a ten-year-old errand boy. "Within a few hours," runs one early recounting of the drama, "he was both a married man and a wanted criminal fleeing to the New World."

This is an agreeably dramatic story, but Pinkerton's account would not have withstood the scrutiny of a sharp-eyed private detective. If the Glasgow police had truly been determined to arrest him, they would have had ample notice of his whereabouts. According to parish records, Pinkerton and Joan Carfrae were married in a public ceremony in a Glasgow church on March 13, 1842. No hint of secrecy or subterfuge is evident in the marriage register, and the Scottish tradition of the "proclamation of the banns"—a public announcement of the intent to marry, posted on three consecutive Sundays so as to allow any lawful impediments to come to light—was duly observed. In fact, the only unusual feature of the wedding appears to have been the bride's age. Though she claimed to be eighteen, Joan Carfrae was, in fact, just two months past her fifteenth birthday.

If Pinkerton romanticized some of the details, his reasons for seeking a fresh start remained clear: "I know what it is to strive and grope along, with paltry remuneration and no encouragement save that of the hope and ambition planted in every human heart," he wrote many years later. "I have been a poor lad in Scotland, buffeted and badgered by boorish masters. I have worked weary years through the 'prentice period, until, by the hardest application, I conquered a trade. I know what it is, from personal experience, to be the tramp journeyman; to carry the stick and bundle; to seek work and not get it; and to get it, and receive but a pittance for it, or suddenly lose it altogether and be compelled to resume the weary search. In fact, I know every bitter experience that the most laborious of laboring men have been or ever will be required to undergo."

Privately, his memories of his start in life were harsher still. In a letter written nearly twenty years later, at the start of the Civil War, Pinkerton expressed a sentiment that would color every aspect of his new life in America. "In my native country," he declared, "I was free in name, but a slave in fact."

Slave was not a word Pinkerton bandied about lightly. Within three years of his flight from Scotland, he would be running a station on the fabled Underground Railroad, helping runaway slaves make their way north to freedom.

CHAPTER TWO
HOW I BECAME A DETECTIVE

•

I am a success today because I had a friend who believed in me,
and I didn't have the heart to let him down.
—quote attributed to ABRAHAM LINCOLN

THE SHARP-DRESSED STRANGER wore a heavy gold ring on his left hand. He was tall, perhaps six feet or so, sixty-five years of age, and "very erect and commanding in his appearance." As he rode his horse through the center of the village on a fine, clear day in July 1847, it was obvious that trouble was coming.

Henry Hunt, the owner of a general store at the center of town, knew all too well what would happen next. Few outsiders ever troubled to visit Dundee, a quiet Illinois farming settlement about fifty miles northwest of Chicago. Lately, the appearance of a visitor signaled that a ruinous flood of counterfeit coins and notes was about to wash over the town. Hunt's business had barely recovered from the last wave of bogus currency, and he was determined not to let it happen again. In his view, there was only one man who had the skills to deal with the matter. Keeping an anxious eye fixed upon the stranger, Hunt sent his errand boy to fetch Allan Pinkerton, the town cooper.

"I was busy at my work," Pinkerton recalled, "bareheaded, barefooted, and having no other clothing on my body than a pair of blue denim overalls and a coarse hickory shirt—my then almost invariable costume—but I started down the street at once."

Arriving at the store, Pinkerton found Hunt and another shopkeeper, Increase Bosworth, waiting behind the counter. "Come in here, Allan," Hunt said, leading him to a room at the back of the store; "we want you

25

to do a little job in the detective line." Pinkerton greeted this proposal with a burst of incredulous laughter. "Detective line!" he cried. "What do I know about that sort of thing?"

It was a fair question. Pinkerton was still a newcomer in Dundee, struggling to make a success in the coopering trade. After his turbulent departure from Scotland five years earlier, he and his bride had alighted briefly in Chicago, where his old friend Robert Fergus helped him land a job at the Lill & Diversey brewery, making beer kegs for fifty cents a day.

Soon, Pinkerton set his sights on a business of his own. In the spring of 1843, he heard talk of a community of Scottish farmers on the Fox River in Kane County, and he realized that there would be plenty of work for a man who could make barrels, churns, and tubs. He told Joan that he would go ahead and "get a roof over my head" while she waited in Chicago.

For Joan, married barely one year, it was a tearful parting. After a lingering farewell on the banks of the Chicago River, Pinkerton turned and crossed a pontoon bridge, his bag of tools slung across his shoulder. Upon reaching the other side, he looked back and waved, then set off into the tall grasses that lay beyond, whistling a Scottish ballad. "I couldna bear it when the great grass swallowed him up so quick," Joan recalled, but long after he disappeared from view, she could hear him whistling, and was comforted by the thought that "there'd be a wee home soon for us."

In Dundee, near a bridge that crossed the Fox River, Pinkerton hand-built a small log cabin and work shed. Farmers and cattle drovers passing on their way to market could not fail to notice the bright new sign: ALLAN PINKERTON, ONLY AND ORIGINAL COOPER OF DUNDEE. After a few weeks, he headed back to Chicago to collect Joan, who soon turned her hand to growing vegetables and tending chickens. "In the little shop at Dundee," she recalled, "with the blue river purling down the valley, the auld Scotch farmers trundling past with the grist for the mill or their loads for the market, and Allan, with his rat-tat-tat on the barrels, whistling and keeping tune with my singing, were the bonniest days the good Father gave me in all my life."

Pinkerton, too, seems to have enjoyed the quiet charms of Dundee, and his hard work soon brought dividends. By 1846, he had eight men working for him, a mix of fellow Scots and more recent German immigrants. "I felt proud of my success," he wrote, "because I owed no man." Pinkerton's family, too, was growing. In April of that year, Joan gave birth to a son—the first of six children—named William, after both of his grandfathers.

Now twenty-seven, Pinkerton became regular, even rigid, in his habits, going to bed each night at 8:30 and rising each morning at 4:30, a schedule that seldom varied for the rest of his life. He neither drank nor smoked, but he might indulge himself at bedtime with a novel by Edward Bulwer-Lytton, whose florid historical melodramas, widely ridiculed today, were hugely popular at the time. Though Pinkerton would surely have read the novel *Paul Clifford*—with its much-parodied "dark and stormy night"—his favorite was *Eugene Aram,* which drew on the career of a real-life murderer and his eventual capture. At the outset, Bulwer-Lytton declared his belief that the case was "perhaps the most remarkable in the register of English crime," and he insisted that the reader must examine the "physical circumstances and condition of the criminal" in order to "comprehend fully the lessons which belong to so terrible a picture of frenzy and guilt." These lessons were not lost on Pinkerton, who judged the novel to be the greatest ever written. As a Dundee friend later recalled, "He didn't think much of you if you disagreed with him on that."

If Bulwer-Lytton fired his imagination, Frederick Douglass sparked Pinkerton's conscience. The newspapers at that time were filled with stories about Douglass, the escaped slave whose 1845 memoir—*Narrative of the Life of Frederick Douglass, An American Slave*—was becoming a touchstone of the abolitionist movement. Pinkerton was deeply moved by Douglass's struggle, as well as by his eloquence. Soon, the political ideals of Pinkerton's Chartist days found a new channel. "This institution of human bondage always received my earnest opposition," he later wrote. "Believing it to be a curse to the American nation, and an evidence of barbarism, no efforts of mine were ever spared in behalf of the slave." The first of these efforts, it appears, was to offer his services to Charles V. Dyer, a leading force in the Chicago chapter of an organization called the American Anti-Slavery Society. Dyer soon found a way for the only and original cooper of Dundee to make himself useful.

The Underground Railroad—a secret network of meeting points, back-channel routes, and safe houses used by abolitionists to ferry runaway slaves north to free states and Canada—had been up and running for many years by this time. Writing in 1860, one former slave claimed that the operation got its name from a disgruntled slaveholder who could not understand how his "escaped chattel" had disappeared so completely: "The damned abolitionists must have a railroad under the ground," he complained. Pinkerton admired the cunning and subterfuge of the enterprise. The circuitous routes were changed frequently to throw marshals and bounty hunters off the track, and the organizers made use of coded railroad terminology to protect the individual components of the system from discovery. The planners of the escape routes were known as "presidents of the road," the guides who escorted the fugitives from place to place were "conductors," the hiding places and safe houses were "stations," and the ever-changing routes were "lines." The fugitives themselves were variously known as "passengers," "cargo," or "commissions."

Within months, Pinkerton's log cabin on the Fox River would become an active station on the Underground Railroad, being a useful stopping point on the journey north to Wisconsin and Canada. Though some of the Illinois stationmasters would be prosecuted for harboring slaves, Pinkerton made little effort to conceal his activities. Some of his passengers stayed long enough to receive instruction in the basics of barrel making, in the hope that the skills might prove useful to them as free men. Years later, Pinkerton spoke feelingly of his efforts at this time, and of his growing awareness that the issue of slavery threatened to divide the nation. "Above all," he said, "I had hoped for the oppressed and shackled race of the South that the downfall of slavery would be early accomplished, and their freedom permanently established. I had the anti-slavery cause very much at heart, and would never have been satisfied until that gigantic curse was effectually removed."

For the moment, at least, Pinkerton had more immediate concerns. Although he claimed to be content with his "quiet, but altogether happy mode of life" in Dundee, he often found himself pressed for cash. "There was plenty of dickering, but no money," Pinkerton complained. "My barrels would be sold to the farmers or merchants for produce, and this I would be compelled to send in to Chicago, to secure as best I could a few dollars, perhaps." A series of bank failures earlier in the decade compounded the problem. "There was but little money in the West," he wrote, and a workingman such as himself "could get but little." Looking to save whatever he could, Pinkerton found ways to scavenge for the raw materials he needed for his barrels and casks. "I was actually too poor to purchase outright a wheelbarrow-load of hoop-poles, or staves, and was consequently compelled to cut my own," he recalled. To this end, he often roamed along the banks of the Fox River, and in time he found a small island a few miles north "where the poles were both plentiful and of the best quality."

One day, as Pinkerton took a raft upriver to cut a fresh supply, he stumbled across the smoldering remains of a campfire. For months, he had heard talk of gangs of counterfeiters in the region and concluded that the island was being used for unlawful purposes. "There was no picnicking in those days," he recalled, "people had more serious matters to attend to, and it required no great keenness to conclude that no honest men were in the habit of occupying the place." Curious, and perhaps offended at the thought of sinister doings on his patch, Pinkerton decided to investigate. He returned again and again over the next few days, hoping to catch sight of the visitors. One evening, hearing a splash of oars as a small boat rowed out of the darkness, Pinkerton hid himself in a stand of tall grass and watched as several men scrambled ashore and lit a fire. After hearing a few snatches of conversation, Pinkerton felt sure he had uncovered a criminal hideout.

The following day, Pinkerton took his suspicions to the sheriff of Kane County. Rounding up a posse of men, Pinkerton and the sheriff led a raid on the island a few nights later and discovered an elaborate counterfeiting ring. "I led the officers who captured the entire gang," Pinkerton reported proudly, "securing their implements and a large amount of bogus coin." The sheriff subsequently discovered that the ringleaders were well-known swindlers, or "coney men," who were also wanted for cattle rustling and for horse theft. The episode brought Pinkerton a great deal of attention, with eager villagers stopping him in the street to hear details of the raid. "In honor of the event," he recalled years later, "the island ever since has been known as 'Bogus Island.'"

The matter would likely have ended there but for the arrival a short time later of the tall, well-dressed stranger. It seemed obvious to the shopkeepers Henry Hunt and Increase Bosworth that Pinkerton, the hero of Bogus Island, would be just the man to prevent another outbreak of counterfeiting. Pinkerton himself, standing barefoot in the back room of the general store, felt dubious. He had no skills, he told the two men, and no experience. "Never mind now," one of the shopkeepers told him. "We are sure you can do work of this sort, if only you will do it." If Pinkerton could catch the stranger in the act of passing bad paper, they insisted, the plague might be cut off at its source.

This, Pinkerton later realized, was the turning point of his career:

> There I stood, a young, strong, agile, hard-working cooper,
> daring enough and ready for any reckless emergency which
> might transpire in the living of an honest life, but decidedly
> averse to doing something entirely out of my line, and which in
> all probability I would make an utter failure of. I had not been

but four years in America altogether. I had had a hard time of it
for the time I had been here. A great detective I would make
under such circumstances, I thought.

Privately, his reservations were more practical. He could see little advantage in neglecting his cooperage for this "will-o'-the-wisp piece of
business." He wavered for a moment or two—"What do *I* know about
counterfeiting?" he asked—but Hunt and Bosworth persisted, certain he
would succeed if he put his mind to it. Pinkerton, flattered by their confidence, made an impulsive decision: "I suddenly resolved to do just that
and no less," he recalled, "although I must confess that, at that time, I
had not the remotest idea how to set about the matter."

For all his reservations, Pinkerton wasted no time. Posing as a "country
gawker," he strolled into town to strike up a conversation with the stranger,
and he soon found himself invited to have a quiet chat on the outskirts
of town, away from prying eyes. There, the visitor opened a cautious line
of questioning, identifying himself as John Craig, a farmer from Vermont, and hinting that he needed a local partner to join him in a lucrative scheme. Not wishing to seem too eager, Pinkerton gave measured
responses, admitting that times were "fearfully hard" and that he would
be open to a scheme "better adapted to getting more ready cash." All the
while, Pinkerton noted, Craig studied him closely with "a pair of the
keenest, coldest small gray eyes I have ever seen." Worse yet, Pinkerton
glimpsed the handles of a pair of pistols protruding from Craig's coat. "I
had nothing for self-protection," he recalled, "save my two big fists." As
Craig continued his questioning, Pinkerton felt "a sense of insignificance"
as he measured himself against the older man. "There I was, hardly more
than a plodding country cooper," he said. "I felt wholly unable to cope
with this keen man of the world."

As it turned out, however, a plodding country cooper was just what
Craig wanted. Turning suddenly, the older man asked point-blank if
Pinkerton had ever passed any counterfeit currency. "Yes, Mr. Craig,"
Pinkerton replied promptly, "but only when I could get a first-class article.
I frequently 'work off' the stuff in paying my men Saturday nights. Have
you something really good, now?"

Craig answered that he had a "bang up article," and passed over a pair
of bogus ten-dollar bills. Pinkerton had never seen a ten-dollar bill—real
or bogus—in his entire life, but for Craig's benefit he pretended to be a

shrewd judge of forgeries. "I looked at them very, very wisely," he recalled, "and after a little expressed myself as very much pleased with them."

Craig now made his proposal. He would sell Pinkerton five hundred dollars' worth of phony bills for twenty-five cents on the dollar, or $125 in genuine "eastern bills." If all went well, he would take Pinkerton on as his local partner, allowing the young cooper a chance to clear more cash in one year than Dundee's most prosperous merchant would see in a decade. Pinkerton took a moment to weigh the offer, then put out his hand to seal the deal. The two men arranged to carry out the exchange later that day at an appropriately remote spot—an unfinished church building in nearby Elgin.

This would be the first great test of Pinkerton's career, and he bungled it badly. As Craig rode off toward Elgin, Pinkerton headed back to Dundee to report to Hunt and Bosworth, who immediately supplied the cash needed to make the exchange, confident that Craig's arrest and prosecution would soon follow. At the deserted church in Elgin, however, Pinkerton's inexperience showed itself. As he passed the bundle of cash over to Craig, the older man asked him to step outside for a few minutes to see if anyone happened to be watching. Pinkerton did as directed, realizing too late that he had "placed myself in the man's power completely" by taking his eyes off the money. A moment later, Craig reappeared, telling an absurd story: A shadowy colleague had swooped in unexpectedly, he claimed, and left a mysterious parcel behind. "He is never seen by any living person with whom I have business," Craig insisted. "Look under that stone over yonder. I *think* you will find what you bought." Pinkerton saw at once that he had been badly outmaneuvered. Craig had arranged matters so that he could not be apprehended in possession of incriminating evidence. Reaching down, Pinkerton took the parcel from under the stone and found fifty ten-dollar bills inside. Glancing at Craig, Pinkerton saw a steely, self-satisfied expression on the older man's face. "Old John Craig is never caught napping, young man," he said pointedly.

Pinkerton hesitated for a moment, badly unsettled, as Craig continued to study him carefully. Recovering himself, Pinkerton saw that he had no choice but to continue playing his role, in the hope that the situation might yet be turned to his advantage. Thumbing through the packet of bills, he asked Craig how much more of his "product" happened to be available. The counterfeiter hedged, but he allowed as how he might be able to get his hands on an additional four thousand dollars. Pinkerton leapt at the opening. "Look here, Craig," he said, "if you wouldn't be in too big a hurry about getting back home, I'll tell you what I'll do. I believe I could make arrangements to buy you out altogether." Clutching the forged notes, Pinkerton hastily improvised a plan. If Craig would allow him a few days to gather up the necessary "eastern bills" from friends in the area, Pinkerton would meet him in Chicago, at a hotel called the Sauganash, to make the exchange. After a moment's consideration, Craig agreed. In the meantime, he said, he would lay low at the home of a friend. "Good-bye, then," said Craig shaking Pinkerton's hand. "But, mind you, be discreet!"

Being discreet was now the least of Pinkerton's problems. He had, in effect, made an all-or-nothing bet on the integrity of a counterfeiter. If Craig were to have second thoughts, or receive a better offer, Pinkerton would have nothing to show for Hunt and Bosworth's money but a pile of worthless paper. Even so, as the two men parted ways, some previously untapped instinct told Pinkerton that Craig could be trusted to keep their bargain: "Criminal though he was, he was a man who, when he had passed his word, would be certain to keep it."

Returning to Dundee, Pinkerton found that Hunt and Bosworth did not share this opinion. Craig had ridden off with a great deal of their money in his saddlebags and they feared that he "would leave us all in the lurch." Shaken by their doubts, Pinkerton went to bed that night filled with dread, "and fully satisfied in my own mind that I was not born to become a detective."

By the following morning, however, he had formed a plan of action. For three days, he devoted "very little attention to my casks and barrels" and gave himself over entirely to "a good deal of nervous plotting and planning." Having learned a bitter lesson at the church in Elgin, Pinkerton anticipated that Craig would arrange matters in Chicago so that no incriminating bills would be found in his hands. "Circumstances and my own youth and inexperience were against me," Pinkerton admitted, but he was determined to atone for his earlier failure. At last, on the appointed day, Pinkerton saddled a horse and rode into Chicago.

The Sauganash, Chicago's first hotel, was a whitewashed log structure at Wolf Point, where the main stem of the Chicago River divides into its north and south branches. Described by one early visitor as a "vile two-storied barrack," the Sauganash featured a tavern on the ground floor, where traders and other visitors were known to gather. Arriving well ahead of time, Pinkerton made a few final arrangements with a pair of Chicago constables. He positioned one of the officers inside the tavern, where the meeting was to take place, while the second would keep watch outside the building for any unexpected arrivals or departures. Satisfied, Pinkerton took a seat in the hotel's front room and waited.

At the appointed hour, John Craig entered the room and "sauntered about for a time," apparently in no rush to acknowledge Pinkerton. Finally, he snatched up a newspaper and dropped into an adjacent seat, pretending to be absorbed in reading. Without taking his eyes off the paper, he asked in a lowered voice if Pinkerton had managed to bring the money. Pinkerton, keeping his eyes fixed straight ahead, acknowledged that he had. Craig instructed him to pass it over, promising that a package of bills would be in his hands "in the course of an hour." Pinkerton was ready for this. Drawing a deep breath, he said that the friend who had loaned him the money, a man named Boyd, was having second thoughts. Boyd insisted on seeing the merchandise in advance, Pinkerton explained, and had accompanied him to Chicago in order to supervise the transaction. In fact, Pinkerton said, he expected Boyd to appear at any moment. The man was a lawyer, and a "stickler for form."

Craig appeared deeply unsettled by this development. He insisted "with some warmth" that he did not want an outsider complicating matters. Pinkerton answered in a tone that suggested the matter was out of his hands. "You know I would trust you with ten times this sum," he said, "but I've placed myself in this damned lawyer's power, and he insists like an idiot on having the thing done only in one way."

As Craig's objections mounted, Pinkerton admitted to himself that his chances of success were now "beginning to look a little misty." The two men adjourned to the hotel's tavern, where Craig knocked back a fortifying drink as Pinkerton continued to plead his case. After a few moments, Craig took himself off to consider the matter in private. Pinkerton later learned, from the constable posted outside, that the older man passed the next half hour walking aimlessly in various directions, making sudden stops and turns, and looking frequently over his shoulder to see if he was being followed. After a time, he drew up short, as though he had come to an abrupt decision, and made his way back to the hotel.

Seeing Craig reappear in the hotel's front room, Pinkerton at once stepped forward. "Well, Craig, are you going to let me have the money?" he asked. The older man looked back at him with an air of polite surprise, as if Pinkerton were a total stranger.

"What money?" Craig asked.

Pinkerton hadn't expected this. At a stroke, all his careful planning appeared to be undone. "The money you promised me," he stammered.

Craig remained unflappable. "I haven't the honor of your acquaintance, sir," he said coolly, "and therefore cannot imagine to what you allude."

Pinkerton was utterly dumbfounded. "If the Sauganash Hotel had fallen upon me," he would later say, "I could not have been more surprised."

Staggered as he was, Pinkerton knew that he had to take action. His entire scheme depended on apprehending Craig in the act of selling the forged bills. Now, with the older man feigning ignorance of Pinkerton and his designs, the would-be detective had no evidence that would stand up in court. Craig, he knew, was far too slippery to allow himself to be apprehended with counterfeit money in his pockets. If the case came before a judge, it would come down to one man's word against another's. The situation appeared hopeless, but Pinkerton felt obligated to follow through with his plans. Otherwise, Craig would simply slip away and return to his home in Vermont, out of the jurisdiction of the local authorities, carrying Hunt and Bosworth's money off with him.

"There was only one thing to do," Pinkerton concluded, "and that was to make Mr. Craig my prisoner." Pinkerton signaled the constable across the room, who hurried over to make the arrest. Craig, still pretending ignorance of both Pinkerton and his accusations, loudly protested his innocence. A large crowd gathered, and "considerable sympathy was expressed for the stately, gray-haired man who was being borne into captivity by the green-looking countryman cooper from Dundee." Pinkerton's first big case—which he would one day recount under the heading of "How I Became a Detective"—ended with a swarm of bystanders raining insults on his head.

As it happened, Pinkerton's flimsy evidence was never tested in court. Although Craig was duly arrested and locked up to await trial, it was discovered one morning that he had mysteriously vanished from his jail cell—leaving, it was said, at least one jailer considerably richer. The episode taught Pinkerton a valuable lesson in what he would call "the perfidy of officials." A second, more personal lesson had already been taken to heart. Writing of the episode many years later, Pinkerton reflected on a moment at the church in Elgin when he found himself lingering over Craig's bundle of fifty ten-dollar bills: "For a moment the greatest temptation of my life swept over me," he admitted. "A thousand thoughts of sudden wealth and a life free from the grinding labor which I had always known, came rushing into my mind. Here in my hands were five hundred dollars, or what professed to be, every one of them as good as gold, if I only chose to use it." He would resist the temptation, but Pinkerton never forgot it. Throughout his career, he claimed that he could never look on those who had fallen prey to greedy impulses without "a touch of genuine human sympathy."

Returning to Dundee, Pinkerton found that his latest exploit brought him even more notice than the Bogus Island adventure. "The country being new, and great sensations scarce, the affair was in everybody's mouth," he wrote, "and I suddenly found myself called upon, from every quarter, to undertake matters requiring detective skill." Before long, Pinkerton was offered the post of deputy sheriff of Kane County. The duties were not terribly demanding, mostly serving court papers and chasing down an occasional horse thief, but his days as a country cooper were coming to an end—"all of which," he later admitted, "I owe to Old John Craig."

CHAPTER THREE
ARDENT SPIRITS

•

Against Lincoln the Democrats put up Peter Cartwright, a famous and rugged old-fashioned circuit rider, a storming evangelist, exhorter and Jackson Democrat. [Lincoln] went to a religious meeting where Cartwright in due time said, "All who desire to give their hearts to God, and go to heaven, will stand." A sprinkling of men, women and children stood up. The preacher exhorted, "All who do not wish to go to hell will stand." All stood up—except Lincoln. Then Cartwright in his gravest voice: "I observe that many responded to the first invitation to give their hearts to God and go to heaven. And I further observe that all of you save one indicated that you did not desire to go to hell. The sole exception is Mr. Lincoln, who did not respond to either invitation. May I inquire of you, Mr. Lincoln, where you are going?"
Lincoln slowly rose: "I came here as a respectful listener. I did not know that I was to be singled out by Brother Cartwright. I believe in treating religious matters with due solemnity. I admit that the questions propounded by Brother Cartwright are of great importance. I did not feel called upon to answer as the rest did. Brother Cartwright asks me directly where I am going. I desire to reply with equal directness: I am going to Congress."
—CARL SANDBURG, on Lincoln's 1846 congressional race

IN THE SPRING OF 1847, a letter appeared in the *Western Citizen*, a Kane County newspaper, accusing Allan Pinkerton of being an "unrepining atheist." The denunciation appeared over the signature of M. L. Wisner, the pastor of the Dundee Baptist Church, and signaled that the town cooper had become persona non grata in the community.

Pinkerton was not a religious man. In Glasgow, he recalled, his parents had been "obliged to take their children to church to be baptized, but otherwise they never went to church; they were what is called Atheists."

Pinkerton, too, had taken his firstborn son to be baptized at Wisner's church in Dundee, but he saw himself in much the same light as his parents. Nevertheless, for the sake of fitting in as a member of the community, he dutifully hitched up a farm wagon each week and drove with Joan to Sunday services.

Pastor Wisner's sudden grievance against his parishioner appears to have had more to do with politics than with church doctrine. A few weeks earlier, Pinkerton had announced himself as a candidate for office in Kane County's Abolitionist party, putting a public face on the clandestine activities he had long pursued with the Underground Railroad. There were many in Dundee who felt as Pinkerton did about slavery, but the young cooper's open, unequivocal stance put him at odds with the village elders, reflecting a clash between factions of the church that would echo through the region.

When Pinkerton's friends rallied to his side, publishing a letter of "collective protest" in the next issue of the *Citizen,* Wisner stepped up his attack. He now insisted that Pinkerton was both using and selling "ardent spirits," placing him at the wrong end of the "moral thermometer" established by the American temperance movement. Pinkerton, a teetotaler, raised an energetic defense, gathering testimonials to the effect that no liquor had ever passed his lips and that spirits were not tolerated in his home. Wisner was unmoved. The pastor demanded a series of open trials at the church, where Pinkerton's moral failings could be paraded in front of the congregation. In one session, Pinkerton was rebuked for circulating blasphemous materials, a charge he strenuously denied.

As the slander and finger-pointing escalated, Pinkerton withdrew from the congregation in disgust, along with a number of sympathetic friends. Pinkerton believed he had left with his honor intact, but the episode placed an uncomfortable strain on his daily life in the small community. Business at the cooperage tapered off, and neighbors looked away as he and Joan passed. Not surprisingly, he began to look for greener pastures.

Soon, his reputation as a rising lawman brought an offer from William Church, the sheriff of neighboring Cook County, to serve as his deputy. Though it meant selling the cooperage, Pinkerton didn't hesitate. He was more than ready to put Dundee behind him and turn his volatile energies to better things. All his life, Pinkerton had been spoiling for a fight; a small man with big fists, he was cunning enough to channel his innate aggression into lofty causes, whether it was the Chartist rebellion of his homeland or the abolitionist movement of his adopted country. He had learned many lessons from John Craig, the wily counterfeiter, and had caught sight of possibilities beyond the banks of the Fox River.

The new position marked a considerable increase in status, as Cook County encompassed Chicago, and with it fully half the population of Illinois. Joan accepted the move stoically, though not without a note of regret. She would never again hear the fondly remembered "rat-tat-tat" of the cooper's hammer as it kept time with her singing. "They were bonnie days," she said of their time in Dundee, "but Allan was a restless one."

With his wife and one-year-old son at his side, Pinkerton and his horse-drawn wagon rolled into Chicago in the fall of 1847. The city was in the midst of a robust expansion—"growth is much too slow a word," one visitor exclaimed—and the population had nearly tripled since Pinkerton's days at the Lill & Diversey brewery. The family settled on Adams Street, between Fifth and Franklin, in one of the thriving neighborhood's two-room "balloon" houses—so named for the speedy manner in which they sprang up.

Pinkerton's family was also expanding rapidly. Twins, Joan and Robert, were born within a year. Pinkerton often spoke of the "unbroken sunshine" his children brought to the house, but storm clouds soon appeared. Another daughter, Mary, would die a few years later at the age of two, and seven-year-old Joan would be carried off by fever soon afterward. Two more daughters followed in time; one of whom, known as Belle, would suffer from poor health all her life, requiring near-constant care.

Professionally, Pinkerton made a fast rise through the ranks. After a year as a deputy sheriff, he won an appointment from Chicago's mayor to serve as the city's first—and, for some time, only—official detective. Already, Pinkerton had carved out a reputation for strength and daring; now, as an official detective, he added a rigid, incorruptible code of ethics to his tough-guy image, setting a pattern for future generations of "untouchable" lawmen. Pinkerton, it was said, could not be bought.

At a time when Chicago still retained much of the character of a frontier town, a lawman's effectiveness could be measured in the number and vehemence of his enemies. By that standard, Pinkerton had no equal. One night in September 1853, as he walked up Clark Street toward home, a gunman stepped out of the darkness and fired a pistol into his back. "The pistol was of large caliber," reported the *Daily Democratic Press*, "heavily loaded and discharged so near that Mr. Pinkerton's coat was put on fire." His survival was largely a matter of luck; he had developed a habit of walking with his left arm tucked behind his back, as if to add ballast to his top-heavy, loping stride. As the gunman fired from behind, Pinkerton's arm caught the full force of the shots, probably sparing his life. "Two slugs shattered the bone five inches from the wrist and passed along the bone to the elbow," according to the *Press,* "where they were cut out by a surgeon, together with pieces of his coat." By the time he returned to duty, Pinkerton's reputation had taken on a mythic dimension: Even bullets couldn't stop him.

Soon, Pinkerton took a position as a special mail agent with the United States Postal Service, where he became embroiled in a sensational, high-profile robbery. At the time, the Chicago post office was all but overwhelmed with complaints from local businessmen about bank drafts and postal orders—representing huge sums of money—that routinely went missing in the mail. Post office officials, fearing legal reprisals, assigned Pinkerton to investigate.

Pinkerton went undercover to get a firsthand look at the situation, an approach he would use again and again in years to come. Posing as a mail sorter, or "piler," he spent several weeks pulling shifts at Chicago's main postal depot. While hauling mailbags and working the sorting table, Pinkerton managed to ingratiate himself with a coworker named Theodore Dennison, praising the "swift and nimble" manner in which his new friend handled letters and packages. Dennison warmed to the flattery, boasting that his fingers were "so sensitive that he knew when a letter contained a penny or a dollar." The remark struck Pinkerton as notably suspicious. Soon, he observed the nimble-fingered clerk slipping envelopes into his pockets.

Dennison, Pinkerton learned, had a brother who had previously been arrested for mail theft. These "familial associations," together with several more incidents of pilfering, led Pinkerton to believe that he'd gathered all the evidence he needed. On the following Saturday morning, he brought a Cook County deputy to the sorting office to make the arrest as Dennison left the building. The postal clerk tried to flee as the deputy moved in, but he soon found himself sprawled facedown in the dirt—"as pale as ashes"—with Pinkerton pinning his arms behind his back.

To Pinkerton's distress, Dennison's familial associations extended upward as well as down. When the suspect was formally charged, it emerged that his uncle was no less a figure than the postmaster of Chicago, who tersely informed Pinkerton that he had better produce some fairly hard evidence to back up his claims. This proved difficult, as no bank drafts or money orders had been found on Dennison's person at the time of his arrest. Pinkerton, it appeared, had fingered the wrong man.

With his future at stake, Pinkerton took two deputies to search the clerk's room at a nearby boardinghouse. The three men spent several hours rummaging through "every stitch and stick," even rolling back the carpet and prying up floorboards, but no evidence surfaced to substantiate Pinkerton's accusation. On the point of despair, Pinkerton took down a picture from the wall and flipped it back to front. There, he found the first of several incriminating bank drafts cunningly folded into the frame. A search of the other pictures in the room produced additional drafts, totaling nearly four thousand dollars. One newspaper offered a giddy tally of the distribution of the sums: "Behind a picture of the Virgin Mary and the Immaculate Conception: $1,503. The Highland Lovers: $900. The Indian Warrior: $1,000. A framed Daguerreotype of his mother: $300."

Chicago took notice. "To Allan Pinkerton is due all the credit for the detection," reported the *Chicago Press*. "For three weeks Mr. Pinkerton scarcely has had repose in the devotion with which he has followed up the criminal . . . until body and brain were nearly exhausted. As a detective police officer, Mr. Pinkerton has no superior, and we doubt if he has any equal in the country. There is danger of expecting too much of his peculiar talent and force, for we suppose there are some impossibilities in the detection of villainy, even for him."

Buoyed by this sudden burst of notoriety, Pinkerton decided to leave the city payroll and strike out on his own. He found a small second-floor suite of rooms at the corner of Dearborn and Washington streets, a few steps from the city courthouse, and set up an office dedicated to the "modern science of thief-taking," soon to be more commonly known as a private detective agency.

It was perhaps inevitable that the only and original cooper of Dundee should become the only and original private detective of Chicago. His friend Robert Fergus, a fellow immigrant, had made the most of Chicago's many opportunities, parlaying a menial printer's job into a successful publishing concern. With his success in the Dennison case, Pinkerton saw a chance to follow Fergus's path to success, leverage his growing fame, and once again become his own master.

Initially, Pinkerton partnered with a local lawyer named Edward Rucker and set up operations as the North-Western Police Agency, but Rucker soon faded from view and the operation continued as the Pinkerton National Detective Agency. Pinkerton would always list the year of the agency's founding as 1850, but it is possible that he fudged the date to create the illusion of longer experience, as the accounts of his post office exploit did not appear until 1855. An early statement of purpose echoed the effusions of the *Chicago Press* story, and offered a broad, somewhat scattershot menu of the fledgling agency's services. Potential clients were informed that Pinkerton's agency would "attend to the investigation and depredation [*sic*], frauds and criminal offenses; the detection of offenders, procuring arrests and convictions, apprehension or return of fugitives from justice, or bail; recovering lost or stolen property, obtaining information, etc."

Pinkerton's agency was not, as many have claimed, the first of its kind, but it would soon eclipse all others. Though this success had much to do with Pinkerton's cunning and his relentless drive, he also benefited from having set up shop in the right place at the right time. Chicago's headlong expansion continued through the 1850s as railroad lines and shipping traffic converged to form what one newspaper called "a hub of industry that, however noisy and malodorous, is undeniably thriving." The new prosperity brought a new type of crime: train robbery. As the nation's disparate railroad lines expanded—covering more and more territory, although not yet linked up under a single authority—they presented an ideal target for opportunistic criminals who preyed on baggage cars and bonded messengers before disappearing into the empty spaces between regional jurisdictions.

Pinkerton, in Chicago, was ideally positioned to combat this new class of criminals. The authority he claimed for himself wasn't bound by county or state lines. With its handpicked operatives and dogged, systematic methods of pursuit, Pinkerton's agency could push into territories where overmatched and undertrained local authorities could not follow, marking the transition between frontier justice and a national authority. The Federal Bureau of Investigation, created to oversee interstate law enforcement, would not come into being for several decades, and the United States Secret Service, originally designed to combat counterfeiting, would not be created until 1865—Abraham Lincoln would sign the legislation on April 14, the date of his assassination. In the absence of federal authority, Pinkerton made up the rules as he went along. He literally designed his own badge.

From his first day in business, Pinkerton took extraordinary measures to stand apart from other lawmen. The bitter lessons of his early years— John Craig's bribing his way out jail; Theodore Dennison's operating under the protection of his powerful uncle—opened Pinkerton's eyes to the realities of official corruption. In response, he worked hard to establish a reputation for honesty and probity, and codified it as a business policy. In the early years of the agency, he hammered out a series of "General Principles," which he hoped would serve as watertight ethical guidelines for his employees:

> The Agency will not represent a defendant in a criminal case except with the knowledge and consent of the prosecutor, they will not shadow jurors or investigate public officials in the performance of their duties, or trade-union officers or members in their lawful union activities; they will not accept employment from one political party against another; they will not report union meetings unless the meetings are open to the public without restriction; they will not work for vice crusaders; they will not accept contingent fees, gratuities or rewards. The Agency will never investigate the morals of a woman unless in connection with another crime, nor will it handle cases of divorce or of a scandalous nature.

Pinkerton also expounded on the character traits—both moral and intellectual—that would be necessary on the mean streets of Chicago and beyond:

> The role of a detective is a high and honorable calling. Few professions excel it. He is an officer of justice and must himself be pure and above reproach. . . . Criminals are powerful of mind and strong of will, who if they had devoted themselves to honest pursuits would undoubtedly have become members of honorable society. The detectives who have to gather the evidence and arrest these criminals must be men of high order of mind and must possess clean, honest, comprehensive understanding, force of will and vigor of body. . . . Criminals must eventually reveal their secrets and a detective must have the necessary experience and judgment of human nature to know the criminal in his weakest moment and force from him, through sympathy and confidence, the secret which devours him.

These principles formed a template for Pinkerton's first generation of "operatives," the term he used to distinguish his employees from common police detectives. Along with his Chartist ideals, Pinkerton also drew on a robust strain of derring-do that he likely gleaned from Eugène-François Vidocq, the legendary French detective. A criminal in his youth, Vidocq later turned his talents to law enforcement, helping to create the Sûreté, the detective bureau of the French police, in 1811. The French detective, whose story would serve as inspiration for the character of Jean Valjean in Victor Hugo's *Les Miserables,* was still active in Paris when Pinkerton opened his doors in Chicago. Widely credited as the first investigator to bring scientific rigor to the detection of crime, Vidocq introduced such innovations as rudimentary ballistics, plaster of paris molds of footprints, and a centralized criminal database. At the same time, he pioneered the use of disguises and cover identities, a technique that Pinkerton would employ in nearly every major operation of his career. Vidocq's dramatic, often fanciful memoir had been a publishing phenomenon both in Europe and the United States, and Pinkerton seems to have studied it closely. Pinkerton would have been especially amused by a chapter in which Vidocq matched wits with a duplicitous cooper from Livry, who was suspected of stealing a fortune in jewels. Posing as a fellow thief, Vidocq plied the cooper with alcohol and eventually wormed his way into the suspect's confidence.

Pinkerton, for his part, advised his operatives against coercing statements by means of alcohol, as these tended to "shake the strength of evidence" when brought into court. The example of Vidocq, however, gave him a firm belief in the possibility of redemption for even the most hardened criminals. Pinkerton believed that lawbreakers were "capable of moral reform and elevation" if treated properly, and he advised his men to "do all in their power" in the interests of rehabilitation. "Unfortunately," he noted, "under our present system, this is too little thought of." If these views were progressive, other aspects of Pinkerton's philosophy reached back to the ancients by way of Machiavelli. Again and again, Pinkerton insisted that "the ends justify the means, if the ends are for the accomplishment of Justice." He understood, however, that this was not a universal view. "Moralists may question whether this is strictly right," he said, "but it is a necessity in the detection of crime."

During his first year of business Pinkerton spent much of his time assembling and training a core team of operatives. From the start, he demonstrated a strong eye for talent, beginning with his first employee, twenty-five-year-old George H. Bangs, a former newspaper reporter, who became Pinkerton's right-hand man. Tall and reserved, Bangs traced his lineage to the *Mayflower* and could mix easily with the rich and power-ful. Bangs proved "very able and efficient" as a detective, according to Pinkerton, and even more talented as a businessman. As general superin-tendent, Bangs oversaw the agency's finances and rapid growth, leaving Pinkerton to concentrate on detective work.

With Bangs minding the store in Chicago, Pinkerton was free to travel wherever his latest case happened to take him. In 1853, when an investi-gation took him to New York City, Pinkerton spotted a man he felt would make an outstanding addition to the team. Pinkerton, who had never been to New York before, had carved out some time to take in the spectacle of America's first world's fair. Characteristically, he was less in-terested in the soaring Crystal Palace exhibition than in the special police force detailed to guard it. Pinkerton was particularly struck by the effi-cient and courteous manner of a young police sergeant on duty inside the main hall. His name, Pinkerton learned, was Timothy Webster; a thirty-two-year-old native of England, he had emigrated with his family as a boy. Webster had set his sights on a career as a New York policeman, but his advancement had been thwarted, he believed, because he had no po-litical connections. Pinkerton, acting on impulse, offered him a job on the spot and handed him train fare to Chicago.

Timothy Webster soon became Pinkerton's best and most resourceful detective. "He was a man of great physical strength and endurance," Pinkerton said, "skilled in all athletic sports, and a good shot." Above all, in Pinkerton's view, Webster possessed "a strong will and a courage that knew no fear." Two other Englishmen, Pryce Lewis and John Scully, soon followed. Pinkerton also brought on a "shrewd hand" named John H. White, who had the useful manner and appearance, in Pinkerton's esti-mation, of a con man rather than a detective. White completed a core team of eight employees—five detectives, two clerks, and a secretary. Apart from Webster, none of Pinkerton's original operatives came from a law-enforcement background, but each had a quality that Pinkerton felt could be turned to his advantage. The men trained on the job, learning how to shadow suspects and gain the confidence of otherwise tight-lipped criminals. Like Vidocq, Pinkerton encouraged his men to adopt whatever persona would be useful for the task at hand, as he himself had done at the Chicago post office, and to inhabit that identity as fully as possible—"acting it out to the life," as he described it. One account of the Pinkerton operation describes the Chicago office as resembling the backstage of a theater, complete with a large closet full of disguises so that the men could easily transform themselves into bartenders, gamblers, horse-car conductors, or newly arrived "greenhorns" fresh off the boat from the old country.

In another corner of the office, Pinkerton pinned up sketches and daguerreotypes of wanted men, the rudimentary beginnings of what would become a storied "rogue's gallery" of hunted criminals. Over time, Pinkerton refined his record keeping to take account of a criminal's modus operandi, distinguishing characteristics, handwriting samples, and known associates. He cultivated an extensive correspondence with police captains and county sheriffs across the country, transforming the Chicago office into a national hub of criminal data. It was a project that would absorb him to the end of his life.

The ever-vigilant Pinkerton "Private Eye."

In time, the soon-to-be famous Pinkerton logo—a stern, unblinking eye—made its appearance on the agency's correspondence and legal documents. For Pinkerton, this aptly chosen symbol expressed the rigid work ethic and eternal vigilance he demanded from a prospective agent: "At an instant's warning, he must be ready to go wherever he may be ordered. Sometimes, for weeks, he may have little or no rest; and he may be called upon to endure hardships and dangers which few men have the courage to face."

Only a few years earlier, a scheming criminal had delivered a stinging rebuke to Pinkerton: "Old John Craig is never caught napping, young man." Now, as he took his place at the head of a rapidly expanding detective empire, Pinkerton turned these words into a statement of purpose, and he had the boldly lettered line placed beneath the image of the watchful, all-seeing eye. He had boiled it down to three simple words: "We Never Sleep."

CHAPTER FOUR
PINK LADY

•

A woman is the only thing I am afraid of that I know will not hurt me.
—ABRAHAM LINCOLN

IN OCTOBER OF 1856, Pinkerton took a momentary break from the reports and correspondence piled on his desk and dashed off a quick note to his friend Henry Hunt, the Dundee shopkeeper who had set him on the track of "Old John Craig" a decade earlier. Much had changed since the day Pinkerton stood barefoot in Hunt's store and admitted that he had never seen a ten-dollar bill. The Pinkerton agency now stretched across the region, with branch offices in Wisconsin, Michigan, and Indiana. The previous year, Pinkerton had signed a contract with the Illinois Central Railroad, undertaking to guard its "road" and rolling stock as the line pushed south to Mobile and the Gulf of Mexico. Several other railroad companies followed suit, employing a growing cadre of Pinkerton men for any "special and sudden exigencies" that might arise. For these services, Pinkerton received annual retainers amounting to ten thousand dollars a year, as well as "several funds hereinafter specified" to help the agency expand. As he told Hunt, "I am overwhelmed with business." The grueling pace sometimes left him so exhausted, he admitted, that he could scarcely stand: "I never removed my clothes this evening but fell across my bed."

That same year, Pinkerton made a decision that would change forever what it meant to be a Pinkerton man. One afternoon, as he sat "pondering deeply over some matters," Pinkerton looked up and saw a young woman standing in the door of his office. The visitor introduced herself as Mrs. Kate Warne and explained that she was a widow seeking employment. Pinkerton estimated her age at twenty-two or twenty-three. "She was above the medium height," he observed, "slender, graceful in her movements, and perfectly self-possessed in her manner." Kate Warne was perhaps the most remarkable person ever to pass through the doors of the Pinkerton National Detective Agency. Her pale, broad face was frank and unassuming, Pinkerton noted, but her dark blue eyes were captivating—sharp, decisive and "filled with fire." She was not a conventional beauty—her features, Pinkerton admitted, were "not what would be called handsome"—but she radiated a quiet strength and compassion. Kate Warne appeared to be the sort of person to whom one would turn in times of distress.

"I invited her to take a seat," Pinkerton recalled. He assumed, understandably, that she had come in hopes of a secretarial position. "I'm afraid there are no openings at present," he said, glancing down at his papers.

Mrs. Warne folded her gloved hands. "I'm afraid you have misunderstood me," she said.

Pinkerton looked up. "Have I?" he asked.

The young widow gave him a level gaze across the cluttered expanse of his desk. Her blue eyes, he saw, were now burning with resolve. "I have come to inquire," she said, "as to whether you would not employ me as a detective."

These words, Pinkerton admitted, left him dumbfounded and thoroughly unsettled. Up to that moment, the possibility of hiring a female operative had simply never occurred to him. The very suggestion was shocking, and entirely outside the compass of his experience. Pinkerton agents, by definition, were rugged men of action, good with their fists and cool in the face of danger. The work was physically demanding, as well; one operative had recently trailed a horse-drawn carriage on foot rather than lose sight of a suspect, covering more than twelve miles at a dead run. This was not Pinkerton's idea of women's work.

To his credit, Pinkerton decided to give Mrs. Warne a fair hearing. "It is not the custom to employ women as detectives," he told her. "How, exactly, do you propose to be of service?" The young widow leaned forward and spoke with sudden urgency. "A female detective may go and worm out secrets in ways that are impossible for male detectives. A criminal may hide all traces of his guilt from his fellow men, but he will not hide it from his wife or mistress. The testimony of these women, then, becomes the sole means of resolving the crimes, and this testimony can be obtained in only one way—a female detective makes her acquaintance, wins her confidence, and draws out the story of the wrongdoing."

Pinkerton nodded his head as Mrs. Warne spoke, and continued nodding after she had finished. In spite of his instinctive reservations, he could not fail to see the merits of her reasoning. "She had evidently given the matter much study," he admitted. Still, as Pinkerton knew all too well, his operatives routinely placed themselves in harm's way—he himself carried scars along the length of his left arm from the night he had been shot in the back. He had grave misgivings about exposing a woman to such dangers.

Mrs. Warne, seeing the indecision in his face, tried to continue pleading her case, but Pinkerton held up a hand to stop her. "Thank you, madam," he said. "I must consider the matter in private. If you will return tomorrow afternoon, I will give you my decision." Mrs. Warne clearly wished to say more, but after a moment's pause, she thought better of it. She gave a polite nod, thanked Pinkerton for his time, and swept from the room. Pinkerton spent several moments gazing at the empty doorway, an uncharacteristic look of puzzlement on his face.

Pinkerton spent a restless night weighing the "moral costs" of employing a female detective, but he admitted that "the more I thought of it, the more convinced I became that the idea was a good one." When Mrs. Warne returned the next day at the appointed time, Pinkerton signed her up as America's first female private eye.

There was no precedent for Kate Warne. The work of Elizabeth Cady Stanton and Susan B. Anthony had barely begun in 1856, and their National Woman's Suffrage Association was more than ten years in the future. The New York City Police Department would not have a female investigator in its ranks until 1903. Nevertheless, Kate Warne at once became an integral part of the Pinkerton agency, and she proved to be a versatile and utterly fearless operative. In one investigation, she posed as a fortune-teller—"the only living descendant of Hermes"—to lure secrets from a superstitious suspect, and on another occasion she forged a "useful intimacy" with the wife of a suspected murderer. "She succeeded far beyond my utmost expectations," Pinkerton admitted, "and I soon found her an invaluable acquisition to my force." Mrs. Warne proved so indispensable that Pinkerton encouraged her to recruit other female operatives. Soon, the Pinkerton agency had a female detective bureau running out of the Chicago office, with Mrs. Warne acting as superintendent.

In later years, Pinkerton chafed at criticism that he should never have hired women to do work that was not only dangerous but also morally compromising. "It has been claimed that the work is unwomanly, that no respectable woman who becomes a detective can remain virtuous," he wrote. "To these theories, I enter a positive denial. I have no hesitation in saying that the profession of a detective, for a lady possessing the requisite characteristics, is as useful and honorable employment as can be found in any walk of life."

At the time of Mrs. Warne's hiring, however, Pinkerton was more concerned with solving cases than with social convention, and his new operative was soon given a chance to test her mettle. In the early months of 1858, Pinkerton received a letter from Edward S. Sanford, vice president of the Adams Express Company, describing the theft of several thousand dollars from a locked courier pouch. The money had been in transit from the Adams Express offices in Montgomery, Alabama, to a branch depot in Augusta, Georgia. Oddly, Sanford did not want Pinkerton to launch an investigation; he simply wanted the detective's advice on how to proceed. After describing the circumstances of the theft in some detail, Sanford expressed a hope that Pinkerton might be able to shed light on how the theft had been managed—based solely on the information contained in the letter—and, if possible, point his finger at the thief.

To Pinkerton, this appeared to be a fool's errand. For all his skill and resourcefulness, he had little hope of cracking the case at a remove of six hundred miles, without ever seeing the crime scene or interrogating the suspects. After reading the letter a second time, however, he found that the challenge stirred his professional pride. Setting aside his reservations, Pinkerton spent a weekend in his office pulling together a nine-page report, an extraordinary attempt at playing armchair detective, his information based solely on an inexperienced observer's account of the matter.

Pinkerton had a solid business reason for making the effort. "Up to that time I had never done any business for the Adams Express," he recalled, "and as their business was well worth having, I was determined to win." Pinkerton's eagerness was understandable, as the Adams Express Company—together with Wells Fargo & Company and American Express—had created a business that was growing as rapidly as the railroads themselves. In spite of the ongoing efforts of Pinkerton and other special mail agents, the United States Postal Service had not yet found a means to guarantee the safe delivery of large parcels and freight, especially when those shipments contained currency or other valuables. As the country's frontiers expanded, the need arose for bonded messenger services that promised both speed and security. These "express service" companies made use of whatever delivery methods were at hand, including horses, stagecoaches, and, later, as the railroads moved west, special train compartments fitted with armor plating. The delivery agents, or "expressmen," who undertook these arduous and often dangerous assignments were, in Pinkerton's words, "men above reproach."

Not surprisingly, Pinkerton paid close attention to the workings of express companies. The presence of cash and other "express material" presented an irresistible target to a rising breed of train robbers. In some cases, bands of outlaws would stop a train, or even derail it, in order to break into its express compartment. Over the next decade, railroad companies would turn again and again to Pinkerton for protection.

There had been no brazen show of force in the Adams Express case, however. Instead, the shipment had simply vanished en route from Montgomery to Augusta. From Edward Sanford's letter, Pinkerton knew that the missing money had been placed in a locked pouch in Montgomery before it was handed over to the expressman. Pinkerton also knew that, as a matter of policy, Adams Express messengers were not informed of the contents of their pouches, nor were they given any access to their cargo while it was en route—the pouches were locked away in armored safes during transport. "The messenger was not furnished with a key to the pouch," Pinkerton noted, "but it was handed to him locked by the agent at one end of the route to be delivered in the same condition to the agent at the other end." As the lock on the pouch boasted a "peculiar construction" and showed no signs of tampering, Pinkerton concluded that the robbery had not actually occurred during the train journey. In all likelihood, he believed, the money had never made it into the pouch at all. Instead, the cash had been stolen before the train ever left Montgomery, and the empty pouch had been placed into the hands of the expressman as a decoy. Based on this theory of the crime, Pinkerton's suspicions fell on a man named Nathan Maroney, the manager of the Adams Express office in Montgomery, who had been the last person to have possession of both the pouch and the key. Though Pinkerton could offer no evidence without a firsthand examination of the scene, he advised Sanford to keep Maroney "under strict surveillance, before he bites you twice."

Pinkerton took a great deal of satisfaction at having provided a probable solution to the case without ever stirring from his desk in Chicago. "The letter was a very long one," he admitted, "but one of which I have always been proud." He heard nothing more from Sanford, however, and in time he put the affair out of his mind. One year later, a cryptic telegram arrived: "Allen Pinkerton: Can you send me a man—half horse and half alligator? I have got 'bit' once more. When can you send him? Edward S. Sanford."

The phrase "half horse and half alligator"—used to describe the type of rugged outdoorsman who was equally at home in the backwoods or on the river—suggested something of the challenge that lay ahead. Pinkerton soon learned that Sanford had taken his advice to heart and had arranged for the arrest of Nathan Maroney, the Montgomery office manager. The evidence against Maroney was shaky at best, but Sanford believed he had no other way to prevent the suspect from slipping out of town with the company's money.

What Sanford had not foreseen was that Maroney's arrest would spark a wave of public outrage. The integrity of the office manager, according to the local press, "had always been unquestioned." Though it was well known that Maroney had a "love for fast horses, which often threw him into the company of betting men," the suspect's friends believed he was being unfairly maligned. The city's leading citizens denounced Adams Express and raised forty thousand dollars for bail. Under fire, and fearful that his case was too weak to stand up in court, Sanford pleaded with Pinkerton to find the proof that would "end this thing for good and all."

In many ways, the Maroney case was an index of a worsening political climate. In May 1858, a scant three weeks after the robbery, the city of Montgomery had convened the highly contentious Southern Commercial Convention, ostensibly to discuss business concerns. The official agenda was soon pushed aside, in the words of a *New York Times* reporter, for "an exhibition of low, contemptible demagogueism and political cant." Amid calls for the removal of "existing prohibitory laws" concerning slavery, the convention became a platform for "denunciations hurled forth against the North." The Nathan Maroney case provided the city with yet another grievance against the North. The local press rallied behind Maroney as a man of "high character and Southern citizenship," while the Adams Express Company—headquartered at that time in New York—was widely seen as a hostile Northern concern launching a campaign of baseless persecution. As the trial date loomed, the consequences for Adams Express were potentially ruinous, as the majority of the company's business was conducted in the South. If he had any hope of defusing the situation, Sanford realized, he would have to tread carefully and construct an airtight case against Maroney.

Responding to Sanford's summons, Pinkerton devised a plan of attack that relied heavily on the talents of Kate Warne. Although Nathan Maroney was free on bail, Pinkerton knew that he would be at pains not to do anything to draw suspicion. The solution, in Pinkerton's view, rested with close observation of Maroney's wife. She undoubtedly knew the truth of her husband's actions, Pinkerton believed, and had probably taken possession of the stolen money during his imprisonment in order to keep it safe from investigators in Montgomery.

Gathering a team of operatives, Pinkerton established a base of operations in Philadelphia, where Mrs. Maroney had gone with her young daughter, Flora, to escape the unwelcome notoriety as her husband awaited trial. There, Pinkerton hoped, Kate Warne might find an opportunity to strike up a useful friendship. "As confidence begets confidence," Pinkerton told her, "Mrs. Maroney will most certainly, in time, unbosom herself to you." In fact, Mrs. Maroney appeared to be unbosoming herself freely in her husband's absence. She ranged from city to city in pursuit of "social pleasures," often in the company of handsome young men. It did not escape Pinkerton's professional eye that Mrs. Maroney was an uncommonly lovely and exotic woman. "She was a medium sized, rather slender brunette," he observed, "with black flashing eyes, black hair, thin lips and a rather voluptuously formed bust."

In time Mrs. Maroney alighted in Jenkintown, Pennsylvania, a convenient stopping point on the road between Philadelphia and Doylestown. She had relatives in the town, Pinkerton learned, and was planning a lengthy visit at a local boardinghouse. To get the lay of the land, Pinkerton sent an operative from house to house; posing as an itinerant clock repairman, he gathered local gossip at each stop. Next, Mrs. Warne took a room at the boardinghouse, posing as the wife of a Southern businessman, and waited for a chance to cross paths with Mrs. Maroney. "The desired introduction was brought about by an accident," Pinkerton recalled. Mrs. Maroney and her daughter, Flora, had been taking their "accustomed stroll through the pleasure grounds" of Jenkintown when the girl, running ahead of her mother, tripped and pitched forward onto a gravel path, badly scraping her hands. Mrs. Warne was close at hand, and she rushed forward to help the girl. By the time Mrs. Maroney caught up with her daughter, Mrs. Warne was binding Flora's wounds with a handkerchief.

Mrs. Warne's kindness brought a "rush of womanly feeling" from Mrs. Maroney, and soon the two women were having tea together at the boardinghouse. In the course of their conversation, Mrs. Warne managed to let slip that she bore a secret sorrow—her husband had been "enticed into committing forgeries," she said, and was now serving a prison term. Mrs. Maroney said nothing of her own husband's circumstances, but she appeared to regard Mrs. Warne with renewed interest.

Meanwhile, another Pinkerton operative appeared on the scene. "A woman of Mrs. Maroney's stamp, while separated from her husband, would most likely desire gentlemen's company," Pinkerton observed, "and as she, like most of her class, would put up with none but the handsomest, it was necessary to select as fine a looking gentleman to be her wooer as could be found." As it happened, Pinkerton had just such a person in his employ, a man named De Forest, who soon joined Mrs. Maroney on her strolls through the pleasure grounds of Jenkintown. Now that all the pieces were in place, Pinkerton believed that Mrs. Maroney would, in time, lead his team to the money her husband had stolen. No sooner had he set the plan in motion, however, than he received word that time was growing short. A letter from Edward Sanford informed Pinkerton that the Adams Express Company's lawyers had lost hope of building an effective case against their suspect. With the trial date fast approaching, the company's hopes now rested entirely on Pinkerton's investigation. "Do not fail us," Sanford wrote.

An unexpected break came when Maroney traveled to New York for a brief rendezvous with his wife. While in the city, he visited a locksmith to have an unusual key duplicated. The key proved to be of the same type used to open messenger pouches, like the one from which the Adams Express company's cash had gone missing. "On discovering this, I saw through Maroney's plan at once," Pinkerton said. "He wished to have a key made similar to the pouch key, and introduce it as evidence at his trial." The appearance of a duplicate key would cloud the prosecutor's assertion that only Maroney could have had access to the missing money. In this way, Pinkerton believed, Maroney might well "overthrow the testimony" of his accusers.

Maroney's attempt to cover his tracks gave Pinkerton an idea. "If we could get him in prison," Pinkerton reasoned, "I could introduce a detective, disguised as a fellow prisoner, whose duty would be to get into his confidence." Pinkerton readily admitted that certain "points of law" did not favor this plan, but he pressed ahead nonetheless. Maroney was taken into custody on unspecified charges and placed in a New York holding cell with one of Pinkerton's men, John White, who posed as a forger. The two men soon developed an easy rapport over countless hands of euchre, but Maroney remained tight-lipped about the Adams Express robbery. Pinkerton stirred the pot further by sending anonymous letters to the prison, informing Maroney that his wife was receiving the attentions of a gentleman caller in Jenkintown. Maroney grew agitated and restless, telling White that he was more anxious than ever to get out of prison so he could rush to his wife's side.

In a few days, a man representing himself as a lawyer—actually Pinkerton's superintendent, George Bangs—appeared to deliver John White's release order. At this, Maroney roused himself to action. Fearing that his wife would run off with her suitor while he languished in prison, Maroney pleaded with White for assistance. White allowed as how he might be able to make himself useful if "the right kind of money" could be found to buy Maroney's way out of trouble. Maroney took the words to heart. If White would agree to go to Jenkintown on his behalf, Maroney said, his wife would provide all the money they would need. After a convincing show of reluctance, White agreed to undertake the mission. Greatly relieved, Maroney sat down and wrote a letter to his wife, instructing her to "hand over everything you have in the packages" to White. "Now, I say to you, trust in him implicitly!" Maroney urged. "He will take care of all."

As White made his way to Jenkintown, however, a fresh complication arose. Initially, Pinkerton had expected that Kate Warne and the handsome Mr. De Forest would have several weeks in which to work their way into Mrs. Maroney's confidence, drawing out incriminating evidence by slow, steady degrees. With Adams Express pressing him for quick results, however, Pinkerton had been forced to adopt the faster, messier expedient of throwing Maroney into jail to extract an admission of guilt. Now, as the twin strands of the investigation crossed, it appeared that Pinkerton had tripped himself up. Mrs. Maroney, having grown fond of De Forest's company, did not seem especially anxious to see her husband released. "I don't know what to do," she told Mrs. Warne. "I am almost crazy!"

Pinkerton realized that the success of the operation now rested entirely with Mrs. Warne. If she could persuade Mrs. Maroney to hand over the mysterious "packages" to White, and if—as Pinkerton assumed—those packages contained the stolen Adams Express money, the case would be solved. Otherwise, Maroney would stand trial in Montgomery without the evidence needed to convict him.

It took three days. During that time, Mrs. Warne "talked incessantly" as she attempted to coax Mrs. Maroney into revealing where she had hidden the packages. "She appealed to Mrs. Maroney's sense of duty," Pinkerton wrote. "She depicted in glowing terms the happiness of the wife who looks only to her husband's interests, and makes sacrifices in his behalf. She drew a touching picture of Maroney's sufferings in jail, and tried to impress upon her the conviction that it was more than probable that he had taken the money so as to be able to place her in a situation where she could command any luxury. 'He loves you,' said she, 'and would do anything for you.'"

Mrs. Maroney was unmoved. She acknowledged that her husband had placed "certain funds" in her care, but she denied any knowledge of wrongdoing. Moreover, she insisted that the money should remain hidden at all costs: "I will burn it before I will give it to White," she declared.

As the hours wore on, Mrs. Maroney "invoked the aid of stimulants" time and time again, growing even less inclined to assist her husband as the alcohol did its work. "I don't want anyone with me but you," she told Mrs. Warne at one stage. "Would you be willing to run away with me? We could go down to Louisiana, where we are not known, buy a small place in some out of the way town and live secluded for four or five years, until our existence was forgotten." Mrs. Warne pretended to fall in with the plan, certain that it would bring the hidden money to light, but even now Mrs. Maroney refused to say where the cash was hidden. Instead, she proposed to live on Mrs. Warne's income until the excitement over the Adams Express robbery died down. Only then, she insisted, would it be safe to recover the hidden banknotes and "make our appearance once more in the fashionable world, with plenty of money to maintain our position." Mrs. Warne gave a heavy sigh, gathered herself, and tried again.

Pinkerton, meanwhile, waited in Philadelphia with Edward Sanford and other officers of Adams Express, who were pressing harder than ever for a resolution. During the long wait, Pinkerton assured his anxious clients that the case was in good hands, as Mrs. Warne's "subtle but very potent" powers of persuasion were far greater than his own. In fact, Mrs. Warne had vowed in a letter to Pinkerton that she would see the money delivered safely to Philadelphia, "even if she had to walk in with it herself."

At the end of three days, Mrs. Maroney's reserves finally broke. "Your duty as a wife is plain and simple," Mrs. Warne told her. "Do as your husband wishes you to do." Mrs. Warne's long hours of pleading and cajoling had done their work, said Pinkerton, "but to Mrs. Maroney it was a bitter pill." Without another word, she led Mrs. Warne to the dirt cellar of the boardinghouse. There, a heavy bundle wrapped in an oilskin cloth was pulled from a deep hole and handed over to John White. This done,

Mrs. Maroney withdrew to her room to seek the consolation of brandy. "This excitement has nearly killed me," she declared.

Within hours, at the La Pierre House, a hotel in Philadelphia, Pinkerton's team gathered one by one, shedding the various disguises they had assumed over the course of the investigation. Edward Sanford summoned the president of Adams Express to count up the recovered money personally. "The package proved to contain thirty-nine thousand five hundred and fifteen dollars," Pinkerton reported, "within four hundred and eighty-five dollars of the amount stolen."

Kate Warne burst into the room shortly after the money had been tallied, still covered in grime from the dirt cellar and hovering at the point of exhaustion from her three-day effort. On being assured that all was well, she sank heavily into a chair. "Her strength seemed suddenly to leave her," Pinkerton wrote. "The victory was complete, but her faculties had been strained to the utmost in accomplishing it, and she felt completely exhausted. She had the proud satisfaction of knowing that to a woman belonged the honors of the day."

IN FACT, THE VICTORY was not yet complete. Even now, Nathan Maroney remained confident that he would be acquitted of all charges at his trial in Alabama. The money found in Jenkintown, he insisted, had nothing to do with any robbery; it had been raised by the sale of his property in Montgomery. As the trial commenced in December 1859, Maroney appeared relaxed and self-assured, smiling broadly at his friends in the courtroom and nodding approvingly as witnesses spoke in glowing terms of his character and service to the community.

Matters took a sudden turn on the second day of testimony, as the clerk of the court rose at the prosecution's behest to summon John White to the witness stand. Only then did Maroney realize that his cell mate was a Pinkerton operative. "His cheek blanched with fear," Pinkerton recalled. "His eyes were filled with horror and he gasped for breath. A glass of water was handed to him. He gulped it down, and, vainly endeavoring to force back the tears from his eyes, in a hoarse, shaky voice he exclaimed, 'Tell the court I plead guilty . . . I am gone!'"

"This," Pinkerton noted with satisfaction, "ended the matter."

Pinkerton and his team had every reason to feel pleased with the operation. "The recovery of forty or fifty thousand dollars today is considered a small operation," he would write, looking back on the case years later, "but in 1859, before the war, the amount was looked upon as perfectly enormous." Though Pinkerton would investigate many high-profile robberies in the years to come, the Maroney case did more than any other to advance his reputation. By the time the verdict was delivered in Montgomery, Allan Pinkerton had become the most famous detective in America.

Every railroad baron in the country took note. The following year, when Samuel Felton—the president of the Philadelphia, Wilmington and Baltimore Railroad—heard vague rumors of a plot to disrupt the forthcoming presidential inauguration, he knew that only one man could be counted on to prevent it.

CHAPTER FIVE
LET US DARE TO DO OUR DUTY

•

John Brown's effort was peculiar. It was not a slave insurrection. It was an attempt by white men to get up a revolt among slaves in which the slaves refused to participate. . . . That affair, in its philosophy, corresponds with the many attempts, related in history, at the assassination of kings and emperors. An enthusiast broods over the oppression of a people till he fancies himself commissioned by Heaven to liberate them. He ventures the attempt, which ends in little else than his own execution.
—ABRAHAM LINCOLN at Cooper Union, February 27, 1860

THE KNOCK ON THE DOOR came at 4:30 A.M. on March 11, 1859. Allan Pinkerton swung open the door in his nightshirt, a revolver in hand. The sight that greeted him was all too familiar: a group of eleven newly liberated slaves—men and women alike—in tattered clothing and worn boots, exhausted after an arduous trudge across miles of frozen prairie. One of the women cradled a cold, hungry baby in her arms, having given birth on the journey, and she and her fellow travelers, according to one man who helped them on their way that night, formed "a portrait of human misery."

Pinkerton stepped back and waved the travelers inside, his eyes darting up and down the street before he shut the door behind them. His wife, Joan, still in her nightclothes and robe, set to work preparing breakfast while Pinkerton turned to the man who had brought them north after a raid in Missouri. Even in his soiled, ragged clothing, the visitor retained the stern and fiery appearance of an Old Testament prophet. Tall and angular, he carried himself with a crisp, military air. He had piercing

59

blue-gray eyes under bristling brows, and a flowing white-gray beard framing his sharp, craggy features. Pinkerton stepped forward and grasped his hands. "John Brown," he said. "We had not expected you, but you are welcome all the same." The notorious fire-and-brimstone abolitionist returned Pinkerton's greeting with uncommon warmth—"more than that," said a friend, he embraced the detective as "brother to brother."

"Old Brown of Osawatomie," as he was known at the time, was no stranger to Pinkerton's home on Adams Street. "John Brown," Pinkerton would write, "was my bosom friend, and more than one dark night has found us working earnestly together in behalf of the fleeing bondsman who was striving for his liberty." Not all abolitionists had such high regard for Brown, who advocated a "holy crusade" of armed insurrection as a means to end slavery. Abraham Lincoln would label him a "misguided fanatic."

The abolitionist John Brown, Allan Pinkerton's "bosom friend."
Courtesy of the Library of Congress

Pinkerton had come to know Brown at the time of the "Bleeding Kansas" crisis, a series of shockingly brutal clashes between abolitionist forces and pro-slavery "Border Ruffians" over the issue of whether Kansas would enter the Union as a free or slave state—a prospect that threatened to tip the balance of political power. In May 1856, Brown had led a raid into Kansas that left five pro-slavery Southerners dead—hacked to death with swords—an act he characterized as a response to recent violence against abolitionists, and a signal of his unflinching stand against the weak and conciliatory policies of the North. The "Pottawatomie Massacre," as the assault came to be known, established Brown's grim resolve to tear apart the increasingly fragile relations between North and South.

Now, warming his hands at Pinkerton's fire, Brown appeared more than ever to be, as Frederick Douglass described him, a man whose "soul had been pierced with the iron of slavery." For all his ferocious passion, he came to Pinkerton as a wanted outlaw. The governor of Kansas was reported to have offered a three-thousand-dollar reward for his capture. President Buchanan had ordered his arrest, and had added $250 to the bounty. As one newspaper declared, John Brown had become "the most notorious brigand our land has yet produced."

Brown's fugitive status did nothing to undercut the support offered him by Pinkerton, America's top lawman. If anything, Pinkerton's growing fame had added heat to his convictions. Even as he gained national renown as a tough and ruthlessly efficient lawman, Pinkerton continued to operate as an agent of the Underground Railroad. Having established himself as a detective, albeit a private one, Pinkerton found that his clandestine activities now carried a serious threat of legal consequences. The Fugitive Slave Act of 1850, intended to bolster earlier legislation that had fallen into disuse, sought to force federal marshals and other officers of the law in the free states to return runaway slaves to their masters. The new law overturned many of the "personal liberty laws" that had been passed in Northern states, and carried a one-thousand-dollar fine for any official who failed to enforce it. At the same time, any person charged with providing food or shelter to a fugitive would be subject to six months in prison and a one-thousand-dollar fine. As the stakes rose, Pinkerton found that he had become a lawbreaker with a badge—"half horse and half alligator," in Edward Sanford's phrase. The contradiction did not trouble him. "I have not a single regret for the course I then pursued," he wrote in later years. To Pinkerton, John Brown was a hero to be emulated, a courageous figure "who almost single handed threw himself into a fight against the Nation." So long as Brown was in Chicago, Pinkerton made sure he would not fight alone.

Pinkerton's two-room clapboard house on Adams Street was now crowded with children, and not as well-suited to Underground Railroad traffic as the cooperage in Dundee had been. There were two sons, twelve-year-old William and ten-year-old Robert, and two younger daughters, Joan—born in 1855 and named after her recently deceased older sister—and the sickly Belle. Even so, Joan Pinkerton worked tirelessly to feed and clothe a steady stream of fugitives, who sometimes appeared in such great numbers that she was forced to find room in the cramped space beneath the floorboards and in the half attic below the roof. When the house overflowed, she enlisted friends and neighbors into the cause. Often, when her husband's detective work took him away from home for long stretches of time, the duty of seeing the runaways safely on to their next destination fell to her. She would have been barely twenty-one years old when the family took up residence on Adams Street, but she threw herself into the struggle, according to one Chicago abolitionist, "as vigorously as did her husband."

With John Brown's latest unannounced arrival, the Pinkertons set to work once again. Joan gathered fresh clothing while her husband took the fugitives who would not fit under their roof and "got them under cover" with sympathetic friends. Brown himself was taken to the home of John Jones, a self-educated black man who was campaigning tirelessly against the state's restrictive "Black Laws." Jones listened along with Pinkerton as Brown informed them that he had arrived in Chicago "without a dollar" and could not continue his journey without financial help. Both Jones and Pinkerton pledged to do what they could. "There is a Democratic meeting in the city today," Pinkerton said. "I'll go down and make them give me enough money to send you and these slaves to Canada."

Pinkerton recalled that he left the house in a "determined frame of mind," but he soon realized that his plan had a serious flaw. The Democratic meeting he had mentioned was, in fact, a session of the Chicago Judiciary Convention. Although many of the participants would undoubtedly be sympathetic to the plight of Brown's runaways, few of them would want to pledge support openly in a legal forum. Pinkerton made some concession to the delicacy of the situation by declining to make the request himself. "I was too well known as being an anti-slavery man," he said, "and I thought my absence from the meeting would be the best thing." Instead, he dispatched a pair of friends to circulate what he called a "subscription list" among the delegates. When they returned without a single donation, however, Pinkerton took the matter into his own hands. "I decided that I must have the money," he said. "I was willing to pay something myself but I could not pay the whole."

Pinkerton's new tactic was nothing if not direct. Bursting into the meeting hall, he jumped to the stage and motioned for silence. "Gentlemen," he began as a stunned silence fell over the room, "I have one thing to do and I intend to do it in a hurry. John Brown is in this city at the present time with a number of men, women and children. I require aid, and substantial aid I must have. I am ready and willing to leave this meeting if I get this money; if not, I have to say this. I will bring John Brown to this meeting and if any United States Marshal dare lay a hand on him he must take the consequence. I am determined to do this or have the money." Folding his arms, Pinkerton stepped back and waited.

For several moments, the audience of "astonished jurists" simply stared at Pinkerton in uncomfortable silence. Then, with a conspicuous clearing of the throat, a young politician rose and made his way forward, holding out a fifty-dollar bill. With a curt nod of thanks, Pinkerton took off his hat and held it out. One by one, the others formed a line and filled the hat with bills. Within minutes, Pinkerton had collected nearly six hundred dollars. When the last man had passed, Pinkerton inclined his head. "Thank you, gentlemen," he said. Placing the hat back on his head, he left the hall without another word.

Later that afternoon, Pinkerton and his elder son, William, collected John Brown and his fugitives from the various homes where they had been lodged the night before and prepared to send them on their way. Pinkerton made arrangements with railroad superintendent C. G. Hammond—"a friend to me and also to the colored people"—to have a special passenger car readied at the Chicago depot. As a grateful John Brown took his leave, he turned and offered a warm farewell, along with a pregnant word of warning: "Friends, lay in your tobacco, cotton and sugar because I intend to raise the prices." When the abolitionist was safely aboard the train, Pinkerton laid a hand on his son's shoulder. "Look well upon that man," he said. "He is greater than Napoleon and just as great as George Washington."

THIS OPINION REGARDING JOHN BROWN would be sorely tested in the months to come. Though Pinkerton had received strong support from Hammond and other powerful railroad men, not all of his colleagues were so sympathetic to the abolitionist cause. One of Pinkerton's closest friends during these years was the vice president and chief engineer of the Illinois Central, a young West Point graduate named George Brinton McClellan. Pinkerton and McClellan were an unlikely pair. In contrast to the rough-hewn Pinkerton, McClellan was sleek, handsome, and dashing, and had led something of a charmed life. Born in Philadelphia in 1826, McClellan had entered the University of Pennsylvania at age thirteen, then transferred to West Point two years later, graduating second in his class. Upon leaving the academy, he served with distinction in the Mexican-American War, even performing reconnaissance missions for Lt. Gen. Winfield Scott, a close family friend. Following the war, McClellan joined Randolph Marcy's expedition to discover the sources of the Red River, only to find upon his return that all the members of the expedition had been given up for dead. The following year, he put his engineering skills to work for Secretary of War Jefferson Davis, exploring possible routes for the transcontinental railroad. In 1855, at the height of the Crimean War, McClellan was dispatched as an official observer of the European armies, later producing a manual on cavalry tactics and a design for a "McClellan saddle," which became standard U.S. Army issue.

When Pinkerton met him in 1857, McClellan had resigned his military commission, capitalizing on his engineering and railroad experience to secure a lucrative position with the Illinois Central. Though McClellan was seven years younger than Pinkerton, his remarkable catalog of achievements made a forceful impression on the detective, who adopted the young officer as a mentor and role model. Soon enough, their relationship would take a new shape on the battlefields of the Civil War, amid lasting controversy. To the end of his life, Pinkerton would be one of McClellan's staunchest supporters, declaring himself "proud and honored in ranking him foremost among my invaluable friends." In terms of political beliefs, however, it is difficult to understand how the seeds of that bond were sown so deeply during their early association in Illinois. Many of McClellan's views would have struck Pinkerton as shortsighted and timid. McClellan had no particular sympathy for the institution of slavery, and he hoped to improve the condition of "those poor blacks," but there were clear limits to his resolve. As he told his wife, "I will not fight for the abolitionists." Even so, Pinkerton embraced him as a kindred spirit. "From its earliest incipiency," the detective wrote, his working relations with McClellan had been of "the most agreeable and amicable nature."

Pinkerton was oddly silent about another of his Illinois Central colleagues of this period. Like Pinkerton, Abraham Lincoln was on retainer with the railroad during these years, and the career of the circuit-riding lawyer—like the detective's—was inextricably linked to the fortunes of the company. Having returned to practice law in Springfield after serving a term in the U.S. House of Representatives, Lincoln often found himself engaged in the legal issues arising from the rapid spread of the railroads across the state, and by the mid-1850s the bulk of his practice was devoted to railroad law.

George McClellan recalled crossing paths with Lincoln on many occasions during these years. "More than once I have been with him in out-of-the-way county-seats where some important case was being tried," wrote McClellan, "and, in the lack of sleeping accommodations, have spent the night in front of a stove listening to the unceasing flow of anecdotes from his lips. He was never at a loss, and I could never quite make up my mind how many of them he had really heard before, and how many he invented on the spur of the moment. His stories were seldom refined, but were always to the point."

Whatever his personal feelings may have been, McClellan made his political views clear during the fateful election campaign of 1858, when Lincoln, as the candidate of the newly formed Republican party, challenged incumbent Stephen Douglas for his seat in the U.S. Senate. McClellan and many other Illinois Central men threw their support behind Douglas, a fact that made itself felt during the famous series of debates that decided the contest. As the candidates had agreed to meet in seven different congressional districts, a great deal of travel on the Illinois Central was required. "At all points on the road where meetings between the two great politicians were held, either a special train or a special car was furnished to Douglas," noted Lincoln's friend Ward Hill Lamon, "but Lincoln, when he failed to get transportation on the regular trains in time to meet his appointments, was reduced to the necessity of going as freight." Lamon recalled one ignominious occasion when a freight car carrying Lincoln was shunted off the main track to allow Douglas's special to thunder past. "The passing train was decorated with banners and flags, and carried a band of music which was playing 'Hail to the Chief.' As the train whistled past, Mr. Lincoln broke out in a fit of laughter and said, 'Boys, the gentleman in that car evidently smelt no royalty in our carriage.'"

At times, Lincoln left a similar impression with the gentlemen in his own car. One passenger who traveled along with him to a debate was startled by the "uncouth, not to say grotesque" appearance of the candidate: "That swarthy face, with its strong features, its deep furrows, and its benignant, melancholy eyes, is now familiar to every American [but] at that time it was clean-shaven and looked even more haggard and careworn than later, when it was framed in whiskers. On his head he wore a somewhat battered stovepipe hat. His neck emerged, long and sinewy, from a white collar turned down over a thin black necktie. His lank, ungainly body was clad in a rusty black frock-coat with sleeves that should have been longer; but his arms appeared so long that the sleeves of a 'store' coat could hardly have been expected to cover them."

It is likely that Pinkerton also crossed paths with Lincoln at some stage during his travels on the Illinois Central, but if so, he did not record it. Pinkerton did, however, follow the debates closely. "The famous contest absorbed public attention throughout the country," he recalled. "The two candidates indulged in open discussions of public policy, which were remarkable for their brilliancy and for the force and vigor with which their different views were uttered. It was during this canvass that Mr. Lincoln made the forcible and revolutionizing declaration that: '*The Union cannot permanently endure half slave and half free.*'"

In fact, Lincoln first made the famous statement while accepting his party's nomination at the start of the race: "A house divided against itself cannot stand. I believe this government cannot endure, permanently, half slave and half free. I do not expect the Union to be dissolved—I do not expect the house to fall—but I do expect it will cease to be divided. It will become all one thing or all the other." Lincoln went on to warn that recent shifts in national policy, including the Dred Scott decision and the Kansas-Nebraska Act, would lead to the spread of slavery throughout the Union if left unchecked.

Even Lincoln's closest allies recognized that these sentiments, which suggested that conflict between the North and the South was inevitable, sounded a note that was far too pointed and clamorous for the times. "It is true," said William Herndon, Lincoln's law partner at the time, "but is it wise or politic to say so?"

Though Lincoln ultimately went down to defeat in the Senate race, his ideas—and the eloquence with which he expressed them—captured the attention of the nation, raising him to national prominence. Lincoln, wrote Herndon, had now become centrally entwined in the issues facing the nation. "His tall form enlarged," said Herndon, "until, to use a figurative expression, he could no longer pass through the door of our dingy office."

Lincoln's increasing prominence signaled what Pinkerton called "a growing sentiment of abolitionism throughout the North," which, in turn, "aroused the advocates of Slavery to a degree of alarm." As a result, the new year of 1860 "opened upon a scene of political agitation." In February, at Cooper Union in New York, Lincoln attempted to elaborate his opposition to slavery while offering reassurance to fractious elements in the South. While he insisted that slavery was "an evil not to be extended" into the new territories of the West, Lincoln acknowledged that the institution was protected by the Constitution where it already existed. He urged his fellow Republicans to "calmly consider" the demands of the Southern states and to "yield to them if, in our deliberate view of our duty, we possibly can." The address ended on a soaring note: "Neither let us be slandered from our duty by false accusations against us, nor frightened from it by menaces of destruction to the government nor of dungeons to ourselves. Let us have faith that right makes might, and in that faith, let us, to the end, dare to do our duty as we understand it."

The speech received a rapturous reception and helped to establish Lincoln in the East as a possible contender in the upcoming presidential contest. "Mr. Lincoln is one of Nature's orators," wrote Horace Greeley, "using his rare power solely and effectively to elucidate and to convince, though their inevitable effect is to delight and electrify as well." Though he had not yet declared himself as a candidate for the Republican presidential nomination, his aspirations were becoming clear. "I will be entirely frank," Lincoln admitted to a friend. "The taste *is* in my mouth a little."

BY THAT TIME, tensions had been further inflamed by John Brown's abolitionist crusade, raising what Pinkerton called "a spirit of fierce opposition in the minds of the Southern leaders." On October 16, 1859—seven months after Pinkerton had put him on a train in Chicago—John Brown led his notorious raid on the federal arsenal at Harper's Ferry, Virginia, in the hope of sparking a slave revolt throughout the South. Brown's tiny force of eighteen men was quickly overwhelmed by a detachment of marines under the command of Col. Robert E. Lee, and six weeks later—on December 2, 1859—Brown went to his death on a scaffold in Charles Town, Virginia. "I am waiting the hour of my public *murder* with great composure of mind, & cheerfulness," he had written to his family a few days earlier, "feeling the strongest assurance that in no other possible way could I be used to so much advance the cause of God; & of humanity."

During the long weeks that Brown spent awaiting execution, there were many rumors to the effect that armed supporters would descend from the North to liberate him and bear him back in triumph. In a memoir written nearly twenty-five years later, Pinkerton would offer his thoughts on the matter: "[H]ad it not been for the excessive watchfulness of those having him in charge, the pages of American history would never have been stained with a record of his execution." These words have been taken by some to suggest that Pinkerton himself planned to rescue Brown from his prison cell, and it has even been reported that he traveled to Harper's Ferry with the intent of thwarting the execution order. There is no firm evidence of this, and Pinkerton himself would likely have waved off the speculation. He admitted only to having been "unceasing" in his efforts to win a stay of execution.

Then as now, John Brown was a controversial and divisive figure;

Abraham Lincoln's "misguided fanatic" was Allan Pinkerton's "bosom friend." Even allowing for Pinkerton's lifelong opposition to slavery, his unflinching support of Brown's methods is difficult to reconcile with his dedication to upholding the law. His complaint of "excessive watchfulness" on the part of Brown's jailers must be counted as extraordinary, coming from a professional watchman whose logo was an unblinking, hypervigilant eye. Though Brown's death was mourned throughout the North with black bunting and prayer meetings, many added a note of remorse over the abolitionist's many acts of horrific violence. Pinkerton entertained no such qualms. The man who had marched with the physical-force Chartists in his younger days believed that violence was, at times, a necessary tool for effecting social change. As he so often said, "The ends justify the means, if the ends are for the accomplishment of Justice."

The "Eye" had its blind spots.

CHAPTER SIX
IT'S COMING YET

•

During the spring of 1860, the counties of Illinois held their conventions. The State Convention met at Decatur a few days previous to the assembling of the National Convention in Chicago. While the delegates were in session Mr. Lincoln came in as a spectator, and was invited to a seat on the platform. Soon afterward a couple of weather-worn fence-rails were borne into the hall, decorated with flags, and bearing the inscription, "Abraham Lincoln, the Rail Candidate for President in 1860." A storm of applause greeted the appearance of the fence rails thus decorated and inscribed. Lincoln was called upon and said, "I suppose I am expected to reply to that. I cannot say whether I made those rails or not, but I am quite sure I have made a great many just as good." . . . From that day forward, Lincoln was hailed as "the Rail-Splitter of Illinois."
—JOSIAH SEYMOUR CURREY, *Chicago: Its History and Its Builders* (1912)

DOZENS OF SPECIALLY CHARTERED TRAINS, many of them decorated with flags and patriotic bunting, converged on Chicago from all points of the compass in May 1860. Some forty thousand people had "said good-bye to their wondering families," wrote Joseph Howard, Jr., in the *New York Times*, "and set off with the world's people on a patriotic mission" to the Republican National Convention. While en route, many of the delegates found themselves in a festive mood. "Time and space would fail me to describe the smoking car, the boxes of cigars, the gin cocktail jugs, the brandy flask and the whisky slings which were freely circulated through the cars," wrote Howard. "I will only allude to the fact that they were there."

Residents along Michigan Avenue illuminated their homes to greet the arriving trains, with rockets fired at regular intervals to create what the *Chicago Press* called a "brilliant tableau of welcome." Much had changed since Allan Pinkerton rode into town as deputy sheriff twelve years earlier. The Sauganash Hotel, where Pinkerton arrested the counterfeiter John Craig, had burned down in 1851, to be replaced in 1860 by a two-story meeting hall known as the Wigwam—so called because the "chiefs" of the Republican party were to gather there to nominate their standard-bearer for the November presidential race. Many saw this event as Chicago's debut on the national stage. No longer simply "a town of meat and mud," as one early visitor had complained, Chicago had transformed itself into a robust and thriving metropolis. "She glistens," observed the *New York Herald,* "and bids fair to outstrip her more complacent eastern cousins."

Abraham Lincoln also had hopes of outstripping his more complacent eastern cousins, though his fortunes were by no means assured. "We are facing a crisis, there are troublous times ahead," the Republican power-broker Thurlow Weed told the conventioneers. Such times called for exceptional statesmanship, Weed insisted, and his choice was the man widely considered to have the nomination locked up: New York's long-time governor, and current senator, William H. Seward. Before the balloting began, however, Lincoln's supporters cunningly positioned their candidate as a more electable alternative to Seward, whose views on slavery were considered too extreme to win the White House. At the same time, the Lincoln men packed the hall with partisans—even printing extra tickets to hand out to Lincoln backers—who greeted his nomination with a "perfectly deafening" show of support. The strategy worked: Seward failed to gain the needed majority on the first and second rounds of balloting, and on the third, Lincoln pulled ahead. By the end of the proceedings, the "gallant son of the West" had secured the nomination, the improbability of which may be gauged by the reaction in Washington, where the House of Representatives adjourned in a "state of confusion." Howard, of the *New York Times,* perhaps overly fortified with gin cocktails and whiskey slings, struggled to find the handle on the story: "Great inquiry has been made this afternoon into the history of Mr. Lincoln," he wrote. "The only evidence that he has a history as yet discovered, is that he had a stump canvass with Mr. Douglas, in which he was beaten." In the absence of other information, the reporter fell back on a hasty reading of Lincoln's campaign biography. "The youngster who, with ragged trousers, used barefoot to drive his father's oxen and spend his days splitting rails, has risen to high eminence," he told his readers, but the nominee's name was rendered as "Abram Lincoln."

"The lines of battle were now drawn," Pinkerton declared. "Never before in the history of the parties was a canvass conducted with more bitterness or with a greater amount of vituperation. The whole country was engrossed with the gigantic struggle." For all of that, Pinkerton declined to say if he was in Lincoln's corner. Quite possibly, his friendship with McClellan pulled his support away from Lincoln, as it would in future elections. In any event, Pinkerton, the failed Abolitionist party candidate, would have followed the goings-on at the Republican National Convention with close interest, as the Wigwam was within a short walk of both his home and his office.

Lincoln remained at home in Springfield during the convention and through the long months of the presidential campaign, in accordance with the traditions of the day, while his supporters made speeches, held marches, and distributed pamphlets and lithographs. Though he considered making an appearance in Chicago after the nomination was announced, even this gesture was discouraged. "Don't come here for God's sake," warned David Davis, his campaign manager. "Write no letters and make no promises till you see me." It was the custom of the time for the candidate to hold himself apart from active campaigning, but in Lincoln's case there were more pressing reasons to keep his own counsel. Any further elaboration of his views, it was believed, would be seized upon and distorted by his opponents, adding fuel to the Southern uproar over his nomination.

Once again, Lincoln's Democratic opponent would be Stephen Douglas, the two men replaying their earlier Senate race on the national stage. Many felt confident that the "steam engine in breeches," as the energetic Douglas was known, would again defeat his rival, with one Democratic-leaning newspaper rejoicing that the Republicans could find no one better than a "third rate Western lawyer." Even among Republicans, there were rumblings that Lincoln wasn't up to the job. "You fellows knew at Chicago what this country is facing," wrote one disillusioned party member. "You knew that above everything else, these times demanded a statesman and you have gone and given us a *rail splitter*."

As the election neared, however, the splintering effect of pro-slavery candidates such as John C. Breckenridge and John Bell made itself felt. "The Southern 'Fire-eaters,' as they were called, fully realized their inability to elect the candidates they had named," Pinkerton noted, "but strove with all their power to prevent the success of the regular Democratic nominees." Soon enough, the Democratic party would split into Northern and Southern factions, all but ensuring the defeat of Douglas.

"When at last the day of election came, and the votes were counted," Pinkerton recorded, "it was found that Abraham Lincoln had been elected." In the South, the result gave fresh ammunition to the Fire-Eaters. "The anti-slavery proclivities of the successful party was instantly made a plausible pretext for secession," Pinkerton noted, "and the withdrawal of the slave-holding States from the Union was boldly advocated." Among those attempting to defuse the crisis was the recently defeated candidate, Stephen Douglas, who selflessly carried a message of unity to hostile audiences in the South, attempting to calm the secessionist fervor and broker a compromise.

In spite of these efforts, many Southern newspapers claimed that all hope of conciliation had been extinguished. "The election was not the Cause," declared Senator Jefferson Davis, "it was but the last feather which you know breaks the Camel's back." The *Charleston Mercury* drew a comparison to Colonial times: "The tea has been thrown overboard; the revolution of 1860 has been initiated." In New York, Horace Greeley captured the nation's mood in a pointed, anxious question: "What next?"

It would be some time before the question could be answered. With Lincoln's election, the nation entered a period of tense apprehension—the "Great Secession Winter of 1860–1861," in Henry Adams's phrase. Until March 4 of the following year—the date designated by the Founding Fathers as Inauguration Day—Lincoln would be caught between two worlds. Though he did not yet have any authority over events, he found himself constantly pressed for hints of the course he would pursue as president. He watched helplessly as several Southern states edged toward secession under President Buchanan's waning stewardship, but he feared to aggravate the situation by speaking out from Springfield. "Much has been said about the propriety of your saying or writing something now that you are President Elect, to satisfy and appease the South," a Pennsylvania congressman wrote to him. "In my judgment anything you could or would say with a view to accomplish any good would be perverted, misconstrued and prove worse than useless. They have hardened their hearts against you." Illinois congressman Elihu Washburne concurred, echoing a phrase coined by Sir James Mackintosh: "What we want most is a 'masterly inactivity.'"

For Lincoln, the wait was agonizing. Writing to a friend, he stated that he would "willingly take out of my life a period in years" equal to the number of months remaining until the inauguration. Pinkerton, watching events unfold from Chicago, felt similar apprehensions. "The political horizon was dark and obscured," he wrote. "The low mutterings of the storm that was soon to sweep over our country, and to deluge our fair land with fratricidal blood, were distinctly heard."

Pinkerton, whose work frequently took him below the Mason-Dixon line, was appalled by what he read in the pages of Southern newspapers. "Especial efforts had been made to render Mr. Lincoln personally odious and contemptible," he wrote, "and his election formed the pretexts of these reckless conspirators who had long been plotting the overthrow of the Union. No falsehood was too gross, no statement too exaggerated, to be used for that purpose, and so zealously did these misguided men labor in the cause of disunion, and so systematically concerted was their action, that the mass of the people of the slave states were made to believe that this pure, patient, humane, Christian statesman was a monster whose vices and passions made him odious, and whose political beliefs made him an object of just abhorrence." Pinkerton worried that the hostile Southern press would tip over into actual violence against Lincoln, which might, in turn, serve as the flash point for armed rebellion.

Though Pinkerton did not know it at the time, "low mutterings" of this kind could already be heard in Baltimore. Already, the city's saloons and drawing rooms buzzed with restless outrage, the first stirrings of a darker purpose to come. For the moment, Pinkerton had no idea that he was fated to play a central role in the coming drama, or that the events of the next few weeks would set his life and career on an entirely new track.

Like Lincoln, Pinkerton found himself caught between two extremes as the war approached. As his work carried him away from home for longer and longer stretches, he became a distant, mercurial figure to his wife and children. At home, he retained the abstemious, early-to-bed habits of his coopering days; in the field, as he assumed the identity of a train worker or traveling businessman, he became a gregarious bon vivant, always ready to share a drink and a smoke, eager to pass an hour or two at the nearest saloon. This radical change of demeanor, more than the altered hairstyles and clothing he adopted, made him effective as an undercover operative, but if Pinkerton had appeared under his own roof while working a case, his wife and children would not have recognized him.

The gulf between his work and home life grew wider over time. One day, Pinkerton's sons would follow him into the detective business, but for the moment he believed it was necessary to keep his two worlds separate, especially at those times when his work required him to get his hands dirty. "It is, perhaps, a matter not to be exultant about," Pinkerton explained, "but, during my life as a detective, I have, for various reasons of a politic nature, become intimately acquainted with the men whom I was most anxious to apprehend, mingling with them in their ordinary walks, entirely unsuspected, until the time for action arrived and arrests were necessary." In order to achieve this, he insisted, a detective was required to assimilate "as far as possible" into the criminal's world, and, by "appearing to know but little, acquire all the information possible."

This ability to blend in with "men of evil intent" would make Pinkerton invaluable to Abraham Lincoln as he made his way to Washington in a climate of gathering danger. As a committed abolitionist, Pinkerton understood the challenges facing the incoming president as well as any man of his time. For all of that, when his path crossed with Lincoln's in the days ahead, politics would be pushed aside. What Lincoln would need most at this defining moment was not a political partisan, but a cunning, hardheaded railroad detective.

Pinkerton might have drawn inspiration for the coming adventure from "Tam o'Shanter," a favorite poem by the Scottish bard Robert Burns, which tells the tale of a wild journey through a dark night, beset by hostile spirits, ending finally in the safety of a river crossing. The poem was also a great favorite of Lincoln, who ranked the plowman poet alongside Shakespeare, and who was said to "quote Burns by the hour" in his Springfield law office. The previous year, on January 25, 1859, Lincoln had participated in a "Burns Night" celebration at Springfield's concert hall, where he marked the centenary of the poet's birth by proposing one of the evening's toasts. "It is said," one of Lincoln's campaign biographies noted, "he now has by heart every line of his favorite poet."

Pinkerton, too, had joined in the Burns celebrations that night, attending a parade through the streets of Chicago, followed by a hundred-gun salute. The evening finished with a gathering of three thousand people at the city's Metropolitan Hall, with tributes from Mayor Haines and former governor McComas. According to one account, a highlight of the evening was the appearance of thirty-one-year-old Joan Pinkerton, who took the stage to lead the Highland Guard of Chicago in a heartfelt rendition of "A Man's a Man for A' That," with its vision of a future in which all men are equals:

> Then let us pray that come it may
> (As come it will for a' that)
> That Sense and Worth o'er a' the earth
> Shall bear the gree an' a' that!

For a' that, an' a' that,
It's comin' yet for a' that,
That man to man the world o'er
Shall brithers be for a' that.

Almost twenty years had passed since Pinkerton had first heard Joan Carfrae's soprano voice in the back parlor of a Glasgow pub. He had come up in the world a great deal since then, but in many ways he was still the barefoot cooper who had marched on Newport for the rights of the workingman. Now, sitting with his sons, William and Robert, on one of his increasingly rare visits home, he listened as his wife's voice filled the hall, singing of honest poverty and independent minds. After a moment, William and Robert heard an unfamiliar sound. Turning away from the stage, they saw that their father's head was lowered and tears were streaming from his eyes.

PART TWO

•

PLUMS and **NUTS**

"If I alone must do it, I shall—Lincoln shall die in this city."

CHAPTER SEVEN
A PIG-TAIL WHISTLE

•

In the day's mail for Lincoln came letters cursing him for an ape and a baboon who had brought the country evil. He was buffoon and monster; an abortion, an idiot; they prayed he would be flogged, burned, hanged, tortured. Pen sketches of gallows and daggers arrived from "oath-bound brotherhoods." Mrs. Lincoln saw unwrapped a painting on canvas, her husband with a rope around his neck, his feet chained, his body tarred and feathered.

—CARL SANDBURG, *Abraham Lincoln: The Prairie Years*

ON CHRISTMAS DAY OF 1860, a forty-nine-year-old sculptor named Thomas D. Jones stepped off a train at the Western Railroad Depot in Springfield. He wore a jaunty wide-brimmed hat and a flowing shawl tossed carelessly across his shoulders. In one hand he carried a cloth artist's bag filled with knives, cutters, and trim tools, and in the other was a leather travel grip. Folded up in a pocket of his velvet frock coat was a commission to create a portrait bust of President-elect Lincoln, who at that moment was spending a final holiday at home with his family before heading to Washington. Jones had no guarantee that Lincoln would agree to pose, but as he took his bearings outside the small brick depot, he felt "a warming sense of optimism."

The sculptor was just one of thousands of visitors trying to catch Lincoln's ear during the hectic final days in Springfield. Ever since the election, Lincoln had been so besieged by people seeking political appointments and other favors—"groveling time-wasters, fawners, sycophants and parasites," as one journalist described them—that he found it difficult to walk the streets. "Individuals, deputations, and delegations from all quarters pressed in upon him in a manner that might have killed a man of less robust constitution," declared his friend Ward Hill Lamon. "The hotels of Springfield were filled with gentlemen who came with light baggage and heavy schemes. The party had never been in office: a clean sweep of the 'ins' was expected; and all the 'outs' were patriotically anxious to take the vacant places. It was a party that had never fed, and it was vigorously hungry."

Jones, the sculptor, who had traveled through a heavy snowstorm to reach Springfield, was pleased with his first view of the town, recalling the "magical effect" of the falling snow as it mingled with steam from the arriving train. Others were less impressed. "None of the streets were paved, and in wet weather, of which a good deal prevailed during that winter, they were simply impassable," noted Henry Villard in the *New York Herald*. "There was but one decent hotel." Villard was being unkind; there were several well-regarded hotels and rooming houses within walking distance of the State House, along with a number of restaurants and saloons, and no fewer than three billiard halls. Still, as Villard remarked, the town was not accustomed to such crowds: "The influx of politicians is so great that a large number are nightly obliged to seek shelter in sleeping cars."

Jones was fortunate to find a room available on the top floor of a serviceable hotel called the St. Nicholas, where he established a makeshift studio. The following day, rising at a "timely hour," he strolled over to the State House in hopes of getting a moment with the president-elect, pausing briefly to take in the building's impressive limestone facade and copper dome. Two years earlier, Lincoln had delivered his now-famous "House Divided" speech from this building. Now, at the invitation of the governor, Lincoln had moved his headquarters from the cramped law office he shared with William Herndon to a spacious reception room on the second floor. As Jones entered, he found the room buzzing with politicians and office seekers. To the artist's surprise, Lincoln himself came forward with a word of greeting and invited him to take a seat. Jones was struck by the "hard and rugged lines" that creased Lincoln's face, the stamp of his early life on the prairie, but noted that the president-elect's features softened as he began to speak. "As he was a prompt man, he lost no time in proceeding to business," the artist recalled, "and inquired how I made my busts." A few months earlier, Lincoln explained, he had posed for a plaster cast of his face, an experience he had found "anything but agreeable." Jones assured the president-elect that his method was different; he intended to execute various pencil sketches during a series of sittings, then craft a likeness from clay. "I like your mode," Lincoln replied, and agreed to make himself available for an hour each morning at the St. Nicholas.

Lincoln had any number of reasons to consent to sit for Jones, but perhaps the most compelling was the chance to display his new beard, which he had begun growing only a few weeks earlier. The change of appearance was intended to mold a new image as he entered the White House, putting the seal on his transformation from prairie rail-splitter to judicious statesman. A popular piece of lore tells of a letter Lincoln received from eleven-year-old Grace Bedell, a girl in upstate New York, who advised him during the campaign that growing out his whiskers would likely tip her family's support in his direction: "[Y]ou would look a great deal better for your face is so thin," Miss Bedell reasoned. "All the ladies like whiskers and they would tease their husbands to vote for you and then you would be President." The letter drew a prompt reply from Lincoln, who expressed regret that he had no daughters of his own to advise him on such matters. "As to the whiskers," he said, "having never worn any, do you not think people would call it a piece of silly affect[ta]tion if I were to begin now?" In fact, Lincoln had been pondering the change for months. "It is allowed to be ugly in this world," he remarked, "but not as ugly as I am." The beard, he believed, would serve to "hide my horrible lantern jaws."

Through the early weeks of January, the newly bearded president-elect dutifully trudged through muddy streets to the St. Nicholas, where he climbed four flights of stairs to the sculptor's room for daily sittings. While Jones sketched, Lincoln reviewed his mail and composed replies. Every so often, Lincoln would hand Jones a pencil and ask him to sharpen it with one of his sculpting knives. The artist soon came to realize that their daily routine provided Lincoln with his "only retreat from the pursuit of the numerous applicants for office, where he could compose his addresses in peace."

The peace would be short-lived. One day, an expressman clambered up the stairs with a small box addressed to Lincoln, wrapped in brown paper and loosely tied with string. "It was neither large nor formidable in appearance," Jones recalled, "but it looked suspicious." Jones at once offered to open the package himself, fearing that it might contain "an infernal machine or torpedo." After some debate, Jones fastened on the plan of "placing it at the back of the clay model on which I was at work, using it as an earthwork, so in case it exploded, it would not harm either of us."

One can only admire the sculptor's bravery, but it is not entirely clear how much protection was to be afforded by a half-completed bust of Lincoln's head. Nevertheless, Jones placed the parcel accordingly, then gingerly cut the strings with one of his sculpting knives. To the surprise of both men, "out tumbled a pig-tail whistle."

Lincoln burst out laughing. A proverb of the day held that "One cannot make a whistle out of a pig's tail," but here was tangible evidence to the contrary. Given what lay ahead in Washington, the gift was a uniquely fitting token of luck, as Lincoln, too, faced a task widely held to be impossible. "Mr. Lincoln enjoyed the joke hugely," recalled the reporter Henry Villard, who came upon the president-elect while he was trying earnestly to produce a few notes on this "masterpiece of ingenuity."

Lincoln later acknowledged the "valuable present" with a note of thanks. "When I get to Washington," he promised, "I will use it to call my cabinet together."

JONES WOULD LATER characterize the episode as an amusing distraction—"Neither did we soak it in a tub of water," he said of the suspicious package, "or say many prayers over it"—but his initial concern was understandable. Even before the election returns were in, Lincoln's postbag in Springfield contained at least a dozen pieces of hate mail each day. According to the *Washington Constitution,* Lincoln's desk was piled high with threats of "flaying alive, assassination, mayhem, fire and brimstone, and getting his nose pulled." Much of this unpleasant correspondence was the direct result of an ever-rising level of vitriol in the Southern press. Though Lincoln gave no sign that the attacks intimidated him, his friend Henry Clay Whitney felt revulsion. "There were threats of hanging him, burning him, decapitating him, flogging him, etc.," Whitney recalled. "Nor had the limner's art been neglected: in addition to several rude sketches of assassination, by various modes, a copy of *Harper's Weekly* was among the collection, with a full length portrait of the president-elect; but some cheerful pro-slavery wag had added a gallows, a noose and a black-cap."

One morning, after reviewing some particularly unpleasant letters in his third-floor law office, Lincoln scooped up an armful of offensive material and carried it down the steps to a cabinetmaker's shop on the ground floor. Pausing in the doorway, Lincoln asked if he might borrow the proprietor's stove to dispose of his burden. The cabinetmaker, who had taken a keen interest in his fellow tenant's rise to the highest office in the land, asked if he might be allowed to keep the letters instead. Lincoln agreed.

These letters, and others like them, provide a chilling index of the passions stirred throughout the country:

Old Abe Lincoln

God damn your god damned old Hellfired god damned soul to hell god damn you and goddam your god damned family's god damned hellfired god damned soul to hell and god damnation god damn them and god damn your god damn friends to hell god damn their god damn families to eternal god damnation god damn souls to hell god damn them and God Alighty God damn Old Hamlin to[o] to hell God damn his god damned soul all over everywhere double damn his God damned soul to hell

 Now you God damned old Abolition son of a bitch God damn you I want you to send me God damn you about one dozen good offices Good God Almighty God damn your God damned soul and three or four pretty Gals God damn you

 And by doing God damn you you

Will Oblige
Pete Muggins

A second, more succinct letter made a grim prediction for the date of the inauguration in Washington:

Abraham Lincoln Esq
Sir
 You will be shot on the 4ᵗʰ of March 1861 by a Louisiana Creole we are decided and our aim is sure.

A young creole.
BEWARE

Other messages, like the one that arrived sometime later from a Mr. A. G. Frick, offered Lincoln a chance at survival if he would agree to resign the presidency:

Mr. Abe Lincoln
If you don't Resign we are going to put a spider in your dumpling and play the Devil with you you god or mighty god dam sundde of a bith go to hell and buss my Ass suck my prick and call my Bolics your uncle Dick god dam a fool and goddam Abe Lincoln who would like you goddamn you excuse me for using such hard words with you but you need it . . .

Many of Lincoln's supporters also urged him to resign, rather than face likely death at the hands of his enemies. Several people warned of potential poisoning, with one correspondent advising the president-elect to "drink hot milk in Large Quantities—in order to frustrate the diabolicol [*sic*] plot." Another cautioned that there might be poison in the ink Lincoln was using to write his letters. An Iowa chemistry professor offered to outfit the president-elect with a special chain-mail shirt, covered with silk and "plated with gold, so that perspiration shall not affect it." He added his assurance that "Napoleon III is constantly protected in this way."

To all outward appearances, the president-elect remained untroubled, if perhaps a little beleaguered by the sheer volume of his correspondence. On one occasion, he was spotted at the post office filling "a good sized market basket" with his latest batch of letters, and then struggling to keep his footing as he navigated the icy streets. Soon, he took on a pair of extra hands to assist with the burden. John Nicolay—a pale, bookish young Bavarian immigrant with thinning hair and a dark goatee—had applied to write Lincoln's official campaign biography, only to find that the job had already been assigned. "Never mind," he was told. "You are to be private secretary."

As he took up his duties, Nicolay was troubled by the growing number of threats that crossed Lincoln's desk. "His mail was infested with brutal and vulgar menace, and warnings of all sorts came to him from zealous or nervous friends," Nicolay wrote. "But he had himself so sane a mind, and a heart so kindly, even to his enemies, that it was hard for him to believe in political hatred so deadly as to lead to murder." From the earliest days, however, it was clear that not all of the warnings could be brushed aside. Even before election returns were in, an unsettling letter had arrived from Fort Leavenworth, Kansas:

Dear Sir:
On a recent visit to the east, I met a lady of high character, who had been spending part of the summer among her friends and relatives in Virginia. She informed me that a number of young men in Virginia had bound themselves, by oaths most solemn, to cause your assassination, should you be elected. Now Sir, you may laugh at this story, and really it does appear too absurd to repeat, but I beg you to recollect, that on "the institution" these good people are most certainly demented, and being crazy, they should be taken care of, to prevent their doing harm to themselves or others—Judicious, prompt and energetic action on the

part of your Secretary of War, will no doubt secure your own safety, and the peace of the country,

> *I have the honor to be,*
> *Very Sincerely,*
> *Your mo. ob.*
> *David Hunter*

The warning from Hunter, a U.S. Army major, stood apart from the garbled threats of the anonymous "young Creole" and the gloriously profane Pete Muggins. Hunter was clearly no zealot: He was a West Point graduate, whose grandfather had signed the Declaration of Independence. Lincoln sent a prompt reply, indicating that he had heard rumblings of this type from another source within the army. "While I think there are many chances to one that this is a hum-bug, it occurs to me that any real movement of this sort in the army would leak out and become known to you," Lincoln wrote. "In such case, if it would not be unprofessional, or dishonorable (of which you are to be judge) I shall be much obliged if you will apprise me of it."

Major Hunter took the president-elect at his word, and he wrote again in December to warn that "careful study of the signs of the times" had inclined him to believe that there was trouble ahead. In particular, Hunter had heard talk of a plot to capture Washington and retain James Buchanan, "the Old Publick Functionary," as president. It would be a wise precaution, Hunter suggested, to enlist 100,000 Wide Awakes—the uniformed citizens brigade that formed during the election to support the Republican cause—and have them "wend their way quietly to Washington" in advance of the inaugural. "The reins once in your hands, I cannot doubt a triumphant result," Hunter wrote, "and that you will preserve every star on our flag."

Hunter's suggestion could hardly be counted as practical at a time when Lincoln was trying to avoid provocation, nor was it at all clear how a force of 100,000 men might wend its way "quietly" into the capital. Nevertheless, Lincoln took the major's concerns seriously, and he invited Hunter to join his entourage for the forthcoming trip to Washington. Hunter readily accepted. It was one of the few times before leaving Springfield that Lincoln gave any sign of concern for his safety. He was keenly aware, as he would later admit, of the many warnings of "people who were intending to do me a mischief," but he chose not to acknowledge these threats. "I never attached much importance to them," he would say, "never wanted to believe any such thing. So I never would do anything about them, in the way of taking precautions and the like. Some of my friends, though, thought differently."

Even as the hate mail piled up, Lincoln continued to maintain an open-door policy at the State House. Soon enough, disgruntled Southerners began to appear. December saw the arrival of a "genuine secessionist" named D. E. Ray, who had traveled all the way from Yazoo, Mississippi, to air his views. Fortified with "divers doses of whiskey," Ray made his way into the governor's reception room, where Lincoln was receiving visitors, as usual. "He walked in with a sullen air," reported journalist Henry Villard, "and plunged into a corner of the sofa, where he reposed for at least a quarter of an hour, without uttering a word." Ray occupied the time by making repeated adjustments to the angle of his hat, so that Lincoln would get an eyeful of his blue cockade—a knot of hanging ribbons that had been adopted throughout the South as the symbol of disunion.

Presently, some of the others in the room engaged the "scowling Southron" in conversation, which soon turned to the subject of secession. Pressed for his views, Ray allowed that the people of his state were not afraid of Lincoln himself, but of the Republicans who had elected him. At this, Lincoln himself entered the debate. "You will find that the only difference between you and me is that I think slavery wrong and you think it right," he declared, "that I am opposed to its extension, while you advocate it." Even so, Lincoln insisted, he would decline to interfere with slavery "where it existed," so that slaveholding states would remain "as secure from encroachments" as they had been under Buchanan.

Lincoln had said much the same thing many times before, but hearing the words from the incoming president's own lips appeared to mollify the secessionist, who "softened down under the influence of these peaceful declarations." As Ray made his way to the exit, Lincoln stopped him and handed over a collection of transcripts of the Lincoln-Douglas debates, recently published in book form. Smiling, Lincoln expressed a hope that having such a book in his possession wouldn't cause trouble for Ray when he got back to Mississippi.

Not all secessionists could be turned aside so amicably. The following day—December 20, 1860—South Carolina became the first state to secede from the Union, with the *Charleston Mercury* issuing a broadside that declared "The Union Is Dissolved." Attention soon focused on South Carolina's claims upon the three federal garrisons strategically located at Charleston Harbor—Fort Sumter, Fort Moultrie, and Castle Pinckney. It now became clear, as John Nicolay reported, that the South Carolinians "intended somehow to get possession of these fortifications, as it was the only means by which they could make any serious resistance to the federal government."

Fort Moultrie, a poorly engineered structure originally built of palmetto logs, was almost impossible to defend, and a rumor reached Lincoln's ears that President Buchanan had instructed its commander, Maj. Robert Anderson, to surrender if attacked. Lincoln wished to maintain his public silence, but he was outraged by Buchanan's posture of submission. "If that is true," he told Nicolay, "they ought to hang him." The president-elect sent a message to Lt. Gen. Winfield Scott, the "Grand Old Man of the Army," urging him to be prepared, by the time of the inauguration, "to either *hold,* or *retake,* the forts, as the case may require."

On the night of December 26, Major Anderson, acting on his own initiative, moved his small garrison from Fort Moultrie across the harbor to the more defensible Fort Sumter. The following day, South Carolina took possession of the abandoned Fort Moultrie, as well as Castle Pinckney. The action threw the capital into turmoil as President Buchanan deliberated over a possible response, and fresh rumors surfaced of an armed insurrection against Washington.

William Seward, Lincoln's former rival for the Republican nomination, sensed a growing mood of panic in the halls of government. Writing from the capital on December 28, he advised Lincoln to make his way east without further delay:

> There is a feverish excitement here which awakens all kind of
> apprehensions of popular disturbance and disorders, connected
> with your assumption of the government. I do not entertain
> these apprehensions myself, but is it worth consideration in our
> peculiar circumstances that accidents elsewhere may aggravate
> opinion here. Habit has accustomed the public to anticipate the
> arrival of the President-elect in this city about the middle of
> February, and evil-minded persons would expect to organize
> their demonstrations for that time. I beg leave to suggest
> whether it would not be well for you keeping your own counsel
> to be prepared to drop into the city a week or ten days earlier.
> The effect would probably be reassuring and soothing.

The following day, Seward wrote again, this time with even greater urgency, sounding very much like a man reporting from behind enemy lines. "It pains me to learn that things there are even worse than is understood," he declared, referring to the possibility that President Buchanan might recall Major Anderson and allow Fort Sumter to fall. Worse yet, he insisted, there was now an unmistakable threat of armed resistance to Lincoln's inauguration, with the support of men in high places. "A plot is forming to seize the Capitol on or before the 4th of March—and this too has its accomplices in the public councils," Seward declared. "I could tell you more particularly than I dare write. But you must not imagine that I am giving you suspicions and rumors—Believe that I know what I write—in point of fact the responsibilities of your administration must begin before the time arrives—I therefore revive the suggestion of your coming here earlier than you otherwise would—and coming in by surprise—without announcement." Seward was so concerned that this letter might be intercepted that he sent it without his signature—"which for prudence is omitted," he explained. In a letter to his son Frederick, Seward was even more blunt about conditions in the capital: "Come when you can," he urged. "It is revolutionary times here."

Seward's messages demanded a delicate response. Lincoln would later claim that he gave no credence to the rumors, but he knew that Seward's warnings would have to be taken seriously, all the more so because he was trying to persuade the senator to join his cabinet as secretary of state. "Yours without signature was received last night," Lincoln replied. "I have been considering your suggestions as to my reaching Washington somewhat earlier than is usual." Lincoln acknowledged the gravity of Seward's concern, but then he swiftly turned to a matter he considered to be of even greater importance. Technically, the election was not yet official; the Electoral College would not assemble in Washington to ratify the victory until February. Lincoln was keenly aware that he had failed to achieve a majority in the popular vote; his total amounted to not quite 40 percent. In the current climate, there was ample reason to fear that the Electoral College might decline to assemble or—in the event of an uprising—be unable do its duty. He told Seward:

> It seems to me the inauguration is not the most dangerous
> point for us. Our adversaries have us more clearly at disadvan-
> tage on the second Wednesday of February, when the votes
> should be officially counted. If the two Houses refuse to meet at
> all, or meet without a quorum of each, where shall we be? I do
> not think that this counting is constitutionally essential to the

election; but how are we to proceed in absence of it? In view of this, I think it is best for me not to attempt appearing in Washington till the result of that ceremony is known.

Though Lincoln had redirected Seward's concern to another channel, William Herndon reported that he was now "annoyed, not to say alarmed" at the threats that he would not reach Washington alive, and the insistence from many quarters that "even if successful in reaching the Capitol, his inauguration should in some way be prevented." Hoping for reassurance, Lincoln decided to take a sounding from General Scott, who was also on the scene in the capital. Lincoln knew that Scott's support would be essential in any coming conflict, especially if the situation at Fort Sumter worsened. Though Lincoln did not say so explicitly, he also sought confirmation that Scott, a Virginia native, would serve under the Lincoln administration even if his state followed South Carolina in seceding from the Union.

Thomas Mather, Illinois's adjutant general, was dispatched to Washington, bearing a letter from Lincoln. Arriving in the capital, Mather called on Scott at his home, but was told that the seventy-four-year-old general was too ill to receive visitors—a discouraging sign. Mather left Lincoln's letter and returned later. This time, he was promptly ushered to the general's bedside. "I found the old warrior, grizzly and wrinkled, propped up in the bed by an embankment of pillows behind his back," Mather recalled. "His hair and beard were considerably disordered, the flesh seemed to lay in rolls across his warty face and neck, and his breathing was not without great labor. In his hand he still held Lincoln's letter." Though the general was pale and visibly trembling from his long illness, it was clear that Lincoln's message had stirred his passions. "General Mather," he declared, straightening his back against his pillows, "present my compliments to Mr. Lincoln when you return to Springfield, and tell him I expect him to come on to Washington as soon as he is ready." Any resistance, the old veteran promised, would be met with all the considerable force at his command.

Greatly reassured, Lincoln announced that he would remain in Springfield until mid-February. He told journalist Henry Villard that plans for his "impending removal to the federal capital" were being laid, though the route and date of departure had not yet been fixed. "I think Mr. Lincoln's preferences are for a southerly route," Villard reported, "via Cincinnati, Wheeling and Baltimore, doubtless to demonstrate how little fear he entertains for his personal safety." Villard allowed that pressure from concerned friends would likely force the president-elect to adopt a more northerly path, but in either case, Lincoln would make "stoppages" along the way to greet his supporters. "He knows that those who elected him are anxious to see how he looks," Villard explained, "and hence is willing to gratify this, their excusable curiosity."

In the coming weeks, the task of planning Lincoln's journey to Washington would prove nearly as complicated as that of assembling his cabinet. Political considerations aside, there was no simple or obvious means of making the trip at the time. Although the nation's railroads continued to expand at a fantastic rate, there was not yet a single direct railway line running from Illinois to Washington, D.C. Instead, Lincoln would have to travel across a rough patchwork of independent regional lines, a relay instead of a marathon. At various stages of the journey, especially in cases where the gauge of a particular railroad's track happened to be incompatible with that of the next line, a change of locomotives and cars would be required. Lincoln and his party would have to make frequent transfers from one railway's terminus to the next, usually riding in open carriages, and sometimes even carrying their own baggage.

Since each of the many regional lines had its own president and officers, Lincoln also had to concern himself with the political loyalties of dozens of powerful railway executives. At least one official—John Work Garrett of the Baltimore and Ohio Railroad, who had more than five hundred miles of track running below the Mason-Dixon line—was believed at the time to have Southern sympathies that might pose a threat to the president-elect's safety. "[Y]our life is not safe, and it is your simple duty to be very careful of exposing it," Horace Greeley warned in a letter to Lincoln. "I doubt whether you ought to go to Washington via Wheeling and the B. & O. Railroad unless you go with a very strong force." Lincoln, however, let it be known that a "martial cortège" was out of the question, as it would signal exactly the sort of warlike posture he had been at pains to avoid. He told Henry Villard that he utterly disliked "ostentatious display and empty pageantry" and would make his way to Washington without a military escort.

John Nicolay, his new secretary, insisted that Lincoln was unwilling to compromise his duty for the sake of personal safety. "He knew," Nicolay explained, "that incitements to murder him were not uncommon in the South, but as is the habit of men constitutionally brave, he considered the possibilities of danger remote, and positively refused to torment himself with precautions for his own safety; summing the matter up by saying that both friends and strangers must have daily access to him; that his life was therefore in reach of anyone, sane or mad, who was ready to murder and be hanged for it." There was no way that Lincoln could guard against all danger, Nicolay concluded, unless he shut himself up in an iron box— "in which condition he could scarcely perform the duties of a President."

At least one railway executive—Samuel Morse Felton, president of the Philadelphia, Wilmington and Baltimore Railroad—believed that the president-elect had failed to grasp the seriousness of his position. Felton, a stolid, bespectacled blue blood whose brother was president of Harvard at the time, was not a man given to saber rattling. Nevertheless, in January 1861, even as Lincoln downplayed the possibility of danger, Felton became convinced of what he called a "deep-laid conspiracy to capture Washington, destroy all the avenues leading to it from the North, East, and West, and thus prevent the inauguration of Mr. Lincoln in the Capitol of the country." For Felton, whose track formed a crucial link between Washington and the North, the threat against Lincoln and his government also constituted a danger to the railroad that had been his life's great labor. Though he had been concerned about secessionist activity for some time, Felton's decisive moment came on a wintry Saturday afternoon in his office in Philadelphia, when he looked up from his desk and saw Dorothea Dix, the celebrated social reformer, standing in the doorway. Nearly sixty at the time, Miss Dix was instantly recognizable in her familiar attire: a plain dark-colored dress with a white ruffle at the throat. She wore her chestnut hair gathered in a coil at the back of her head, setting off a "sweet grave face, lighted up by not too frequent smiles."

Felton jumped to his feet and showed his visitor to a seat. For more than twenty years, Felton knew, Dorothea Dix had been a vigorous crusader for the rights of the mentally ill, visiting hundreds of jails, hospitals, and almshouses to report on the treatment of sufferers, and advocating the benefits of "moral treatment," as opposed to the "heroic" measures of the time, which often featured painful physical restraints and dangerous narcotics. "I had known her for some years," Felton recalled. "Her occupation had brought her in contact with the prominent men of the South. In visiting hospitals she had become familiar with the structure of Southern society, and also with the working of its political machinery."

Miss Dix claimed to have no political agenda—"I have no patience and no sympathy either with northern Abolitionists or southern agitators," she declared—but after Lincoln's election, she had begun to hear rumors that alarmed her greatly. Fearing that her concerns would not be taken seriously in Washington, she brought her case to Felton instead, knowing that he would give her a fair hearing. Impatient to speak, she brushed Felton's pleasantries aside and told him she had "an important communication to make." Seeing the urgency in her expression, Felton closed the door to his office and settled himself behind his desk. Miss Dix promptly launched into a chillingly clear and concise outline of a Southern plot to topple the government of the United States. She spoke for more than an hour, her blue-gray eyes fixed intently on Felton's face, giving a "tangible and reliable shape" to what Felton had previously heard only in scattered rumors. "The sum of it all," Felton recalled, "was that there was then an extensive and organized conspiracy throughout the South to seize upon Washington, with its archives and records, and then declare the Southern conspirators *de facto* the Government of the United States. The whole was to be a *coup d'etat*. Mr. Lincoln's inauguration was thus to be prevented."

As Felton listened with growing alarm, his visitor gave additional details. The agitators, she told him, planned to disrupt all of the railroad lines connecting Washington with the North—not just Felton's—which would not only sever communication and commerce but also "prevent the transportation of troops to wrest the capital from the hands of the insurgents." Felton's railroad, Miss Dix went on to explain, would be easily captured. Several paramilitary drill teams were already conducting exercises at various points along the track, "pretending to be Union men." In truth, Miss Dix insisted, these so-called committees of safety had pledged their loyalties to the South: "They were sworn to obey the command of their leaders, and the leaders were banded together to capture Washington."

A heavy snow had begun to fall by the time Miss Dix finished speaking. Stepping to the tall windows, Felton looked down as one of his own trains rolled into the nearby terminus, trailing a column of sparks and vapor. After a moment, he turned and clasped Miss Dix by the hands, thanking her warmly for coming to see him. As he showed her to a waiting carriage, Felton promised immediate action.

Returning to his office, Felton drew up a hasty report to General Scott and sent it on to Washington in the hands of a trusted employee. The general's response to the railway executive was considerably less reassuring than the one he had sent to Lincoln. Scott indicated that he was well aware of the danger and was taking steps to reinforce Washington, but he allowed that he had not been able to rouse the Buchanan administration to any further action, which left him fearful of "the worst consequences." As of yet, nothing had been done to secure the routes into the city—not even those that skirted or passed through potentially hostile territory in states such as Maryland, where sentiment was running strongly toward the South. Given the circumstances, Scott admitted to Felton, "he feared nothing would be done . . . and that Mr. Lincoln would be obliged to be inaugurated into office at Philadelphia," rather than risk the dangerous journey south to Washington.

Disheartened, Felton resigned himself to the fact that the government would offer no assistance. "I then determined," he said, "to investigate the matter in my own way." What was needed, he realized, was an independent operative who had already proven his mettle in the service of the railroads. Snatching up his pen, Felton dashed off an urgent plea to "a celebrated detective, who resided in the west."

By the end of January, with barely two weeks remaining before Lincoln departed Springfield, Allan Pinkerton was on the case.

CHAPTER EIGHT
MOBTOWN

•

Should that little craft fall into the hands of pirates, one broadside from the Pennsylvania four-decker will clear the road to Washington. Lincoln, if living, will take the oath of office on the steps of the National Capitol on the 4th of March. My State will guarantee him a safe passage to the White House!

—SENATOR SIMON CAMERON of Pennsylvania (later Lincoln's first secretary of war)
on the prospect of Maryland's secession, January 1861

PINKERTON LOST NO TIME. Felton's letter landed on his desk on January 19, a Saturday. The detective set off within moments, flashing one of the many courtesy railroad passes he carried as he hopped aboard the next available train. He reached Felton's office in Philadelphia only two days later, an impressively rapid response for the time.

Felton had only hinted at the scope of the problem in his letter. Now, as Pinkerton settled into a chair opposite Felton's broad mahogany desk, the railroad president spelled out the details. According to Miss Dix and other reliable sources, he explained, there was a plot afoot among "the roughs and secessionists of Maryland" to destroy the Philadelphia, Wilmington and Baltimore Railroad. If successful, Washington might well fall into the hands of "rebel insurgents."

Shocked by what he was hearing, Pinkerton listened in silence. For all his commitment to the abolitionist cause, he had been slow to grasp, as he later admitted, that the country stood at the brink of war. "I entertained no serious fears of an open rebellion, and was disposed to regard the whole matter as of trivial importance," he explained. "I was inclined to believe that with the incoming of the new administration, determined or conciliatory measures would be adopted, and that secession and rebellion would be either averted or summarily crushed." Felton's plea for help, the detective said, "aroused me to a realization of the danger that threatened the country, and I determined to render whatever assistance was in my power."

For the moment, the detective needed time to consider how to attack the problem. Pinkerton and his operatives had thwarted every imaginable type of train robbery by this time, but never a "deliberate and calculated design" to disrupt a railroad for political reasons. As he reviewed the situation from Felton's office in Philadelphia, the full weight of the dilemma became clear. Much of Felton's line was on Maryland soil. In recent days, four more states—Mississippi, Florida, Alabama, and Georgia—had followed the lead of South Carolina and seceded from the Union. Louisiana and Texas would soon follow. Maryland had been roiling with anti-Northern sentiment in the months leading up to Lincoln's election, and at the very moment that Felton poured out his concerns to Pinkerton, the Maryland legislature was debating whether to join the exodus.

There was little reason to hope that the Old Line State would vote to remain in the Union. In the November election, several Maryland counties had recorded only a single vote for Lincoln, and in two districts he had received no votes at all. Even these meager showings stirred indignation. When a band of six intrepid Republicans in Charles County was found to have cast their votes for Lincoln, angry neighbors ordered them to pack up and leave.

The importance of Maryland, with the Mason-Dixon line squaring off its northern and eastern borders, was obvious to all. It now seemed inevitable that Virginia would secede, and many assumed that Maryland would automatically follow its neighbor. The previous year, a joint committee of the Maryland legislature had responded to the first stirrings of secession in South Carolina with a forceful resolution of support: "[S]hould the hour ever arrive when the Union must be dissolved," it stated, "Maryland will cast her lot with her sister states of the South and abide their fortune to the fullest extent." If Maryland made good on this promise and pledged her loyalties to the South, Washington would be hemmed in by secessionist territory and entirely cut off from the North. In that case, as General Scott had suggested to Felton, the federal government might have to abandon its capital city and reestablish itself in Philadelphia or New York.

With the Virginia General Assembly calling for a vote on secession, it appeared that Maryland's decisive moment was at hand. "The people of the District are looking anxiously for the result of the Virginia election," noted Frederick Seward, who had joined his father in the capital. "They fear that if Virginia resolves on secession, Maryland will follow; and then Washington will be seized. Meantime the anxiety of the citizens is almost ludicrously intense."

Pinkerton grasped at once that Felton's "great connecting link" between Washington and the North must be kept open at all costs. If war came, Felton's PW&B would be a vital conduit of troops and ammunition. The problem, as Felton explained, was the line's extreme vulnerability at the many points where it crossed over water. The wooden railroad bridges spanning Maryland's Gunpowder River and smaller streams could be easily demolished, perhaps even at the moment that a train entered the span. The danger was even greater at Havre de Grace, at the headwaters of Chesapeake Bay, where the line traversed a mile-wide expanse of the Susquehanna River. Although a single-track bridge was under construction, it would not be completed for another five years. In the meantime, railcars arriving at Havre de Grace were uncoupled and placed on ferryboats, which shuttled them across to the opposite bank, a slow and painstaking process and one that could easily be scuttled. As soon as the rumors of sabotage reached his ears, Felton understood that any attack would most likely come at one of these crossings.

For all their concern about the railroad, both Felton and Pinkerton appear to have been blind, at this early stage, to the possibility of violence against Lincoln. They understood that the secessionists sought to prevent the inauguration, but they had not yet grasped, as Felton would write, that if all else failed, Lincoln's life was to "fall a sacrifice to the attempt." Instead, as Felton recalled, he did nothing more than supply "a few hints" before Pinkerton set to work. The full degree of peril was beyond his imaginings; "The half," he admitted, "had not yet been told."

In this climate of rumor and uncertainty, Pinkerton accepted the commission with a somewhat blinkered view of what was at stake. For the moment, his only concern was the protection of Felton's railroad. He returned to Chicago to consider the problem, drawing up a seven-page report with recommendations on how to proceed. His proposal made it clear that the situation was changing moment by moment, and that as of yet there had been no tangible proof of a threat against Felton's line.

"Should the suspicions of danger still exist," Pinkerton wrote, he would assemble a team of operatives and dispatch them at once to "the seat of danger" in Maryland. Once there, they would assess the risk and attempt to confirm the truth of the plot against the railroad. If successful, Pinkerton and his operatives would go undercover to "become acquainted" with the plotters. In this way, they would soon "learn positively who the leading spirits are that would be likely to do the *Active Labor.*" With this information in hand, Pinkerton could take whatever steps were necessary to thwart the design, either by arresting the plotters or by heightening security at the intended point of attack.

In many respects, the plan Pinkerton presented to Felton was a simple variation on the template he had been using for years, whether pulling shifts as a mail "piler" at the Chicago post office or assigning Kate Warne to pose as the wife of a forger. As Pinkerton explained to Felton, it would be necessary to keep the suspects under the tightest possible surveillance—"an *unceasing Shadow,*" as he called it—in order to worm out their secrets. This meant placing men in saloons, hotels, and billiard halls to catch the suspects in unguarded moments, when they would be most likely to spill their secrets.

From the outset, Pinkerton realized that he would be racing the clock. If the plotters intended to disrupt Lincoln's inauguration—now only five weeks away—it was evident that any attack would come soon, perhaps even within days. Given this time constraint, Pinkerton worried that his usual methods would prove ineffective. "The only danger which I perceive to our operating is in the short time we have to work in," he explained. "Our operations are necessarily tedious—Nay, frequently very slow." This was to be expected, he said, because the success of his technique relied upon "attaining a controlling power over the mind of the suspected parties," as when Kate Warne had persuaded Nathan Maroney's wife to disclose the location of the stolen money. In such cases, however, Pinkerton had had the luxury of time. The capture of Maroney had unfolded at a stately pace over several months. By contrast, Felton's case would be a wind sprint.

Accordingly, Pinkerton planned to tackle Felton's problem with an unusually large team of detectives. "Had I plenty of time to work in, I might probably be able to ascertain all that you require with two or three operatives," he explained. As matters stood, however, "the time is too brief for me to work safely in this manner." To have any chance of success, he would have to send a wave of men flooding across Maryland, so as to "attack on every point we can find."

Pinkerton closed his long letter to Felton by urging him to keep the matter entirely confidential, since any indiscretion would likely expose his detectives to danger. "Our strength lays in the secrecy of our movements," he warned. "As I have before remarked, Secrecy is the Lever of any success which may attend my operations, and as the nature of this service may prove of a character which might to some extent be dangerous to the persons of myself, or any operatives, I should expect that the Fact of my operating should only be known to myself or such discreet persons connected with your Company as it might be absolutely necessary should be entrusted." Experience had taught Pinkerton that Felton would not be able to keep the matter entirely quiet, so he added a final heartfelt plea: "But on no conditions would I consider it safe for myself or my operatives were the fact of my operating known to any Politician—no matter of what school, or what position." Possibly this remark struck Felton as a gratuitous swipe, but, in fact, Pinkerton's distrust of politicians was well founded. He had dealt with shady elected officials for more than a decade, beginning with the corrupt jailer who had released John Craig at the close of his first case. As a result, Pinkerton had learned to play his cards close to the vest.

Felton agreed at once to give his full support and financial backing to Pinkerton's plan, and the detective departed immediately for "the seat of danger" with a crew of top agents. To a casual observer, Pinkerton and his team would have looked like an ordinary group of travelers as they boarded the train in Chicago that day. The English-born Timothy Webster, with his bright blue eyes and dark, wavy hair, appeared to be just another attentive husband helping his young wife navigate an unsteady set of wooden platform steps. When the compartment door closed behind them, however, the pair quickly separated and took seats on opposite benches. Webster, a married man, was simply playing a role. The young woman was actually a twenty-four-year-old beauty named Hattie Lawton, a recent addition to Kate Warne's so-called Female Detective Bureau, who would pose as Webster's bride in the days ahead. "Her complexion was fresh and rosy as the morning, her hair fell in flowing tresses of gold," Pinkerton wrote of her. "She appeared careless and entirely at ease, but a close observer would have noticed a compression of the small lips, and a fixedness in the sparkling eyes that told of a purpose to be accomplished."

Kate Warne was also at Pinkerton's side that day, preparing to play her signature role of the Southern belle with a kindly nature and a sympathetic ear. She had become one of Pinkerton's most trusted confidants by this time, and it is likely that the two of them spent much of the journey conferring over maps and case files, laying plans for the task ahead. Close at hand was another new recruit, Harry Davies, a fair-haired young man whose ruddy, open face and unassuming manner belied a razor-sharp mind. Davies had traveled widely, spoke many languages, and had a gift for adapting himself to any situation. He had trained as a Jesuit priest,

Pinkerton noted, which lent him an "insinuating manner" that proved useful in dealing with sinners. Best of all from Pinkerton's perspective, Davies possessed "a thorough knowledge of the South, its localities, prejudices, customs and leading men, which had been derived from several years residence in New Orleans and other Southern cities."

As his team headed east, Pinkerton seized the chance to get the lay of the land. "I took passage on one of the trains of the road, intending to see for myself how affairs stood, and to distribute my men in such a manner as to me seemed best," he said. "I resolved to locate my men at the various towns along the road, selecting such places where, it was believed, disaffection existed." Not surprisingly, the signs of political unrest grew more pronounced as the train pushed toward Maryland and crossed the Mason-Dixon line. At Havre de Grace, the vital crossing point of the Susquehanna River, Pinkerton and his operatives mingled among the locals and heard open expressions of hostile intent. When the train pulled away, a Pinkerton man was left behind to conduct further observation.

Across the river in Perrymansville, twenty-seven miles outside of Baltimore, Pinkerton found an even more intensely warlike mood. The village had long been a hub of railroad workers, but the Fort Sumter crisis had transformed it into a staging area for a makeshift unit of armed cavalry. Pinkerton soon realized that these freshly minted soldiers, though "professedly sworn to protect the railroad," had a different agenda. "Under the influence of bad men the secession movement had gained many supporters and sympathizers," he noted. "Loud threats were uttered against the railroad company, and it was boastfully asserted that 'no damned abolitionist should be allowed to pass through the town alive.'" Though he heard much talk of this kind, Pinkerton knew better than to take such pronouncements at face value. "I have always found it a truism that 'a barking dog never bites,'" he said, "and although I had but little fear that these blatant talkers would perform any dangerous deeds, I considered it best to be fully posted as to their movements." Accordingly, Pinkerton made a snap decision to post Timothy Webster in Perrymansville. Webster would look for work among the railroad workers, while Hattie Lawton, in her role as his wife, would seek out "useful friendships" among the women of the community. After a few last-minute arrangements, Pinkerton took his leave of the two operatives and pressed on toward Baltimore, where Felton's line terminated.

As Pinkerton's train rolled into Baltimore during the first week of February, the detective observed that the mood of opposition to Lincoln's inauguration became "manifestly more intense." Pinkerton took rooms at a boardinghouse on Howard Street, near the Camden Street train station, and he and his remaining operatives fanned out across the city, mixing with crowds at saloons and restaurants to listen to the "grumblings and grouses" of the citizenry. "I soon found that the fears of the railroad officials were not wholly without foundation," he reported, but he insisted that he had no firm evidence of imminent danger. Even so, the depth of secession-ist feeling in Baltimore persuaded him that the possibility of some kind of organized plot was very real. "The opposition to Mr. Lincoln's inauguration was most violent and bitter," he wrote, "and a few days' sojourn in this city convinced me that great danger was to be apprehended."

It was inevitable that Pinkerton's focus should come to rest on Balti-more. The city, as one of Lincoln's advisers would note, was "the back door of the National Capital." Three separate rail lines converged to form a hub at the center of the city, creating a choke point for all passenger and freight traffic moving through the region. Felton's brick-fronted depot on President Street was the southern terminus of his Philadelphia, Wilmington and Bal-timore Railroad; roughly a mile to the south was the Baltimore and Ohio line's Camden Street Station, running south to Washington; and lying be-tween the two, half a mile to the west, was the Calvert Street Station of the Northern Central line, running up to Harrisburg, Pennsylvania. So long as these three rail lines remained in operation, Baltimore would have unparal-leled strategic importance in the event of war.

At the time, Baltimore had a population of over 200,000—nearly twice that of Pinkerton's Chicago—making it the nation's fourth-largest city, after New York, Philadelphia, and Brooklyn, which at that time was a city in its own right. As a major port, Baltimore was not only a thriving center of shipping but also the arrival point for huge numbers of immi-grants from Ireland and Germany, giving rise to a deeply entrenched gang culture much like that of New York City. Allegiances were forged accord-ing to neighborhood, nationality, and trade, and battles were fought on much the same lines. Gangs with colorful names such as the Rip Raps, Blood Tubs, and Black Snakes ruled the streets, and even reached out to form political alliances. On election days, the gangs took to the streets to intimidate voters and stuff ballot boxes. According to the *Baltimore Re-publican,* the "gutters flowed with rivers of blood."

The violence had intensified during the 1856 presidential election: Eight men were killed in the streets and more than 250 others were in-jured, reducing a proud community to what one observer called "the

Pandemonium of American Cities." Though Mayor George William Brown had launched a series of reforms by the time of the 1860 election, the city's bloody reputation persisted. Three decades earlier, President John Quincy Adams had praised Baltimore as the "Monumental City." At the time of Lincoln's election, it was known far and wide as "Mobtown."

The city's prominence as a rail hub guaranteed that it would feature in the planning for Lincoln's inauguration, since virtually any route that the president-elect chose between Springfield and Washington would necessarily pass through Baltimore. Few people imagined that Lincoln would receive a cordial reception. In April of the previous year, when the Republican State Convention gathered to elect delegates for the Chicago convention, a group of "local roughs" had stormed the meeting and flipped over the desks and benches. The delegates retreated under a shower of ink pots. "The whole scene was extremely disgraceful," wrote a correspondent for the *New York Times*. "For God's sake let every man and all parties—religious, political or otherwise—when respectful, entertain and express their own sentiments free from molestation."

The plea went unheeded. After Lincoln's nomination, his supporters in Baltimore were subject to further violence, as a diehard Republican named Worthington G. Snethen reported to Lincoln himself. "Our people behaved nobly," said Snethen, recounting an assault on a torchlight procession of Wide Awake marchers. "There were some 300 of them. They walked their whole distance amid showers of eggs, brick-bats and injurious epithets from the mob." Snethen refused to be discouraged. Following the election, he wrote again, in the hope that Lincoln would reward his "gallant little band" of supporters with a stop in Baltimore on his way to Washington. Snethen promised a courteous reception, but the city's treatment of President-elect James Buchanan four years earlier suggested otherwise. Traveling from his home in Pennsylvania, Buchanan was said to have received a merciless heckling from Baltimore's street gangs, with the result that he cut his visit short and departed for Washington on an earlier train.

Four years on, there was little reason to hope that Lincoln would fare better. "The city of Baltimore was, at this time, a slave-holding city," Pinkerton noted, "and the spirit of Slavery was nowhere else more rampant and ferocious." Horace Greeley concurred, adding that the city's rich and powerful were particularly eager to see the Republican agenda derailed. If the Union were dissolved, he explained, Baltimore would emerge as a dominant power in the new South: "In a confederacy composed exclusively of the fifteen Slave States, Baltimore would hold the position that New York enjoys in the Union, being the great ship-building, shipping, importing and commercial emporium, whitening the ocean with her sails, and gemming Maryland with the palaces reared from her ample and ever-expanding profits." For this reason, Greely concluded, the city's upper classes were "ready to rush into treason."

This created an additional problem for Pinkerton. It would not be enough simply to infiltrate the violent gangs at the lower end of Baltimore's social strata; he would also have to find a find a way of moving among members of the wealthier classes, who would be likely to provide the money needed for any large-scale plot. Accordingly, Pinkerton decided to set up a cover identity for himself as a Southern stockbroker newly arrived in Baltimore. It was a canny choice, as it gave him an excuse to make himself known to the city's businessmen, whose interests in cotton and other Southern commodities often gave a fair index of their political leanings.

In order to play the part convincingly, Pinkerton hired a suite of offices in a large building at 44 South Street, at the center of the triangle formed by the city's three train stations. From this vantage point, he could easily gather reports from all quarters and send instructions to his agents in the field. It would not be seen as unusual for a stockbroker to receive frequent visitors, but Pinkerton took care to select a location that would help to shield the identities of his operatives. The building on South Street had entrances on all four sides and could be accessed inconspicuously through an alley at the back. Pinkerton's agents would be able to assemble in his office without being seen in one another's company as they passed in and out of the building. If one agent should be compromised, the others would not automatically fall under suspicion. This feature would become especially important as the operation grew in size; Pinkerton's first order of business on South Street was to wire to Chicago for an additional force of men.

Soon enough, Pinkerton was trading under the name of John H. Hutchinson—which he originally spelled as Hutcheson, Hutchesontown being the name of a district in the Gorbals. By all accounts, he played the role with convincing gusto. To all outward appearances, he was now "an outgoing gentleman of southern birth," with a resolved but sympathetic demeanor that would encourage people to confide in him. "The detective must *always* be an actor," Pinkerton wrote, "and nine-tenths of the actors on the stage today would do well to take lessons in their own profession from him."

From the office on South Street, Pinkerton assigned new identities to each member of his team. "I distributed my Operatives around the City," he recalled, after giving each one a distinct set of characteristics "for the purpose of acquiring the confidence of the Secessionists." Harry Davies, the aristocratic former seminarian, was to assume the character of "an extreme anti-Union man" newly arrived from New Orleans, and put himself up at one of the best hotels in the city. From this platform, Davies was to make himself known as a man willing to pledge his loyalty and his pocketbook to the interests of the South. Kate Warne was to assume the identity of "Mrs. Barley," passing herself off as a visitor from Montgomery, Alabama—drawing on knowledge gained during the Adams Express robbery case. "Mrs. Warne displayed upon her breast, as did many of the ladies of Baltimore, the black and white cockade," Pinkerton wrote, "which had been temporarily adopted as the emblem of secession." Her job was to cultivate the wives and daughters of suspected plotters. "Mrs. Warne was eminently fitted for this task," Pinkerton noted. "She was a brilliant conversationalist when so disposed, and could be quite vivacious, but she also understood that rarer quality in womankind, the art of being silent."

Not all of Pinkerton's agents were comfortable with their assigned roles. One operative, to whom Pinkerton gave the name of Charles Williams, was instructed to pass himself off as a transplant from Mississippi. He promptly hit a snag when he ran across a native of Jackson who appeared determined to engage him in a lengthy discussion of their home state. Fearful of being exposed, Williams excused himself and made his way back to South Street, where he duly recorded the incident in his field report. "I was afraid I could not play my part," he wrote, but Pinkerton assured him that "there was no danger, and all I wanted was self confidence." After receiving a few additional pointers, Williams squared his shoulders and returned to work. Pinkerton himself suffered no qualms about playing his role. For the moment, the task at hand appeared relatively straightforward. His goal, as he had described it to Samuel Felton, was to forge a relationship with anyone suspected of belonging to a secessionist group of any kind. The next step would be to "apply the necessary test" by expressing opinions and sympathies designed to tease out any plans for violence. Such methods had worked well in the past, he explained, allowing him "to penetrate into the abodes of crime in all classes of society."

Even as Pinkerton wrote these words, however, the focus of his operation began to shift beneath his feet. From the first, Pinkerton's plan of action rested on the assumption that Baltimore's secessionists intended to attack the railroads as part of a larger plan to capture Washington. Many believed that if Lincoln could be prevented from taking the oath of office in the capital, even if he were to be sworn in at Philadelphia or New York, the Union cause would be lost before the new administration had begun. By keeping Felton's "road" open, Pinkerton would be doing his part to ensure an orderly inauguration, sending a strong message of Lincoln's resolve. Even as Pinkerton made his initial report to Felton, however, he caught the first scent of a darker design. On January 27, in Springfield, the president-elect offered up the first details of the itinerary for the forthcoming trip to Washington. Until that moment, the specifics of Lincoln's journey to the capital had been a subject of furious speculation and debate. Would the newly elected president be able to make a public procession to Washington, as his predecessors had done? Would he be able to set foot in his native Kentucky? Would he even dare to show his face in a slaveholding state? Now, with the date of the inaugural fast approaching, Lincoln announced that he would travel in an "open and public" fashion, with frequent stops along the way to greet the public.

The message was clear: Lincoln was standing firm in the face of the secession crisis. As the *Baltimore Sun* reported:

> It is now positively settled that Mr. Lincoln will depart for Washington on the 11th of February. He will go hence via Lafayette to Indianapolis, where he will receive the hospitalities of the Indiana Legislature; thence he will proceed, probably, by way of Cincinnati to Columbus, Cleveland, Buffalo and Albany. From Albany he intends to make for Harrisburg direct, thence to Baltimore and the Federal Capital; but a tour to New York and Philadelphia is not impossible.
>
> Arrangements for special trains all the way through are making. No military escort will be accepted.

In the days to come, the itinerary would be fleshed out and elaborated upon until every moment of Lincoln's time was cataloged for the public. By the date of departure, it would be known that Lincoln intended to arrive at Baltimore's Calvert Street Station at 12:30 on the afternoon of Saturday, February 23, and that he would depart from the Camden Street Station at 3:00. "The distance between the two stations is a little over a mile," Pinkerton noted darkly. "No provision for his reception had been made by any Public Committee in Baltimore. The few Union men that were there at the time were over-awed by the Secessionists, and dared not make any demonstration."

Instantly, the announcement of Lincoln's imminent arrival became the talk of Baltimore. Of all the stops on the president-elect's itinerary, Baltimore was the only slaveholding city apart from Washington itself, and there was a distinct possibility that Maryland would vote to secede by the time Lincoln's train reached her border. In that case, what sort of reception might the president-elect expect? The *Baltimore Sun* expressed a hope that the city would rein in any hostile impulses:

> It is of great concern to all who love and would honor the State of Maryland and the city of Baltimore that no demonstration whatsoever should be made, even by a single individual, inconsistent with our self-respect. We would a thousand times rather see the most elaborate exhibition of official courtesy, unbecoming as it would be in such a case, than that the slightest personal disrespect should mar the occasion, or blur the reputation of our well-ordered city. . . . Let it be the part of every man to sustain the honorable status we profess; and so to illustrate before the eyes of the President elect the self-respect of a people who cordially dissent from his political opinions.

No doubt there were many in the city who shared this noble sentiment. As Pinkerton would soon learn, however, there were some who saw Lincoln's passage through Baltimore as an open challenge, a red rag trailed before a stirring bull. As of yet, Pinkerton had no idea if the angry talk would resolve itself into a credible threat, or what form that threat might take, but he was now convinced that Baltimore's secessionists could not be ignored. "Every night as I mingled among them I could hear the most outrageous sentiments enunciated," he wrote. "No man's life was safe in the hands of those men."

CHAPTER NINE
SUSPICIONS OF DANGER

•

You are respectfully invited to participate in the courtesies extended to Hon.
Abraham Lincoln, President elect, by the several Railroad Companies,
from Springfield to Washington.
—Inscription on the official train pass issued to riders of the
Lincoln Special

ON HIS LAST FULL DAY in Springfield—Sunday, February 10, 1861—Abraham Lincoln paid a final visit to his law partner, William Herndon, at the office they had shared in the town's Capitol Square. Having done no legal work for several months, Lincoln had promised to have "a long talk" with Herndon before setting off for the White House.

Lincoln's final days in Springfield had been hectic. Two days earlier, he and his family had vacated their house at the corner of Eighth and Jackson streets, the only home Lincoln had ever owned, and moved into a two-dollar-a-day hotel suite. Most of the family furniture had been sold off to friends and neighbors, and the house had been rented. The extra cash would be needed in the days to come, as the government at that time did not underwrite a president-elect's travel expenses. Lincoln made a withdrawal of four hundred dollars at the Springfield Marine and Fire Insurance Company to see him safely to Washington.

Now, sitting in the cluttered law office with Herndon, Lincoln went over the firm's books and reviewed unfinished case files. In a few instances, he gave instructions to his younger partner on "certain lines of procedure," which Herndon dutifully recorded in his ledger. When his business was finished, Lincoln seemed reluctant to leave. He threw himself down on a battered sofa, now so decrepit that it stood braced against a wall for support, and lay there for some moments, telling stories of the "ludicrous features" of his early days on the law circuit. "I never saw him in a more cheerful mood," Herndon reported, but by the end of their interview, Lincoln's mood had darkened. "He said the sorrow of parting from his old associates was deeper than most persons would imagine," Herndon recalled, "but it was more marked in his case because of the feeling which had become irrepressible that he would never return alive."

After a time, as Lincoln prepared to take his leave, he drew his partner's attention to the wooden signboard swinging on rusty hinges at the foot of the stairway. "Let it hang there undisturbed," he told Herndon in a strangely hushed voice. "Give our clients to understand that the election of a President makes no change in the firm of Lincoln and Herndon. If I live I'm coming back some time, and then we'll go right on practicing law as if nothing had ever happened."

Lincoln's nostalgic afternoon with Herndon marked the end of his career as a "prairie lawyer," though he had long since ceased to take an active role in the practice. In the previous weeks, the president-elect had spent almost all of his time laying the groundwork for his administration, assembling his cabinet, and crafting his inaugural address. Lincoln had also set his mind to the delicate task of planning his journey to Washington. After weeks of "masterly inactivity" in Springfield, Lincoln knew that every word and gesture of his reemergence into public view would be parsed for signs of how he intended to meet the secession crisis. Having invested so much care in the message of his inaugural address, Lincoln intended to tread lightly in the meantime, hoping to avoid making statements about policy until he reached Washington. In announcing the details of his inaugural journey, Lincoln emphasized that he wished to avoid elaborate ceremonies, as he knew that any suggestion of pageantry would be received poorly in the South. Even the date of departure was likely chosen with an eye to appearances. Lincoln would be well under way on February 13, the date on which the Electoral College would assemble to formally ratify his election as president. Privately, he had expressed fears that the outcome might cast doubt on the legitimacy of his election, but publicly he would signal that he considered the proceedings a mere formality.

Though he wished to avoid antagonizing the secessionists, Lincoln cannily shaped his itinerary to underscore the traditions of the presidency. The proposed route would take him through the state capitals of Indiana, Ohio, New York, New Jersey, and Pennsylvania, with stops in a number of other major cities where he had received strong support in the election. An appearance in New York City had been added to the itinerary in the latter stages of the planning, as well as a side trip to raise a flag over Independence Hall in Philadelphia, artfully timed to coincide with George Washington's birthday.

In a sense, Lincoln was following in Washington's footsteps. Lincoln had long admired a particular biography that described Washington's grand procession from Mount Vernon to New York, where his first inauguration took place, and the rapturous reception he received along the way: "The inhabitants all hastened from their houses to the highways, to have a sight of their great countryman; while the people of the towns, hearing of his approach, sallied out, horse and foot, to meet him." William Seward and others had advised Lincoln to make his way to the capital quietly, even secretly, but the president-elect believed that by traveling in an open fashion, he would lay emphasis on the continuity of the government of the United States, as well as the legitimacy of his own election.

The decision drew welcome support from Ohio governor Salmon P. Chase, another contender for the Republican presidential nomination in Chicago, whom Lincoln now hoped to bring into his cabinet. "I am glad you have relinquished your idea of proceeding to Washington in a private way," wrote Chase. "It is important to allow full scope to the enthusiasm of the people just now." Like Chase, Lincoln believed that the public, especially those who felt skittish about the election of a relatively unknown "western" politician, would welcome the chance to come out and see him in the flesh. He hoped that "when we shall become better acquainted," as he would soon tell a group of fellow politicians, "we shall like each other the more."

The initial announcement of Lincoln's plans had claimed that the entire journey would be made "inside of ten days." That optimistic prediction fell by the wayside as invitations to receptions and dinners along the route flowed into Springfield. Lincoln was eager to accept as many as possible, with the result that his itinerary expanded to include overnight stays in Pittsburgh and Cleveland, and numerous stops in smaller towns along the way. Each new invitation that Lincoln accepted added a fresh layer of complication to the planning. By the time the arrangements were settled, Lincoln's intended route would crisscross over two thousand miles on eighteen different railroad lines, occasionally looping back on itself, as opposed to a journey of roughly seven hundred miles as the crow flies.

Lincoln himself acknowledged that this "rather circuitous route" left much to be desired. Mindful of time constraints, he urged one supporter to schedule "no ceremonies that will waste time," and in some instances he promised only to "bow to the friends" at a particular stop if circumstances permitted. "Will not this roundabout way involve too much fatigue and exhaustion?" asked Salmon Chase, but Lincoln pressed ahead regardless. In the end, he would deliver more than a hundred speeches, sometimes at a clip of more than a dozen in a single day.

The unenviable job of adapting Lincoln's ballooning agenda to the realities of railroad travel fell to Superintendent of Arrangements William S. Wood. A suave, silver-haired New York railroad man, Wood surfaced in Springfield after the election and offered to coordinate the irksome details of Lincoln's journey, perhaps hoping to be rewarded with a patronage job in Washington. Wood undertook the thankless task with uncommon zeal. He promptly embarked on a scouting trip across the disjointed network of rail lines that connected Springfield to Washington, crafting a route that would allow Lincoln to make his desired "stoppages" while keeping the train to a tight, sometimes grueling schedule. At the same time, Wood made arrangements for the special trains and carriages that would be necessary at each phase of the journey, and negotiated with hotels in each city to ensure the "comfort and safety" of the presidential party.

At a time when hundreds of powerful men were jostling for position at Lincoln's elbow, Wood's duties required enormous tact and diplomacy, two qualities that were conspicuously absent in his overbearing, "relentlessly executive" nature. According to Henry Villard, Wood was "greatly impressed with the importance of his mission and inclined to assume airs of consequence and condescension." There would be many more snappish comments by the time the Lincoln Special got rolling, but it is probably closer to the truth to say that Wood simply carried out Lincoln's private wishes. At a time when the president-elect was going to heroic extremes to make himself available to all callers, Wood took on the unpopular role of gatekeeper.

Some of Wood's high-handed behavior reflected the growing concern for Lincoln's safety. To anticipate potential dangers, Wood looked to the example of a recent cross-country tour of America made by Britain's Prince of Wales. Many of the same safeguards, Wood realized, could be adapted for Lincoln's journey. The presidential train, like the royal one, would be preceded by special "pilot engines," running a short distance ahead to scout for obstructions or hidden hazards. Once the advance crew passed safely over a section of track, the switches governing that portion of the line would be "spiked and guarded" until the Lincoln Special swept through. Wood also consulted with the presidents of the various railroads along the route, receiving promises that Lincoln's train would be entitled to the exclusive use of the road—*"all other trains,"* ordered one executive, *"must be kept out of the way."*

In an additional nod to security concerns, Wood printed up a detailed, if rather autocratic, "Circular of Instructions," laying down a set of guidelines for Lincoln's fellow travelers as well as the officials receiving him in each of the host cities. "Gentlemen," he wrote, "Being charged with the responsibility of the safe conduct of the president-elect and his suite to their destination, I deem it my duty, for special reasons which you will readily comprehend, to offer the following instructions." As it happened, Wood's recommendations had more to do with protocol than safety, with a heavy emphasis on the niggling details of carriage rides and private dining rooms and "contiguous" hotel rooms. Aware that he risked raising hackles along the route, Wood added a plea for unity: "Trusting, gentlemen, that inasmuch as we have a common purpose in this matter, the safety, comfort and convenience of the President elect, these suggestions will be received in the spirit in which they are offered."

Amid all his fussing over seating charts, however, Wood made one pronouncement—possibly at Lincoln's suggestion—that cut to the heart of safety concerns: He designated twenty-three-year-old Elmer Ellsworth as the point man for the president-elect's security. It was an inspired decision. A dashing, Byronic figure, Ellsworth had captured the nation's attention at the head of a flashy military drill team, the "U.S. Zouave Cadets," who were rakishly attired in scarlet trousers and blue jackets with gold braiding, modeled on the uniforms of a celebrated French battalion that fought in the Crimean War. Ellsworth's guardsmen traveled the country, whipping up patriotic fervor with their acrobatic parade-ground drills. As one admirer related, "They would fall to the ground, load their guns, fire, turn over on their backs, fire again, jump up, run a few steps, fall, then crawl on their hands and feet as silent and quick as cats, climb high stone walls by stepping on each other's shoulders, making a human ladder." Ellsworth, with his trim, compact build and dark good looks, soon achieved a sort of heartthrob status. "His pictures sold like wildfire in every city of the land," noted *The Atlantic Monthly*. "Schoolgirls dreamed over the graceful wave of his curls."

Ellsworth had come to Lincoln's attention the previous year, when his unit staged an exhibition before an appreciative crowd in Springfield.

"The predominance of crinoline was particularly notable," observed the *Illinois State Register,* in a nod to Ellsworth's many female devotees. The young officer also found an admirer in Lincoln, who stood and watched the spectacle for two hours in the shade of a cottonwood tree. Ellsworth had become an enthusiastic campaigner for Lincoln by that time, and the grateful candidate came to take a fatherly interest in his fortunes. Within a month of the Zouave exhibition, Ellsworth was back in Springfield, working as a clerk in the offices of Lincoln and Herndon. He soon became a frequent presence in the Lincoln home and "a great pet in the family," according to one relation. Ellsworth had been at Lincoln's side on Election Day, even escorting the candidate to the polling station, and his voice had been one of the loudest in cheering the result.

Entered according to Act of Congress in the year 1861, by M. B. Brady, in the Clerk's office of the District Court of the U.S. for the So. District of New-York

Colonel Elmer Ellsworth, the dashing young Zouave. *Courtesy of the Library of Congress*

In private moments Ellsworth wrote long letters to his fiancée, Carrie Spafford, alternating between expressions of undying love and snippets of practical advice: "take PLENTY of EXERCISE, and AVOID TIGHT LACING." Now and then Ellsworth would touch on the growing apprehension in Springfield over Lincoln's safety. "People here are in a huge sweat about secession matters," he wrote, adding that it was now a common belief "among the better informed" that some sort of attempt on Lincoln's life "will surely be made."

As the weeks passed, Ellsworth's continued presence in Springfield gave rise to rumors that Lincoln would be escorted to Washington by a full complement of fifty Zouaves, resplendent in their scarlet-and-blue attire. This would have been exactly the type of saber rattling that Lincoln wished to avoid. Soon, a denial appeared in the *Herald.* "Mr. Lincoln," readers were assured, "has too much common sense to entertain so ridiculous a scheme for a moment."

If there was no room on the train for a corps of rifle-twirling cadets, however, a place was easily found for their charismatic leader. William Wood, in his role as superintendent of arrangements, saw at once that Ellsworth's renown and his close ties to Lincoln could be turned to his own uses. The presence of the much-admired officer would signal that protective measures were in place, even if largely ceremonial in form. Lincoln, for his part, could scarcely object to the presence of a man who had become, as many friends would remark, "like a son" to him.

In his "Circular of Instructions" to the reception committees along the train's route, Wood attempted to give shape to Ellsworth's duties:

> The President-elect will under *no circumstances* attempt to pass
> through any crowd until such arrangements are made as will
> meet the approval of Colonel Ellsworth, who is charged with the
> responsibility of all matters of this character, and to facilitate this,
> you will confer a favor by placing Col. Ellsworth in communica-
> tion with the chief of your escort, immediately upon the arrival
> of the train.

Ellsworth would be the only member of the entourage with any official security designation, but in the days leading up to departure, several other military men would vie for seats on the train, with an eye toward protecting the president-elect. Capt. John Pope, like Ellsworth, managed to straddle the line between family circle and armed escort—the future general was a relation of Mrs. Lincoln's. David Hunter, the army major who had written to advise the deployment of 100,000 Wide Awakes to Washington, received a cordial but unequivocal invitation from Lincoln himself: "I expect the pleasure of your company." A friend of Hunter's, Col. Edwin Vose Sumner, also intended to be on hand. "I have heard of threats against Mr. Lincoln," Sumner declared, "and of bets being offered that he would never be inaugurated. I know very well that he is not a man to live in fear of assassination, but when the safety of the whole country depends upon his life, I would respectfully suggest to him whether it would not be well to give this matter some attention." At sixty-four years of age, Sumner was nearly three times as old as Ellsworth, and believed himself to be the senior man in Lincoln's security retinue.

Lincoln also had a number of self-appointed bodyguards among his civilian friends, including two of his closest advisers: Norman Judd, an Illinois state senator whose imperious manner and thrusting white beard reminded some of a Russian czar, and Judge David Davis, a three-hundred-pound giant with "a big brain and a big heart" to match. Both men had had a hand in Lincoln's election; Davis had managed the campaign, and Judd had been instrumental in bringing the Republican National Convention to Chicago. Both intended to see their man safely to Washington.

Far more vocal in his concern was Ward Hill Lamon, a gregarious, hard-drinking, banjo-playing companion of Lincoln's days on the legal circuit. Like Judd and Davis, Lamon had been a major force in the presidential race, and he is generally credited with one of the more celebrated maneuvers of the Chicago convention—printing up duplicate tickets to ensure that the Wigwam would be packed with Lincoln supporters. In a memoir written many years later, Lamon recalled answering a summons to Springfield after the election. It was known that he had hopes of a diplomatic appointment in Paris, but, as Lamon reported it, Lincoln had other plans: "It looks as if we might have war," Lincoln told him. "In that case I want you with me. In fact, I must have you. You must go, and go to stay."

Lamon, no stranger to barroom brawling, seems to have believed that he would meet whatever dangers lay ahead with his fists and a scattering of concealed weapons. A physically commanding presence—over six feet tall and weighing nearly three hundred pounds—he arrived in Springfield carrying "a brace of fine pistols," along with a set of brass knuckles, a large bowie knife, and a blackjack. "The fear that Mr. Lincoln would be assassinated," Lamon recalled, "was shared by very many of his neighbors at Springfield," and because of his long friendship with the president-elect, Lamon considered himself to be foremost in the chain of protectors. "No one knew Mr. Lincoln better," he insisted, "none loved him more than I." In later years, Lamon would often tell a story about being at Lincoln's side as he prepared to depart for Gettysburg, where he would deliver his famous address at the scene of the pivotal battle. Upon being informed that he was in danger of missing his train, Lamon recalled, Lincoln offered a characteristic response: "Well, I feel about that as the convict did in Illinois, when he was going to the gallows. Passing along the road in custody of the sheriff, and seeing the people who were eager for the execution crowding and jostling one another past him, he at last called out, 'Boys! You needn't be in such a hurry to get ahead, for there won't be any fun till I get there.'"

The anecdote underscored the central difficulty of planning Lincoln's safe passage to Washington. In making the arrangements, William Wood had drawn up a detailed timetable for the journey and supplied copies to the press. The gesture was in keeping with Lincoln's desire to make himself visible after the long winter in Springfield, but it also presented an enormous dilemma for the friends and advisers who wished to keep him safe. From the moment Lincoln's train departed Springfield, anyone wishing to cause harm would be able to track his movements in unprecedented detail—even, at some stages of the journey, down to the minute. At a time when Lincoln was receiving daily threats of death by bullet, knife, poisoned ink, and spider-filled dumpling, the degree of precision in Wood's timetable appeared to play into the hands of his enemies. So long as the trains ran on time, anyone intent on mischief would now have a window of opportunity calculated to the instant.

Of all the stops on Lincoln's itinerary, only one would be made in a place where he had not actually been invited to appear. For the most part, as his secretary John Nicolay would attest, Lincoln's movements had been planned at the invitation of various governors and state legislators. "No such call or greeting, however, had come from Maryland," Nicolay observed, "no resolutions of welcome from her Legislature, no invitation from her Governor, no municipal committee from Baltimore." Private citizens like Worthington Snethen, the resolute Wide Awake marcher, would make a few overtures. A Mr. R. B. Coleman, the manager of Baltimore's Eutaw House hotel, went so far as to invite Lincoln to stay "for a week or more," so as to give ample evidence that he was "not afraid to stop in a slave state." Maryland's elected officials, however, were conspicuous in their silence.

Capt. George Hazzard, a West Point graduate who had served with distinction in Mexico, was one of the first to apprehend danger behind that silence. Hazzard had been writing to Lincoln for some months with advice on matters ranging from election strategy to the strengthening of federal arsenals. When the itinerary for the inaugural journey became public, Hazzard turned his sights on Baltmore. "I hope the interest I feel in your personal safety and in the success of your administration will be a sufficient excuse for my addressing you this unsolicited communication," he wrote. "I have the very highest respect for the integrity and abilities of your master of transportation, Mr. Wood, and did I not feel that *a residence of several years* in the city of Baltimore and four trips up and down the Potomac from its mouth to Washington City had given me some personal knowledge of the citizens and the geography of Maryland that Mr. Wood does not possess, I would not utter one word by way of advice or suggestion."

Given the circumstances, however, Hazzard felt compelled to warn

Lincoln about the likely perils of passing through Maryland, adding that "the greatest risk" would surely come in Baltimore, where there were many men who would "glory in being hanged" for having murdered an

GREAT WESTERN RAILROAD.

TIME CARD

For a Special Train, Monday, Feb. 11, 1861,

WITH

His Excellency, Abraham Lincoln, President Elect.

Leave SPRINGFIELD,	8.00	A. M.
" JAMESTOWN,	8.15	"
" DAWSON,	8.24	"
" MECHANICSBURG,	8.30	"
" LANESVILLE,	8.37	"
" ILLIOPOLIS,	8.49	"
" NIANTIC,	8.58	"
" SUMMIT,	9.07	"
Arrive at DECATUR,	9.24	"
Leave DECATUR,	9.29	"
" OAKLEY,	9.45	"
" CERRO GORDO,	9.54	"
" BEMENT,	10.13	"
" SADORUS,	10.40	"
Arrive at TOLONO,	10.50	"
Leave "	10.55	"
" PHILO,	11.07	"
" SIDNEY,	11.17	"
" HOMER,	11.30	"
" SALINA,	11.45	"
" CATLIN,	11.59	"
" BRYANT,	12.07	P. M.
" DANVILLE,	12.12	"
Arrive at STATE LINE,	12.30	P. M.

This train will be entitled to the road, *and all other trains must be kept out of the way.*

Trains to be passed and met must be on the side track at least 10 minutes before this train is due.

Agents at all stations between Springfield and State Line must be on duty when this train passes, and examine the switches and know *that all is right before it passes.*

Operators at Telegraph Stations between Springfield and State Line must remain on duty until this train passes, and immediately report its time to Chas. H. Speed, Springfield.

All Foremen and men under their direction must be on the track and know positively that the track is in order.

It is very important that this train should pass over the road in safety, and all employees are expected to render all assistance in their power.

Red is the signal for danger, but any signal apparently intended to indicate alarm or danger must be regarded, the train stopped, and the meaning of it ascertained.

Carefulness is particularly enjoined.

F. W. BOWEN,
Supt.

A moment-by-moment time card for the first day of Lincoln's journey.
Courtesy of the Alfred Whital Stern Collection, Rare Book and Special Collections Division, Library of Congress

abolitionist president. Hazzard laid out three possible "courses of conduct" to meet the danger. The first, he suggested, would be to travel "openly and boldly" through the city, exactly as Lincoln planned to do at all the other stops on his route, but with the added security of a highly visible military escort. Clearly, Hazzard did not favor this plan. "It would take an army of 50,000 men and a week's preparation to make a perfectly safe passage through a hostile city as large as Baltimore," he believed. "Thousands of marksmen could fire from windows and housetops without the slightest danger to themselves."

That being the case, Hazzard presented a second option: bypassing Baltimore entirely. The methods of doing so were limited at best, he explained, since the only viable alternate railroad route would pass into Virginia, a state that promised to be no less hostile than Maryland. To avoid both states, Lincoln might consider a voyage by steamboat from Philadelphia, making the final leg of the journey along the Potomac River, charting a middle course between the two unfriendly territories. The journey would be plagued by difficult navigation, Hazzard admitted: "In many places the scene is narrow and commanded by eminences from which an enemy could seriously annoy if not disable a single ship." If Lincoln found himself compelled to go ashore, Hazzard warned, "the inhabitants would be very likely to detain you" until after the date of the inauguration had passed.

The third option, and the one that Hazzard appeared to favor, was a plan for catching Lincoln's potential attackers off guard. Having studied the railroad routes and timetables carefully, Hazzard put forward a scenario that would allow the president-elect to deviate from his published timetable and pass through the city ahead of schedule. According to this plan, Lincoln would slip away from his entourage in Philadelphia or Harrisburg—"privately and unannounced with a very few friends"—and take a sleeper car through to Washington. If this could not be managed, Lincoln might stop outside of the city and board a different train, or perhaps even arrange for a horse and buggy to carry him the rest of the way to Washington. Any of these options, Hazzard explained, would allow the president-elect to avoid the point of greatest risk: riding in an open carriage from one depot to another in Baltimore, through a large and hostile crowd.

Not satisfied with a change of itinerary, Hazzard also suggested a change of appearance. He insisted that Lincoln should adopt a disguise for added security before showing himself on the streets of Baltimore. Apparently unaware that his correspondent had recently grown a beard, Hazzard suggested that a "false mustache" could be provided, along with "an old slouched hat and a long cloak or overcoat for concealment." Even then, he maintained, Lincoln would have to be shadowed by a phalanx of guards walking "eight or ten paces" to the front and rear of him. If all of these precautions were adopted, Lincoln might be able to pass safely through the city. "This could be accomplished," Hazzard concluded.

Significantly, all of Hazzard's suggested "courses of conduct" rested on the assumption that Lincoln would come under fire in Baltimore. In weighing the risks, he compared Lincoln to an emperor at the gates of a conquered city, as opposed to the democratically elected president he was. Hazzard was clearly aware of the enormity of what he was proposing, and recognized that Lincoln had many reasons to resist any change of plan. "If after reading this communication you and your advisors shall think proper to go *openly* through Baltimore," he concluded, "I shall feel fully satisfied that *all* the information in your possession justifies such a course and I will follow you to the last." He closed with a final courtesy: "No answer is expected."

Lincoln did reply, however. It is often supposed, given his later statements and his serene lack of concern at the time, that Lincoln was unaware of any stirrings of danger in Baltimore as he set forth from Springfield. In fact, the receipt of Hazzard's letter made Lincoln aware of the looming trouble in January 1861—perhaps even before Allan Pinkerton caught wind of it. It is impossible to gauge how much credence Lincoln gave to Hazzard's warning, but it is plain that he did not dismiss it out of hand. At a time when scores of politicians and office seekers were scrambling for passage on the inaugural train, Lincoln offered a seat to Hazzard. Like Ward Lamon, the young captain came prepared for whatever contingencies he might face. In his pockets he carried protective eyewear, brass knuckles, and a dagger. "In any event," he told Lincoln, "I shall do myself the honor to witness your inauguration."

CHAPTER TEN
HOSTILE ORGANIZATIONS

•

*He soon became a welcome guest at the residences of many of the first families of that
refined and aristocratic city. His romantic disposition and the ease of his manner
captivated many of the susceptible hearts of the beautiful Baltimore belles, whose eyes grew
brighter in his presence, and who listened enraptured to the poetic utterances which were
whispered into their ears under the witching spell of music and moonlit nature.*
—ALLAN PINKERTON on the efforts of Detective Harry Davies in Baltimore

DURING THE EARLY WEEKS of February 1861, Pinkerton operative
Harry Davies began spending a great deal of time in a Baltimore house
of prostitution. The dimly lit wooden house at 70 Davis Street, in the
shadow of the Calvert Street train station, had a narrow hallway at the
front that opened onto a parlor filled with dark curtains, narrow divans,
and gilt-framed paintings of wood nymphs and water sprites. Annette
Travis, the proprietor, would greet her patrons with a warm smile and a
glass of strong spirits. Behind her, two or three young women sat quietly
on a painted bench, sometimes busying themselves with needlework. After a few pleasantries, the visitor was led to one of three upstairs chambers, where the business of the evening would be carried out.

It was not the sort of place one would expect to find Davies, the former seminarian. For more than a week, however, the detective had been
working hard to cultivate the friendship of a young man named Otis K.
Hillard, a sallow-faced, hard-drinking regular of the establishment. Hillard, according to Pinkerton, "was one of the fast 'bloods' of the city." On
his chest he wore a gold badge stamped with a palmetto, the symbol of
South Carolina's secession. It was known that Hillard had recently signed

on as a lieutenant in the "Palmetto Guard," one of several secret military organizations springing up in Baltimore.

Pinkerton had targeted Hillard, who came from a prominent family, as one of the Fire Eaters who regularly gathered at Barnum's Hotel on Fayette Street, just off Monument Square. "The visitors from all portions of the South located at this house," Pinkerton noted, "and in the evenings the corridors and parlors would be thronged by the tall, lank forms of the long-haired gentlemen who represented the aristocracy of the slavehold-ing interests. Their conversations were loud and unrestrained, and any one bold enough or sufficiently indiscreet to venture an opinion contrary to the righteousness of their cause, would soon find himself in an unenvi-able position and frequently the subject of violence."

On Pinkerton's orders, Davies took a room at Barnum's and used the "ready passport" of his New Orleans birth to ingratiate himself with the Southern element. Davies claimed to have come to Baltimore on business, but at every turn, he quietly insinuated that he was far more interested in matters of "rebeldom." Whenever the crowd at Barnum's gave voice to anti-Union sentiments, Davies would offer a raised glass and a crisp nod of the head.

Of all the regulars at Barnum's, Otis Hillard appeared to be the most promising source of information. Davies worked to forge a useful bond, buying drinks with a free hand, and seeking advice on the amusements of Baltimore. Soon, the two men became inseparable. A typical day in-cluded dinner at a favorite chophouse called Mann's, followed by bil-liards and cigars at Harry Hemling's, a second-floor "chalk and sawdust" room on Fayette Street. The two were often seen at a concert saloon known as the Pagoda, enjoying the latest in "popular song and genteel merriment." In the latter stages of the evening, depending on which way Hillard's moral compass happened to be pointing, they would attend vespers at a local Catholic church or seek the company of Anna Hughes, Hillard's favored companion at Annette Travis's establishment. After a particularly eventful evening, if the consumption of alcohol had been such as to render navigation difficult, the two men would sleep in the same room.

"By reason of his high social position," Pinkerton observed, "Hillard was enabled to introduce his friend to the leading families and into the most aristocratic clubs and societies of which the city boasted, and Davies made many valuable acquaintances through the influence of this rebel-lious scion of Baltimore aristocracy." Though these connections proved useful, Hillard himself soon became a source of frustration, as his commitment to the secessionist cause proved to be tenuous. "Because of a weak nature and having been reared in the lap of luxury, he had entered into this movement more from a temporary burst of enthusiasm, and because it was fashionable," Pinkerton noted. Hillard often spoke of winning fame and glory for himself, but as the calls for armed rebellion grew louder, he appeared to think better of it. "He was inclined to hesitate," Davies reported, "before the affair had gone too far." Davies hoped to exploit Hillard's doubts, pressing him for useful information under the guise of sympathizing with his fears. Hillard, for his part, seemed to enjoy toying with Davies's obvious interest in Baltimore's secret cabals. He refused to confide fully in his new friend, preferring instead to dangle his forbidden knowledge just out of reach, always suggesting that he knew more than he could tell, for reasons of personal honor. Undeterred, Pinkerton instructed Davies to keep trying. He was convinced that Hillard would soon become "a pliant tool in our hands."

Pinkerton appeared willing to go to any lengths. In Chicago, he had often discouraged his operatives from using alcohol as a means of loosening a suspect's tongue, but in Baltimore, he relied heavily on the "unbridled talk" of the barroom. By the same token, he would later defend against charges that he and his operatives preyed on the weak-willed, exchanging false friendship for information. "Such a technique was distasteful to me," Pinkerton said of one such case, "but the course pursued was the only one which afforded the slightest promise of success, hence its adoption. Severe moralists may question whether this course is a legitimate or defensible one, but as long as crime exists, the necessity for detection is apparent. In this righteous work the end will unquestionably justify the means adopted to secure the desired result." Many would disagree, but in this instance—perhaps more so than any other—Pinkerton held himself above criticism. The clock was ticking.

A report from Charles Williams, the operative who had been concerned about passing himself off as a Mississippian, underscored the urgency of the situation. Williams had been trawling for information at Sherwood's, a "small and rather prim" hotel at the corner of Harrison and Fayette streets, when he noticed that the bartender—Howell Sherwood, the landlord's brother—appeared visibly troubled, as if struggling with a difficult decision. Taking a seat at the bar, Williams struck up a conversation and found that Sherwood was eager to unburden himself. He began by saying that he was a peaceful man and had no desire to fall in with the

"Seces-crowd" of the city. If possible, he insisted, he would prefer to see the Union preserved, but if forced to "give up the Stars and Stripes," he would pledge his loyalty to the South. Williams allowed as how he felt the same way. Was it inevitable, he asked, that war must come? Sherwood fell silent for several moments, apparently considering his answer carefully. At length, he gave a heavy sigh and began to speak in a halting voice, as if the words themselves were causing him pain. He had overheard murmurs of a horrifying plot against the government, he said—"the vilest proposition that ever was heard of." In Washington in a few days time, the members of the Electoral College would gather in the United States Capitol to ratify the election of Abraham Lincoln. On that day, Sherwood said, a group of agitators from Baltimore intended to detonate a bomb inside the Capitol, striking a devastating blow to the government and throwing the peaceful transition of power into chaos. "Oh, my God, it is so," Sherwood insisted. "If anyone had said there was such a conspiracy in this or any other city, I would not have believed it."

When Williams hurried back to South Street with this information, Pinkerton listened with an air of mounting frustration. He pointed to a stack of reports on his desk, filled with wild stories and outlandish rumors. Alarming as the claims were, none could be confirmed definitively. After more than a week in Baltimore, Pinkerton had yet to achieve the first of the goals he had outlined to Felton—proof of the existence of a plot.

Pinkerton felt certain that Otis Hillard could provide a badly needed shard of evidence, if only he could be induced to do so. A few days earlier, Hillard had been summoned to Washington to answer questions about the rumors surrounding the inauguration. It is likely that Hillard's summons to Washington was the red flag that caught the attention of the Pinkerton team, but the experience left him more than usually cautious about sharing confidences. Despite Harry Davies's best efforts, Hillard continued to play coy, offering nothing more than broad hints and vague insinuations.

A significant break came on Tuesday, February 12, when Hillard introduced Davies to a man named Hughes, a daguerreotype photographer recently arrived from New Orleans. As the newcomer gave an enthusiastic report of how matters stood in his home state—Louisiana having seceded the previous month—Davies seized the opening to steer the conversation toward Maryland's prospects. The visitor warmed to the subject immediately, claiming that officials in Washington had sent out spies to keep an eye on agitators throughout the state. "I understand," he said, "that they have men watching the railroad bridges between here and Philadelphia. The railroads are afraid that they will be destroyed—but I do not know if it will do any good." This last remark was accompanied by a significant wink in the direction of Hillard. Davies pressed for more information, but neither man would elaborate on the statement.

For the rest of the day, as the two men made their familiar round of restaurants and saloons, Davies tried to draw Hillard out on the subject. The encounter appeared to have put Hillard in a melancholy mood, and he refused to take the bait. Instead, he brooded on the declining state of his health. Davies, trying to move the conversation forward, suggested that perhaps Hillard's fondness for prostitutes might be a contributing factor. Hillard drew back and "seemed horrified."

After a restorative dinner and a round of billiards, Hillard recovered his better humor. His earlier concerns were forgotten as he proposed a visit to Annette Travis's establishment on Davis Street. Davies willingly tagged along, hoping to maneuver his friend into a more talkative frame of mind. Once again, Hillard arranged to enjoy the company of Anna Hughes, a pale, dark-haired woman who said little but giggled incessantly. Davies turned to leave as the young woman led Hillard toward the stairs, but Hillard laid a hand on his sleeve and asked him to stay. There were still important matters to be discussed, Hillard said with a wink. Reluctantly, Davies followed the couple as they made their way upstairs.

Davies perched awkwardly on a chair in the corner of the room as Hillard made himself at home. "Hillard and his woman seemed very much pleased at meeting," Davies reported delicately, "and hugged and kissed each other for about an hour." Even in this setting, Hillard refused to give up his claim to Davies's attentions. Several times, Davies rose to excuse himself from the room, but each time his friend called him back, suggesting that there was more to be said about "forthcoming events." As the evening wore on, Hillard teased Davies with hints and preened for Anna Hughes, portraying himself as a man burdened with many secrets, the nature of which would astonish the world. Davies, squirming on his chair in the corner of the room, tried to play along. He alternated words of encouragement with notes of skepticism, suggesting that perhaps Hillard didn't know as much as he claimed. Try as he might, however, he could not get Hillard to enlarge on his boasts.

Finally, Davies lost patience. Jumping to his feet, he told Hillard that he was leaving, and his tone suggested that the two men would not be seeing each other again. "I started for the door," Davies said, but as he turned the handle, Hillard called after him, telling him to wait. He seemed to realize, belatedly, that he had pushed his friend too far. For several days, he had been playing a game of cat and mouse, hinting at grand designs of which he dared not speak. Now, it appeared, Davies was prepared to turn his back. All other urgencies were forgotten as Hillard disentangled himself from Miss Hughes and followed Davies out onto the street. At last, he was ready to talk.

The two men made their way back to Davies's room and sat talking into the early hours of the morning. Hillard spent considerable time describing his activities with the Palmetto Guard, one of the many rifle-toting "committees of safety" that were springing up across the state. He mentioned that his unit would be drilling the following evening at a secret gathering place and that he would be obliged to join with them. Davies listened with rising impatience. Though this was more than Hillard had ever revealed before, it was hardly earth-shattering news. Timothy Webster, the detective Pinkerton had stationed among the railroad crews in Perrymansville, had already managed to join a unit of National Volunteers there, marching along the banks of the Susquehanna River.

Davies changed tactics. Playing up his role as an ardent secessionist, he chided Hillard for being sluggish in his response to the Northern threat. His home state of Louisiana, he reminded Hillard, had already withdrawn from the Union. The practice drills of the Palmetto Guard, by contrast, seemed little more than empty posturing.

Hillard fell silent, apparently stung. He gave a sidelong glance at his friend, then cleared his throat. When he spoke again, his manner had changed. He affected a breezy tone, as if remarking on the weather, but he fixed Davies with an intense gaze, indicating the true import of his words. "He then asked me," Davies said, "if I had seen a statement of Lincoln's route to Washington City."

Davies lifted his head, at last catching sight of a foothold amid all the slippery hearsay. It was the first time that Hillard had made direct reference to Lincoln's passage through Baltimore, much less suggested a link—oblique as it was—between the president-elect's movements and the activities of a Maryland militia unit. Struggling to remain composed, Davies said only that he had seen a statement of Lincoln's itinerary in the newspapers.

The answer appeared to encourage Hillard. "By the by," he said lightly, "that reminds me that I must go and see a certain party in the morning the first thing."

Again, Davies was careful not to appear overeager, so as not to put Hillard off. "What about?" he asked.

"About Lincoln's route," Hillard replied. "I want to see about the telegraph in Philadelphia and New York and have some arrangements made."

"How do you mean?" Davies asked.

Hillard gave a shrug to suggest that he was merely speculating, but then he went on to outline a coded system that would allow the progress of the president-elect's train to be tracked from stop to stop, even if telegraph communications were being monitored for suspicious activity. "We would have some signs to telegraph by," he explained. "For instance, supposing that we should telegraph to a certain point 'all set up at 7,' that would mean that Lincoln would be at such a point at 7 o'clock."

Davies fell silent, nodding his head. He realized at once that the existence of a cipher of this type signaled a well-developed plot, or "mature arrangement," involving Lincoln's train. Once again, he shaped his reply in a manner that would strike at Hillard's pride, in hopes of drawing out additional details. Why should the guardsmen bother with codes and signals, he asked, when there did not appear to be any specific scheme for using them? "It is very singular," Davies said, "that some plan of action has not been proposed."

Hillard chafed at this, his mask slipping a bit. He insisted that there was, in fact, a carefully plotted strategy in place. The codes, he continued, were only a small part of a larger design. "I asked him what it was," Davies reported, but Hillard would not divulge anything more.

"My friend," he said grimly, "that is what I would like to tell you, but I dare not—I wish I could—anything almost I would be willing to do for you, but to tell you that I dare not."

Davies continued to hammer at Hillard's vanities and insecurities, peppering him with heavily barbed questions for the better part of an hour. At length, it became clear that Hillard would say nothing more, and that he now regretted revealing as much as he had. As the two men parted, Hillard cautioned Davies to say nothing of what had passed between them. Looking pale and fretful, he set off once again to seek comfort in the arms of Anna Hughes. Davies waited until Hillard had passed out of sight, then headed to Pinkerton's office to make his report.

IN EXTRACTING EVEN THESE SMALL GLIMMERS of information from Hillard, Davies had succeeded where an official government inquiry had failed. Hillard's trip to Washington one week earlier had come in response to a summons to appear before an imposing congressional select committee. President Buchanan had reluctantly authorized the inquiry as a response to "alleged hostile organizations" operating within the District of Columbia, and their plans to attack the Capitol or disrupt the forthcoming inauguration. "It is said that serious apprehensions are, to some extent, entertained, in which I do not share, that the peace of this District may be disturbed before the 4th of March," declared the president in a characteristic display of fence-sitting. "In any event, it will be my duty to preserve it, and this duty shall be performed . . . and whatever the result may be, I shall carry to my grave the consciousness that I at least meant well for my country."

While hardly a clarion call, the president's concerns were sufficient for the purpose. The select committee was impaneled on January 9, 1861. From the first, the investigators approached their task with a certain anxious diffidence, paddling about on the surface of various rumors but never plunging to any depth. Over the course of five weeks the committee heard testimony from two dozen witnesses. The possibility of violence was raised several times but never pursued with any vigor, suggesting that the committee members were reluctant to fan the flames.

The witnesses ranged from concerned government officials such as Winfield Scott and James Berret, the mayor of Washington, to those believed to have knowledge of sinister designs, many of them hailing from Baltimore. Otis K. Hillard, one of the latter category, appeared before the committee on February 6. In spite of what he would tell Harry Davies one week later, Hillard testified under oath that he was "not a member of any military organization," and he firmly denied any knowledge of plans to interfere with Lincoln's inauguration. Hillard did tell the committee that he was aware, "altogether from hearsay," of the doings of a formidable organization known as the National Volunteers. According to Hillard, this group, numbering some six thousand men, had sprung up in Baltimore to prevent "any armed body" from passing through Baltimore with Lincoln. Curiously, in Hillard's construction of the events, the National Volunteers had no quarrel with Lincoln himself, only with the prospect of a military escort. "Mr. Lincoln will not be interrupted as a citizen alone," he told the committee. "Individually, they have the greatest respect for Mr. Lincoln, and I think there would not be a solitary thing done, unless some military comes with him, which they look upon in the light of a threat." Hillard went so far as to say that it made no difference whether these military men came from the North or the South; Baltimore would object in either case. Strangely, the committee sought little clarification on this point, but it instead asked repeatedly for the names of the leaders of the National Volunteers. Hillard declined for "prudential reasons" to give an answer, indicating that he did not wish to compromise his friends. When pressed, he gave a series of Bartleby-like refusals: "I would rather not answer that question," he declared.

Astonishingly, the select committee accepted this rebuff without demur. Hillard was excused from further testimony, though the investigators reserved the right to recall him should it become necessary to compel him to answer. Though he had come through unscathed, Hillard returned to Baltimore feeling thoroughly rattled. In the circumstances, it is not surprising that he was reticent when the amiable Harry Davies popped up at his elbow a few days later.

As Davies chipped away at Hillard's defenses in Baltimore, the select committee in Washington turned its attention to a bigger fish. As the secession debate in Maryland intensified, Thomas H. Hicks, the governor of the state, emerged as a central figure in the national crisis. In his inaugural address three years earlier, Hicks had attempted to claim the middle ground: "The people of this State yet know of no grievances for which disunion is a remedy," he declared, "and they have always, in the words of Washington, discountenanced whatever might suggest even the slightest suspicion that Union can, *in any event*, be abandoned." At the same time, however, the new governor insisted that the people of Maryland "will hearken to no suggestion inimical to the slaveholding States, for she herself is one of them."

This balancing act, a political expedient in 1858, had become untenable after Lincoln's election, with many of Hicks's most powerful constituents clamoring for Maryland to withdraw from the Union. As the state legislature pushed Hicks to convene a special session—at which a vote on secession was expected—the governor engaged in a series of desperate stalling and blocking measures. This "sulphurous dithering" infuriated his colleagues and many of his constituents, but it won praise from the Northern press. "We know of no man who occupies a more prominent position at the present time than the Governor of the State of Maryland," declared the February 16 issue of *Harper's Weekly*. "To his wise and patriotic action, in firmly resisting the tide of partisan feeling in his State, he has so far averted civil war, and preserved Maryland as a nucleus about which, if politic counsels prevail, our glorious Union may be preserved."

It is perhaps closer to the truth to say that Hicks was trying to gauge which way the wind was blowing. A slave owner himself, Hicks was fiercely committed to the preservation of what he called "southern ideals," and he had recoiled at the election of Abraham Lincoln. A letter attributed to him at that time, quite possibly written in jest, offered a startling suggestion for a recently formed Maryland militia unit: "Will they be good men to send out to kill Lincoln and his men?" Whatever his private feelings may have been, however, he saw clearly that secession would bring disastrous consequences for his state. The previous December, after South Carolina announced its withdrawal, Hicks was told that Southern leaders were intent on "hurrying Maryland out of the Union," so as to set the stage for a Southern takeover of Washington. "If this can be accomplished before the 4th of next March," Hicks was informed, Southern forces would succeed in "divesting the North of the seat of Government."

Hicks regarded the prospect with dread. At the beginning of January he issued a startling but little-heeded proclamation to the people of Maryland, stating that he had been warned "by persons having the opportunity to know" that secessionist power brokers in Washington intended to force Maryland to cast her lot with the cotton states. "They have resolved to seize the Federal capital and public archives, so that they may be in a position to be acknowledged by foreign governments," he declared. "The assent of Maryland is necessary, as the District of Columbia would revert to her in case of a dissolution of the Union. The plan contemplates forcible opposition to Mr. Lincoln's inauguration, and consequently civil war upon Maryland soil, and a transfer of its horrors from the States which are to provoke it."

The nature of these horrors was clear enough. If a war was to be fought for control of Washington, Hicks knew, Maryland would likely be flattened in the process. On the other hand, if war was avoided, Maryland would be made to suffer the consequences if she declared for the South. Hicks continued to stall for time, hoping, as many others did, that a compromise would be reached before Lincoln took office. Publicly, he declared that the people of Maryland would not consent to secession "until every honorable, constitutional and lawful effort" had been exhausted.

As the calls for a special session of the legislature grew louder, Hicks tried desperately to hold his ground. "The people of Baltimore are all tired of waiting," a witness told the select committee in Washington. "They believe that they have the right to speak upon this subject." As the stonewalling dragged on, an angry group of National Volunteers attempted to batter down the door to the governor's office.

Lincoln himself was well aware of Hicks's dilemma. "The pressure there upon Hicks is fearful," he was told by Alexander K. McClure, a Pennsylvania Republican. "Indeed, so embittered are the disunionists in Maryland that Gov. Hicks is seriously concerned for his personal safety. He has been advised that his assassination has been plotted, & is still entertained, in order to throw the government into the hands of the Speaker of the Senate, who is a ranting Secession disunionist." The governor's struggle, McClure believed, had serious implications for the president-elect. "If he should be compelled to yield," he told Lincoln, "you could never get to Washington except within a circle of bayonets."

At the height of Hicks's standoff, a disturbing letter crossed his desk. Sent from Annapolis on February 7, it was written by George Stearns, an employee of Samuel Felton's Philadelphia, Wilmington and Baltimore Railroad, and concerned the passage of Lincoln's train through Maryland:

> *Dear Sir*
> *On Sunday last a man who said he was from Baltimore called on our Bridge tender at Back River and informed him an attempt would be made by parties from Baltimore and other places to burn the bridge just before the train should pass, which should have Mr. Lincoln on Board and in the excitement to assassinate him. The man who imparted this information will not give his name.*

It is not known whether Hicks took any action or even made a reply to this remarkable warning. It is reasonably certain, however, that the letter was on the governor's mind the following week, when he was compelled to testify before the select committee investigators in Washington. Hicks had come to Washington under duress. In the previous weeks, he had ignored repeated calls to appear—even when the committee offered to take his testimony in Annapolis—using the same dodges and feints with which he had confounded his own state legislature. On the morning of February 13, having exhausted every avenue of escape, Hicks was finally sworn in. The governor's testimony proved to be a masterpiece of half-truths and contradictions. He admitted to having heard open declarations that "the installation of Lincoln and Hamlin would never come off," but he insisted that he attached no great importance to such talk. When asked if he had knowledge of plans to attack Washington, he offered unsupported reassurances: "I have not; although I believe it was decidedly contemplated at one time . . . I think it was the settled determination some time ago to make an attack; but I do not believe there is the slightest danger of it now." He declined to give the names of any men suspected in these plots, as it might, he said, "deprive me of sources of information which may be important hereafter."

At one stage, Hicks briefly touched on darker concerns, only to dismiss them as unimportant:

> *Now I have letters going to show that there is a design contemplated to burn a particular bridge and to assassinate particular individuals. All this is to be done in the State of Maryland. But I attach no consequence to this information. I have no doubt these things are talked over, but by a set of men who, in my opinion, cannot organize a system that they can carry out. But that the matter is talked over in secret conclave, I have no doubt.*

The select committee, anxious to move on to other business, somehow chose not to press the point. The official report notes only that "[a]fter further discussion, the question was overruled." It is entirely possible that Governor Hicks believed, or wished to believe, the substance of his testimony before the committee. His own life had been threatened repeatedly during this period, which may well have inured him to warnings of this type. In omitting certain details, however, he had denied the investigators the opportunity to exercise their own judgment. Hicks freely admitted receiving letters that detailed plans for hostile acts against the government, but he pointedly refused to make them available. "If I believed for a moment that it would conduce to the public interest and safety, I would leave all this pile of letters with the committee," he stated, "but I refrain from doing so, that, as one of the guardians at least of the public interest and safety, I may keep the way open hereafter for advice and information." The William Stearns letter, with its unequivocal threat against Lincoln, would remain buried among the governor's papers for years to come.

Governor Hicks would be the select committee's final witness. To a large extent, his testimony had come too late to be of any practical use. One of the committee's principal concerns had been to chase down the threat of "persons or hostile organizations" with designs to prevent the Electoral College from ratifying Lincoln's election. By the time Hicks finally appeared, after several weeks of evasions, that mission had been rendered all but moot. The governor wrapped up his long-delayed testimony shortly before noon on February 13, 1861. The Electoral College was scheduled to convene later that same afternoon. If the investigators appeared to gloss over some of the governor's more provocative statements, it had much to do with the fact that they had already formed their conclusions at this late date, and looked to Hicks for nothing more than an eleventh-hour confirmation. The select committee's official report, released the following day, would state that the investigation had found no proof of "the existence of a secret organization here or elsewhere hostile to the government," and foresaw no "interruption of any of the functions of government."

By that time, Lincoln's train was already under way.

CHAPTER ELEVEN
THE MAN AND THE HOUR

•

We have known Mr. Lincoln for many years; we have heard him speak upon a hundred different occasions; but we never saw him so profoundly affected, nor did he ever utter an address which seemed to us so full of simple and touching eloquence, so exactly adapted to the occasion, so worthy of the man and the hour.

—EDWARD L. BAKER, editor of the *Illinois State Journal*

JUST BEFORE 7:30 ON THE MORNING of Monday, February 11, 1861, Abraham Lincoln ducked into the office of the Chenery House, the hotel in Springfield where his family had spent the past three nights, and began knotting a hank of rope around his traveling cases. When the trunks were neatly bundled, he attached a series of hotel note cards and hastily scrawled an address: "A. Lincoln, White House, Washington, D.C." This done, the president-elect stepped outside and climbed aboard a horse-drawn omnibus coach. The Lincoln Special was due to depart for Washington in half an hour's time.

The weather had been frigid for several days, but there was a thaw in the air that morning. In spite of the early hour, the residents of Springfield were already stirring, eager to pay their respects. As Lincoln made his way toward the Great Western depot on the east side of town, a group of well-wishers trailed along behind, growing larger as it wound through the streets. Arriving at the depot, Lincoln was surprised to find an enormous throng of supporters waiting to see him off—"almost all of whom," he later said, "I could recognize." The boys in the crowd let loose with a chorus of cheers at his arrival.

Stepping down from the omnibus, Lincoln gazed out over the crowd. "His face was pale, and quivered with emotion," declared journalist Henry

Villard, "so deep as to render him unable to utter a single word." The bulky Ward Lamon and the diminutive Colonel Ellsworth appeared suddenly at Lincoln's side, stepping smoothly into their bodyguard roles. Gripping the president-elect lightly by the elbows, they led him into the small brick depot building, where friends and neighbors were waiting to say their good-byes. As he made his way through the small waiting room, Lincoln paused every few steps to grasp hands and exchange a few words.

Lincoln also said a brief farewell to his wife at the depot. With her porcelain skin and glossy auburn hair, Mary Todd Lincoln had been a striking beauty in her youth—"one who could make a bishop forget his prayers," said one admirer. Now, though thickened with age, Mrs. Lincoln could still captivate a roomful of callers. Behind her back, however, there were whispers about her anxious, stormy disposition. She had, a cousin remarked, "an emotional temperament much like an April day."

It had been decided that Mrs. Lincoln would not be on board as her husband's train left Springfield, a last-minute change of plan ascribed to a preinaugural shopping trip in St. Louis. The announcement had prompted unwelcome speculation to the effect that Mrs. Lincoln was afraid to make the journey, owing to the "many vapory rumors" of an assassination attempt. According to one account, Mrs. Lincoln had considered remaining behind with her two younger sons until the Lincoln Special arrived safely in Washington, but she was persuaded otherwise by a telegram from Winfield Scott. The general warned that her absence would draw much comment, as it "might be regarded as proceeding from an apprehension of danger to the President." Instead, it was decided that she, along with Tad and Willie Lincoln, would skip only the first leg of the journey, joining the train in Indianapolis the following day. Writing in the *New York Herald*, Henry Villard gave a gentle polish to Mrs. Lincoln's change of plan:

> A number of lady friends of Mrs. Lincoln have, with characteristic solicitude, taken up the newspaper rumors of intended attacks upon the President-elect while on his way to the Federal capital, and used them as arguments to induce her to delay her removal to Washington until her husband was safely installed in the White House. But the plucky wife of the President met all these well meant propositions with scorn, and made the spirited declaration before she started on her Eastern trip that she would see Mr. Lincoln on to Washington, danger or no danger.

Privately, Villard was glad to be rid of her, however briefly. In a memoir written many years later, he lambasted Mrs. Lincoln as greedy and utterly lacking in propriety, and accused her of accepting gifts for "the use of her influence with her husband" in securing political appointments. Villard claimed that Mrs. Lincoln had nearly delayed her husband's departure that morning, throwing herself on the floor "in a sort of hysterical fit" until he yielded to yet another of her demands.

Whatever may have transpired privately, the Lincolns gave a convincingly affectionate show of parting at the depot. This done, William S. Wood, the self-styled superintendent of arrangements, stepped forward. Eager to keep to schedule, Wood led the president-elect toward the tracks, where a three-car train pulled by a gleaming Rogers steam-powered locomotive waited. It was only the first of several well-appointed trains upon which Lincoln would travel over the next two weeks, as each of the railroad companies transporting the president-elect vied to set new benchmarks for speed and comfort. Descriptions of the lavish trappings of the special cars—including walnut furniture, whale-oil lamps, and crystal flower vases—would become a regular feature of the coverage of the journey. On one segment of the trip, Lincoln would occupy a rolling stateroom with a large portrait of George Washington at one end and a likeness of himself opposite it. On another, Lincoln would recline on a splendid lounge "covered with a mazarine of dark blue cloth of fine texture, trimmed with tri-colored gimp braid and tassels." The latest technology was also in evidence, including a portable telegraph machine, so that the president-elect's party could send and receive messages en route.

The roster of friends and political worthies who would be joining Lincoln on the journey had been shuffled and revised up until the moment of departure. The newspapers estimated that "about fifteen persons" boarded the train that morning, along with a fair number of "special reporters for the leading newspapers." One Lincoln intimate complained that the guest list was "very badly made up," but another chose to make light of the situation, claiming that the train now carried representatives of all parties and political views, "with the exception of the secessionists." Even so, there was little in the way of military trappings, as Lincoln had wished. Though Colonel Ellsworth, in his Zouave garb, hovered protectively at Lincoln's side, the rest of the uniformed escorts were conspicuously absent. Colonel Sumner, Major Hunter, and Captain Pope had all been sent ahead to join the train in Indianapolis.

A great deal of press attention focused on seventeen-year-old Robert

Lincoln, a Harvard freshman, whose striking good looks had drawn much attention from the young women of Springfield. A head shorter than his father, Bob had a smooth round face with dark, hooded blue eyes and the beginnings of a gallant mustache. In contrast to the rough-hewn image of his rail-splitter father, the younger Lincoln's dapper polish inspired the newsmen to dub him the "Prince of Rails." Also joining the Lincoln party was Mrs. Lincoln's brother-in-law, William S. Wallace—"an elderly and amiable personage," according to the *New York Times*—who was also the family doctor. A decade earlier, Dr. Wallace had tended to the Lincolns's second son, Eddie, during the illness that claimed his life five weeks short of his fourth birthday. Ten months later, when the couple's third son arrived, he had been named William Wallace Lincoln, in the doctor's honor.

With so many seats on the train claimed by family and members of the press, only a limited number remained for the advisers and confidants who had received personal invitations from Lincoln himself, a group William Wood had designated as the president-elect's "suite." John Nicolay, Lincoln's private secretary, was expected to be close at hand throughout the journey. Nicolay had pushed hard to find space for his best friend, twenty-two-year-old John Hay. An aspiring poet with wavy, unkempt hair and a quick, ingratiating smile, Hay had been admitted to the bar only one week earlier but had long since made himself indispensable as Nicolay's assistant. Even so, Lincoln was reluctant to add Hay to the traveling party. "We can't take all of Illinois with us down to Washington," he is said to have remarked, though he soon relented: "Well, let Hay come."

John Nicolay (seated) and John Hay, secretaries to Abraham Lincoln.
Courtesy of the Library of Congress

At the stroke of eight, the train bells sounded, signaling that it was time for departure. Mounting the steps of the passenger car, Lincoln turned to face the crowd from the rear platform. The previous day, he had remarked to the press that he did not plan to say anything "warranting their attention" to mark his departure.

Now, humbled by the outpouring of support from his friends and neighbors, he bared his head and prepared to speak. As he did so, a ripple of movement passed through the crowd as hundreds of men removed their own hats. Lincoln paused to gather himself. "His own breast heaved with emotion," reported James Conkling, a neighbor who was in the crowd that morning, "and he could scarcely command his feelings sufficiently to commence."

At last he began to speak:

> My friends, no one, not in my situation, can appreciate my feeling
> of sadness at this parting. To this place, and the kindness of
> these people, I owe everything. Here I have lived a quarter of a
> century, and have passed from a young to an old man. Here my
> children have been born, and one is buried. I now leave, not
> knowing when or whether I may return, to a task before me
> greater than that which rested upon Washington. Without the
> assistance of that Divine Being who ever attended him, I cannot
> succeed. With that assistance, I cannot fail. Trusting in Him,
> who can go with me, and remain with you and be everywhere
> for good, let us confidently hope that all will yet be well. To His
> care commending you, as I hope in your prayers you will
> commend me, I bid you an affectionate farewell.

Speaking without notes or evident preparation, Lincoln somehow managed to capture in a few brief lines the full weight of his emotion at this fateful hour, and his resolve in the face of the task ahead. As Lincoln turned and stepped through the doorway of the train, the crowd burst into three rousing cheers. "Many eyes were filled to overflowing," Conkling wrote, "as Mr. Lincoln uttered those few simple words. He is now fairly on his way for weal or woe of the nation."

THAT SAME DAY, EVEN AS THE LINCOLN Special gathered steam and pushed east toward Indianapolis, a second, oddly parallel journey was launched in Mississippi, some five hundred miles to the south. Climbing aboard a small boat rowed by slaves, Jefferson Davis took leave of Brierfield, his plantation home in Warren County, to catch a steamboat bound for Vicksburg. It was the first leg of a five-day journey to Montgomery, Alabama, where he had been selected as the provisional president of the newly formed Confederate States of America.

For Davis, a former United States senator and secretary of war under Franklin Pierce, it was a bitter turn of events. In Washington the previous month, upon being notified of his home state's secession, Davis had delivered a solemn farewell address on the floor of the Senate. He sorely regretted, as he told his colleagues, that Mississippi's secession had forced his resignation. Throughout his career, Davis held to a firm belief that each state had a sovereign right to secede, but he had also argued forcefully for the preservation of the Union. "I hope," he told his colleagues from the North, "for peaceful relations with you, though we must part. . . . The reverse may bring disaster on every portion of the country." Privately, he feared that armed conflict was now inevitable. It was, as he told a friend, "the saddest day of my life."

Even as Lincoln and Davis set off on their separate journeys, there were many who believed that the secession crisis would yet be defused. One week earlier, on February 4, a widely publicized Peace Convention had convened at Willard's Hotel in Washington. One hundred and thirty-two delegates from twenty-one states assembled under the gavel of former president John Tyler, a pro-slavery Virginian, to consider "some suitable adjustment" to the nation's policies. It was by no means clear how this adjustment was to be reconciled with the platform upon which Lincoln had been elected. Some believed that the Peace Convention would buy time for the secessionist fervor to run its course. Others viewed the gathering as a calculated and even treasonous effort to undermine the incoming president. Lincoln himself anticipated "no good results," though he expressed these doubts privately. In spite of the misgivings, the proceedings opened on a hopeful note. "What is party when compared to the task of rescuing one's country from danger?" Tyler asked the delegates. "Do that, and one loud, long shout of joy and gladness will resound throughout the land."

As it happened, few shouts of gladness were heard that day. Even as Tyler's Peace Convention came to order in Washington, thirty-eight representatives of the six states that had seceded were convening in Montgomery to organize a provisional government—one that would "declare its independence of the late United States, as the Congress of the thirteen colonies declared their independence of Great Britain."

Even now, as the rising Confederacy drew up its constitution, many remained convinced that the North would not take up arms. "There will be no invasion of Southern soil," insisted an editorial in the *New York Times*. "Such a project is as impracticable as it would be unwise—and no one looks to it as a remedy for any of the evils which afflict or threaten the country." This conviction rested in part on a belief that the border states would continue to act as a buffer, preventing a "hostile collision" between North and South: "It is unquestionably true that, whatever may be their sentiments on the general subject—whatever they may think of the policy of secession, or of the advantages of the Union—neither Maryland, Virginia, Kentucky nor Tennessee would assent to the advance of armies from the North through their borders." If these states cast their lot with the Confederacy, the *Times* warned, their interests and wishes would be dashed against the "bold and unprincipled ambition" of the movement's leaders.

THIS WAS PRECISELY THE DILEMMA that plagued Maryland's governor Hicks, who continued to engage in stalling maneuvers as his constituents rallied to join the new Southern Confederacy. As frustrations mounted, the Maryland state legislature resolved to sidestep the governor, announcing that a special convention would be held on February 18 to address the matter of Maryland's secession—with or without Hicks. By that time, Lincoln would be seven days into his inaugural journey, and only five days away from Baltimore.

Allan Pinkerton, posing as the gregarious stockbroker John Hutchinson, had found a way to turn the controversy to his own purposes. At his office on South Street, Pinkerton was engaged in a running debate with a businessman named James H. Luckett, who had been elected as a delegate to the special convention of the legislature. Luckett, who occupied a neighboring office, proudly told Pinkerton that he had won the position on the strength of a speech calling for immediate secession. "Let them call it Treason," he told Pinkerton, "but let us act."

Pinkerton nodded vigorously as Luckett spoke, and he went on to express impatience with the obstructive tactics of Governor Hicks. Luckett appeared highly pleased. "I tell you, my friend," he said fervently, "it will be but a short time until you will find Governor Hicks will have to fly, or he will be hung. He is a traitor to his God and his Country." Troops were being readied to move on Washington in tandem with Maryland's secession, he continued, "and then see where General Scott would be."

Pinkerton, eager to keep his new friend talking, "cordially sympathized" with everything Luckett said. As Luckett became more and more expansive, the detective steered the conversation toward Lincoln's impending passage through Baltimore, hoping to untangle the threads that Harry

Davies had picked up during his revels with Otis Hillard. At the mention of Lincoln's journey, Luckett turned suddenly cautious. "He may pass through quietly," Luckett said, "but I doubt it."

Pinkerton pressed the point, mentioning that the Baltimore police had promised Lincoln safe transit through the city. "Oh," said Luckett dismissively, "that is easily promised, but may not be so easily done."

Pinkerton was unnerved by this sudden reticence. Luckett had been eager enough to talk about secession matters and the capture of Washington, but the subject of Lincoln's travels appeared to be off-limits. Pinkerton felt certain that his companion knew more than he was willing to say. Hoping to force the issue, the detective pulled out his wallet and counted out twenty-five dollars with a dramatic flourish. "I am but a stranger to you" Pinkerton said, "but I have no doubt that money is necessary for the success of this patriotic cause." Pressing the bills into Luckett's hand, Pinkerton asked that the donation be used "in the best manner possible for Southern rights." Shrewdly, Pinkerton offered a piece of advice along with his largesse, seizing on the occasion to warn his new friend to be "cautious in talking with outsiders." One never knew, Pinkerton said, when Northern agents might be listening.

The ploy worked. Luckett took the warning—along with the money—as proof of Pinkerton's trustworthy nature. He told the detective that he and his colleagues were "exceedingly cautious as to whom they talked with," and that only a small handful of men, members of a secret cabal sworn to the strictest oaths of silence, knew the full extent of the plans being laid. Luckett might have stopped there, but Pinkerton's display of caution had inspired a new level of confidence. Perhaps, Luckett said, Pinkerton might like to meet the "leading man" of the secret organization. Leaning forward, Luckett disclosed in a confidential whisper that the gentleman concerned was a "true friend of the South" who stood ready to give his life for the cause. His name was Capt. Cypriano Ferrandini.

Pinkerton's records give no hint as to whether he had considered Cypriano Ferrandini a credible suspect before this moment. The name was familiar to him—perhaps all too familiar—as that of the barber who plied his trade in the basement of Barnum's Hotel, the preferred gathering place of the city's secessionist element. An immigrant from Corsica, Ferrandini was a dark, wiry man with a jet-black chevron mustache and watery eyes that were dimmed by shortsightedness. Ferrandini was a popular figure among the hard-drinking crowd at Barnum's, and his modest shop drew some of the city's most prominent citizens. There, as Ferran-

dini deftly wielded his blades and brushes, his courtly manner drew forth
a great many confidences. It was known that the Corsican barber always
had the latest gossip, and the shop became a regular stopping place for
the city's "young sports." Otis Hillard had taken Harry Davies around to
the barbershop, but Ferrandini had not been there that day to receive
them.

Later, as Pinkerton studied him more closely, he would conclude that
the charismatic Ferrandini was involved in more than idle gossip. Ferrandini was said to be an admirer of the Italian revolutionary Felice Orsini,
a leader of the secret brotherhood known as the Carbonari. In Baltimore,
Pinkerton believed, Ferrandini was channeling the inspiration he drew
from Orsini into the Southern cause. Sixteen months earlier, when John
Brown seized the federal arsenal at Harper's Ferry, Ferrandini had signed
on with a group of Baltimore militiamen who determined to proceed at
once to the "seat of war." Though the crisis passed before they could mo-
bilize, Ferrandini's passions had been inflamed. It was also said that he
had briefly decamped for Mexico City the previous winter to join the revolutionary forces of Benito Juárez. Upon his return to Baltimore, he rose
rapidly through the ranks of the National Volunteers, acquiring the hon-
orary title of captain. Ferrandini's activities had been conspicuous enough
to elicit a summons earlier that month to appear before the select committee in Washington. There, Ferrandini steadfastly denied any knowledge of a plot to interfere with Lincoln or his inauguration, but—like Otis
Hillard—he readily acknowledged that Maryland militiamen planned to
"prevent northern volunteer companies from passing through" the state. It
may have seemed unlikely that Ferrandini—a humble immigrant who
plied a simple trade—could be what Luckett had called him, the driving
force in a maturing conspiracy, but Pinkerton would not have dismissed it
out of hand. Only a few years earlier, he himself had been a humble immigrant plying a simple trade.

Now, sitting in his South Street office, Pinkerton was considering how
best to proceed, when James Luckett made an unexpected suggestion. Ferrandini, Luckett said, was very particular about taking strangers into his
confidence, but, as it happened, the barber considered Luckett to be "a particular friend" of the cause. "Mr. Luckett said that he was not going home
this evening," Pinkerton reported, "and if I would meet him at Barr's Saloon on South Street, he would introduce me to Ferrandini." This sudden
impulse of Luckett's, Pinkerton realized, might well lead to hard evidence
of a conspiracy. He gratefully accepted the offer.

As it turned out, Luckett still had more to say. The decision to bring Pinkerton and Ferrandini together, along with the detective's twenty-five-dollar contribution, appeared to dispel the last of Luckett's inhibitions about speaking freely. Before returning to his own office, he paused with his hand on the doorknob to offer one further revelation about the barber. Luckett counted himself lucky, he said, to be among the privileged few who were cognizant of Ferrandini's secret designs, which would soon change the course of history. Pinkerton, being a man of high Southern character and dedication to the cause, would undoubtedly rejoice in knowing the full extent of these grand deeds. Pinkerton nodded vigorously and motioned for his visitor to continue.

Luckett lowered his voice to a reverential hush, as if delivering a benediction. Captain Ferrandini, he said, "had a plan fixed to prevent Lincoln from passing through Baltimore." He would see to it that Lincoln would never reach Washington, and would never become president. "Every Southern Rights man has confidence in Ferrandini," Luckett declared. "Before Lincoln should pass through Baltimore, Ferrandini would kill him." Smiling broadly, Luckett gave a crisp salute and left the room, leaving a stunned Pinkerton to stare after him.

EVEN NOW, PINKERTON had heard nothing that rose to the level of definitive proof of danger, but Luckett's revelations marked a turning point. Pinkerton had come to Baltimore to protect Samuel Felton's railroad. Now, with Lincoln's train already under way, he found himself forced to consider the possibility that Lincoln himself was the target.

Luckett had handed him an opportunity to assess for himself whether Ferrandini was a credible threat and, if so, to lay plans to foil his scheme. "This was unexpected to me," Pinkerton admitted, "but I determined to take the chances." Whatever the outcome of this meeting, it was clear to Pinkerton that a warning must be sent. He knew that any communication made directly to Lincoln could not be kept private, as it would pass through the hands of any number of secretaries and advisers. For the present, in order to be effective, Pinkerton remained determined to protect the secrecy of his operation. He would have to find another point of contact.

Years before, during his early days in Chicago, Pinkerton had often crossed paths with Norman Judd, the former Illinois state senator who had been instrumental in Lincoln's election. Judd, Pinkerton knew, was now aboard the special train as a member of the president-elect's "suite."

Snatching up a newspaper, Pinkerton consulted an account of Lincoln's travels and decided that the best chance of intercepting the train would be in Indianapolis, at the president-elect's first overnight stop. Tossing the paper aside, Pinkerton reached for a telegraph form. Addressing his dispatch to Judd, "in company with Abraham Lincoln," Pinkerton fired off a terse message:

```
I have a message of importance for you—Where can it reach
you by special Messenger.—Allan Pinkerton
```

The telegram would put Judd on notice. In the meantime, Pinkerton sat down to compose a longer message. If all went well, he would be able to fill in the missing details in a few short hours.

CHAPTER TWELVE
IF I ALONE MUST DO IT

·

Such crowds . . . blessing Old Abe, swinging hats, banners, handkerchiefs, and every possible variety of festival bunting, and standing with open mouths as the train, relentlessly punctual, moved away. The history of one is the history of all; depots in waves, as if the multitudinous seas had been let loose, and its billows transformed into patriots, clinging along roofs and balconies and pillars, fringing long embankments, swarming upon adjacent trains of motionless cars, shouting, bellowing, shrieking, howling, all were boisterous; all bubbling with patriotism.

—JOHN HAY, in the *New York World*, February 1861

WARD HILL LAMON, Lincoln's "particular friend" and self-appointed bodyguard, was known to enjoy the balm of alcohol now and then. "Hill," as Lincoln called him, could toss back a staggering quantity of rye whiskey without showing any ill effects. After a session of particularly hard drinking, he would draw himself up—resplendent in his swallow-tailed coat and thick ruffled shirt, a heavy gold watch chain cresting his stomach—and demonstrate his sobriety with a tongue twister that left all others sputtering: "She stood at the gate welcoming him in." Lamon also had a reputation as a lively banjo player. "Sing me a little song," Lincoln would say during their days on the legal circuit, and Lamon would oblige with a spirited rendition of "Camptown Races" or "Oh! Susanna." "Abe was fond of music," Lamon would recall, "but was himself wholly unable to produce three harmonious notes together."

Both Lamon's banjo and his capacity for drink were very much in evidence as the Lincoln Special pushed toward the Indiana border on the first leg of its journey. Lamon probably took advantage of the temporary absence of Mrs. Lincoln and her younger sons to trot out a few of the off-color

145

verses for which he was notorious, though journalist Henry Villard recalled only that he "amused us with negro songs," such as "The Blue Tail Fly." After the solemnity of the departure from Springfield, Lamon's spirited playing ushered in a more festive mood, as did the tinkling of whiskey glasses. "Refreshments for the thirsty are on board," Villard reported. "The cheers are always for Lincoln and the Constitution." Robert Lincoln, Villard noted, "adheres closely to the refreshment saloon, the gayest of the gay."

Ward Hill Lamon, Lincoln's "particular friend." *Courtesy of the Library of Congress*

Lincoln himself was otherwise engaged. Even before the train pulled away from the Springfield depot, Villard and the other reporters on board had pressed Lincoln for a transcript of his farewell remarks, even though he had been speaking off the cuff. Lincoln obliged, taking out a pad and pencil to record an "official" version of the speech, with the help of secretary John Nicolay. The resulting document, marked with blotches and slips of the pen caused by the lurching of the cars, was then handed over to the operator of the train's portable telegraph. Lincoln's comments would be widely circulated in the press, to a generally enthusiastic reception. "Thousands and tens of thousands read them with tearful eyes," wrote one admirer.

Having completed this piece of business, Lincoln sat back to enjoy the ride in his private car at the rear of the train, gazing out the window at the crowds of well-wishers gathered for a glimpse of the train as it thundered past. "The enthusiasm all along the line was intense," recalled Thomas Ross, the train's brakeman on the first leg of the journey. "As we whirled through the country villages, we caught a cheer from the people and a glimpse of waving handkerchiefs and of hats tossed high into the air."

"There were many way stations where the train halted for a few moments," John Nicolay added. "At all these temporary halts there would be lusty cheering and unceasing calls for Mr. Lincoln." Lincoln answered these calls time and time again—"wherever the iron horse stops to water himself," as he described it—waving from the rear platform of the passenger car, bowing and doffing his hat to the ladies, and sometimes even stepping down from the train and wading into the throngs to shake hands. Later, when Mary Lincoln had come aboard the train, she would occasionally join her husband on the rear platform, her small stature in marked contrast to his towering height, to provide what he called "the long and the short of it."

Amid all the cheering and flag-waving, Lincoln hoped to avoid giving speeches. On a few occasions, he was "bullied" into saying a few words, as the new secretary John Hay recalled, but he kept his comments as innocuous as possible. "It would of course be impossible for him to make speeches everywhere," Hay explained, "and yet no sooner would he make his appearance on the rear platform of the car than calls for a speech would come out of every throat. The people wanted not only to look upon their President-elect, but to hear his voice." Lincoln soon devised a ploy to extricate himself from these situations. He would wait until the train was already under steam before he made his appearance, "hat in hand," leaving just enough time to bow in all directions before the train pulled away. Not all calls to speak were so easily turned aside. According to one source, the train was forced to make an unexpected stop outside of Decatur when eager supporters placed a section of rail fence across the track. An unflappable Lincoln stepped out to exchange greetings with the crowd while the train crew cleared away the obstruction.

Later, when concerns for Lincoln's safety became a matter of public debate, there would be an attempt to recast this episode in a more sinister light. "An attempt was made . . . to wreck the train bearing the president-elect and suite, about one mile west of the State line," the *New York Times* would report on February 26. The article went on to detail an Illinois railroad employee's account of spotting an obstruction shortly before Lincoln's train was due to arrive: "A machine for putting cars on the track had been fastened upon the rails in such a manner that if a train ran at full speed and struck it, the engine and cars must have been thrown off, and many persons killed."

The story of Lincoln's supposed narrow escape would be repeated and embroidered upon in the days to come. None of these later accounts made mention of the pilot engine that was supposed to be running ahead of the train to scout for irregularities, though it is possible that this extra precaution had not yet been put in place. In any case, no one on board Lincoln's train made any mention of the episode at the time, and Ward Lamon would later dismiss the reports as nonsense. "It has been asserted that an attempt was made to throw the train off the track between Springfield and Indianapolis," he would write. "None of the Presidential party ever heard of these murderous doings until they read of them in some of the more imaginative reports of their trip."

At the time, the passengers and crew did not appear overly troubled by thoughts of danger. "I remember that, after passing Bement, we crossed a trestle, and I was greatly interested to see a man standing there with a shotgun," recalled Thomas Ross, the brakeman. "As the train passed he presented arms. I have often thought he was there, a volunteer, to see that the President's train got over it in safety." In fact, the gunman was likely a member of the Illinois state militia, who had been charged by Republican governor Richard Yates with the task of guarding the vulnerable bridge crossings.

Yates's forces were able to stand down shortly after noon on February 11 as the Lincoln Special crossed the Indiana state line to a thirty-four-gun salute, one for each state of the Union—including the controversial Kansas Territory, which had been admitted as a free state only two weeks earlier. As the travelers enjoyed a quick lunch, the train cars were hitched to a fresh engine, which was capable of reaching speeds of up to thirty miles per hour—a breakneck pace for the time—on the straight track of the Toledo and Wabash line.

William Wood, settling into his role as superintendent of arrangements, was determined to keep to schedule in spite of the frequent stops, even at the risk of embarrassment to the president-elect. This became evident at a stop in Thorntown, outside of Lafayette, as Lincoln came to the rear platform as usual and apologized for declining to make a speech. By way of explanation, he launched into an anecdote concerning an aspiring politician who owned a sluggish but sure-footed horse. "The horse was so confoundedly slow, however," he continued, but just at this moment—before Lincoln could deliver his punch line—the train lurched away from the depot, cutting him off in mid-sentence. At the next stop along the line, in Lebanon, Lincoln was informed that some of his supporters from Thorntown had chased after the train and were now literally "panting to hear the conclusion of the story." Lincoln cheerfully took up where he had left off, explaining that he himself shared the dilemma of the owner of the plod-ding horse. If he stopped at every station to make a stump speech, he in-sisted, he would not arrive in Washington until the inauguration was over.

In that spirit, Lincoln would have been pleased to note the train's on-time arrival in Indianapolis at 5:00 that evening, to another thirty-four-gun sa-lute. It was here, however, that Superintendent Wood's elaborate plans be-gan to break down. As a large and boisterous crowd converged on the train, it became evident that Wood's instructions to the Committee of Arrange-ments in Indianapolis had gone unheeded. No precautions had been taken to protect the president-elect from "insolent and rough curiosity," reported Henry Villard. Instead, Lincoln "was almost overwhelmed by merciless throngs before he reached his hotel." Colonel Ellsworth and Ward Lamon managed to bundle him into a waiting carriage, but the rest of the travelers were left to fend for themselves. Most, including Robert Lincoln, were obliged to walk from the station, carrying their own luggage.

Matters were no better at the Bates House, where Lincoln planned to spend the first night of his journey. The four-story brick hotel was be-sieged by "turbulent congregations of men," wrote John Hay, "all of whom had too many elbows, too much curiosity, and a perfectly gushing desire to shake hands." The entrances and stairways were so clogged with "im-movable humanity," said Villard, that Lincoln managed to get inside only by "wedging himself through in a determined manner."

Once inside, Lincoln steeled himself for the first of the many "hand-shaking levees" he would endure on his journey, a seemingly endless re-ceiving line of callers and local dignitaries. The process, as Hay described it, seldom varied: "The crowd came up one staircase, crossed the corridor bowing to Mr. Lincoln, and descended by another staircase to the street. Occasionally one of the sovereigns would address the President in an in-formal manner, eliciting always a prompt, sometimes a felicitous, repar-tee." Almost all of the men who passed in front of Lincoln insisted on pumping his hand, with the result that his fingers were soon sore and swollen. According to Hay, he maintained his affable spirits throughout the ordeal: "From what I saw of the President's coolness under the inflic-tion of several thousand hand-shakings, I should say that he unites to the courage of Andrew Jackson the insensibility to physical suffering which is usually assigned to bronze statues."

Be that as it may, the scenes at the train station and the hotel had ex-posed an unsettling truth. Lincoln's traveling party, with its well-intentioned but disorganized cadre of friends acting as bodyguards, was simply not equipped to handle the sheer crush of people who wished to see, hear, and touch the president-elect as he made his way to Washington. Lamon and Ellsworth might well have been able to stand firm against a crowd of five or six, but not thousands. Even after the rest of the military adjuncts—Colonel Sumner, Major Hunter, and Captain Pope—rejoined the group in Indianapolis, there would be serious concerns about crowd control. Lincoln himself seemed inclined to entrust this matter to the reception committees of each town the train passed through, but his protectors were concerned that any large crowd—even a friendly one—could turn dangerous at any moment. The problem would grow worse in the days to come. "In the push and crush of these dense throngs of people, in this rushing of trains, clanging of bells, booming of guns, shouting and huzzas of individuals and crowds . . . a false step even might bring danger to life and limb under wheels of locomotives or carriages," John Nicolay would write. In some instances the very officials who had invited Lincoln to stop would prove to be the most reckless in matters of safety. "These committees generally seemed consumed by a demon of impatience," Nicolay observed. "They would sometimes tumble pell-mell into a car and almost drag Mr. Lincoln out before the train had even stopped, and habitually, after stoppage, before the proper police or military guards could be stationed around a depot or stopping place to secure necessary space and order for a comfortable open path to the waiting carriages." In a letter to his fiancée, Nicolay was even more blunt: "It has been a serious task for us of his escort to prevent his being killed with kindness."

Lincoln himself was not inclined to protest. As the incoming president, he believed he had an obligation to make himself accessible to the public. He had declined invitations to stay in private homes during the journey, where he would have had more privacy and a better chance of rest, and opted instead to stop in public lodgings where open receptions could be held. "The truth is, I suppose I am now public property," he told Ward Lamon, "and a public inn is the place where people can have access to me."

Lincoln also knew, after his long silence in Springfield, that he would not be able to limit his public pronouncements to cheery anecdotes about slow-moving horses. The public would expect to hear something of how he intended to address the secession crisis once he took office. Toward that end, he planned to deliver short addresses at most of the major stops along the way to the capital, giving a limited preview of the course his administration would pursue. In this way, the Lincoln Special would become something of a rolling laboratory, testing the themes and sentiments of his inaugural address in advance of March 4. Whenever possible, however, he would emphasize that matters were still in flux, and that he had not yet claimed the right to speak as the chief executive. As he would later tell a crowd in Buffalo, "[I]t is most proper I should wait and see the developments, and get all the light possible, so that when I do speak authoritatively, I may be as near right as possible."

Accordingly, during a lull in the reception at the Bates House, Lincoln pulled himself away from the receiving line and stepped out onto the hotel's balcony. A crowd of some twenty thousand people waited on the street below. The speech they heard is thought to have been composed earlier that day on board the train. If so, perhaps Lincoln's exhaustion and sadness at leaving Springfield cast a shadow over the composition, which struck many listeners as strangely off-key. He began with a hairsplitting discussion of the exact meaning of the words *coercion* and *invasion,* with reference to the events at Fort Sumter, and went on to suggest that the secessionists had misunderstood the obligations of statehood: "In their view, the Union, as a family relation, would seem to be no regular marriage, but rather a sort of 'free-love' arrangement, to be maintained on what that sect calls passionate attraction."

Though the crowd laughed heartily at this gibe, the comment would land with a thud in the press. Worse yet, after his earlier efforts to strike a conciliatory posture, Lincoln's careful parsing of the terms of conflict sounded very much like a man sharpening his saber. Lincoln himself appeared to realize that he had said too much. He made some effort to backpedal, insisting that he simply wished to give the crowd something "to reflect upon."

John Hay scrambled to cast the episode in a positive light, insisting that Lincoln's remarks had met with universal approval and that shouts of "That's the talk" and 'We've got a President now" were heard from the crowd. Even so, the speech drew many denunciations, especially in the Southern press. The *Louisville Journal* accused the president-elect of "sporting with fire-balls in a powder magazine." Lincoln would give two more speeches from the hotel balcony before leaving Indianapolis, both of which contained elements designed to soften the message of the first.

Matters went downhill for the rest of the evening. After the long day of travel, Lincoln hoped to enjoy a quiet meal with his inner circle. William Wood's instructions to the reception committee had called for a private dining room, but, as Lincoln now discovered, the request had been ignored.

In the absence of a quieter venue, Lincoln entered the hotel restaurant, where he took in the chaotic scene, with waiters handing out plates of food seemingly at random, without regard to what had been ordered. Lincoln looked on as one man who had asked for tea was given a pickle, and another had a bowl of sugar poured down his back. Hay noted that the spectacle "seemed to amuse the President quite as highly as the gentlemen, whose perception of the fun of the thing was sharpened by getting nothing whatever to eat."

Afterward, in his hotel room, Lincoln's amusement turned to horror. In Springfield, he had carefully packed away the working draft of his inaugural address in a black oilcloth carpetbag, along with the text of several of the other speeches he intended to give on the journey to Washington. The bag had been entrusted to the care of Robert Lincoln, who, perhaps as a consequence of his close adherence to the refreshment car earlier in the day, had now lost track of it. Under close questioning, Robert admitted that he had handed the bag to a waiter during the melee in the dining room and that the waiter, in turn, had placed it on a pile of other baggage behind the hotel counter. "A look of stupefaction passed over the countenance of Mr. Lincoln," recalled John Nicolay, who knew that the president-elect's head was filling with visions of his inaugural address appearing prematurely in the next day's newspapers, or perhaps lost forever. Without a word, Lincoln threw open the door of his room and forced his way along the corridor, which was still packed with well-wishers. Making his way to the hotel office, he swung himself over the baggage counter with "a single stride of his long legs" and fell upon a pile of black carpetbags that had accumulated there. Taking a small key from his pocket, he began snatching up bags one by one and testing the locks. A number of them opened to Lincoln's key, with the result that several pints of whiskey, packs of playing cards, and spare shirt collars were exposed to view before Lincoln at last recovered his own bag. Robert received a "somewhat stern admonition," and for the rest of the trip the bag remained in the hands of Lincoln himself.

While Robert Lincoln licked his wounds, Ward Lamon received a stern admonition of his own. The first day of the journey had exposed the president-elect to dangers no one had foreseen. As the evening drew to a close, some officials from Illinois, most of whom would return home the following day, took Lamon aside to express their concern. As Lamon recalled, the group pulled him into a hotel room and, locking the door, "proceeded in the most solemn and impressive manner to instruct me as to my duties as the special guardian of Mr. Lincoln's person during the rest of his journey to Washington." Jesse Dubois, a longtime friend who had served with Lincoln in the Illinois legislature, finished the remarks with an impressive vow: "We intrust the sacred life of Mr. Lincoln to your keeping; and if you don't protect it, never return to Illinois, for we will murder you on sight." Lamon recognized this as "an amiable threat, delivered in a jocular tone," but he acknowledged that it arose from a "feeling of deep, ill-disguised alarm for the safety of the President-elect." Only after Lamon had promised to protect Lincoln at all costs was the door unlocked so that the party from Illinois could take their leave. "If I had been remiss in my duty toward Mr. Lincoln during that memorable journey," Lamon declared, "I have no doubt those sturdy men would have made good some part of their threat."

IN BALTIMORE, ALLAN PINKERTON was hearing threats that were considerably less amiable. As the Lincoln party made its way east—possibly that same night—Pinkerton was meeting face-to-face with Cypriano Ferrandini, the man who, according to James Luckett, had vowed that the president-elect would not survive his passage through Baltimore.

Pinkerton had a couple of hours to fill before his appointment at Barr's Saloon. He spent a few moments jotting down notes on his meeting with Luckett, then turned to the reports he had received from his agents in the field. Kate Warne, posing as Mrs. Barley of Alabama, had been able to engage a number of the "prominent ladies of Baltimore" in conversation over the news of the Confederate convention in Montgomery. As a result, she heard many vague rumblings about sympathetic doings in Maryland. Pinkerton felt sure that she would soon uncover something more substantial, if given sufficient time.

Timothy Webster and Hattie Lawton, posing as a married couple among the railroad workers of Perrymansville, had also made promising strides. In a remarkably short time, Webster had managed to gain the "entire confidence" of the members of the tightly knit community, whose suspicions of the stranger in their midst had been lulled to a great extent by the presence of his beautiful young wife. A single man might well be a Northern spy, but Webster, posing as a newly married man in search of work, had been able to mingle freely, and was "generally looked upon as a man who could be trusted." Soon after his arrival, Webster learned of a local militia unit with anti-Union leanings. "In twenty-four hours thereafter he had enrolled himself as a member of the company,"

Pinkerton noted, "and was recognized as a hail fellow among his rebel associates."

As the evening shadows fell across his desk, Pinkerton locked his files away in a drawer and stepped around the corner to Barr's Saloon to keep his appointment with Luckett. Entering quietly, he spent several moments studying the scene before moving forward to join his friend. Luckett was standing at the bar, along with several other men, engaged in animated conversation. At the center of the group was the man Pinkerton knew to be Ferrandini. Pinkerton had glimpsed him once or twice in his barbershop, but Ferrandini seemed a different, altogether more commanding presence in this setting. The others turned to him for approval each time they spoke, and hung on his responses with expressions of reverence. "All seemed to regard him as an important personage," Pinkerton noted, "and one who was eventually to perform giant service in the cause."

After a moment, Pinkerton stepped toward the bar and called out a greeting to Luckett, who came forward to present him to Ferrandini. "Luckett introduced me as a resident of Georgia, who was an earnest worker in the cause of secession," Pinkerton recalled, "and whose sympathy and discretion could be implicitly relied upon." In a lowered voice, Luckett reminded Ferrandini of Mr. Hutchinson's generous twenty-five-dollar donation. As the two men shook hands, Pinkerton sized Ferrandini up, as he often did in such situations, in terms of his ethnic heritage. "He shows the Italian in I think a very marked degree," Pinkerton said, "and although excited, yet was cooler than what I had believed was the general characteristic of Italians."

Pinkerton may have worried that Ferrandini would be cautious about speaking freely in the presence an outsider, but Luckett's endorsement had the desired effect. Ferrandini seemed to warm to the detective immediately. After ordering drinks and cigars, the group withdrew to a quiet corner of the saloon, where the conversation turned swiftly to politics. Within moments, Pinkerton noted, his new acquaintance was expressing himself in terms of high treason. "The South must rule," Ferrandini insisted. He and his fellow Southerners had been "outraged in their rights by the election of Lincoln, and freely justified resorting to any means to prevent Lincoln from taking his seat."

Pinkerton and his team had heard similar sentiments expressed many times since their arrival in Baltimore, but Pinkerton found he could not dismiss Ferrandini as just another crackpot. "As he spoke his eyes fairly glared and glistened," the detective wrote, "and his whole frame quivered, but he was fully conscious of all he was doing." Pinkerton noted the steel in his voice, and the easy command of the men clustered about him, and recognized that this potent blend of fiery rhetoric and icy resolve made Ferrandini a dangerous adversary. "He is a man well calculated for controlling and directing the ardent minded," the detective admitted. "Even I myself felt the influence of this man's strange power, and wrong though I knew him to be, I felt strangely unable to keep my mind balanced against him."

As Ferrandini held forth, he kept an appraising eye on Pinkerton, apparently measuring his responses to what was being said. At last, when he appeared satisfied that Pinkerton was in earnest, the conversation edged toward the crucial information that Luckett had hinted at earlier in the day: the possibility of an attempt on Lincoln's life. Ferrandini and his men, Pinkerton would recall, spoke as if the matter had already been settled.

"Are there no other means of saving the South except by assassination?" Ferrandini was asked. He paused, as if weighing the question. "No," he replied. "Never, never shall Lincoln be president. He must die—and die he shall. If necessary, we will die together."

Another man spoke up. "There seems to be no other way, and while bloodshed is to be regretted, it will be done in a noble cause."

Ferrandini's eyes filled with approval. "Yes, the cause is a noble one, and on that day every captain will prove himself a hero. With the first shot the chief traitor, Lincoln, will die, then all Maryland will be with us, and the South will be forever free."

Even as he listened to these incendiary words, Pinkerton realized that he still had no proof of what Ferrandini planned. Gathering himself, he addressed a question to Ferrandini that was intended to draw out the particulars. "But have all the plans been matured, and are there no fears of failure?" he asked. "A misstep in so important a direction would be fatal to the South and ought to be well considered."

The answer shed no light on the situation: "Our plans are fully arranged and they cannot fail. We shall show the North that we fear them not."

Before Pinkerton could speak again, a fresh problem arose. As Ferrandini held forth, a pair of strangers appeared in the saloon and took seats close by. Luckett immediately became suspicious and called Ferrandini's attention to the newcomers, suggesting that they might be eavesdropping. Ferrandini decided to be cautious. He led his followers up to the bar, where a fresh round of drinks was purchased at Pinkerton's expense, and then settled the group in a different corner of the room, waiting to see if the strangers followed. "Whether by accident or design, they again got near us," Pinkerton reported. By now, Ferrandini's suspicions were fully roused. He concluded that the two men must be spying on him, and he refused to say anything more on the subject of Lincoln's visit to Baltimore. For Pinkerton, this was the very worst piece of luck possible. He tried in vain to guide the conversation back to its original channel, but Ferrandini refused to say anything more.

At length, Ferrandini rose to leave, hinting that he had a secret meeting to attend elsewhere. Glancing at the two strangers, he expressed concern that he might be followed as he left the saloon. Once again, Pinkerton's luck took a turn for the worse as Luckett volunteered that he and Pinkerton would stay behind to keep an eye on the newcomers. As it was now clear that Pinkerton would learn nothing more that evening, he contented himself with playing his role as convincingly as possible. "I assured Ferrandini that if they did attempt to follow him, that we would whip them," Pinkerton said. He may well have wished to do so in any case.

Ferrandini and his followers left to attend the meeting, Pinkerton reported dolefully, "and anxious as I was to follow them myself, I was obliged to remain with Mr. Luckett to watch the strangers." After about fifteen minutes, Luckett also rose to excuse himself, leaving Pinkerton alone at his post. Disappointed that he had not been able to trail Ferrandini to his secret gathering, Pinkerton made his way back to his hotel to compile notes on all that he had heard that night.

There was much to consider. At one stage, as Ferrandini became swept up in his own eloquence, he had insisted that his own life was of no consequence, and that he would gladly trade it for Lincoln's—just as his hero, Felice Orsini, had given his life for Italy. This mention of the Italian revolutionary carried a particularly dark resonance under the circumstances. Three years earlier, in January 1858, Orsini had attempted to assassinate Napoléon III by means of three fulminate of mercury bombs hurled at the emperor's imperial carriage. Eight people were killed and dozens injured in the blasts, but the emperor and empress escaped unhurt, thanks in part to the bulletproof construction of their carriage. Orsini soon fell into police hands and was executed two months later, becoming a hero in the eyes of Ferrandini, who now styled himself as a successor to the "much-honored martyr."

Lincoln would not have use of a bulletproof carriage as he traveled from one train station to the next in Baltimore. If he followed the pattern set at the other stops on his inaugural journey, he would ride in an open conveyance, raising his tall form to a standing position at regular intervals to make himself more visible to the crowd. If Ferrandini intended to emulate Felice Orsini, Lincoln would make a far easier target than had Napoléon III.

"If Italy *truly* rises, she *must* conquer," Orsini wrote in his autobiography, published the year before his death; "but to arrive at this end, men of *capacity* and *decision* must be at the head of the revolution; *practical* men, and not *dreamers;* men who are not *intriguers, ambitious,* or afraid of *death* . . . Without this there is no hope of redemption."

Orsini had sought redemption through political assassination. An uncomfortable echo could be heard in the words Ferrandini spoke to Pinkerton that night. "Murder of any kind," he said, "is justifiable and right to save the rights of the Southern people."

Later, he stated his conviction with an even more chilling clarity. "If I alone must do it, I shall," he told Pinkerton. "Lincoln shall die in this city."

CHAPTER THIRTEEN

A POSTPONED REBELLION

•

All governments have their crises. Our republic never escaped one more alarming than that of February 13th, 1861. It was the day appointed for the seizure of Washington. Preparations had been made; armed bodies of men had been enlisted and drilled, and many of them had reported in the city pursuant to orders. When the managers were compelled to postpone the rebellion, these recruits declined to accept the necessity or to put off the opening drama. They had assembled for a revolution with its natural consequences—booty and plunder.
—LUCIUS CHITTENDEN, *Recollections of President Lincoln*, 1891

TUESDAY, FEBRUARY 12, was Abraham Lincoln's fifty-second birthday, though little mention was made of it at the time. The president-elect awoke in Indianapolis to face another long day of travel, speeches and handshaking levees, beginning with breakfast at the governor's mansion. Afterward, Lincoln called in at the capitol to pay his respects to the state legislators. He rounded out his morning with yet another short speech from the balcony of the Bates House, at the conclusion of which the crowd began shouting for a glimpse of Robert Lincoln, whose charm and good looks continued to draw notice in the press. "Bob, with a fine display of pluck, came forward," reported John Hay, "and with a still firmer display of pluck declined to make a speech. He waved his hat, however, bowed, and retired, his debut being pronounced a success."

William Wood had scheduled a late departure from Indianapolis that morning to allow for the arrival of Mary Lincoln, who had taken an overnight train with Willie and Tad to catch up with the inaugural party. They found a scene of frantic confusion at the depot. "The railway people," explained the *New York Times*, "without permission, invited some two hundred guests, which has caused some feeling, and hereafter none but those invited by Mr. Wood will be allowed upon the train." In the tumult, the arrival of the rest of Lincoln's unofficial military escort—Colonel Sumner, Major Hunter, and Captain Pope—went largely unnoticed. Officially, Captain Pope was now absent without leave from his army post, which sent a citation for court-martial across the desk of President Buchanan. In the circumstances, no punitive action would be taken.

As the military men took their places at Lincoln's side, the Springfield contingent that had accompanied him on the first day prepared to return home. Lincoln's old Illinois friends "took hold of him in a melodramatic manner," wrote Henry Villard. "They hugged him and told him to behave himself like a good boy in the White House, and lastly even cut a lock of hair off his head with which they rushed triumphantly out of his room."

By 10:30, having extracted himself from the "hydraulic embraces" of his friends, Lincoln arrived at Indianapolis's Union Depot. A fresh train adorned with presidential portraits and patriotic bunting waited to transport him over the Indianapolis and Cincinnati Railroad. A substantial crowd—"apparently," said Hay, "the entire population of Indianapolis and the surrounding territory"—gave a raucous cheer as the train lurched out of the station at 11:00 sharp. Once again, conspicuous security measures could be seen along the track. "Flagmen are stationed at every road and crossing, and half way between them," reported the *Philadelphia Inquirer,* "they display the American flag as the signal for 'all right.'"

On board the train, Lincoln appeared to be in high spirits. "He has shaken off the despondency which was noticed during the first day's journey," said Hay, "and now, as his friends say, looks and talks like himself." No doubt Lincoln was cheered by the arrival of Willie and Tad, and perhaps amused as they hatched a plan to confound reporters at various stops along the way. Taking advantage of the fact that their father's appearance was not yet widely known, the Lincoln boys would stop random newspapermen and ask, "Do you want to see Old Abe?" Then, instead of pointing out their father, they would direct the victim's attention to some random bystander. At times, as the trip wore on, the boys grew restless and quarrelsome. On one occasion, when a trackside audience called for a sight of the Lincoln sons, Robert dutifully stepped forward, but seven-year-old Tad refused to appear. "[T]he young representative of the house of Lincoln proved refractory," said a reporter, "and the more his mother endeavored to pull him before the window the more he stubbornly persisted in throwing himself down on the floor of the car." Norman Judd, alluding darkly to his poor opinion of the younger Lincoln sons, would write to his wife that Willie and Tad were behaving fairly well on the journey—"considering what they are."

The behavior of the Lincoln boys would not have been Judd's foremost concern as the train thundered toward Cincinnati that morning. Moments before leaving the Bates House, Judd had received Allan Pinkerton's telegram asking where to send his "message of importance" by special messenger. Pressed for time, Judd cabled back a terse reply, informing Pinkerton that the Lincoln train would be in Columbus the following day, and Pitts-

The Lincoln family in 1861. *Courtesy of the Library of Congress*

burgh the day after. Judd must have been disconcerted by Pinkerton's cryptic tone, but he knew the detective well enough to take his message seriously. For the moment, he did not mention the telegram to anyone on board the train.

While Judd kept his own counsel, the Lincoln Special pressed on toward Ohio, pausing at four points along the way so that Lincoln could deliver brief speeches and "bow to friends." In Lawrenceburg, the last stop before leaving Indiana, Lincoln's route skirted the northern edge of Kentucky, the state of his birth. Lincoln was keenly aware of how important Kentucky would be in any coming conflict. "I hope to have God on my side," he would remark later that year, "but I must have Kentucky." Before leaving Springfield, Lincoln hoped to arrange a brief detour so that he might stop in the state. He took pains to prepare an appropriate speech, blending passages from the forthcoming inaugural with a special appeal to his fellow Kentuckians' sense of fair play. Lincoln promised that he would live up to his campaign vow of upholding the Constitution, as surely any right-thinking resident of Kentucky would wish him to do, no matter which candidate they had supported in the election. "What Kentuckian, worthy of his birthplace, would not do this?" Lincoln planned to say. "Gentlemen, I too am a Kentuckian."

In the end, the foray into Kentucky was deemed impractical, which meant that Lincoln's first opportunity to address an audience in a slaveholding state would come in Baltimore. For the moment, in Lawrenceburg, Lincoln had to content himself with pointing across the Ohio River to Kentucky and declaring his intent of "doing full justice to all," on both sides of the water.

At 3:00 that afternoon, outside Cincinnati's Fifth Street depot, the crowd of people that had gathered to greet Lincoln grew so large that it spilled over onto the railroad track, blocking the progress of the presidential train. Police and military forces had to be called in to clear the way. Joseph Howard, Jr., the *New York Times* correspondent who joined the party in Cincinnati, reported that the crowd "cheered, huzzahed and roared a hearty welcome" as the president-elect made his way to the open carriage that would carry him to the Burnet House hotel. "Mr. Lincoln stood up bareheaded, holding on by a conveniently arranged board, and bowed his backbone sore, and his neck stiff, all the way to the hotel." After a two-hour procession, Lincoln arrived at the Burnet House, where he found an even more chaotic scene than the one he had faced the day before, with every resident of the town seemingly determined to shake his hand "as if it were a pump handle."

Though Howard would describe the day as "one continual ovation," his account made it clear that security concerns remained. Readers were told that a "queer-looking box" had been left for Lincoln at his hotel that afternoon under suspicious circumstances, and was handed over to the police for disposal. Later it would also be reported that "a grenade of the most destructive character" had been found aboard Lincoln's train in Cincinnati. Concealed in a carpetbag, the device was said to be "so arranged that within fifteen minutes it would have exploded, with a force sufficient to have demolished the car and destroyed the lives of all the persons in it." Ward Lamon would later dismiss this story as a fabrication, like the report of the attempt to throw the train off the track the previous day. At the time, Lamon insisted, he had heard nothing of the sort.

At the Burnet House, Lincoln's itinerary unfolded much as it had the previous day in Indianapolis—a speech from the hotel balcony, a handshaking levee and a reception for a "plethora of politicians" that had gathered in the city. "Some of them are much given to embracing the President, as if he required a little of that sort of affectionate fortification," wrote Hay. "He puts up with it gravely, although I think he wishes they wouldn't." Toward the end of this greeting period, Lincoln was urged to stand on a chair to make a speech, so that everyone would get a chance to have a look at him. Lincoln reluctantly did so, seizing the occasion to bid farewell to the crowd. "Instantly a ring of policemen and friends was formed around him," wrote Howard, "and with some difficulty he was escorted to his room."

AT 2:00 IN THE MORNING, long after Lincoln and his colleagues had gone to bed, the heavy wooden doors of the Burnet House swung open once again to admit a young Pinkerton agent named William H. Scott, acting as a special messenger for his boss. The resourceful operative had straggled into Cincinnati on an overnight train, in hopes of catching up with Norman Judd before the Lincoln Special departed for Columbus in the morning. He managed to intercept Lincoln's party sooner than anticipated by the simple expedient of tracking their movements through the newspapers. As Pinkerton himself had now come to realize, it was all too easy for anyone—friend or foe—to determine where Abraham Lincoln would be at any given moment.

Pinkerton had been extremely cautious about making contact. In the field, he and his operatives invariably used a simple word-substitution cipher for telegraph communications in order to keep sensitive information from being intercepted in transit. The cipher keys were changed at regular intervals, with the code words drawn from random lists of topics—gardening terms, figures from Greek mythology, or simple fruits and vegetables. One cipher found the Pinkertons replacing the word *forger* with the name Irene, and the title *superintendent* with the name Dolores. The resulting transmissions would have been suitably innocuous, if perhaps a bit nonsensical.

Pinkerton's telegram to Judd had been a simple matter of arranging a rendezvous with his "special messenger." Nevertheless, the wire had gone out using the latest cipher, so as to avoid drawing suspicion to the operation in Baltimore. Since Judd did not have a copy of the cipher key, and would not have been able to decode the message, Pinkerton sent the telegram to George Bangs in Chicago, who decrypted the message before forwarding the contents to Indianapolis—across presumably friendly wires. It would not do for "John H. Hutchinson" of Georgia to be seen communicating directly with a colleague of Abraham Lincoln.

For all of this effort, William Scott would not be able to place the "message of importance" in Judd's hands until the following morning. Scott was informed at the front desk of the Burnet House that Judd had retired at 11:00 P.M. and had left instructions he did not want to be disturbed. The night clerk refused to wake him, and would not give out the room number. Exhausted, Pinkerton's messenger took a room for the night.

The next morning, Scott pounced. "I got up at 7 o'clock," he reported, "and waited until 8 o'clock, when I saw Judd and gave him Pinkerton's letter." Judd tore open the envelope and studied the message carefully, the color draining from his face. Though the original of the letter is now lost, perhaps destroyed on Pinkerton's instructions, the detective would later summarize its contents: "I had reason to believe that there was a plot on foot to murder the President on his passage through Baltimore." Pinkerton promised to advise Judd further as soon as a personal meeting could be arranged.

Judd had been expecting grim tidings of this type ever since Pinkerton's telegram had reached him in Cincinnati the previous day. Gathering himself, he told Scott that "he had been looking for this," and wondered aloud what to do next. It is reasonable to suppose, given Pinkerton's passion for secrecy, that he offered little in the way of corroborating detail. He would have been wary of revealing too much in a letter, especially one sent to a politician. As Pinkerton had told Samuel Felton at the start of the operation, "on no conditions would I consider it safe for myself or my operatives were the fact of my operating known to any Politician—no matter of what school, or what position."

Judd, by contrast, appeared willing to take Pinkerton at his word until further information could be given. "He spoke feelingly of Pinkerton," Scott recalled, "and said they had trained in the same school together." Scott apparently misunderstood Judd on this point, as Pinkerton had not attended a school of any kind since his boyhood in Scotland. Judd likely meant to suggest that the two of them had moved in the same political circles in Chicago.

In any case, once he recovered from his initial shock, Judd told Scott that he was "very much obliged" for the information, and would await further details from Pinkerton himself. Scott offered Judd the chance to send a telegraphic reply to the detective in Baltimore, using the agency's latest cipher. After a moment's reflection, Judd decided against it, saying instead that he would contact Pinkerton when he had more time to consider the situation.

As Scott rose to take his leave, he reminded Judd of the need to hold the information in strictest confidence, so as not to endanger the operation in Baltimore. Though Judd would later be criticized for his silence, for the moment he chose to honor the request. As Pinkerton explained it, "Mr. Judd did not divulge [the information] to anyone, fearing to occasion undue anxiety or unnecessary alarm, and knowing that I was upon the ground and could be depended upon to act at the proper time." From Judd's point of view, this was also a politically expedient course. Although he himself was willing to take Pinkerton's warning on faith, Lincoln and his other advisers would need proof. He was counting on Pinkerton to provide it before the Lincoln Special reached Baltimore.

AS JUDD WELL KNEW, Lincoln himself had other concerns pressing on his mind that morning. Wednesday, February 13, was a date Lincoln had awaited with a mixture of eagerness and trepidation throughout the long winter months. At noon, in Washington, a joint session of Congress would convene to witness the formal proceedings of the Electoral College. Even at this late date, as Lincoln had previously admitted to William Seward, there remained a lingering concern that the Electoral College might decline to assemble, or that it would be prevented from doing so by an uprising of some kind. In Washington, conspicuous measures were being taken to calm the public. Along with "other fears," declared the *New York Times,* "the blowing up of the Capitol was regarded as an event not impossible." Readers were assured, however, that police were conducting nightly inspections "to be sure that no explosive materials had been there clandestinely deposited for such purpose." Lincoln made a show of good cheer as he climbed on board the train in Cincinnati, but his thoughts would be focused on Washington that morning.

The Lincoln Special pulled out of the depot at 9:00 sharp, with Pinkerton's agent William Scott watching from the platform. "The arrangements here throughout were admirable," John Hay noted. "Cincinnati has honored herself in her manner of honoring the President." Henry Villard reported that Lincoln, "although somewhat stiffened in his limbs by his handshaking exertion last night," appeared to be in excellent spirits, though vocal strain and a bad head cold had reduced his speaking voice to a croak. Mrs. Lincoln was reported to be "in her most pleasant mood," chatting and laughing with guests, while Robert "did not seem to feel any worse from the sparkling Catawba with which the Republican youths of Cincinnati had plied him so liberally the previous evening." To all outward appearances, the only dark cloud that morning was the discovery that no provision had been made for lunch. The sudden appearance of two baskets of baked goods shortly after noon, said Villard, was therefore "the signal of great rejoicing among the company."

BY THAT TIME, the counting of the electoral vote was under way in Washington. It had already been an eventful day on Capitol Hill. The select committee wrapped up its inquiry into "alleged hostile organizations" that morning, having finally completed its examination of Maryland's governor Hicks. The press issued a reassuring summary of its findings: "The Special Committee are unanimously of the opinion, whatever combination of intents may have existed at any earlier period, that for the last six weeks there has been no appearance or vestige of an organization with a hostile intent on Washington or the public property therein." Not everyone was reassured. "The air was filled with rumors," wrote Lucius Chittenden, a Vermont delegate to the ongoing Peace Convention at Willard's Hotel. "Few Northern men in the city doubted that a conspiracy to seize the government existed . . . that the force to execute it was organized, armed, and to be furnished by the adjacent states of Maryland and Virginia. Whether any adequate preparations had been made for the defense of the city against such a force, we did not know. There was, consequently, a general feeling of uneasiness; and if a revolution had broken out at any time, it would not have caused much surprise."

Chittenden was a member of a group of younger Republicans who had taken it upon themselves to act as an "independent committee of safety" to chase down the rumors of attacks on Washington and the threats against Lincoln. In that capacity, Chittenden had called on Gen. Winfield Scott the previous week to see what measures were being taken to ensure the safety of the electoral count. The general had now recovered from his earlier illness and was in a resolute frame of mind: "It is my duty," he declared, "to suppress insurrection—*my duty!*" General Scott had said much the same thing in a letter to Lincoln the previous month, promising his "utmost exertions" to ensure an orderly transfer of power. Now that the date of the vote had finally arrived, the general made good on his promise with a conspicuous display of artillery, including two batteries of cannon outside the Capitol. "At every entrance to the building stood a guard of civil but inflexible soldiers, sternly barring admission," wrote Chittenden. "Prayers, bribes, entreaties, oaths, objurgations, were alike unavailing. No one could pass except senators and representatives, and those who had the written ticket of admission signed by the Speaker of the House or the Vice-President. Even members could not pass in their friends. Consequently the amount of profanity launched forth against the guards would have completely annihilated them if words could kill."

Chittenden, a Vermont state senator, managed to secure a seat in the gallery of the House chambers. Although there were many disgruntled faces among the Southern electors, Chittenden observed few expressions of open dissent, even from the many secessionists present. "To one who knew nothing of the hot treason which was seething beneath the quiet exterior," he wrote, "the exercises would have appeared to be tame and uninteresting." General Scott had let it be known that disruptions would not be tolerated and that any man who attempted to interfere with the count risked being "lashed to the muzzle of a twelve-pounder and fired out of a window of the Capitol." Furthermore, Scott promised, "I would manure the hills of Arlington with fragments of his body."

As it happened, the hills of Arlington received no fresh manure that day. At the appointed hour, Vice President Breckinridge, in his role as president of the Senate, stepped forward to tally the official election certificates from each state, which had been in his custody since the election. This duty can only have been a bitter one for Breckinridge, a future Confederate general and secretary of war. As vice president under Buchanan, he had contended for the presidential nomination himself after the split within the Democratic party, finishing second in the electoral tally, well ahead of Stephen Douglas. On this day, however, Breckinridge conducted himself with "marked dignity and courtesy," according to the *New York Times*, having repeatedly declared that he would perform the duties of his office under the sanction of his oath until the end of his term. "If he could be remembered only for his services on that day, Vice President Breckinridge would fill a high place in the gallery of American statesmen," said Chittenden. "[H]e had determined that the result of the count should be declared, and his purpose was manifested in every word and gesture. Jupiter never ruled a council on Olympus with a firmer hand. It was gloved, but there was iron beneath the glove."

Under Breckinridge's resolute gaze, each of the ballot envelopes was opened and its contents read aloud. As the results were tallied, an "absolutely profound" silence settled over the chamber. The vice president rapped his gavel and declared that "Abraham Lincoln, of Illinois, having received a majority of the whole number of electoral votes, is duly elected

President of the United States for the four years beginning on the fourth day of March, 1861."

Their duty completed, the members of the Senate rose and silently filed out of the chamber. Then, according to Chittenden, chaos erupted. "A dozen angry, disappointed men were on their feet before the door had closed upon the last senator, clamoring for recognition by the speaker," he recalled. "For a few minutes the tumult was so great that it was impossible to restore order. . . . There were jeers for the 'rail-splitter,' sharp and fierce shouts for 'cheers for Jeff Davis,' and 'cheers for South Carolina.' But hard names and curses for 'Old Scott' broke out everywhere on the floor and in the gallery of the crowded hall. The quiet spectators seemed in a moment turned to madmen. 'Superannuated old dotard!' 'Traitor to the state of his birth!' 'Coward!' 'Free-state pimp!' and any number of similar epithets were showered upon him."

If such a scene occurred, it escaped the notice of the journalists in the room. "There were no manifestations of applause, disapprobation or uneasiness," insisted the *New York Times*. "The vast audience, satisfied that the interesting event was consummated in peace, arose silently and withdrew in an orderly manner from the chamber."

In either case, all parties agreed that any signs of discord—both in and outside of the Capitol—were short-lived. "Thus has vanished one of the supposed points of danger to the public peace," the *Times* concluded, "and the public pulse beats freer. There really has been so much apprehension that many families left town. Such fears are now dissipated, and people are flocking to town in crowds. True, we hear occasional foolish rumors of plots to take the city, blow up the public buildings, and prevent the inauguration of Lincoln, but they disturb nobody."

AS WASHINGTON'S JITTERS SUBSIDED, tempers flared in Maryland. Until that moment, many in Baltimore had expected that Southern lawmakers would seize upon the electoral vote to thwart Lincoln's inauguration and bring the secession crisis to its boiling point. Now that the occasion had passed without incident, the more vocal contingent of Baltimore agitators—including Cypriano Ferrandini and his followers—believed that it now fell to them to secure the rights of the South. Even the normally ambivalent Otis K. Hillard, from whom Pinkerton's Harry Davies was still trying to extract information, appeared hardened in his resolve. "What a pity," he told Davies, "that this glorious Union must be destroyed all on account of that monster Lincoln."

CHAPTER FOURTEEN
A RABID REBEL

•

*The President-elect will need no armed escort in passing through or sojourning within the
limits of this city or State, and, in my view, the provision of any such at this time would be
ill-judged. The insult offered to President Buchanan in the streets of this city on the eve of
his inauguration, to which reference has been made as the ground for apprehending a
similar indignity to the President-elect, it is well known, was the act of two or three
members of one of the fanatical clubs of his political opponents which at that time infested
our city, but which have long since been numbered among the things that were.*
—GEORGE PROCTOR KANE, marshal of the Baltimore police, January 16, 1861

LINCOLN HAD NOT YET heard the news of the electoral results when
his train rolled into Columbus at two o'clock on the afternoon of February 13. Eager to carry on with business as usual, he kept to a now-familiar
round of processions, speeches, and receptions. Republican governor William Dennison, Jr., led him on a tour of the newly completed state capitol,
where Lincoln offered a few remarks to the legislature, touching on the
subject of his so-called "masterly inactivity" in Springfield. "I have not
maintained silence from any want of real anxiety," Lincoln told the Ohio
lawmakers. "It is a good thing that there is no more than anxiety, for there
is nothing going wrong. It is a consoling circumstance that when we look
out there is nothing that really hurts anybody. We entertain different
views upon political questions, but nobody is suffering anything . . . all we
want is time, patience, and a reliance on that God who has never forsaken
this people."

Once again, in attempting to strike a reassuring note, Lincoln had mis-
fired. Though he intended to suggest that the crisis had not yet advanced
to the point where it could not be resolved peaceably, his comments gave

the impression that he was out of step with the nation's concerns. "Nothing going wrong?" asked the *New York Herald*. "Why, sir, we may more truly say there is nothing going right."

Adding to the cares of the day was another pointed reminder of safety concerns. "At Columbus," wrote John Nicolay, "Mr. Lincoln's friends had a chance to observe how necessary it was to look carefully to his personal surroundings at every moment." The trouble arose at a public reception in the state capitol, where plans had been laid for a receiving line that would cross in a straight line through the spacious rotunda, allowing an orderly progression of guests from the entrance on one side to the exit at the opposite end. As Nicolay related, however, "an inadequate police force" had been detailed to guard the building's other entrances, with the result that eager visitors began swarming in from all directions. Soon, to Nicolay's dismay, Lincoln was at the center of a swirling mass of admirers, "which threatened to crush him and those about him." It fell to Ward Lamon to rescue the situation: "Fortunately Colonel Lamon, a man of extraordinary size and Herculean strength, was able to place himself before him and by formidable exertion to hold back the advancing pressure until Mr. Lincoln could be hurried to a more secure place." It would not be the only time that Lamon quite literally pulled Lincoln out of a tight spot.

Even casual observers could see that the hectic pace of the inaugural trip was taking a toll on Lincoln. "For his own sake, it is to be regretted that this excursion is being made," wrote Joseph Howard in the *New York Times*. "His original plan, which was to proceed directly and quietly to Washington, was much better, and it was with great reluctance that he acceded to the desires of his friends, who are now thoughtlessly and foolishly wearying him, and wearing the life out of him by inches." Howard may have been wrong about Lincoln's own wishes in the matter, but he was sincere in his belief that the tumultuous journey had placed an unnecessary strain on the new president. "Mr. Lincoln submits with pleasure to the infliction," he wrote, "but it is a terrible ordeal through which to pass, when bound as he is not to a place of rest and easeful quiet, but to a scene of discord, trouble and possible danger."

At last, during a lull in the events at the rotunda, a telegram arrived bearing the Electoral College results from Washington: "The votes have been counted peaceably," it read. "You are elected." A small crowd of friends gathered around as Lincoln studied the message. "When he read it he smiled benignly," wrote one witness, "and looking up, seeing everyone waiting for a word, he quietly put the dispatch in his pocket." Pausing for a moment, Lincoln deflected his satisfaction into an innocuous comment about the new state capitol, as if to suggest that the outcome had never been in doubt: "What a beautiful building you have here, Governor Dennison," he said.

The news had a bracing effect on Lincoln, who appeared cheerful and relaxed the following day at a stop near Rochester, Pennsylvania, where a local "coal-heaver" proposed a friendly contest: "Abe, they say you are the tallest man in the United States, but I don't believe you are any taller than I am." Lincoln, peering down from the rear platform of the train, immediately took up the challenge. "Come up here," he called, "and let us measure." The miner pushed his way through the crowd and climbed aboard. At Lincoln's direction, he spun around and the two men stood back-to-back. Colonel Ellsworth, the dashing young Zouave officer, was hovering nearby as the spectacle unfolded. Turning toward him, Lincoln asked for a verdict: "Which is taller?" It was an awkward moment for Ellsworth, who stood barely five feet tall. Unable to see the tops of the taller men's heads from his vantage point, Ellsworth scrambled onto a guardrail for a better view, amid much laughter from the crowd. "I believe," he called out, "they are exactly the same height." The locals cheered this diplomatic solution as Lincoln pumped the miner's hand.

It marked a bright spot in an otherwise gloomy and rain-soaked day. Henry Villard believed that Lincoln felt relief at the sight of the "perfect torrents" of rain that began falling that morning, as the foul weather promised to reduce the size of the "uncomfortable crowds as had pestered him" in the previous days. This proved to be a vain hope. "Immense multitudes" turned out to greet the Lincoln Special as it cut through eastern Ohio toward Pennsylvania, where Lincoln would make an overnight appearance in Pittsburgh. Making light of his crisscrossing route and rapid pace, Lincoln trotted out a joke that would become familiar over the course of the journey. "I understand that arrangements were made for something of a speech from me here," he told a crowd in Newark, Ohio, when the train accidentally overshot its scheduled stop, "but it has gone so far that it has deprived me of addressing the many fair ladies assembled, while it has deprived them of observing my very interesting countenance."

In Pittsburgh the following morning—Friday, February 15—some five thousand people gathered outside the stately Monongahela House hotel to see the newly elected president. Lincoln stepped out onto the balcony of his second-floor room, only to find that the grim weather had followed him from Ohio, transforming the crowd below into an "ocean of umbrellas." Though he had prepared some remarks of local interest, Lincoln once again paused to address the secession crisis, attempting to recast some of his ill-received sentiments of the previous days. "Notwithstanding the troubles across the river," he began, pointing a finger in a southerly direction, "there is really no crisis springing from anything in the Government itself. In plain words, there is really no crisis, except an *artificial* one. What is there now to warrant the condition of affairs presented by our friends 'over the river'? Take even their own view of the questions involved, and there is nothing to justify the course which they are pursuing. I repeat it, then—*there is no crisis,* excepting such a one as may be gotten up at any time by turbulent men, aided by designing politicians. My advice, then, under such circumstances, is to keep cool. If the great American people will only keep their temper on both sides of the line, the troubles will come to an end."

Once again, Lincoln's effort to downplay the nation's troubles fared poorly in the press. The *New York Herald* despaired over his suggestion that "the crisis was only imaginary" and went on to list the many challenges facing his administration, including the potential dissolution of the Union, an empty public treasury, and "a reign of terror existing over one-half of the country." It was worrying, the *Herald* claimed, that the new president seemed to regard these conditions as "only a bagatelle, a mere squall which would soon blow over."

At the Pittsburgh train depot, Lincoln stood in the rain "without any signs of impatience" to shake hands with admirers, even pausing to bestow a kiss on a child who was passed over the heads of the crowd. At this, Henry Villard reported, "three lassies also made their way to him and received the same salutation." As members of Lincoln's escort stepped forward to offer a similar greeting, they were "indignantly repulsed amidst the laughter of the spectators." When the time came to board the train, however, Lincoln and his party found their way barred by a "solid mass of humanity." Herded forward by local Republican James Negley, later a Union general, they managed with difficulty to thread their way through the crowd "one by one in Indian file."

The Lincoln Special pulled out of Pittsburgh at 10:00 A.M., with Lincoln bowing and doffing his hat from the rear platform. Up to this stage of the journey, the train had made a reasonably direct progress toward Washington, veering to the north and south as necessary to stop at the major cities along the way, but always keeping to an easterly heading. Now, instead of cutting directly across Pennsylvania toward Harrisburg, the itinerary took a wild, looping swing to the north to allow for stops in New York—"the greatest, richest and most powerful of the states," as John Hay noted. As if to emphasize the impracticality of this leg of the journey, the day began with the train backtracking across the previous day's route, heading west into Ohio for an overnight stop in Cleveland.

The driving rain had turned to snow by the time the Lincoln Special reached Cleveland at 4:30 that afternoon, but "myriads of human beings" turned out nonetheless, their ranks swelled by several companies of firemen and soldiers. "The anxiety to greet Honest Old Abe was evidently intense," noted Villard. Heedless of the swirling snow, Lincoln stood and bowed as usual as an open carriage conveyed him along Euclid Avenue to the Weddell House, the five-story "Palace of the Forest City."

By now, it had become the established custom that Lincoln's arrival would be marked by a speech from the balcony of his hotel room. In Cleveland, he took the opportunity to repeat the substance of what he had said in Pittsburgh. "I think that there is no occasion for any excitement," he insisted. "It can't be argued up, and it can't be argued down. Let it alone, and it will go down of itself." This last remark drew appreciative laughter from the crowd but a good deal of acid from the press. The lead column of the *Cleveland Plain Dealer* the next day featured an "Epitaph" for the Union: "Here lies a people, who, in attempting to liberate the negro, lost their own freedom." As an exercise in public relations, designed to reassure the North and placate the South, Lincoln's inaugural trip had hit its lowest point. Writing in his diary, Congressman Charles Francis Adams—the son of one president and the grandson of another—expressed a fear that Lincoln's speeches were "rapidly reducing" the public's confidence. "They betray a person unconscious of his own position as well as the nature of the contest around him," Adams wrote. "Good natured, kindly, honest, but frivolous and uncertain."

The following day—Saturday, February 16—began on a disturbing note. Soon after the Lincoln Special left Cleveland, word came that a man had been killed during preparations for yet another thirty-four-gun salute along the route. The travelers were greatly relieved when a subsequent report corrected the first, informing them that the unfortunate man had merely been injured. By this time, however, Lincoln had cause to be thoroughly disenchanted with ceremonial displays of artillery. The previous day, while lunching at a hotel in Alliance, Ohio, the percussion of a nearby cannon salute shattered a window in the dining room, showering Mrs. Lincoln with glass. She recovered her composure quickly but came away thoroughly shaken by the experience.

By early Saturday afternoon, the Lincoln Special had pushed through the upper reaches of Pennsylvania and arrived at "the porch of the Empire State," in the remote northwesterly village of Westfield, New York. "It was like entering St. Peter's through a trap door," wrote Hay. As it happened, Westfield was the home of Grace Bedell, the eleven-year-old girl who had written to advise Lincoln to grow his "whiskers" as a means of improving his appearance. "Some three months ago, I received a letter from a young lady here," he declared from the rear of the train. "It was a very pretty letter, and she advised me to let my whiskers grow, as it would improve my personal appearance. Acting partly upon her suggestion, I have done so; and now, if she is here, I would like to see her." Lincoln was immediately pointed in the direction of a girl who stood "blushing all over her fair face." He climbed down from the platform and bent low to give her "several hearty kisses," amid cheers from the crowd. "You see," he told her, "I let these whiskers grow for you, Grace."

As it happened, there was another celebrated set of whiskers to be seen aboard the Lincoln Special that day. Horace Greeley, whose "absurd fringe of beard" was the delight of editorial cartoonists, had come aboard earlier that morning at Girard, Pennsylvania. Though his arrival was unexpected, the famous editor of the *New-York Tribune* would have been hard to miss. He wore his trademark white coat—"that mysteriously durable garment," as Hay described it—and carried a bright yellow case that announced his name "in characters which might be read across Lake Erie."

The influence of Greeley and his pro-Republican *Tribune* was unparalleled. The previous year, his opposition to William Seward had helped to tip the presidential nomination to Lincoln. Accordingly, the editor's sudden appearance aboard the Lincoln Special created "no little sensation," according to Villard. "He was at once conducted into the car of the President-elect, who came forward to greet him." After conferring privately with Lincoln, Greeley hopped off the train some twenty miles down the line to file an enthusiastic report: "His passage through the country has been like the return of grateful sunshine after a stormy winter day. The people breathe more freely and hope revives in all hearts." Greeley had grave concerns, however, about Lincoln's safety. A few days later, he would report that "substantial cash rewards" were on offer in the Southern states to any-

one who succeeded in murdering the president-elect before the inauguration. Lincoln, he believed, was "in peril of outrage, indignity, and death."

AS THE LINCOLN SPECIAL PRESSED on toward Buffalo on Saturday
afternoon, Allan Pinkerton's investigation in Baltimore was also gaining
on speed. Even as Lincoln said farewell to young Grace Bedell, Pinkerton
was again mingling among the patrons at Barnum's Hotel, hoping to pick
up the trail of Cypriano Ferrandini, the self-professed revolutionary who
had sworn that Lincoln would not live to become president. Pinkerton's
earlier meeting with Ferrandini had been interrupted before the detective
could extract any details of Ferrandini's "fully arranged" plan. Now,
Pinkerton hoped to uncover the facts he would need to thwart the conspiracy.

Though Ferrandini was nowhere to be seen that day, Pinkerton found
himself unexpectedly presented with a chance to take the measure of one
of Baltimore's most-talked-about citizens. George P. Kane, a resolute-
looking man with a dark beard and
military bearing, was holding court at
Barnum's with a group of drinking
companions. As the newly appointed
marshal of Baltimore's police force,
Kane would play a central role in Lincoln's passage through the city, and
Pinkerton was anxious to know if he
could be trusted.

Marshal Kane had become a key
figure in Baltimore's effort to erase
its "Mobtown" image. The previous
year, a reform committee within the
state legislature had enacted a bill to
address the city's "unchecked ruffian-
ism," and it had selected Kane to lead
a newly revitalized police force. Kane
was known to be a man of strong
convictions as well as great personal
courage. Years earlier, while on duty

GEORGE P. KANE.
MARSHAL OF POLICE BALTIMORE.

Baltimore's police marshal George P.
Kane, whose loyalties Pinkerton doubted.
Courtesy of the Library of Congress

in Annapolis with his state militia unit, Kane had been called to the
City Dock when fighting broke out between local townsmen and a group

of "incorrigibles" aboard a Baltimore ship. Stones and bricks were thrown, and the matter soon escalated to the point where cannons were being readied to fire upon the ship. Kane and a pair of fellow officers coolly stepped forward and placed themselves at the mouths of the cannon to prevent the townsmen from firing. This display of unflinching bravery quieted the mob and defused the crisis.

By February 1861, Kane had been marshal of police for barely one year, but already he had made a dramatic impact. The new marshal, wrote one local journalist, "was perhaps the best man in the city for the task confided to him, and the new force organized by him, uniformed and thoroughly drilled, was the best and most efficient the city had ever known. Old abuses were done away with, and the citizens began to look back upon the period of ruffian rule as a terrible nightmare."

With his reforms still in their early stages, however, Marshal Kane understood that the arrival of Abraham Lincoln in Baltimore would present a harsh test. Conscious of a possible eruption of violence, Kane had already made some questionable decisions. As the *Baltimore American* would report, members of the city's Republican Committee—"a few hundred men, particularly obnoxious to the people and public sentiment of Baltimore"— were forming plans to greet the president-elect with a ceremonial procession from the Calvert Street Station. Although marches of this type were being staged in every other city on the Lincoln Special's route, the Baltimore committee was well aware of local feeling against Lincoln and his supporters. Accordingly, they applied to Marshal Kane for police protection. In Kane's view, a public display of this type was an invitation to disaster. "He advised against the proceeding," the *American* noted, "assuring the parties that while Mr. Lincoln, in his passage through Baltimore, would be treated with respect due to him personally and to his high official position, there was no guarantee that the proposed procession would be similarly respected." In fact, as Marshal Kane knew perfectly well, the procession was almost certain to be showered with rocks and rotten eggs, just as earlier Republican marches had been. Kane strongly advised the organizers to abandon their plan, "lest it might provoke some indignity which would involve the character of Baltimore and be very unpleasant to the President-elect." Kane would even carry this argument down to Washington, where he discussed the matter with prominent Lincoln supporters. To go forward, he feared, would "place the people of Baltimore in a false position, as neither they nor the citizens of Maryland sympathized with Mr. Lincoln's political views."

Kane had expressed similar views in a letter to the mayor of Washington, in response to rumors that Baltimoreans were planning to disrupt the inauguration. The mere suggestion, he insisted, ran counter to the "conservative and law-abiding" nature of the city's residents, who sincerely believed that "the day for mobs and riots in their midst has passed, never to return." Although the citizens of Maryland were in "strong sympathy with their Southern brethren," as Kane freely admitted, he rejected any suggestion that they would "tolerate or connive at the unlawful doings of a mob," or countenance an act of "violence or indignity" toward any public official passing through her borders. "The whole thing is probably a political *canard*," he said, "receiving a slight coloring of reality from the thoughtless expressions of a class of people who, in times of excitement, are mostly to be found at street corners or in public barrooms." That being the case, Kane concluded, it would be unnecessary, and perhaps even provocative, to supply Lincoln with an armed escort in Baltimore.

At best, Kane's comments reflect a naïve and perhaps overweening confidence that his reforms alone would be proof against violence on the day of Lincoln's arrival. He may well have believed that the crowds at the Calvert Street Station would show due deference to the office of the president, in spite of their hostility toward the man who was about to occupy it, so long as they were not provoked by overt displays of Republican pageantry or military force. Right or wrong, it should be remembered that Lincoln himself had also been at pains to avoid provoking the secessionists with any suggestion of a "martial cortège." Only a few days earlier, Otis K. Hillard had testified to the Washington select committee that Lincoln would be treated with respect in Baltimore so long as he did not bring a military escort—"which they look upon in the light of a threat." Seen through this prism, Marshal Kane's resistance to a procession by local Republicans, which would all but demand a heavy police presence, might be seen as a peacekeeping measure. One can argue the wisdom of such a position, but it does not necessarily stand as an indictment of Kane's intentions.

There would be many, however, who saw a darker purpose in Kane's maneuverings. Although the marshal had publicly guaranteed Lincoln's safety, there were those who believed that Kane, a strong advocate of secession, could not be trusted to do his duty. For Pinkerton, the question of whether Kane was reliable would loom large in the days ahead, as he tried to determine how to proceed in the face of the emerging threat against Lincoln's life.

Pinkerton's doubts about Kane had been sparked by a comment from

James Luckett, his neighbor at the office on South Street. When Pinkerton mentioned Kane's vow to see the president-elect safely through the city, Luckett gave a high-handed dismissal. "Oh, that is easily promised, but may not be so easily done," he declared. "Marshal Kane don't know any more than any other man, and not so much as some others—but time will tell—time will tell." Others would go further, claiming that Kane was either actively colluding with anti-Union conspirators or that he would turn a blind eye to their designs.

Now, watching Kane through a haze of cigar smoke at Barnum's Hotel, Pinkerton hoped for some indication of whether the marshal could be relied upon. As he tried to edge closer without drawing suspicion, Pinkerton could only make out snatches of Kane's conversation, but these few words seemed to confirm his darkest suspicions. The specifics were not clear, but Pinkerton heard Kane tell his companions that he saw no need for "giving a Police Escort" at some forthcoming event. Pinkerton assumed that Kane was referring to Lincoln's arrival at the Calvert Street Station, because he knew of no other event "likely to transpire in Baltimore which might require a police escort." Though Kane had not explicitly said so, Pinkerton took his words to mean that he "would detail but a small police force to attend the arrival," as opposed to a cordon of armed officers, leaving Lincoln woefully underprotected. As he later explained to his employer Samuel Felton, "[I]t was impossible for Marshal Kane not to know that there would be a necessity for an Escort for Mr. Lincoln on his arrival in Baltimore." If Kane failed to provide one, Pinkerton concluded, "I should from this time out doubt the loyalty of the Baltimore Police."

Then, as now, opinions were strongly divided as to whether Kane was actually "disloyal" in the sense that Pinkerton assumed. It seems that Pinkerton never considered—at the time or at any later date—that Kane's words might have referred to the plans of the Baltimore Republicans for a procession, which the marshal had done so much to discourage. It could easily be argued that any failure to protect the marchers would also, by the same fact, constitute a failure to protect Lincoln. What Pinkerton did not know, however, was that Kane was hatching a private scheme to make good on his guarantee of safe passage, one that would render the necessity of "giving a Police Escort" irrelevant.

Every action that Pinkerton took from this point forward would flow from his belief that the ranking officer of Baltimore's police force could not be trusted to do to his duty. In other circumstances, Pinkerton would have recognized many of his own characteristics in Kane, who was a secretive man, supremely confident in his own judgment and abilities, and very much accustomed to being in charge. If Kane had not been so outspoken in his support of secession, Pinkerton might have found him to be a useful ally. As matters stood, Pinkerton's early doubts now hardened into an implacable suspicion, one that never left him. In later years, he would miss no opportunity to describe Kane as a "rabid Rebel" who commanded a police force composed almost entirely of men with "disunion proclivities." An account published in *Harper's New Monthly Magazine* toward the end of the decade—based on Pinkerton's own writings but highly embellished—would carry these suspicions to a new extreme. In this retelling of the events, one of Ferrandini's men was said to have drawn Pinkerton aside at the height of the drama to deliver a fateful bulletin: "It is determined that that God damned Lincoln shall never pass through here alive!" the detective was told. "The damned abolitionist shall never set foot on Southern soil but to find a grave." To underscore this declaration, Pinkerton's informant was said to have added a chilling coda, suggesting that the plot had been sanctioned at the highest levels: "I have seen Colonel Kane, Chief of Police, and he is all right, and in one week from today the North shall want a new President, for Lincoln will be dead."

In Baltimore, however, Pinkerton offered a far more measured assessment. "He is a man with some fine feelings," the detective allowed, "but thoroughly Southern, and in that respect unscrupulous." That being the case, Pinkerton could not be certain which way the marshal would jump at the critical moment. If Lincoln's life was to be spared, Pinkerton believed he would have to do it himself.

CHAPTER FIFTEEN
A SINGLE RED BALLOT

•

When the train entered the depot, and Mr. Lincoln attempted to pass through the narrow passage leading to the streets, a party already delegated were to engage in a conflict on the outside, and then the policemen were to rush away to quell the disturbance. At this moment—the police being entirely withdrawn—Mr. Lincoln would find himself surrounded by a dense, excited and hostile crowd, all hustling and jamming against him, and then the fatal blow was to be struck.
—ALLAN PINKERTON, *The Spy of the Rebellion*, 1883

"THE MAN AND THE HOUR have met," announced one local politician as the flag-draped train pulled into yet another depot on the evening of February 16. "The whole city is agog," declared another. "Crowds are pouring in from every direction." The journey thus far, observed the *New York Times,* had been "one continuous ovation," an unbroken chain of stirring speeches from train platforms and hotel balconies, and "rapturous audiences" filled with ladies who were "equally enthusiastic with the gentlemen."

Though the praise had a familiar ring by this time, in this instance it was being heaped upon Jefferson Davis—"the other President," as the *Times* referred to him—whose arrival in Montgomery, Alabama, marked the end of his five-day inaugural trip from Mississippi. In two day's time, while Lincoln continued his halting progress through New York, Davis would take his oath as president of the Confederate States of America. "The time for compromise is past," Davis declared upon arrival in Montgomery, "and we are now determined to maintain our position, and make all who oppose us smell Southern powder, feel Southern steel."

The *New York Herald*, while objecting to the warlike tone, nevertheless believed that Davis had acquitted himself well on his inaugural journey, in pointed contrast to Lincoln: "Mr. Davis made five and twenty speeches en route, but we do not hear that he told any stories, cracked any jokes, asked the advice of the young women about his whiskers, or discussed political platforms." This difference in styles, the *Herald* went on to say, owed much to the fact that Davis was a graduate of West Point and a hero of the Mexican-American War, while Lincoln was merely "a splitter of rails, a distiller of whiskey, a story teller and a joke maker."

Even as Davis made his triumphant appearance in Montgomery that Saturday, Lincoln found a near disaster looming in upstate New York. Ten thousand people were massed outside Buffalo's Exchange Street Station as the Lincoln Special approached at 4:30 that afternoon. At trackside, a delegation headed by no less a figure than former president Millard Fillmore stood waiting to receive Lincoln, but the planned exchange of greetings would soon descend into pandemonium. Although the front doors to the station had been barred, with soldiers in position to guard the access points, the eager crowd outside began swarming through the track portals as the train pulled in, resulting in what Henry Villard called "the most ill conducted affair witnessed since the departure from Springfield."

"As Lincoln's train approached, the mass of people gathered in the depot became alarming," reported Buffalo's *Commercial Advertiser.* "The rush was tremendous. A squad from Company 'D' threw themselves around Mr. Lincoln and his immediate party and measurably protected them, but it was impossible to protect anyone else."

"A scene of the wildest confusion ensued," wrote Villard. "To and fro the ruffians swayed and cries of distress were heard on all sides." John Hay saw the soldiers and a line of local policemen struggling valiantly against the surging crowd, but they were soon "swept away like weeds before an angry current." As Major Hunter leaped down from the train and struggled to open a path to a waiting carriage, Lincoln narrowly escaped being swept into the crush and "macerated" as hordes of people outside the station sought to force their way into a receiving area that was already filled to capacity. By comparison, Hay insisted, "the hug of Barnum's grizzly bear would have been a tender and fraternal embrace." Villard believed that Lincoln got through safely only due to the desperation of the small circle of men surrounding him. "The pressure was so great that it is really a wonder that many were not crushed and trampled to death," he wrote. "His party had to struggle with might and main for their lives." The truth of his words may be judged by the injury to Major Hunter, who was "crushed violently against the wall, receiving serious injuries." Hunter came away with a dislocated shoulder, and he would spend the rest of the trip with his arm in a sling. An elderly man in the crowd was also badly pummeled, and before he could be pulled free, he had broken ribs and blood streaming from his nose and mouth. "Women fainted, men were crushed under the mass of bodies, and many others had their bones broken," reported the *Commercial Advertiser*. "Once out of the depot every man uttered a brief 'Thank God!' for the preservation of his life. More with personal injuries were carried away and the fainted women were recovering under a free use of hydrant water."

After this calamitous scene, Lincoln and his traveling party were thankful that the following day—Sunday, February 17—had been set aside as a day of much-needed rest. Lincoln went to church twice that day, once in the company of Millard Fillmore, and later dined at the home of the former president. By all accounts Lincoln was grateful that the relatively light schedule gave him a chance to rest his speaking voice, which by this time had been worn to a ragged croak.

While Lincoln recuperated in Buffalo, the Peace Convention at Willard's Hotel in Washington had also adjourned for the Sabbath. "We are getting along badly with our work of compromise—badly!" one discouraged delegate wrote to his wife. "Will break up, I apprehend, without anything being done. God will hold some men to a fearful responsibility. My heart is sick."

While his fellow delegates rested, Lucius Chittenden turned his attention to the rumors drifting down to Washington from Maryland. Chittenden, the "independent committee of safety" member who had kept an anxious eye on the electoral count a few days earlier, had reason to believe that a fresh crisis was brewing. "Lincoln is to be assassinated—I know it," he was told by a local journalist. "It is not even an independent plot; it is part of the conspiracy of secession." On Sunday afternoon, Chittenden reported, a "duly authenticated" messenger arrived bearing a cryptic message from "reliable friends," urging him to hurry at once to Baltimore. The reason for the summons, the messenger explained, would be revealed on arrival. "It was too important to be trusted to the mails or the telegraph," Chittenden was told, "or even to be put upon paper." Chittenden departed at once for Washington's B&O Railroad Station, where he boarded a late train for Baltimore. As the train neared its destination, he recalled, "a stranger half-stumbled along the aisle of the dimly lighted car, partially fell over me, but grasped my hand as he recovered himself and apologized for his awkwardness." As the man moved away, Chittenden realized that a piece of paper had been pressed into his hand. He with-drew into the passenger car's "dressing-room" to read the note without being observed. "Be cautious," it read. "At the station, follow a driver who will be shouting 'Hotel Fountain,' instead of 'Fountain Hotel.' Enter his carriage. He is reliable and has his directions."

Chittenden followed the directions to the letter. Soon he found him-self being driven to a private residence that he did not recognize, where a "true Republican"—whom he identified only as "Mr. H."—stepped for-ward to greet him. "Our friend of the train came soon after," he reported, whereupon he was led upstairs and introduced to half a dozen "reliable citizens of Baltimore." "No time was wasted," Chittenden continued. No sooner had the group assembled than the mysterious Mr. H. announced his reason for summoning Chittenden from Washington: "We want you to help us save Baltimore from disgrace, and President Lincoln from assassina-tion." Before the startled Chittenden could gather himself to respond, Mr. H. pressed on to explain that he and his colleagues had uncovered details of a credible threat to Lincoln but were unable to take measures to prevent it from being carried out. "We are watched and shadowed so that we cannot leave the city without exciting suspicion," he explained. "We have sent mes-sengers to leading Republicans in Washington, notifying them of the plot against the President's life, but they will not credit the story, nor, so far as we can learn, take any action." Worse yet, it appeared for the moment that Lincoln was determined to pass openly through Baltimore—even if "he loses his life in consequence."

According to Mr. H., the details of the plan were chillingly clear. Within ten minutes of his arrival, Lincoln would be surrounded by a mob of "roughs and plug-uglies" who would murder him where he stood. "We have every detail of the plot," Chittenden was told, "[and] we know the men who have been hired to kill him; we could lay our hands upon them to-night. But what are we to do if our friends will not believe our report?"

Chittenden was dubious. In spite of the many similar rumors he had heard in Washington, he had trouble accepting the existence of such an audacious scheme. "You call the plot a certainty," he said. "What proof have you? Direct proof, I mean?" His hosts were prepared for this. Mr. H. explained that he had arranged for Chittenden to hear directly from one of the conspirators, an "unscrupulous character" who had now turned infor-mant. Chittenden had qualms about accepting the testimony of such a man at face value, but he agreed to hear what he had to say. "Two men en-tered the room with the supposed assassin," Chittenden reported. He noted that the informant "looked the character," and went on to give a description that would not have been out of place in one of the lurid "penny dreadfuls" of the day: "He represented a genus of the human family seen in pictures of Italian bandits. His square, bull-dog jaws, ferret-like eyes, furtively looking out from holes under a low brow, covered with a coarse mat of black hair; a dark face, every line of which was hard, and an impudent swagger in his carriage, sufficiently advertised him as a low, cowardly villain."

Speaking in the halting, heavily accented English of a recent immigrant, the informant described how he had come to be swept up in the plot. "A bad president was coming," he began, and when he took power he would "free the negroes and drive all the foreigners out of the country. The good Americans wanted him killed." The instrument of this plot was to be a man known as "Ruscelli," a barber who likened himself to the Italian revolutionary Felice Orsini, and who had gathered a group of like-minded men around him. These men, the informant went on to explain, had formed a plan that could not fail. If, as many believed, the railcar carrying Lincoln was to be uncoupled at the Calvert Street Station and pulled through the city by horses, Ruscelli and his men would create a sudden obstruction to block its progress. "When the President's car stopped at the obstruction," Chittenden was told, "the assassins were to follow their leader into the rear of the car [and] pass rapidly through it, each knifing the president." They would then make their way out of the car and pass through the crowd to a rum shop at the harbor's edge. Hurrying through to the rear of the shop, the assassins would climb aboard a waiting schooner for a quick getaway. For added cover, bombs and hand grenades would be set off to create general panic and confusion.

The informant went on to say that every stage of the plot had been carefully rehearsed to avoid mistakes or hesitation at the crucial moment. "The whole work," Chittenden learned, "from arresting the car to the departure of the schooner, could be done in five or six minutes." If, on the other hand, Lincoln left his train car at the Calvert Street Station and boarded an open carriage, the work of the assassins would be even simpler. Within five minutes, the carriage would be surrounded by "a crowd of rowdies," who would "swoop down upon it like vultures [and] have ample time to tear him to pieces."

Chittenden took a moment to reflect on this grim scenario as the "miscreant" was led away. Turning to the others in the darkened room, he asked why the information had not been taken to the authorities. Mr. H.

and his colleagues shifted uncomfortably. Ruscelli and his men, they explained, were simply tools of a much larger cabal that stretched from "pot-house politicians of a low order" to an "admixture of men of a better class, some of them in the police." It was thought that many of the city's leading citizens were privy to the plot, having "argued themselves into the belief that this was a patriotic work which would prevent greater bloodshed and possible war." These well-heeled supporters kept the conspirators abundantly supplied with money, while the city's police force—"from superintendent to patrolmen"—looked the other way. "No," Mr. H. insisted, summing up his frustrations, "we have done everything in our power!" Chittenden, he believed, was their last hope. "If the government itself will not interfere," he concluded, "and if, as he declares he will, Mr. Lincoln insists on passing through Baltimore in an open way, on the train appointed, his murder is inevitable." Chittenden agreed at once to carry the group's concerns back to Washington, and to do all that he could to convince General Scott and others of the seriousness of the threat. He passed the rest of the night talking the matter over with the Baltimore group, until it was time to catch the early-morning train back to the capital.

MANY OF THE DETAILS OF CHITTENDEN'S ACCOUNT are dubious and others are open to interpretation, but it seems probable that the ringleader he described as "Ruscelli" was, in fact, Cypriano Ferrandini, as it is unlikely—even in a city the size of Baltimore—that there were two Italian barbers invoking the name of Felice Orsini as a justification for murdering Lincoln. Chittenden would also assert that one member of the league of assassins was "an actor who recites passages from the tragedy of Julius Caesar," raising the tantalizing specter of the noted Shakespearean actor John Wilkes Booth, a Maryland native who was known to patronize Barnum's Hotel in Baltimore. Booth was performing in Albany that month, and may have been in the crowd as Lincoln passed through that city, but there is no evidence to place him in Baltimore during the inaugural journey. Lucius Chittenden, whose account was published many years after the events at Ford's Theatre, and who was much inclined toward elaborate conspiracy theories, drew no connection to the notorious assassin.

Allan Pinkerton would note, however, that "a sample of the feeling" among the people of Baltimore could be found in the person of Otis K. Hillard, a theater devotee who missed few opportunities to quote a favorite line from Shakespeare's play: "Not that I loved Caesar less, but that

I loved Rome more." As Pinkerton recounted, Hillard took solace in these words "when his conscience roused him to a contemplation of the awful crime" under consideration. The "young Lieutenant," as Pinkerton called him, came to believe that Brutus's struggle with the conflicting demands of honor and patriotism mirrored his own. The points in common between Chittenden's story and Pinkerton's—including the Orsini-inspired barber and the Shakespeare-quoting plotter—suggest that the two men were tangled in the same thread of conspiracy. If nothing else, Chittenden's account would seem to confirm that Lincoln's supporters in Baltimore harbored a deep mistrust of the authorities, suggesting that Pinkerton's own suspicions toward Marshal Kane and his men were not entirely without foundation.

Chittenden's interlude in Baltimore came just as Pinkerton's own investigation was drawing near to the heart of Ferrandini's plot. By Sunday, February 17, Pinkerton had "resolved upon prompt and decisive measures to discover the inward workings of the conspirators," because he had only a few days remaining in which to act. The detective sent another report to Norman Judd, in Buffalo, advising him that "the evidence was accumulating," then summoned his resourceful operative Harry Davies, whose efforts to draw further information from Otis Hillard had reached a frustrating impasse.

By piecing together various rumors and reports, Pinkerton had managed to form a working theory of Ferrandini's plan. Though he did not know it at the time, the broad strokes were disturbingly similar to those reported by Lucius Chittenden. "A vast crowd would meet [Lincoln] at the Calvert Street depot," Pinkerton stated. "Here it was arranged that but a small force of policemen should be stationed, and as the President arrived a disturbance would be created which would attract the attention of these guardians of the peace." While the police rushed off to deal with this diversion, he continued, "it would be an easy task for a determined man to shoot the President, and, aided by his companions, succeed in making his escape." All that remained now, Pinkerton believed, was to select the man who would "commit the fatal deed." This was to be determined by a drawing of ballots, "and as yet no one knew upon whom might devolve the bloody task."

Pinkerton was convinced that Otis Hillard held the key to uncovering the final details of the plot, as well as the identity of the designated assassin. Hillard, he believed, was the weak link in Ferrandini's chain of command. The grim realities of the plot were "preying heavily" on the young lieutenant's mind, the detective noted, causing him to sink "still deeper into dissipation." At such times, Hillard invariably turned to Harry Davies, whom he still believed to be an ardent secessionist. Davies's sympathy and support, Pinkerton wrote, "had now become a necessity to him, and they were scarcely ever separated." Though Hillard continued to dangle hints about Ferrandini and his band of conspirators at every opportunity, he had so far refused to take Davies fully into his confidence, claiming that he was bound by a solemn oath of secrecy.

Hillard appeared to regret keeping his friend in the dark. One afternoon, as Hillard appeared at Davies's door, carrying a pair of "worked slippers" as a peace offering, the detective saw a chance to get Hillard talking. Davies accepted the gift readily enough, but his distracted, serious manner was calculated to put Hillard off balance.

"You look sober," Hillard said, "what is the matter with you?"

Davies gave an answer designed to get Hillard talking. "I am thinking about what a damned pretty tumult this country is in," he replied. "I have had all kinds of bad thoughts shoot through my mind."

"What have you been thinking about?" Hillard asked.

Davies gave his answer as if unburdening himself of a difficult secret. If only a man had sufficient courage, he began, he might immortalize himself "by taking a knife and plunging it into Lincoln's heart." It was regrettable, he continued, that a man could not be found "with the pluck to do it." Turning Hillard's oft-quoted Shakespeare reference back on him, Davies bemoaned the fact that things were not as they were "in the time of Brutus and Caesar." The men of the South, he said, lacked the courage of the noble Romans.

Hillard was dismayed by his friend's words. "There *are* men who would do it!' he insisted. Davies pretended to be skeptical: "I will give five hundred dollars to see the man who will do it," he declared.

Hillard, rankled by the aspersions Davies had cast on Southern manhood, rose to the bait. "Give me an article of agreement," he said, "and I will kill Lincoln between here and Havre de Grace." Davies smiled to himself and offered his friend a drink. At last they were getting somewhere.

By any measure, this was an astonishingly reckless exchange on the part of both men. In effect, Davies had goaded Hillard into making a vow to assassinate the president-elect. It is difficult to gauge, based on the dry and uninflected language of Davies's field report, the degree to which either man was in earnest. As the two continued talking, however, it became evident that Hillard had no intention of carrying out the deed alone and unabetted, but Davies's offer appeared to have strengthened his determination to assist in Ferrandini's designs, if so ordered. As he turned the matter over in his mind, Hillard's enthusiasm grew. The money Davies had pledged would be of no use to him personally, he explained, but that was of no concern. "Five hundred dollars would help my mother," he said, "because I would expect to die, and I would say so soon as it was done: 'Here gentlemen take me, I am the man who [has] done the deed.'"

Hillard returned to the subject several times over the course of the day. By evening, Davies's bold statement had inspired further confidences. As the two men dined together at Mann's Restaurant, Hillard at last confirmed that his unit of the National Volunteers might soon "draw lots to see who would kill Lincoln." If the responsibility fell upon him, Hillard boasted, "I would do it willingly."

Davies was keenly aware that he had reached an important crossroads, as Hillard had never before spoken so openly. After offering assurances that he had no wish to pry, Davies gingerly admitted to a natural curiosity—"being a Southern man"—as to the true extent of the plans Hillard had mentioned.

Hillard hesitated. "I have told you all I have a right to tell you," he said at last. "Do not think, my friend, that it is a want of confidence in you that makes me so cautious. It is because I have to be." The reason for this was simple, Hillard explained as he glanced about the restaurant: There were "government spies here all the time." As evidence of this, he mentioned his summons to testify before the select committee two weeks earlier. Hillard could not recall having spoken of the National Volunteers to anyone outside of the organization, but nevertheless he had been called to Washington to give evidence. To his mind, this was proof of spies in their midst. That being the case, the Volunteers had to be on their guard at all times. "We have taken a solemn oath," he explained, "which is to obey the orders of our Captain, without asking any questions, and in no case, or under any circumstances, reveal . . . anything that is confidential." Hillard was careful not to mention the names of Ferrandini or any other member of the secret order, not realizing that Davies and Pinkerton had already identified the key figures.

Davies continued to press. "It is none of my business to ask you questions about your Company," he admitted, but he wondered if perhaps the young lieutenant could go so far as to reveal "the first object" of the organization. Hillard weighed the question for a moment. "It was first organized to prevent the passage of Lincoln with the troops through Baltimore," he said after a time, "but our plans are changed every day, as matters change.

What its object will be from day to day I do not know, nor can I tell. All we have to do is to obey the orders of our Captain—whatever he commands we are required to do." Hillard took a significant pause, apparently wrestling with a desire to confide something further, but after a moment's struggle he restrained himself. "Rest assured I have all confidence in you," he said, but "I cannot come out and tell you all. I cannot compromise my honor."

AS HILLARD RETREATED ONCE AGAIN behind his oath to the National Volunteers, Davies fell into despair. On Pinkerton's orders, Davies had pushed as far as he dared, even pledging money to a potential assassin in his urgent pursuit of information. Pinkerton, who had passed over twenty-five dollars to James Luckett a few days earlier, clearly believed that such measures were an accepted component of undercover work, and a necessary concession to the limited time in which he had to work. For the moment, however, the aggressive tactics appeared to have failed. The surviving portion of Davies's field report ends with Hillard's refusal to compromise his "solemn oath." According to Pinkerton's recollections, however, the situation soon took a more favorable turn. On hearing what had transpired, Pinkerton saw that Hillard's revelation about the ballot drawing had provided them with a tool to overcome the young lieutenant's intransigence. In an account published many years later, Pinkerton claimed that he instructed Davies to demand to be taken to this fateful meeting, insisting that he, too, wished to be given the "opportunity to immortalize himself" by murdering Abraham Lincoln. "Accordingly," Pinkerton wrote, "that day Davies broached the matter to Hillard in a manner which convinced him of his earnestness, and the young Lieutenant promised his utmost efforts to secure his admission." Hillard then withdrew, apparently to plead his friend's case to Ferrandini. Soon, Hillard returned in exuberant spirits. If Davies would be willing to swear an oath of loyalty, he could join Ferrandini's band of "Southern patriots" that very night.

As evening fell, Pinkerton's account continues, Hillard conducted Davies to the home of a man who was well known among the secessionists. The pair were ushered into a large drawing room on the ground floor, where a group of twenty men stood waiting. "The members were strangely silent," Pinkerton declared, "and an ominous awe seemed to pervade the entire assembly." At last, Davies found himself being led forward to meet their "noble Captain," as Hillard repeatedly called him, whose identity had been so closely guarded. As Pinkerton and Davies had expected, this proved to be Cypriano Ferrandini, who had dressed for the occasion in funereal black from head to toe. Ferrandini greeted Davies with a crisp nod, but no words passed between them. As Pinkerton had noted earlier at Barr's Saloon, the others treated their solemn-faced leader with marked deference. Each new man who entered crossed the room to pay his respects, and sought his approval before speaking.

At a signal from Ferrandini, heavy curtains were drawn tight across the windows. In the flickering light of candles, the "rebel spirits" formed a circle as Ferrandini instructed Davies to raise his hand and swear allegiance to the cause of Southern freedom. "Having passed through the required formula," Pinkerton wrote, "Davies was warmly taken by the hand by his associates, many of

Pinkerton operative Harry Davies takes his oath as a member of Ferrandini's band.

whom he had met in the polite circles of society." With the initiation completed, Ferrandini proceeded to the main business of the evening. Climbing onto a chair, he explained in hushed tones that he had assembled this sacred trust of patriots to ensure the preservation of the Southern way of life. Ferrandini's voice gathered force as he spoke, and he carefully reviewed each step of the plan to divert the police at the Calvert Street Station, allowing their chosen assassin to strike. After elaborating on the design, he reminded his followers of the importance of their mission. "He violently assailed the enemies of the South," as Davies reported to Pinkerton, "and in glowing words pointed out the glory that awaited the man who proved himself the hero upon this great occasion." Davies noted that all present appeared to draw courage and resolve from Ferrandini's words. Beside him, Hillard stood with a straight back and steadfast expression, as if his earlier fears were now forgotten. As Ferrandini brought his remarks to a "fiery crescendo," he drew a long, curved blade from beneath his coat and brandished it high above his head. "Gentlemen," he cried to roars of approval, "this hireling Lincoln shall never, never be President!"

When the cheers subsided, Ferrandini turned at last to the selection of Lincoln's killer. "For this purpose the meeting had been called," as Davies well knew, "and tonight the important decision was to be reached." A wave of apprehension passed through the room. "Who should do the deed?" Ferrandini asked his followers. "Who should assume the task of liberating the nation of the foul presence of the abolitionist leader?"

Ferrandini explained that a number of paper ballots had been placed into the heavy wooden chest that sat on the table in front of him. One of these ballots, he continued, was marked in red to designate the assassin. "In order that none should know who drew the fatal ballot, except he who did so, the room was rendered still darker," Davies reported, "and everyone was pledged to secrecy as to the color of the ballot he drew." In this manner, Ferrandini told his followers, the identity of the "honored patriot" would be protected until the last-possible instant.

One by one, the "solemn guardians of the South" filed past the wooden box and withdrew a folded ballot slip. As each man passed, Ferrandini smiled approvingly and murmured a few words of encouragement. Ferrandini himself took the final ballot and held it high in the air, telling the assembly in a hushed but steely tone that their business had now come to a close. There should be no further discussion of the matter until the very moment of Lincoln's arrival, he reminded them, to ensure that nothing should happen to compromise their plan. With a final word of praise for the strength and conviction of their "Southern ideals," Ferrandini brought the meeting to a close.

Hillard and Davies walked out into the darkened streets together, after first withdrawing to a private corner to open their folded ballots. Davies's own ballot paper was blank, a fact he conveyed to Hillard with an expression of ill-concealed disappointment. As they set off in search of a stiffening drink, Davies pretended to feel anxiety as to whether the plan could succeed. He told Hillard that he admired the strategy but was worried that the man who had been chosen to carry it out—whoever he might be—would lose his nerve at the crucial moment. Hillard waved the objection aside. Ferrandini had anticipated this possibility, he said, and had confided to him that a safeguard was in place to prevent such a failure. The wooden box, Hillard explained, had contained not one red ballot, but eight, and all eight were now in the hands of Ferrandini's men. Each man would believe wholeheartedly that he alone was charged with the task of murdering Lincoln, and that the cause of the South rested solely upon "his courage, strength and devotion." In this way, even if one or two of the chosen assassins should fail to act, at least one of the others would be certain to strike the fatal blow. For Hillard's benefit, Davies feigned relief over the ingenuity of Ferrandini's deception. Soon, after reviewing the events of the evening over a glass of whiskey, Davies found an excuse to withdraw for the evening.

Moments later, Davies was hurrying along the back alley behind Pinkerton's South Street building, with the collar of his overcoat drawn tight around his face. He clambered up the rear stairs and burst into the office, launching into his account of the evening's events even before the door had closed behind him. Pinkerton sat at his desk, furiously scribbling notes as Davies spoke, breaking in every so often to ask a question or confirm a detail.

When Davies had finished, Pinkerton sat back in his chair and pondered his next move. He found himself forced to admit to a grudging admiration for the murderous plot as Ferrandini had outlined it. "It was a capital one," he acknowledged, and it would require his best effort if it were to be averted. It was now clear that the period of "unceasing shadow," as he had described his operations in Baltimore, had come to an end.

"My time for action," he later declared, "had now arrived."

CHAPTER SIXTEEN
WHITEWASH

•

For the benefit of laymen I will state that in a crowd as great as the greatest, you can always be sure of getting through it if you follow these instructions: Elevate your elbow high, and bring it down with great force upon the digestive apparatus of your neighbor. He will double up and yell, causing the gentlemen in front of you to turn halfway round to see what is the matter. Punch him in the same way, step on his foot, pass him, and continue the application until you have reached the desired point. It never fails.

—JOSEPH HOWARD of the *New York Times*, from aboard the Lincoln Special

KATE WARNE, IN THE PERSON of Mrs. Barley of Alabama, had become a familiar sight in the hotel parlors and tearooms of Baltimore by this time. The young widow invariably found a seat at the edge of a large group of women and busied herself with a book or a piece of needlework, nodding pleasantly as she settled herself. With the dangling black and white ribbons of a Southern cockade pinned to her breast, Mrs. Warne, whose kindly blue eyes seemed to resonate with the laughter and animated comments nearby, would allow herself by slow degrees to be drawn into the neighboring conversations. She had "an ease of manner that was quite captivating," Pinkerton observed, "and had already made remarkable progress in cultivating the acquaintance of the wives and daughters of the conspirators."

As a rule, Pinkerton's operatives avoided one another in public, so as reduce the risk of exposure if suspicion fell on a particular detective. It came as a surprise, therefore, when Pinkerton himself appeared suddenly in the parlor of Mrs. Warne's hotel on the morning of February 18, signaling an urgent need to speak in private. Taking leave of her latest group of new friends, Mrs. Warne rose and quietly made her way to her room. Moments later, Pinkerton followed, unobserved.

As soon as the hotel room's door closed behind him, Pinkerton began to speak in a rush. Mrs. Warne was to leave immediately, he told her, in order to rendezvous with Abraham Lincoln's party in New York. Although Pinkerton had already been in touch with Norman Judd by telegraph and special messenger, the information he now planned to send would require delicate handling to ensure that it arrived safely and received the attention it deserved.

Reaching into his coat pocket, Pinkerton handed over a fresh letter for Norman Judd. It warned that the danger waiting for Lincoln in Baltimore could no longer be ignored, and urged him to take protective measures. It was essential, Pinkerton insisted, that Mrs. Warne place the letter directly into Judd's hands, and that she bring all of her considerable powers of persuasion to bear as he read it. Above all, she must convince Judd of one essential fact: If Lincoln passed through Baltimore as planned in five day's time, his safety could not be guaranteed. If necessary, the detective continued, he would arrange to meet with Judd personally to advise on a course of action.

Pinkerton also passed over a letter to be carried to Edward Sanford, the man who had hired him to investigate the Adams Express Robbery three years earlier. Sanford, he explained, was now president of the American Telegraph Company, and he would be able to assist in controlling the flow of crucial information in and out of Baltimore. If Mrs. Warne had trouble making contact with Lincoln's entourage, Sanford would also be able to assist in getting access to Judd.

Glancing at his pocket watch, Pinkerton began pacing the room. In order to intercept Lincoln's party, he said, Mrs. Warne would have to take a late train, leaving Baltimore just after five o'clock that evening. There was still much to do in the few hours remaining, but he promised to see her off at the depot with any further information that might come to hand. As Pinkerton turned to take his leave, the strain of the past few days showed in his ashen features and reddened eyes. Mrs. Warne offered no comment; she knew full well that Pinkerton would not rest for more than two or three hours a night until Lincoln had passed safely though Baltimore. Instead, she tucked the letters away and promised to carry out his instructions to the letter.

LEAVING MRS. WARNE TO PREPARE for her journey, Pinkerton hurried back to his office and dashed off an urgent warning to Samuel Felton, instructing him to tighten the patrols around his bridges and ferries. The railroad president would have needed little persuading. He remained deeply concerned about the militia groups carrying out their training drills alongside his track. "One of these organizations was loyal," he believed, "but the other two were disloyal, and fully in the plot to destroy the bridges."

By this time, Felton had received corroboration from a second informant. This unknown "gentleman from Baltimore" had walked five miles out of the city to deliver a warning to one of Felton's bridge keepers. According to his information, some of the militiamen were secretly preparing "combustible materials" to pour over the wooden bridges, so that they could be more easily destroyed when the time came. In the event that Northern troops were brought by train to reinforce Washington, the militiamen would set fire to the bridges just as the Lincoln Special came within range. "The bridge was then to be burned [and] the train attacked," the informant claimed, "and Mr. Lincoln to be put out of the way." Every detail of the scheme had been carefully worked out, Felton's informant claimed, including the means by which the saboteurs would "disguise themselves as negroes" to avoid detection.

It is fair to wonder if this last detail would have passed entirely unnoticed. If the plan lacked a certain element of plausibility, however, Felton had absolute confidence in his unnamed informant. "I have never been able to ascertain who he was," Felton wrote in later years, but he "appeared to be a gentleman, and in earnest, and honest in what he said." The man declined to give his name, he said, because "his life would be in peril were it known that he had given this information."

Felton's account jibed with reports coming in from Timothy Webster, the agent Pinkerton had stationed in nearby Perrymansville, where the "loud threats" reported earlier had now taken a more tangible form. In a report dated Tuesday, February 19, Webster detailed the manner in which an ordinary game of "Ten-pins" had erupted into a heated debate over Lincoln's prospects for survival, with one of the players stating darkly that if any Northern troops dared to show themselves, "Lincoln would never get to Washington." Another man—a railway worker named Springer—heartily concurred, warning that "he had better not come over this road with any military, for if he did that boat would never make another [trip] across the River." This was understood to be a reference to the *Maryland*, the small steamer used in the painstaking process of ferrying railcars across the Susquehanna River at Havre de Grace.

Later that day, Springer expanded on his remarks, telling Webster that he had heard talk from Baltimore of "about one thousand men, well organized and ready for anything." When Lincoln arrived in the city, Springer explained, there would be calls for him to step out from his train to give a speech. If Lincoln complied, Springer said, he "would not be surprised if they killed him." Webster pressed for details about the leaders of this plot, but, as he reported to Pinkerton, "I could not learn from him any of their names."

In a later account, Pinkerton claimed that the men of Perrymansville saw themselves as key figures in a larger web of conspiracy. In their view, as Pinkerton reported it, little good would be accomplished by Lincoln's assassination alone. His death would only "hasten a disaster they were anxious to avoid," because the forces of the Union "would rise as one man to avenge the death of their leader." That being the case, it would be necessary to work in concert with the Baltimore plotters to hamper and perhaps prevent Northern retaliation. "As soon as the deed had been accomplished in Baltimore," Pinkerton reported, "the news was to be telegraphed along the line of the road, and immediately upon the reception of this intelligence the telegraph wires were to be cut, the railroad bridges destroyed and the tracks torn up, in order to prevent for some time any information being conveyed to the cities of the North, or the passage of any Northern men." In this way, the Union would be unable to bring its forces south with any speed or efficiency.

Pinkerton readily acknowledged that the scheme was "wild" and "reckless," but Webster's reports left him in no doubt that an attack on Samuel Felton's railroad was imminent. He advised Felton to assemble a force of men "to guard the various bridges and ferries, who could be warned in time to resist attack should such be made." Felton raised a group of some two hundred workers, who were "drilled secretly" for the task ahead. Felton was anxious to tread lightly, for fear that a conspicuous display of force would draw a violent response. Accordingly, he sent out his forces in the guise of work crews assigned to whitewash the bridges, as if sprucing up the line in advance of Lincoln's arrival. In the course of this seemingly innocent labor, Felton's men coated the vulnerable crossings with a flame-retardant solution of salt and alum, designed to render the wood nearly fireproof. Felton's crews worked with extraordinary speed, he reported, and managed in some places to cover the bridges with six or seven layers of protective material. The whitewashing was "so extensive in its application," Felton recalled, that it "became the nine-days wonder of the neighborhood."

IN BUFFALO, AFTER THE RELATIVE DAY of quiet on Sunday, William Wood's ambitious itinerary resumed with a vengeance. On Monday, February 18, the "peculiar exigence of time tables" required the travelers to rise at 4:00 A.M. "At that hour the waking human heart yearneth to behold its enemy," grumbled John Hay, adding that the cluster of men gloomily assembled in the dim corridors of the hotel "thirsted for the blood of Wood, as the hart thirsteth for the running brooks." Lincoln and his family were spared to some extent, as Wood had provided them with a sleeper car at the rear of the departing train.

Complaints aside, the morning unfolded smoothly, thanks to well-run trains and straight stretches of track, allowing the Lincoln Special to attain speeds of nearly sixty miles per hour. John Hay declared that the "vital history" of the day amounted to three words: "Crowds, cannon, and cheers." Lincoln's speeches, too, appeared to be running more smoothly, or at least drawing better notice in the press. He had now recast his poorly received remark about the "artificial crisis," clarifying his intent of stating that there had been an unhealthy degree of panic over the situation. "I do not mean to say that this artificial panic has not done harm," he insisted. "That it has done much harm I do not deny." Having admitted this much, however, Lincoln went on to assure his audiences that he would "take such grounds as I shall deem best calculated to restore peace, harmony and prosperity to the country." The *New York Times* approved: "There is not the slightest doubt that, in its origin and its political aspect, the present crisis is what Mr. Lincoln styled it, an artificial one, got up by demagogues for selfish and partisan purposes."

Lincoln had also become more adept at turning aside the calls to address the crowds at every stop. If he could not avoid speaking altogether, he devised artful explanations for the brevity of his remarks. In Hudson, New York, he declined to mount a nearby speaker's platform, but joked with his audience that he did not intend to make a habit of it: "You must not on this account draw the inference that I have any intention to desert any platform I have a legitimate right to stand on."

Henry Villard observed that Lincoln had also developed a relaxed manner with the "impertinent individuals" who spoke up during his speeches, answering their "rough courtesies" with good-natured humor, which invariably drew cheers and laughter. By now, Lincoln's trackside pleasantries had been honed to a tidy formula, a fact that greatly pleased the clock-watching Wood. "Short-hand would express it thus," wrote Joseph Howard in the *Times*. "Crowds—enthusiasm—little speech—little bow—kissed little girl—God-blessed old man—recognized old friend—much affected."

This crisp routine fell to pieces as the Lincoln Special reached Albany at 2:30 that afternoon. A company of soldiers had been summoned to maintain order, but when these men failed to appear, the crowd swelled to unmanageable proportions, resulting in yet another ugly scene. An overmatched squad of policemen was swept aside, reported Villard, as "little boys and big men climbed under and over the train, only to be kicked and thrown back." Lincoln remained safely inside his train compartment, awaiting the late arrival of the soldiers as his fellow travelers watched the brawl outside, commenting on the "relative muscle of the policemen and the crowd." At last, the reinforcements appeared and quickly fell upon the "enthusiasts," using clubbed muskets to clear a path from the train. Even so, as Lincoln climbed into a waiting carriage for his trip to the capitol, a few determined supporters slipped through the cordon. A man named Fennessey, "being more or less influenced by liquor," pushed his way forward and pumped Lincoln's hand until police ushered him away. "All was confusion, hurry, disorder, mud, riot and discomfort," remarked a disgusted Villard.

Arriving at last at the capitol's rotunda, Lincoln received a warm welcome from Governor Edwin Morgan, the influential chairman of the Republican National Committee. In response, Lincoln expressed a hesitation to speak in such an august setting, as he felt himself to be "the humblest of all individuals" ever elected to the White House. At the insistence of his hosts, Lincoln managed a few brief words, but he took pains to avoid a detailed discussion of "our present difficulties" until he had "enjoyed every opportunity to take correct and true ground."

Lincoln would elaborate on this theme the following day, answering critics who continued to call for an elaboration of future policy. "I have not kept silent since the Presidential election from any party wantonness," he declared, "or from any indifference to the anxiety that pervades the minds of men about the aspect of the political affairs of this country. I have kept silent for the reason that I supposed it was peculiarly proper that I should do so until the time came when, according to the customs of the country,

I should speak officially." In other words, Lincoln remained determined to keep his powder dry for the inaugural address in Washington, allowing for any further "shifting of the scenes" in the interim, and giving his best and most fully considered statement of intent only when he had officially ascended to the presidency.

Several observers in Albany would remark that Lincoln seemed "much wearied" as he was rushed through his paces. One reporter went so far as to say that he looked like a man who had recently awakened from a nap. If Lincoln appeared more careworn than usual that day, he had good reason. At the capitol, Governor Morgan had handed him a disturbing letter from Worthington G. Snethen, one of his few supporters in Baltimore. Earlier, Snethen had written to report on a torchlight parade of Lincoln men, who conducted themselves "nobly" even when pelted by eggs and brickbats. Now, however, Snethen appeared to be waffling on whether he and his colleagues would be able to mount a similar procession for Lincoln's arrival. Although he did not report as much to Lincoln, he had now learned that George Kane, Baltimore's marshal of police, would not provide any police protection, which placed Snethen and his "gallant little band" of supporters in a very delicate position.

"On consultation with some of our leading Republican friends," Snethen wrote, "it has been deemed inadvisable, in the present state of things, to attempt any organized public display on our part." Instead, Snethen proposed that he and a few others should go to Philadelphia or Harrisburg and return with Lincoln to the city, so as to escort him quietly to his planned lunch at the Eutaw House hotel. He added, significantly, that they would be pleased to offer this service "should you decide to stop in Baltimore." If Lincoln chose instead merely to change trains in the city, Snethen continued, he and his group would convey him from one depot to the next. Snethen went on to express hope, even at this late date, that the city's officials might yet come forward to provide Lincoln with a formal welcome to Baltimore, complete with "the necessary conveyances and escort," as had been done at all of the previous stops on his journey. He admitted, however, that so far there had been "no intimations" of this kind. "The city authorities are all opposed to us," he said, "and some of them are even hostile."

Snethen had couched his letter in terms of unflagging support, but the underlying message was unmistakable: Lincoln was not welcome in Baltimore. The following morning, as the Lincoln Special's route turned toward Washington, Lincoln would be headed due south for the first time.

Maryland lay directly in his path, but the political establishment of the state had yet to acknowledge his approach. Governor Hicks, still trying to maintain his partisan balancing act, had been especially notable in his silence. Only Snethen and his plucky fellow Republicans had troubled to extend a hand of welcome, and even they appeared to be thinking better of it.

AS IT HAPPENED, the man who would have best understood Lincoln's concerns was not on board when the Lincoln Special pulled out of Albany at eight o'clock the following morning. Norman Judd, who had already received two warnings about conditions in Baltimore from Pinkerton, found himself left behind when the train departed ahead of schedule. Judd had "never felt so mortified in all his life," he admitted, and hastily bought a ticket on a regular passenger train to catch up with the Lincoln Special in New York City later that afternoon.

It was felt by some that Lincoln's early departure reflected his disgust with the hectic arrangements in Albany—"a miserable botch," in Villard's words—but it was more likely a concession to difficult travel conditions. Ice floes in the Hudson River had made the original route inadvisable, so Wood adjusted the timetable to allow for a detour. Whatever the official reason, both Lincoln and his wife were said to be grateful for "safe deliverance" from their overeager hosts, and vowed never to return.

At three o'clock that afternoon, after another day of "cheers and hurrahs," the train pulled into New York City's Hudson River Railroad terminal at West Thirtieth Street. It was a significant milestone for the man whose name had been misreported as "Abram Lincoln" at the time of election. Nearly one year had passed since his previous visit to the city, when he had delivered his pivotal address at Cooper Union. On that occasion, he had been virtually unknown, and he had walked to the Astor House hotel on foot. Now, as John Nicolay reported, the city's streets, doorways, windows and rooftops were lined with a "continuous fringe of humanity" as residents jockeyed for a clear view of the incoming president.

New York City's police superintendent, John Kennedy, greeted Lincoln at the station, signaling an unparalleled level of security and crowd control. Lincoln's arrival had been an occasion of bedlam at every previous stop, but Kennedy had imposed a system of ticketed admission at the station, limiting the crowd to invited guests. Maj. David Hunter, who still wore his arm in a sling after the melee in Buffalo, looked on with obvious approval as he climbed down from the train.

Kennedy's security measures remained in evidence outside the station, where a line of thirty-five coaches stood waiting for a procession of three and a half miles through the city streets. Lincoln submitted to a brief grooming from his wife, who attempted to smooth his unkempt hair and beard, before stepping into an ornate carriage at the head of the column, drawn by six black horses. As the procession rounded onto Ninth Avenue from Thirtieth Street, squads of mounted police took up positions at the front and rear, with patrolmen on foot flanking the carriages, and hundreds of additional men lining the parade route. "The police arrangements were among the most perfect," Nicolay reported. "Broadway had been kept clear, so that the double line of carriages which made up the procession moved in perfect order."

Significantly, New York Mayor Fernando Wood was not on hand to greet Lincoln that day. The previous month, Wood had proposed that New York declare a form of independence during the secession dispute, so as to continue "uninterrupted intercourse with every section" of the country. "When Disunion has become a fixed and certain fact," he declared, "why may not New York disrupt the bands which bind her to a venal and corrupt master?" The suggestion drew bitter criticism. "Wood evidently wants to be a traitor," wrote Horace Greeley. "It is lack of courage only that makes him content with being a blackguard." Lincoln's response, expressed privately, was equally cutting. "I reckon," he said, "it will be some time before the front door sets up housekeeping on its own account."

If Mayor Wood's views were extreme, they reflected New York's mood, which had turned anxious and pessimistic in the wake of the election. Businesses were faltering and the stock market had plummeted. Many New Yorkers believed that their troubles rested squarely on Lincoln's shoulders, and they greeted his arrival with "much respect," according to one reporter, but "little enthusiasm." Signs of the city's ambivalence could be seen clearly along the route to the Astor House. RIGHT MAKES MIGHT read one banner, a reference to Lincoln's triumphant Cooper Union address, but another urged the incoming president to show caution: WELCOME ABRAHAM LINCOLN, it read. WE BEG FOR COMPROMISE.

After bowing and doffing his hat for an hour and a half as the procession rolled slowly along, Lincoln arrived at last at the Astor House, located on Broadway between Vesey and Barclay streets. Across the street, watching from the top of a Broadway omnibus, the poet Walt Whitman looked on as Lincoln stepped out of his carriage. "The figure, the look, the gait, are distinctly impress'd upon me yet," Whitman wrote many years later. "All was comparative and ominous silence. The newcomer look'd with curiosity upon that immense sea of faces, and the sea of faces return'd the look with similar curiosity. In both there was a dash of something almost comical. Yet there was much anxiety in certain quarters. Cautious persons had fear'd that there would be some outbreak, some mark'd indignity or insult to the President elect on his passage through the city, for he possess'd no personal popularity in New York, and not much political. No such outbreak or insult, however, occurr'd." The poet went on to take a bit of license with the scene, looking back over the intervening years to suggest a presentiment of roiling dangers: "I had no doubt (so frenzied were the ferments of the time) many an assassin's knife and pistol lurk'd in hip or breast-pocket there—ready, soon as break and riot came."

While Whitman watched from the street, Kate Warne looked down on the scene from the top floor of the hotel. "Lincoln looked very pale and fatigued," she noted in her field report. "He was standing in his carriage bowing when I first saw him. From the carriage he went directly into the house, and soon after appeared on the balcony." As had become his habit, Lincoln attempted to deflect the calls for an impromptu speech, insisting that he had "nothing to say just now worth your hearing," but the crowd persisted. Mrs. Warne looked on as he ventured a few remarks, but "there was such a noise it was impossible to hear what he said."

For Mrs. Warne, it had been a day of frustrations. Her train ride from Baltimore had been an eleven-hour crawl, finally reaching New York at the inhospitable hour of 4:00 A.M. She then made her way to the Astor House, where, "after much trouble," she succeeded in getting a room. Weary from the unpleasant journey, she tried to get a few hours of rest but found herself unable to sleep. She rose and breakfasted at 7:30, then settled down in her room, awaiting the chance to meet with Norman Judd. In the meantime, Mrs. Warne hoped to make contact with Edward Sanford to deliver the other message Pinkerton had left in her care. Summoning a messenger boy, she sent a note to Sanford's office to arrange a meeting, and waited with increasing impatience for a reply. Finally, at three o'clock that afternoon, she sent a second message, underscoring the urgency of her errand. At this, Sanford replied, saying that he was unavailable but would call on Mrs. Warne that evening. In the meantime, upon seeing Lincoln arrive, Mrs. Warne dispatched a note to Judd, asking him to come to her room as soon as convenient. "I gave the note to the bell-boy and told him to deliver [it] immediately," she noted in her field report, but her hopes for a prompt meeting were dashed when the messenger returned with the news that Judd had been left behind in Albany. Exasperated, Mrs. Warne pulled a chair to the window and resumed her vigil.

Several hours later, as Judd belatedly straggled into the Astor House, the hotel bellboy pressed Mrs. Warne's note into his hand. Judd lost no time in answering the summons, having been well primed by his earlier messages from Pinkerton. "I followed the servant to one of the upper rooms of the hotel," he recalled, "where, upon entering, I found a lady seated at a table with some papers before her. She arose as I entered."

Judd took a moment to assess the agreeable, if understated, young woman standing before him, likely wondering why Allan Pinkerton had sent a woman to do a man's job. Seeing his hesitation, Mrs. Warne hurried forward and offered her hand. "Mr. Judd, I presume," she said crisply.

Judd gave a curt nod. "Yes, madam," he replied, but before he could speak further, Mrs. Warne guided him firmly to a chair, explaining that Pinkerton had sent her to New York because he "did not like to trust the mail in so important a matter." Judd had been expecting as much, and he apparently felt the need to steel himself for the contents of Pinkerton's letter. On the long journey from Springfield, John Hay and others had become accustomed to seeing Judd with an unlighted cigar clamped between his teeth. Now, as Mrs. Warne passed over the envelope from Pinkerton, Judd asked for her permission to light up.

Judd tore open the letter and read through it with visible agitation. Once again, Pinkerton had been sparing with his details. New evidence of a plot against Lincoln had come to light, he insisted, but the particulars were too sensitive to be shared in a letter. It was imperative, however, that Judd be prepared to take whatever action would be necessary when the time came. In the meantime, Pinkerton and his operatives would gather information and form a plan to meet the crisis. Mrs. Warne had been instructed to arrange a face-to-face meeting with Pinkerton at Judd's earliest-possible convenience. At that time, the detective promised, all would be revealed.

For several moments, Judd said nothing. He read through the letter a second time, sending up a thick plume of cigar smoke, then allowed the paper to dangle from his fingers. Up to this point, he had kept his own counsel about the bulletins Pinkerton had sent from Baltimore, so as to "avoid causing any anxiety on the part of Mr. Lincoln." Now, after staying silent for nearly a week, he worried that he had badly misjudged the seriousness of the situation. Pinkerton had made it plain that nothing more could be revealed until they met in person, but Judd was not willing to wait. Desperate for more detail, he rounded on Mrs. Warne. What, exactly, was this new evidence? How many conspirators were in on the plot? Why had Pinkerton not gone to the police?

"Mr. Judd asked me a great many questions, which I did not answer," Mrs. Warne recalled. "I told him that I could not talk on the business." Instead, she promised Judd that she would hand-carry a message directly to Pinkerton in Baltimore. The two of them could speak in person the following day so that "all the proofs relating to the conspiracy could be submitted."

This did nothing to calm Judd's fears. "He said he was much alarmed and would like to show the letter I had given him to some of the party," Mrs. Warne wrote, "and also consult the New York police about it." Mrs. Warne stood firm. She told Judd that he was "to do no such thing," and advised him to "keep cool" until the meeting with Pinkerton could be arranged.

Pinkerton had feared just such a response from Judd, and was counting on Mrs. Warne's considerable powers of persuasion to keep him in check. Pinkerton earnestly believed that bringing others in on the plot would pose a danger to his agents in the field, and limit his options in dealing with the threat. Secrecy, as he had told Samuel Felton, was the lever that guaranteed his success. Any wider discussion of his discoveries within Lincoln's circle would almost certainly spark rumors in the press. If that were to happen, the conspirators might well abandon their current plan and form a new one, and Pinkerton's hard-won information would become useless.

For the moment, Mrs. Warne's arguments appeared to be having little effect. Judd began to pace the room, puffing hard at his cigar. After a moment, he asked if Pinkerton couldn't be summoned to New York immediately. Mrs. Warne calmly pointed out that Pinkerton couldn't possibly reach the city before Lincoln was scheduled to depart. This served only to deepen Judd's gloom. He repeated that he "did not know what to do" and felt he must "consult with one of his party" to determine a course of action. Mrs. Warne furrowed her brow and said nothing. She now feared that Pinkerton's decision to confide in Judd was about to backfire.

At that moment, help arrived from an unexpected quarter as Edward Sanford, Pinkerton's client in the Adams Express robbery, appeared at the door of Mrs. Warne's room. The last time Sanford had seen Mrs. Warne, she had been streaked in grime from digging in a dirt cellar for his company's stolen money. Meeting her again now, Sanford swept into the room and clasped Mrs. Warne's hands in a warm greeting, praising her lavishly as someone to whom he owed a great debt.

Sanford's effusive words seemed to have a calming effect on Norman Judd. After Mrs. Warne made the introductions, she handed Sanford his letter from Pinkerton, asking for his assistance in making arrangements to conduct Lincoln safely through Baltimore. When Sanford finished reading the letter, he passed it over to Judd. Although this second message offered no new information, Judd took added reassurance from the fact that Pinkerton was already laying plans with Sanford to meet the crisis. As his mood brightened, Judd told Sanford that everything appeared to be "all right" now. Pinkerton, it appeared, was a man of sound judgment. Sanford heartily agreed, and he offered Judd the use of the American Telegraph Company's lines for any communication he might wish to make. Judd declined, saying that he would withdraw to his room for the moment to consider the matter further.

Mrs. Warne was filled with misgivings as Judd rose to leave. She repeated her warning about keeping Pinkerton's concerns quiet. Judd offered no promises, saying only that he would return with further instructions later that evening. This was far from reassuring, but for the moment Mrs. Warne had little choice but to stand aside and hope that he would honor Pinkerton's wishes. As the door closed behind Judd, Mrs. Warne found herself alone with Edward Sanford, whose own curiosity had been inflamed by Pinkerton's message. Based on his business relationship with the agency, Sanford believed he was entitled to Mrs. Warne's full confidence. "Now," he said, with an air of getting down to business, "what is the trouble?" Once again, Mrs. Warne found herself deflecting questions about the drama unfolding in Baltimore. She insisted that she had merely come to New York as a courier for Pinkerton, and "that was all I had to say on [the] business." Sanford was far from satisfied with this answer. As he pressed harder, Mrs. Warne grew impatient, having covered much of the same ground with Judd moments earlier. "There is no reason why I should tell all I know," she said tersely. "I have no more to say."

Sanford pounced on this statement as an admission that Mrs. Warne knew more than she was telling. "There *is* something more," he insisted, his temper flaring. "If you will only tell me how you are situated, and what you are doing at Baltimore, I can better judge how to act." Mrs. Warne held firm, repeating only that she had "nothing more to say." Sanford grumbled at this, complaining that Mrs. Warne was taking unfair advantage of him. Perhaps, he said, she had entangled so many men with her wily deceits that she could no longer be "roped" herself. Mrs. Warne answered him with a laugh. "It is as easy to 'rope' me as anyone else," she admitted, "but just now I really have nothing to say." Her lighthearted response had the desired effect: "Mr. Sanford laughed at this, and said that I was a strange woman." To her relief, his anger had vanished, and he now "seemed good-natured again."

In fact, Mrs. Warne was paying the price for carrying out Pinkerton's orders to the letter and adhering to his increasingly impracticable demands for secrecy. Both Sanford and Judd were powerful men who were used to getting their own way, and who would have been unaccustomed to such treatment from a young woman, no matter how skilled at "roping" she may have been. Pinkerton had placed her in the untenable position of securing their cooperation on a vague promise of evidence to come. Her skill and tact may be gauged by the fact that Sanford now turned to her for advice in writing a dispatch to Pinkerton, pledging his full support in whatever lay ahead. Sanford also offered the services of a "young attaché" named George H. Burns, who had carried messages back and forth to Mrs. Warne earlier in the day. Burns, Sanford explained, would be able to take full control of the telegraph wires carrying messages in and out of Baltimore, allowing Pinkerton to monitor the lines or cut off communications entirely if he saw fit. "He was [now] very friendly," Mrs. Warne wrote, "and stayed until after 10:00, when he bade me good night."

Pausing at the door, Sanford tried one last time to draw out further information, expressing surprise that Pinkerton and Mrs. Warne were so "frightened" by what they had discovered in Baltimore. "I suppose he thought now that I would go on and tell him all I knew, but I said nothing," Mrs. Warne declared, "only that we were not frightened, and what was more I had never known Mr. Pinkerton to *be* frightened." Sanford took this rebuff in good humor, then left, promising to keep in close contact.

Sanford had barely closed the door behind him when a telegram arrived from Pinkerton. Mrs. Warne read it with rising dread, knowing that it would touch off a fresh round of difficulties. "I immediately sent for Judd," she recalled, "who came at once to my room." Closing the door behind her, Mrs. Warne passed over the folded telegraph slip, which read:

```
"Tell Judd I meant all I said, and that today they offer ten
for one, and twenty for two."
```

Judd did not have to be told the meaning of this cryptic message. Pinkerton was simply reporting the latest word from the streets of Baltimore, where the local "sporting men" were setting odds that Lincoln would not pass through the city with his life.

CHAPTER SEVENTEEN
THE MUSIC AGENT

·

I was advised on Thursday morning of a plot in Baltimore to assassinate the President-elect on his expected arrival there. . . . I sent Fred to apprise him of it.
—WILLIAM H. SEWARD, in a letter to his family, February 23, 1861

AS THE SUN ROSE on the clear and chilly morning of Wednesday, February 20, New York's City Hall and the Astor House hotel appeared to be staring each other down across the wide expanse of Broadway. The imposing bulk of City Hall put its best face forward with a brilliant facade of Massachusetts marble, but at the rear the building gave way to more economical Newark brownstone, reflecting a shortage of funds during construction. By contrast, the stolid granite exterior of the Astor House—with its Doric columns and entablature—masked a gleaming modern interior of black walnut, with a tree-shaded central courtyard under a high rotunda of cast-iron and glass. In between the two landmarks, white slabs of a shiny pavement known as Russ created a slick surface, treacherous in wet weather, where even the horses were known to lose their footing.

At eleven o'clock that morning, Lincoln emerged from the Astor House and was driven the short distance across Broadway in an open carriage, "amid the most enthusiastic cheering" of the crowds gathered outside, to attend a reception at City Hall. On this occasion, Lincoln's host would be Fernando Wood, the charismatic and crafty mayor of New York City, whom a colleague would recall as "the handsomest man I ever saw, and the most corrupt man that ever sat in the Mayor's chair."

Mayor Wood, who had pointedly declined to welcome Lincoln to the city the previous day, now received him in the lavish Governor's Room on the second floor, availing himself of the many symbolic features of the room: "Mr. Lincoln entered, hat in hand, and advanced to where Mayor Wood was posted," reported the *New York Times,* "behind Washington's writing desk, and immediately in front of Governor Seward's portrait." Backed by the stern full-length image of Seward, New York's most outspoken proponent of compromise, Wood took the occasion to deliver a lecture on the "political divisions" that had "sorely afflicted" his city, and expressed concern that "the present supremacy of New York may perish" if the Union should be dissolved. "To you," he told the president-elect, "we look for a restoration of fraternal relations between the States, only to be accomplished by peaceful and conciliatory means—aided by the wisdom of God."

A murmur of disapproval ran through the room at this high-handed moralizing, but Lincoln, according to the *Times,* managed to preserve his "characteristically thoughtful look" until Wood concluded his remarks. Now, as he made to reply, he "brightened his face with a pleasant smile," and expressed gratitude for the kind reception he had received in a city whose residents "do not, by a large majority, agree with me in political sentiment." Nevertheless, he continued, he believed that New Yorkers stood with him in support of the "great principles" underpinning the government. "In regard to the difficulties that confront us at this time," he declared, "I can only say that I agree with the sentiments expressed by the Mayor. In my devotion to the Union, I hope I am behind no man in the nation . . . There is nothing that could ever bring me to consent— willingly to consent—to the destruction of this Union, in which not only the great City of New York, but the whole country has acquired its greatness, unless it would be that thing for which the Union itself was made." He then expanded on this last remark with a graceful play on the familiar metaphor of a "ship of state": "I understand that the ship is made for the carrying and preservation of the cargo, and so long as the ship is safe with the cargo it shall not be abandoned. This Union shall never be abandoned unless the possibility of its existence shall cease to exist, without the necessity of throwing passengers and cargo overboard."

For many New Yorkers, these aptly chosen words marked a turning point. The previous day, the Reverend Irenaeus Prime, an editor of the *New York Observer,* had expressed "overwhelming" disappointment at the sight of Lincoln, "looking weary, sad, feeble and faint" as he passed along Fifth Avenue. "He did not look to me to be the man for the hour." Today, however, the Reverend Prime found himself duly converted. "Mr. Lincoln's reply was so modest, firm, patriotic, and pertinent, that my fears of the day before began to subside, and I saw in this new man a promise of great things to come."

That sense of promise was much in evidence at the reception that followed Lincoln's remarks, during which some five thousand New Yorkers were hurried through the Governor's Room as if "discharged by a piece of ordnance." It was amusing, said the *Times,* to see "the bewildered look of the injected visitors" as they were hustled through the receiving line by police and soldiers. Lincoln shook hands and exchanged pleasantries for the better part of two hours, then followed this effort with a speech from the second-floor balcony of City Hall. Once again, the careful preparations of Superintendent John Kennedy were much in evidence. At the conclusion of the speech, a line of officers "suddenly faced outwards," rapidly clearing a path for Lincoln's exit.

Under Kennedy's watchful eye, Lincoln enjoyed one of the smoothest days of his journey as he made his rounds in New York. At the Astor House that morning, he had greeted a ninety-four-year-old supporter who had voted in every presidential election to date, going all the way back to George Washington. That afternoon, he accepted a pair of new hats from rival manufacturers, and diplomatically avoided expressing a preference between the two: "They mutually surpassed each other," he managed to say. Mrs. Lincoln and the boys, meanwhile, accepted an invitation from P. T. Barnum to visit his celebrated "American Museum" on Broadway at Ann Street, where the exhibitions at that time included Major Little Finger—a "less intelligent" relation of Tom Thumb—as well as "The Great Grizzly Mammoth Bear Samson," said to weigh two thousand pounds. Seven-year-old Tad declined to join the visit at the last moment, claiming that he had seen more than enough bears back home in Springfield.

That evening, Lincoln dined in unaccustomed luxury at the Astor House with vice president–elect Hannibal Hamlin, whose own inaugural journey from Maine had brought him to New York that afternoon. Hamlin would recall that Lincoln appeared bemused when confronted with a plate of oysters on the half shell. "Well," he remarked, "I don't know that I can manage these things, but I guess I can learn." Afterward, both men attended a performance of Verdi's *A Masked Ball* at the Academy of Music, slipping into their box after the curtain rose on the first act. Curious patrons subjected the pair to a "double-barreled opera glass attack," which was followed, as word of their presence spread, by a rousing chorus of

"The Star-Spangled Banner." Lincoln, exhausted by the day's labors, ducked out before the end of the performance, and gave Hamlin the job of addressing a crowd of supporters gathered outside the hotel.

KATE WARNE, also exhausted from her exertions in New York, had made her way back to Baltimore to report to Pinkerton by that time. "I went to bed tired," she said of her efforts the previous evening, after talking long into the night with Norman Judd at the Astor House. Judd's concerns about Lincoln's safety had been reignited by Pinkerton's "ten for one" telegram, reporting the odds given in Baltimore's betting shops that Lincoln could not pass through the city alive. Though Pinkerton had intended simply to impress Judd with the gravity of the situation, so as to ensure the politician's full cooperation, the message brought Judd to the edge of panic. Though he stopped short of carrying the message straight to Lincoln, he told Mrs. Warne that he wanted her to meet with Hannibal Hamlin as soon as he reached New York. "I said that it would never do," Mrs. Warne reported, adding firmly "that I could not say anything more to Hamlin than I had said to him." Seeing that she would not budge, Judd's anxiety eventually exhausted itself. It was agreed that Mrs. Warne would leave for Baltimore on a morning train, as planned, and make arrangements for Pinkerton to rendezvous with Judd in Philadelphia, Lincoln's next stop. The time and place of the meeting would have to be arranged on arrival, but Judd knew that he would not be hard to find: "I informed her," he later recalled, "that I should be in the carriage with Mr. Lincoln" as he greeted the citizens of Philadelphia.

Mrs. Warne would not have been the only detective working late that night. New York's police superintendent, John Kennedy, was also said to be laboring "deep into the weary hours" to ensure that Lincoln's remaining time in the city passed without incident. According to the *Times,* Lincoln had "frequently expressed his admiration of the excellent police arrangements" throughout his stay, and he even had Kennedy brought to the Astor House so that he "might be complimented as he deserved." Kennedy accepted the thanks gladly, but assured Lincoln that he and his men had simply been carrying out their duty. "Well," Lincoln is reported to have said, "a man ought to be thanked when he does his duty right well."

In fact, Kennedy was doing far more than his duty. The previous month, he had been summoned to Washington to accept a politically sensitive commission. Capt. George W. Walling, later a chief of police, joined him on the express train to the capital. "During the journey the Superintendent told me of the condition of affairs," Walling recalled. "I learned that the Washington authorities were uneasy. They had requested that some of the most trustworthy officers of the New York police should be detailed for service in Baltimore to ascertain what grounds there were for such suspicions." The reason for the concern, Walling continued, was "the state of public feeling in Maryland, especially in Baltimore, through which Mr. Lincoln was to pass on his way to Washington to assume office. Riots were feared, and there were sinister rumors of threatened attempts to assassinate the President-elect."

On reaching Washington, the two men received a briefing from an official they later declined to name. "With secret instructions from this gentleman we went to Baltimore," Walling reported. "Mr. Kennedy's duty was a very delicate one. We were soon satisfied that Baltimore was bitterly irritated, but whether the feeling against Mr. Lincoln was personal enough to make his passage through the city dangerous was hard to determine. The situation demanded closer investigation." Digging deeper, Kennedy sought out his counterpart in the local police force, Marshal George P. Kane, a man whose loyalties he had already come to doubt. "I ascertained from Marshal Kane himself the plan by which Maryland was to be precipitated out of the Union, against the efforts of Governor Hicks to keep it there," Kennedy would write. "He told me Maryland would wait for the action of Virginia, and that action would take place within a month; and 'that when Virginia seceded through a convention, Maryland would secede by gravitation.'"

Kennedy, like Pinkerton, declined to place his confidence in a man who publicly advocated secession. Instead, he instructed Captain Walling to dispatch a pair of detectives to Baltimore to begin working under cover. After giving the situation much "anxious thought," Walling selected two experienced officers, Thomas Sampson and Ely DeVoe, who began operating under the names of Anderson and Davis. "They were instructed to go to Baltimore, look over the ground and ingratiate themselves with disaffected persons," Walling wrote. "In other words, to use their own discretion and find out all they could." The two detectives were to report their findings to Col. Charles P. Stone in Washington. Stone was one of two men serving as a "right hand" to Gen. Winfield Scott. The other, as fate would have it, was Col. Robert E. Lee. ("I do not know what induced me to select Stone in preference to Colonel Lee," Kennedy would later admit, "but I did so.")

•

BY THEIR OWN ADMISSION, Sampson and DeVoe played their roles with gusto. "As soon as we reached our destination we assumed the role of Southern sympathizers and mixed freely with the secessionists," Sampson recalled. "We were well supplied with money, very swaggering and loud-mouthed, and soon made friends with a certain class of Southerners whose talk was 'fight to kill.' We stayed at the Fountain Inn and for some weeks had a good time. By degrees we worked our way into the confidence of our new friends."

By the time Allan Pinkerton and his Chicago detectives reached Balti-more in early February, Sampson and DeVoe were already hard at work. For more than two weeks, Kennedy's men and Pinkerton's were working on parallel tracks, but the two teams were unaware of each other's efforts for most of that time. It is likely, given the many points of intersection between the two investigations, that at times Pinkerton's men were liter-ally tripping over Sampson and DeVoe. Had Pinkerton known of their efforts, he would likely have admired their ingenuity. Though Pinkerton had more men on the ground, the New Yorkers had managed in a very short time to infiltrate Baltimore's secret societies and military units. The major difference lay in what the two teams were doing with the intelli-gence they gathered. Pinkerton was communicating directly with Lin-coln's suite as they made their way across the country, while Kennedy funneled his information down to Washington. The fact that Sampson and DeVoe were headquartered at the Fountain Hotel, the name of which had been used to signal Lucius Chittenden on his mysterious dead-of-night errand to Baltimore in mid-February, suggests that Chittenden's "committee of safety" had direct ties to the Kennedy network.

As matters stood, however, the two teams were likely working at cross purposes on more than one occasion. Both Otis Hillard and Cypriano Ferrandini complained to Pinkerton's men of being under constant ob-servation by "government spies," and it is possible that the presence of the New York investigators contributed to this climate of suspicion. On the evening of Pinkerton's meeting with Ferrandini at Barr's Saloon—during which the Italian barber had declared that "Lincoln shall die in this city"—the detective's efforts had been hampered by a "pair of strangers" who appeared to be eavesdropping on the conversation. Their presence had caused Ferrandini to cut his remarks short, and Pinkerton was greatly annoyed at having to remain behind to keep watch over the interlopers. It is entirely possible that the two strangers were none other than Sampson and DeVoe.

In any event, while Sampson and DeVoe worked their way into a company of "Southern Volunteers," Superintendent Kennedy dispatched a third man to Baltimore, an officer named David S. Bookstaver, who took the identity of a "music agent" with interests at the city's theaters and concert halls. While Sampson and DeVoe mixed with "rebel roughs," Kennedy wrote, "Bookstaver gave particular attention to the sayings and doings of the better class of citizens and strangers who frequent music, variety, and book stores."

For Bookstaver, the situation reached a crisis point on Wednesday, February 20, the same day that Kate Warne returned from New York under orders from Norman Judd. On that day, according to Kennedy, Bookstaver obtained information that "made it necessary for him to take the first train for Washington." Arriving in the capital early on Thursday morning, Bookstaver sought out the team's Washington contact, Col. Charles P. Stone. By some accounts, Bookstaver was so eager to make his report that he tracked Stone to his rooming house and pulled him out of bed. In any case, the New York detective soon had Stone's full attention.

Bookstaver gave Stone a hurried summary of what he had learned during his three weeks in Baltimore. During that time, he had often "heard threats of mobbing and violence," but he had dismissed much of this talk as empty barroom chatter. Now, he said, he had cause to believe otherwise. Within the past few days, he had learned of a "serious danger of violence" in Baltimore, as well as a concrete plan for "the assassination of Mr. Lincoln" during his passage through the city. Unless something was done, Lincoln would surely die before he reached Washington.

Afterward, Bookstaver declined to record the precise details that had convinced him of the sudden urgency of the situation, nor did he give any accounting of how he had acquired the information. Whatever he said that morning, however, left Colonel Stone thoroughly convinced. As soon as Bookstaver finished speaking, Stone rushed the warning directly to General Scott, who now considered the threat in Baltimore to be an established fact. Bookstaver, he said, had provided "the closing piece of information" that confirmed the dark suspicions he and his men had formed in the previous weeks, being "entirely corroborative" of the thick file of warnings and rumors "already in our possession."

Time was growing short. Lincoln was due to reach Baltimore in two day's time, at 12:30 on the afternoon of Saturday, February 23. As a military man, Scott realized that the Baltimore plotters had a crucial advantage. Lincoln's itinerary had been a matter of public record for weeks, making it all too easy for potential assassins to lay their plans. In order to foil these designs, Scott knew, Lincoln would have to break away from the moment-by-moment timetable he had followed since leaving Spring-field. As Colonel Stone declared, "All risk might be easily avoided by a change in the travelling arrangements."

If this seemed plain enough to a military man, General Scott knew that a politician would see the matter differently. He told Stone that Lincoln's "personal dignity would revolt" at the idea of making any change to his plans, even "on account of danger to his life." Stone objected strenuously. "Mr. Lincoln's personal dignity was of small account in comparison with the destruction, or, at least, dangerous disorganization of the United States government," he insisted, "which would be the inevitable result of his death by violence in Baltimore." If the planned assassination were to succeed, Stone declared, "we should find ourselves in the worst form of civil war, with the Government utterly unprepared for it."

General Scott needed no persuading on this point. The difficulty, he believed, lay in making the case to Lincoln, and convincing him to take the necessary steps. Although Scott had already been in touch with Lincoln several times since the election, he saw that this task would have to be entrusted to someone with greater influence than he had. He quickly decided that Senator Seward, who was also known to be concerned for Lincoln's safety, offered the best chance of success. In the months following the election, Lincoln had been extremely solicitous of his defeated rival, seeking the senator's advice on cabinet appointments and submitting a draft of his inaugural address for Seward's approval. General Scott reasoned that if Seward put his weight behind the assassination concerns, Lincoln might be convinced that he was "not coming to Washington to be inaugurated as quietly as any previous President."

Having decided on this course of action, Scott jotted a note to Seward. He told the senator that Colonel Stone, a "distinguished young officer," was acting on his behalf: "He has an important communication to make." Stone took the message to Seward at the Capitol and then gave him a summary of what he had learned from Bookstaver. Seward "listened attentively to what I said," Stone recalled, and asked a number of questions. Like General Scott, the senator took Bookstaver's warning as confirmation of his own fears. He asked Scott to write down his information and invited him to add any suggestions he cared to make. Once this was done, Seward took the paper and hurried from the room.

Seward wanted to get the message into Lincoln's hands as soon as possible, but he also believed that the situation's "peculiar sensitiveness," as he phrased it, required him to remain in Washington. Since he could not carry the message to Lincoln himself, and because he felt that the telegraph wires couldn't be trusted in such circumstances, he needed a messenger in whom he could place his full confidence. As it happened, there was someone close at hand: Seward's thirty-year-old son, Frederick.

The younger Seward, an editor of the *Albany Evening Journal*, was seated in the gallery of the Senate Chamber when a page approached and touched him lightly on the arm, whispering that his father wished to see him. "Going down I met him in the lobby," he recalled. In hushed tones, the elder Seward explained the situation and passed over a brief note he had written to Lincoln, along with the messages from Scott and Stone. "Whether this story is well founded or not, Mr. Lincoln ought to know of it at once," Senator Seward told his son, "but I know of no reason to doubt it. General Scott is impressed with the belief that the danger is real. Colonel Stone has facilities for knowing, and is not apt to exaggerate." The senator paused, glancing around to make certain he was not being overheard. "I want you to go by the first train," he continued. "Find Mr. Lincoln wherever he is, and let no one else know your errand!"

The younger Seward set off at once for the station and boarded a train for Philadelphia, his mind churning with anxiety and regret. "The time had not yet come," he would later write, "when Americans in general could realize that a crime at once so nefarious and so foolish as the assassination of the Chief Magistrate was possible."

Seward was fully convinced that Abraham Lincoln's survival rested on his shoulders, and he had no way of knowing, as he passed through Baltimore on his way north, that Allan Pinkerton was already speeding toward Philadelphia on the same mission.

CHAPTER EIGHTEEN
A FEW DETERMINED MEN

·

PRESIDENT ABRAHAM LINCOLN departs today for Washington, and the
WINDOWS AND BALCONIES OF THE MUSEUM afford a fine view of him as
HE LEAVES THE ASTOR HOUSE AND PASSES DOWN BROADWAY, directly
in front of the Museum, so that he will be seen plainly and distinctly. Who will not
embrace the opportunity to look upon the NATION'S HEAD, the NATION'S
DELIVERER, the PEOPLE'S FAVORITE and FRIEND?
Remember, this is the last chance in New York.
—advertisement for Barnum's American Museum, February 21, 1861

EARLY ON THE MORNING of February 21, even as David Bookstaver made his report to Charles Stone in Washington, Abraham Lincoln boarded a steam ferry at New York's Cortlandt Street terminal for a brief, choppy crossing of the Hudson River to New Jersey, the first leg of that day's travel to Philadelphia. It was soon apparent, as Lincoln came ashore to a familiar scene of chaos at the landing in Jersey City, that he had passed out of Superintendent John Kennedy's efficient jurisdiction. "The Jersey police were overwhelmed," reported the *New York Times*. "Vainly did they brandish their clubs and push the crowd back." As Lincoln moved toward the train that would carry him south, an enthusiastic "Son of Erin" barreled out of the crowd in a giddy effort to shake his hand. The police detail quickly surrounded the eager Irishman and duly "punched him off the platform" with their clubs, much to the amusement of the crowd. As the multitudes surged again, however, the police line gave way. "It was like being in a hydraulic press," wrote Joseph Howard. "Verily, our reporter's bowels ache when he mentally recalls that excruciating collapse." As Howard and the other "compressed unfortunates" howled with pain, their cries were taken to be cheers for Lincoln.

Lincoln, shielded by his escorts, would have been pleased to hear any sound that could be mistaken for cheering that morning. For the first time, he had entered a state that he had not carried in the election. New Jersey had gone to Stephen Douglas by a narrow margin, and signs of ambivalence, if not outright hostility, were plainly visible along the route. In Newark, where Lincoln paused to give a pair of speeches later that morning, his carriage passed a black-bearded effigy swinging by the neck from a lamppost, together with a placard reading THE TRAITOR'S DOOM.

By noon, Lincoln had reached Trenton, where a heaving crowd at the train depot "beat down the line of feeble constables" with a mighty rush, swarming forward as Lincoln entered his carriage. Howard reported himself sorry to see Lincoln and his suite struggling in the crush, but he admitted to a certain satisfaction in the distress of the local worthies: "It did me good to see them pummeled, pushed and squeezed," he wrote.

In the first of two speeches at the New Jersey State House, Lincoln departed from his prepared remarks to offer a fond recollection of childhood. He spoke of the pleasure he had found in his early reading of Weem's *Life of Washington,* with its epic description of the general crossing the Delaware River in advance of the Battle of Trenton. After recalling the manner in which the "struggle here at Trenton" had fixed itself in his imagination, Lincoln deftly linked Washington's triumph to the crisis ahead. "I am exceedingly anxious that this Union, this Constitution, and the liberties of the people shall be perpetuated," he declared, "in accordance with the original idea for which that struggle was made."

Lincoln made the point even more forcefully in his second speech, this time before the state senate. "The man does not live who is more devoted to peace than I am," he declared, drawing a round of cheers from the legislators. "None would do more to preserve it. But it may be necessary to put the foot down firmly." At this, John Hay reported, Lincoln "lifted his foot lightly, and pressed it with a quick, but not violent, gesture upon the floor." Wild applause and cheers greeted this display, and several moments passed before he could resume. "And if I do my duty, and do right, you will sustain me, will you not?" As a second wave of cheers passed through the chamber, Lincoln reminded his audience of the enormity of the task ahead. Recalling his comments in New York the previous day, he asked for assistance in "piloting the ship of State through this voyage, surrounded by perils as it is." If the ship should suffer attack now, he warned, "there will be no pilot ever needed for another voyage."

ALLAN PINKERTON HAD ALREADY put in a long day in Philadelphia by this time, rushing from place to place—head bent forward, one arm tucked behind his back—as he tried to put the finishing touches on a "plan of operation" he had devised in Baltimore. Much had changed since Pinkerton's previous visit to the Quaker City, some three weeks earlier, when he had first learned of Samuel Felton's concerns for the safety of his railroad. In light of what he had now uncovered in Baltimore, Pinkerton believed that Lincoln could no longer be tethered to William Wood's moment-by-moment timetable, as this ready catalog of his movements played directly into the hands of the conspirators. It had become an "absolute necessity" to abandon the well-publicized itinerary and proceed directly to Washington that very night, under the detective's personal protection. If Pinkerton could spirit Lincoln through the city ahead of schedule, the assassins would be caught off guard. By the time they took their places for the scheduled arrival in Baltimore, Lincoln would already be safe in Washington.

Pinkerton knew that what he was proposing would be risky and perhaps even foolhardy. Even if Lincoln departed ahead of schedule, the route to the capital would pass through Baltimore in any case. If any hint of a change of plan leaked out, Lincoln's position would become far more precarious. Instead of traveling openly with his full complement of friends and protectors, he would be relatively alone and exposed, with only one or two men at his side. That being the case, Pinkerton knew that secrecy was even more critical than ever. He suspected that Lincoln was being watched at every moment by "rebel spirits," who sent regular reports of the president-elect's movements to "sympathetic parties" in the South. Any suggestion of a break from the published timetable would sound alarms that would be heard in Baltimore.

The dark weight of Pinkerton's mission contrasted sharply with the cheery scenes all around him. "The streets were alive with the eager populace, all anxious to do honor to the new President," he reported. Philadelphia had been a late addition to Lincoln's itinerary, and the city's politicians and "committee men" had scrambled to get ready in time. "Great preparations had been made," Pinkerton wrote, "and the military, of which Philadelphia was justly proud, were to escort the President-elect from the depot to the Continental Hotel, where quarters had been engaged for him, and where he would receive the congratulations of the people." The Continental, a six-story showplace completed one year earlier, had been fully booked in anticipation of Lincoln's arrival, so Pinkerton took a room at the nearby St. Louis, a quieter and more understated hotel and one that better suited his purpose. He also reserved a room for Kate Warne, who would be joining him in Philadelphia. If Pinkerton's plan came together as he hoped it would, Mrs. Warne would be playing her most challenging role yet.

Shortly after 9:00 A.M., Pinkerton met up with Samuel Felton in front of a hotel on Broad Street, and walked along with him toward the depot of the PW&B Railroad. The two men had much to discuss. Pinkerton was deeply conscious of the fact that everything he had learned over the course of the previous weeks had come at Felton's instigation, and that the railroad president had financed the operation at great expense to his company. Pinkerton had always operated on the principle that any information he gathered in the field belonged to the man who had hired him. Though the discovery of the assassination plot had sent Pinkerton's efforts along a different track, the detective felt a clear responsibility to his employer even at this crucial moment. "I deemed it my duty," Pinkerton said, "to communicate the [facts] to Mr. Felton. I said to him that I knew this information was theirs but I knew of no reason why it should not be imparted to Mr. Lincoln or his friends with a view to avoiding the peril."

As the two men walked through the streets, Pinkerton outlined everything he had learned in Baltimore. He told Felton that his investigation left no room for doubt: "[T]here would be an attempt made to assassinate Mr. Lincoln." Even if some of the intelligence he had gathered was untrustworthy, he said, there had been such an accumulation of evidence that Pinkerton had no question of the overarching threat. Pinkerton enumerated all of the disparate elements—his distrust of Marshal Kane, Harry Davies's report on Ferrandini's secret meeting, Timothy Webster's dispatches from Perrymansville—but he was careful not to exaggerate the scope of the plot. While some rumors placed the number of active conspirators in the thousands, Pinkerton insisted that he did not believe there was "any large organization or body of men who would be willing to go so far." Instead, based solely on the information he could verify, he concluded that there were no more than twenty men "who would be reckless enough to attempt anything of the kind." This was far from comforting, however, since the detective had no doubt that "a few determined men" working in concert could easily succeed. He reminded Felton that all mobs, "especially a Baltimore mob," were dangerously volatile: "[T]he first shot fired, the first blow struck, and the whole became a living mass of mad, ungovernable people." Moreover, Pinkerton concluded, returning to the original purpose of his investigation, if the plot were successful, Felton's railroad would be destroyed to prevent retaliation by Northern troops.

To Pinkerton's relief, Felton gave his full support to the detective's plans. "Mr. Felton approved of what I had said and of the view I had taken of the case," Pinkerton reported. The railroad president also agreed "that there would be bloodshed in Mr. Lincoln's attempting to pass through Baltimore openly by the route proposed." Felton hoped it would be possible for Lincoln to depart for Washington that evening, perhaps taking a sleeping car through Baltimore in the dead of night. Felton assured Pinkerton that all of the resources of the PW&B would be placed at Lincoln's disposal.

Until that morning, Pinkerton had likely not realized the extent to which Felton's fears for Lincoln's safety had already been inflamed. In addition to Pinkerton's own reports, Felton had heard dire warnings from other sources, including the mysterious "gentleman from Baltimore" who had walked for miles to pass information to one of Felton's bridge keepers. Felton had become so concerned by these disparate threads of evidence that he had already mentioned the possibility of danger to a Philadelphia newspaper editor, Morton McMichael of the *North American*. Not surprisingly, McMichael had taken "a deep interest" in the matter. In fact, as Felton now told Pinkerton, the editor had left Philadelphia that morning to intercept the Lincoln Special, so that he might deliver a timely warning of the situation.

With effort, Pinkerton kept his temper in check. He had repeatedly told Felton that no one could be informed of the doings in Baltimore without placing his operatives at risk. Now, at this vital moment, Felton had placed the entire effort at the mercy of a newspaperman. Seeing Pinkerton's distress, Felton assured him that he had told McMichael not to mention the subject to anyone but Norman Judd—"not even to Mr. Lincoln himself"— but Pinkerton knew that it could only be a matter of hours before whispers began to appear in the press. This, in turn, would put the Baltimore plotters on alert.

Pinkerton was now more determined than ever to take control of Lincoln's itinerary and spirit him off to Washington that evening. Leaving Felton at his office, the detective hurried back to the St. Louis and told

Kate Warne to stand by for further instructions. Next, Pinkerton went in search of George H. Burns, the "young attaché" whom Edward Sanford had sent to assist. If Pinkerton's plan had any chance of success, he would need to meet with Norman Judd as soon as the Lincoln Special pulled into Philadelphia. Burns, who had acted as a courier between Sanford and Mrs. Warne in New York, was now given the job of carrying messages from Pinkerton to Judd. "I requested Mr. Burns to go to the Kensington Railroad Depot, and await the arrival of the Presidential Party [to] arrange for a meeting with myself and Mr. Felton at the earliest possible moment," Pinkerton noted in his field report. Knowing that there would be a vast crush of people waiting to see Lincoln at the Continental, Pinkerton decided that his room at the St. Louis would be the "best and safest" place to meet with Judd.

After dispatching Burns, Pinkerton rejoined Samuel Felton, whose concerns had now been further inflamed by a "curious telegram" from Hannibal Hamlin. The vice president–elect had wired to request a special car on the noon train from Philadelphia to Baltimore the following day, which would send him through the city a day ahead of Lincoln's scheduled passage on Saturday. For Pinkerton, this raised yet another dilemma. Hamlin's request suggested that security concerns had surfaced within Lincoln's inner circle. Pinkerton could only guess at the source, but, as Kate Warne had reported, Norman Judd had wanted to warn Hamlin the previous day. Although Judd had promised at the time to honor Pinkerton's request for discretion, Hamlin's telegram suggested that alarms had been sounded in any case.

Pinkerton knew that any change of plan for Hamlin would complicate the arrangements he hoped to make for Lincoln, especially if news of the change found its way to the press. Hoping to contain the information, Pinkerton arranged to use Edward Sanford's influence to prevent the item from being released over the wires of the American Telegraph Company. This would buy a bit of time, but if Hamlin was determined to press ahead with his change of plan, Pinkerton knew that "it would be advisable for us to meet Mr. Judd as early as possible and lay the whole matter before him."

As it happened, the chance to do so was now at hand. "Just at this time I heard the sound of music," Pinkerton reported, which meant that the city's marching bands had swung into action. Lincoln had at last reached Philadelphia.

AT THE KENSINGTON DEPOT, noted a reporter for the *Philadelphia Inquirer,* a "wild mass of human beings" jostled for a glimpse of the president-elect, "swaying to and fro in a manner which was equally destructive to the integrity of one's temper and one's integuments." Even as he struggled to preserve his poise and outer coverings, the newsman had praise for the manner in which Lincoln's honor guard of Hunter, Pope, and Hazard kept their heads in "frantic" circumstances, and he singled out the dashing young Colonel Ellsworth for his gallant efforts to protect Lincoln from "the importunities of curious crowds." As it happened, the military men also prevented George H. Burns, Pinkerton's young messenger, from delivering the detective's note to Norman Judd. Thrown back by the crowd and the security detail, Burns hurried outside, looking for a chance to intercept Judd as Lincoln's line of carriages made its four-mile procession toward the Continental Hotel.

The "pummeling, pushing and squeezing" continued along the parade route. "There were old men and young men, wives and maidens, matrons and children," noted the *Inquirer,* "all anxious for a sight of the hero of the hour." Mixing in with the throng were Pinkerton and Felton, drawn by the sounds of the approaching pageant. "All was excitement," Pinkerton observed, taking careful note of the security measures. "On each side of the carriage in which Mr. Lincoln was seated, accompanied by Mr. Judd, was a file of policemen whose duty it was to prevent the mass of people from pressing too closely to the vehicle." The unbroken line of policemen stood with linked arms along the entire length of the parade route, holding back the surging crowd while a squad of cavalry surrounded the carriage.

Impressive as these precautions were, George H. Burns remained determined to get Pinkerton's note into the hands of Norman Judd. As Lincoln's carriage rolled slowly through the streets, pulled by four plumed horses, Burns threaded his way through the crowd alongside, leaping up and down as he attempted to attract Judd's attention. Pinkerton looked on as Burns made a frantic effort to reach the carriage, heedless of the fact that he appeared for all the world to be a crazed assailant launching an attack on Lincoln himself.

"As the procession reached the corner of Broad and Chestnut streets," Pinkerton reported, Burns summoned all his strength and powered his way past the cordon of policemen. "I saw Mr. Burns break through the ranks of the officers, and coming to the side of the carriage, he handed to Mr. Judd a slip of paper on which was written: 'St. Louis Hotel, ask for J. H. Hutchinson.'" Shrugging off the approaches of nearby officers, Burns trotted alongside the carriage as Judd read the message and gave a verbal response. Then, gathering himself to reverse course, Burns plunged back through the police ranks and lost himself in the dense crowd, eventually finding Pinkerton outside the nearby La Pierre Hotel. Breathlessly, Burns told the detective that he had managed to fix a time for the meeting at 7:30 that evening. Pinkerton's face fell. If there was to be any hope of getting Lincoln on a train that same night, a 7:30 meeting would be too late. "I requested Mr. Burns to endeavor once more to see Mr. Judd," Pinkerton recalled, "and say to him that some circumstances had transpired which rendered it advisable to meet earlier." Hearing this, the young messenger turned and looked again at the line of policemen with linked arms and the squad of mounted soldiers. It must have seemed to Burns that he had been asked to take a second lap across the Hellespont.

Squaring his shoulders, Burns launched himself back into the fray. "How Mr. Burns was to get through the crowd and overtake the carriage I could not see, nor how he would again break the ranks of the police I could not tell," Pinkerton admitted, "but he left me and with superhuman strength I saw him go through the crowd like nothing, and bursting through the ranks of the police again reach the carriage. In a few minutes he returned and said that Mr. Judd would see me immediately at the St. Louis." Pinkerton nodded his approval, though the young messenger's heroics could not have eased his concerns about what lay ahead. If Burns could so readily reach Lincoln's side with a message, surely an assassin would be able to reach him with a knife.

As Lincoln's procession continued on to the Continental, Pinkerton returned to his room at the St. Louis and lit a fire. Samuel Felton arrived shortly afterward, but it was already 6:45 by the time Norman Judd managed to pull free and make his way to Pinkerton's room. Pinkerton, anxious about the hour, hastily introduced Judd to Felton and hurried both men into chairs by the fire. Felton would recall that he and Pinkerton were both so eager to get down to business that they began speaking at once: "We lost no time in making known to him all the facts which had come to our knowledge in reference to the conspiracy."

Judd listened attentively as Pinkerton elaborated on details that he had only hinted at in his earlier messages. The detective, looking to make his case in the most effective manner possible, took care to emphasize that the plot against Lincoln had come as a surprise to him. He had gone to Baltimore, he said, with no other purpose in mind than the protection of

Felton's railroad. Only in the course of pursuing that investigation had he "discovered the fact that some persons meditated the assassination of the President Elect." Felton, meanwhile, confirmed that corroborating information had come to him from other sources, and he insisted that he had no doubt that "there would be blood-shed in Baltimore" if Lincoln adhered to his published itinerary. At the same time, Pinkerton was careful not to exaggerate the scope of the threat. Again and again, he stressed that "a few resolute men" scattered through the crowd in Baltimore would be sufficient to precipitate a disaster. He asked Judd to imagine the likely consequences if Lincoln's party were to be "hemmed in" by the crowd and surrounded by "a small number of men acting in concert." It had been difficult enough, at the earlier stops on the itinerary, to get Lincoln safely through. In Buffalo, amid a crowd of enthusiastic supporters, the chaos had been so great "as to seriously injure Major Hunter." If the Baltimore crowd sheltered men who were bound and determined to strike Lincoln down, "even if they had to give a life for a life," it would be all but impossible to stop them.

Pinkerton spoke at length about such secessionists as Otis K. Hillard, "whose every sympathy was with the South and would deem it an honor to become martyrs in their cause." Though it was tempting, Pinkerton admitted, to dismiss Hillard and his kind as toothless firebrands, the same might also have been said of the abolitionist John Brown, "who almost single-handed threw himself into a fight against the nation." The men in Baltimore, Pinkerton insisted, were no less devoted to their cause. Hillard and his kind would do whatever their leaders called upon them to do, "without asking a why or wherefore," to guarantee "that Lincoln should not pass through Baltimore alive."

Adding to his fears, Pinkerton explained, was the fact that he did not expect the Baltimore police to provide effective protection, based on the remarks he had overheard Marshall Kane make. Even if Kane's men were to "make a decent show to preserve order," Pinkerton reasoned, it would not be enough. A single determined individual might yet thwart their efforts, as George H. Burns had demonstrated that very afternoon. Pinkerton also had blunt words about the inadequacies of Lincoln's own arrangements. He asked pointedly what was known of William S. Wood, who had seemingly appeared from nowhere to assume complete control of Lincoln's movements. Judd admitted that he knew nothing at all of Wood's background or credentials, and that he had raised much the same questions with Lincoln himself.

Pinkerton concluded that, "as things stood now," the prospects for a safe passage through Baltimore were bleak. He earnestly believed that he himself—"nameless and unknown as I was"—would stand a better chance in similar circumstances. "I at least had some of my own men with me," he said, "who would die in their boots before I should be injured." Ellsworth, Lamon, and the others—well-intentioned as they might be—were simply not prepared for what awaited them. In Pinkerton's view, Lincoln would be reasonably safe while still on board the train, but from the moment he landed at the Baltimore depot, and especially while riding in the open carriage through the streets, he would be in mortal peril. "I do not believe," he told Judd, "it is possible he or his personal friends could pass through Baltimore in that style alive."

"More than an hour was occupied in going over the proofs," Pinkerton said. During this time Judd said very little. Occasionally, he broke in to ask a question or seek clarification of a detail, but for the most part he sat and stared into the fireplace, stroking his beard and puffing intently at a cigar. At last, when Pinkerton had finished speaking, Judd turned to him with an expression of utter resolve. He was "fully convinced that the plot was a reality," he said. The question now was what to do next.

This was the moment for which Pinkerton had been planning all day. "My advice," he told Judd, "is that Mr. Lincoln shall proceed to Washington this evening by the eleven o'clock train." Judd made to object, but Pinkerton held up a hand for silence. He went on to explain that if Lincoln altered his schedule in this manner, he would be able to slip through Baltimore unnoticed, before the assassins made their final preparations. "This could be done in safety," Pinkerton said. In fact, it was the only way.

Judd's face darkened. "I fear very much that Mr. Lincoln will not accede to this," he said. He explained that although he himself was "deeply impressed with the danger which surrounded Mr. Lincoln," he doubted that the president-elect would be willing to change his plans in any way. "Mr. Judd said that Mr. Lincoln's confidence in the people was unbounded," Pinkerton recalled, "and that he did not fear any violent outbreak; that he hoped by his management and conciliatory measures to bring the secessionists back to their allegiance."

Though Judd did not say so, there was an additional reason for sticking to the published schedule. Lincoln had less than two days left on his meticulously planned itinerary, and those final hours were packed with emotional resonance. George Washington's birthday would be celebrated the following day, and Lincoln planned to mark the occasion with a flag raising at Independence Hall, followed by a hectic dogleg journey to Harrisburg to address the state legislature. He had traveled many miles out of his way to make these two important stops, having missed no opportunity throughout the journey to emphasize the symbols and traditions of the presidency. At that very moment, even as Judd sat talking with Pinkerton and Felton, Lincoln was giving one of his characteristic addresses from the balcony of the Continental Hotel, seizing on the historic totems of Philadelphia as he promised to "listen to those breathings rising within the consecrated walls" where the Constitution and Declaration of Independence had originally been framed. Lincoln would not abandon Philadelphia easily.

In Judd's view, the best chance of getting Lincoln to change his mind rested with Pinkerton himself. He didn't think it likely that Lincoln would yield, he said, "but as the President is an old acquaintance and friend of yours, and has had occasion before this to test your reliability and prudence, suppose you accompany me to the Continental Hotel in person and abide by his decision?"

There is nothing in Pinkerton's reports to suggest that he expected to take his concerns directly to Lincoln, nor is it likely, given his long-established passion for secrecy, that he welcomed the prospect. He had made a career of operating in the shadows, always taking care to disguise his appearance, identity, and methods. Worse yet, he had launched the Baltimore operation with a pointed declaration that he would not "consider it safe for myself or my operatives were the fact of my operating known to any politician—no matter of what school, or what position." Now, with time running short, he would have to break cover and plead his case to the nation's leading politician, together with his many advisers. Though Judd insisted that Pinkerton's involvement would remain a closely guarded secret—"whatever the consequences might be"—the detective knew that this would be a difficult promise to keep. Looking back on that night a few years later, Pinkerton was characteristically terse about the decision: "After a long conversation and discussion, Mr. Judd desired that I should go to the Continental Hotel with him and have an interview with Mr. Lincoln. We did so."

It was now almost 9:00 P.M. If they were going to get Lincoln on a train that night, they had barely two hours in which to act.

CHAPTER NINETEEN
AN ASSAULT OF SOME KIND

•

*Only begirt with a mighty army or disguised like a fugitive felon or spy, could the elected
Chief Magistrate of Thirty Millions of Freemen pass through eight or ten of the States
which he has been chosen to lead.*
—HORACE GREELEY in the *New York Independent*, February 21, 1861

ALLAN PINKERTON, A VETERAN of the Newport Rising in his native
Britain, had never seen a mob like the one that surrounded the Continental Hotel that evening. "A dense crowd of people filled Chestnut Street," he
wrote, "every square inch of ground was occupied." For a few moments, he
and Judd attempted to force their way through the jam at the front doors.
When this proved fruitless, Pinkerton took Judd around the corner to the
servant's entrance on Sansom Street. Even then, it was only with "the utmost difficulty that we were able to get into the building."

Pinkerton hoped to complete the final details of his plan before meeting
with Lincoln. Leaving Judd at the hotel, Pinkerton pushed his way back
out onto the street to make additional arrangements, a task made inordi-
nately difficult by the "denseness of the crowd." Returning a few minutes
later, he dived into the throng once more and caught sight of Lincoln in the
midst of one of his handshaking levees on the second floor, which had
produced a tidal surge of people moving through the hotel. "The interior
of the house was as densely crowded as was the outside," Pinkerton wrote,
"and I found that all were 'getting up stairs.' When I reached the last of
the stairs I found that Mr. Lincoln was in a balcony at the head of the first
landing, bowing to the people as they passed up the stairs. There was no
way for me to get up but to go into the jam and go up with the human
tide, so I went in—but *such* a jam."

Carried along with the flow, Pinkerton came within sight of Lincoln as the receiving line churned through the hallway and down a second set of stairs. "The people were kept moving in a steady stream around through a double file of police to the stairway on Tenth Street, and thus out," Pinkerton noted. For a few moments, it looked as if Pinkerton himself would be swept back out onto the street, but after a brief struggle, the detective managed to break free of the current. "I managed to get outside of the file of police and soon found Mr. Judd's room, where I found him waiting for me," the detective said. Judd promised that he would send Lincoln a note, asking him to join them as soon as he had finished with the receiving line.

While waiting, Pinkerton continued to lay his plans. He sent messengers to place officers of the telegraph companies on alert. He also arranged for the Adams Express Company to bulk up the security on its runs in and out of Baltimore. Should an attack on Lincoln occur, Pinkerton reasoned, professional thieves might seize on the resulting scenes of confusion "with a view to plunder." As he made these arrangements, however, Pinkerton had to be cautious of giving out too much information. He asked his contacts at Adams Express to give no explanation of the extra measures to Samuel Shoemaker, their representative in Baltimore. It was not that he doubted Shoemaker's honesty or loyalty, Pinkerton explained, "but that I feared his discretion." Even as he took these precautions, Pinkerton kept an anxious eye on the clock. As the hour of ten passed, his hopes of getting Lincoln on a train that night were fading. He considered asking Samuel Felton to provide a special train, but feared that this would make the change of plan far too conspicuous, even if it could be managed in time.

Finally, at 10:15, Pinkerton got word that Lincoln had retired for the evening. Judd dashed off a note, asking the president-elect to come to his room "so soon as convenient on private business of importance." Pinkerton himself carried the message to Lincoln's room, but he was prevented from delivering it by Colonel Ellsworth, who stood guard at the door. After what one imagines to have been a heated discussion, Pinkerton dragged the young colonel to see Judd, who "at once ordered Ellsworth to deliver the note." Ten minutes later, Ellsworth took up his post outside Judd's room as Lincoln himself ducked through the doorway.

At the sight of Lincoln, Judd hurried forward to make the necessary introductions. According to Pinkerton, however, Lincoln waved the formalities aside. He "at once recollected me" from the days when both men

had given service to the Illinois Central Railroad, Pinkerton said, and—
"as usual"—had a kind word of greeting for his old acquaintance. "Lincoln liked Pinkerton," Judd observed, and "had the utmost confidence in him as a gentleman—and a man of sagacity." For his part, Pinkerton noted that Lincoln appeared "rather exhausted from the fatigues of travel and receptions."

After showing the president-elect to a chair, Judd began to speak, briefly outlining the circumstances that had sent Pinkerton to Baltimore. "Whilst Mr. Judd was talking," Pinkerton noted, "Mr. Lincoln listened very attentively, but did not say a word, nor did his countenance, which I watched very closely, show any emotion. He appeared thoughtful and serious, but decidedly firm."

When Judd finished, he asked Pinkerton to take up the thread and lay out the details of what he had learned, much as he had for Felton and himself earlier in the day. "I did so," Pinkerton said, carefully reviewing "the circumstances connected with Ferrandini, Hillard and others," who were "ready and willing to die to rid their country of a tyrant, as they considered Lincoln to be." Again, Pinkerton stressed that the danger rested with a small group of men who were "thoroughly devoted to Southern rights, and who looked upon the north as being aggressors." In the eyes of these men, Pinkerton explained, Lincoln stood as "the embodiment of all those evils, in whose death the South would be largely the gainers."

It is probably fair to say that Lincoln did not need a civics briefing from Pinkerton. Understandably, the detective wished to stress the powder-keg conditions in Baltimore, but Lincoln would have been more interested in hearing the specifics of the threat, rather than a catalog of Southern grievances. Pinkerton quickly returned to the main point, telling Lincoln in blunt terms that if he kept to the published itinerary, "an assault of some kind would be made upon his person with a view to taking his life."

The outlines of what Pinkerton told Lincoln that night are best reflected in a report by Joseph Howard that appeared in the *New York Times* a few days later. Although Howard was not in the room that night, he would soon learn that "a celebrated Western detective" had brought warnings of three possible assassination plans, "by one of which the conspirators expected to prevent the safe conveyance of Mr. Lincoln to Washington."

The first of these plans involved a fatal train derailment. "The argument in favor of this plan was its obviously easy execution," Howard reported. "The objection to it was that the destruction of so many innocent lives was an unnecessary murder." The second plan involved "an infernal machine," which would "blow up the car in which Mr. Lincoln was to ride." This method, it was suggested, might possibly spare innocent lives, but it was also thought to be unreliable. The third plan, in Howard's view, was the only feasible one. In this scenario, "a large and organized crowd of roughs" would surround Lincoln's open carriage as he rode through the streets. As Lincoln bowed or "extended his dexter hand for a friendly shake," an assassin concealed within the crowd would strike: "[T]he keen stiletto would be buried in the heart of the President-elect, and aided by his fellows, the assassin, slipping into the surrounding mass of brother conspirators, would avoid recognition or detection, while the end would be accomplished and the fate of the country sealed."

Though Howard did not report it, Pinkerton would have added a possible variation to this third design. Even before Lincoln reached his carriage, there would be a clear opportunity to strike as he passed through the narrow vestibule leading from the Calvert Street Station to the street. "A row or fight was to be got up by some outsiders," Pinkerton explained, and the "few policemen at the Depot would rush out" to quell the disturbance, "thus leaving Mr. Lincoln entirely unprotected and at the mercy of a mob of secessionists who were to surround him at that time." Once the fatal deed was done, the assassins would slip away: "A small steamer had been charted and was lying in one of the bays or little streams running into the Chesapeake, to which the murderers were to flee and it was immediately to put off for Virginia."

In Judd's room that evening, Pinkerton outlined not only the particulars of these separate designs but also the methods by which he had uncovered them. "During the entire interview, he had not evinced the slightest evidence of agitation or fear," Pinkerton said of Lincoln. "Calm and self-possessed, his only sentiments appeared to be those of profound regret, that the Southern sympathizers could be so far led away by the excitement of the hour, as to consider his death a necessity for the furtherance of their cause."

Pinkerton would recall only one brief interruption during the meeting, when Ward Lamon ducked into the room to hand a note to Lincoln. In his field report, Pinkerton expressed irritation that Lamon addressed him by name, as he had been at pains to preserve his anonymity as "J. H. Hutchinson." It would not be the last time Pinkerton had cause for annoyance with Lincoln's self-described "protector."

For the moment, desperate to secure Lincoln's consent to leave that night, Pinkerton brushed the interruption aside. "After Mr. Lincoln had been made fully acquainted with the startling disclosures," the detective said, "Mr. Judd submitted to him the plan proposed by me, that he should leave Philadelphia for Washington that evening." Judd emphasized that the action would have to be carried out in total secrecy, "as it will involve the lives of several devoted men now on Mr. Pinkerton's force."

In addition, Judd said, there would be serious political ramifications. "If you follow the course suggested," he warned, "you will necessarily be subjected to the scoffs and sneers of your enemies, and the disapproval of your friends who cannot be made to believe in the existence of so desperate a plot." Even worse, Judd continued, it would not be possible to offer any defense. Pinkerton's evidence, convincing as it was, "could not be laid before the public." To do so would endanger the very agents "who were at that moment playing their wise game among the Secessionists." It was one thing for well-meaning advisers to urge the change of plan, Judd said, but Lincoln would be the one to "bear the burthen of the thing." There was no doubt, he said, but that "the world will laugh at you."

Lincoln did not appear troubled by thoughts of ridicule, and he gave his assurance that he "could stand anything that was necessary." Having said that much, Pinkerton was distressed to find that Lincoln didn't seem inclined to say anything more. Instead, Pinkerton recalled, "Mr. Lincoln remained quiet for a few minutes, apparently thinking." After a time, Judd broke the silence to ask Lincoln if there was anything further that he or Pinkerton could say that would convince him to pick up and make an immediate departure for Washington.

Lincoln rose from his chair. "I cannot go tonight," he said firmly. "I have promised to raise the flag over Independence Hall tomorrow morning, and to visit the legislature at Harrisburg in the afternoon—beyond that I have no engagements. Any plan that may be adopted that will enable me to fulfill these promises I will accede to, and you can inform me what is concluded upon tomorrow." With these words, he turned and left the room, promising to decide the matter in the morning.

"The firmness of tone in which Mr. Lincoln spoke shewed that there was no further use in arguing the proposition," a dejected Pinkerton wrote in his field report, "and Mr. Judd inquired of me what I thought best to do in the emergency." The detective saw no alternative but to yield to Lincoln's wishes, and he immediately set to work on a new plan, hoping that it would win Lincoln's approval. Struggling to anticipate "all the contingencies that could be imagined," Pinkerton would work through the entire night.

THOUGH IT WAS NOW PAST 11:00 P.M., the upstairs corridors of the Continental Hotel were still packed with people. Emerging from Judd's room, Lincoln slowly threaded his way through the jam, pausing here and there for the necessary handshakes and greetings. When at last he reached his own suite, Lincoln found that his long and wearing day had not yet finished. Frederick Seward, freshly arrived with his urgent messages from Washington, sat waiting by the fire, having been ushered directly to Lincoln's room by Ward Lamon to catch a few moments with Lincoln before he retired for the night.

Exhausted as he was after a day that had begun early that morning in New York City, Lincoln managed "a few words of friendly greeting" for his unexpected visitor. After brief inquiries about Seward's father and affairs in Washington, Lincoln took the bundle of letters Seward carried and sat down by a gas lamp to read. "Although its contents were of a somewhat startling nature he made no exclamation," Seward observed, "and I saw no sign of surprise on his face." Indeed, the substance of the communication would have been all too familiar by this time. In addition to a brief note from General Scott attesting to the bona fides of the information, Lincoln found an anxious message from the elder Seward:

> My son goes express to you—He will show you a report made by our detective to General Scott—and by him communicated to me this morning—I deem it so important as to dispatch my son to meet you wherever he may find you.
>
> I concur with General Scott in thinking it best for you to reconsider your arrangement. No one here but Genl. Scott, myself & the bearer is aware of this communication.

Also included was Colonel Stone's report, based on what he had learned from David Bookstaver, Superintendent John Kennedy's "music agent" operative in Baltimore:

> A New York detective officer who has been on duty in Baltimore for three weeks past reports this morning that there is serious danger of violence to and the assassination of Mr. Lincoln in his passage through that city should the time of that passage be known—He states that there are banded rowdies holding secret meetings, and that he has heard threats of mobbing and violence, and has himself heard men declare that if Mr. Lincoln was to be assassinated they would like to be the men—He

states further that it is only within the past few days that he has considered there was any danger, but now he deems it imminent—He deems the danger one which the authorities & people in Baltimore cannot guard against. All risk might be easily avoided by a change in the traveling arrangements which would bring Mr. Lincoln & a portion of his party through Baltimore by a night train without previous notice.

Unwelcome as these alarms may have been, it now appeared that Pinkerton's discoveries—as well as his suggested plan of action—had been affirmed by two of the most powerful men in Washington. To Lincoln's mind, however, the warnings had curious parallels that demanded further scrutiny. After reading the messages through a second time, he turned back to his visitor. "Did you hear anything about the way this information was obtained?" Lincoln asked. "Do you know anything about how they got it? Did you hear any names mentioned? Did you, for instance, ever hear anything said about such a name as Pinkerton?"

Seward replied that he had heard no names other than those of General Scott and Colonel Stone. Lincoln considered this for a moment. "I may as well tell you why I ask," he said. "There were stories or rumors some time ago, before I left home, about people who were intending to do me a mischief. I never attached much importance to them—never wanted to believe any such thing. So I never would do anything about them, in the way of taking precautions and the like. Some of my friends, though, thought differently—Judd and others—and without my knowledge, they employed a detective to look into the matter. It seems he has occasionally reported what he found; and only today, since we arrived at this house, he brought this story, or something similar to it, about an attempt on my life in the confusion and hurly-burly of the reception at Baltimore."

"Surely Mr. Lincoln," Seward insisted, "that is a strong corroboration of the news I bring you." Lincoln did not appear convinced. "That is exactly why I was asking you about names," he told Seward. "If different persons, not knowing of each other's work, have been pursuing separate clews that led to the same result, why then it shows there may be something in it. But if this is only the same story, filtered through two channels, and reaching me in two ways, then that don't make it any stronger. Don't you see?"

This logic was unanswerable, Seward admitted, but he told Lincoln that he believed strongly that the two investigations had been conducted independently. In his view, it would be "prudent to adopt the suggestion, and make the slight change in hour and train which would avoid all risk." Even now, Lincoln was not prepared to make that decision. Just as he had with Pinkerton and Judd, he rose from his chair to signal the end of the discussion. "Well," he told Seward, "we haven't got to decide it tonight, anyway, and I see it's getting late."

Seeing the disappointment on Seward's face, Lincoln hastened to assure him that he would take the warning seriously. "You need not think I will not consider it well," he said. "I shall think it over carefully, and try to decide it right, and I will let you know in the morning."

BOTH SEWARD AND PINKERTON had been forcefully impressed by Lincoln's icy calm in the face of these unexpected revelations. "I never saw him more cool, collected and firm than he was on that evening," Pinkerton would recall. To the end of his life, Pinkerton would believe that he had been the first to alert Lincoln to the peril. "Up to this time Mr. Lincoln had been kept in entire ignorance of any threatened danger," the detective would write, "and as he listened to the facts that were now presented to him, a shade of sadness fell upon his face. He seemed loath to credit the statement, and could scarce believe it possible that such a conspiracy could exist. Slowly he went over the points presented, questioning me minutely the while, but at length finding it impossible to discredit the truthfulness of what I stated to him, he yielded a reluctant credence to the facts."

Lincoln may well have been reluctant, but he was far from ignorant of the threat. His challenge in Philadelphia was not to accept a painful truth, but to judge the degree of the threat. Though he made no mention of it that evening, Lincoln had been hearing concerns about Baltimore for weeks, long before Pinkerton's investigation had even begun. In fact, the previous month, Capt. George Hazzard had proposed a plan very much like Pinkerton's, suggesting that Lincoln take a night train through the city, "privately and unannounced with a very few friends." Clearly, Lincoln had not dismissed these concerns out of hand, as Hazzard had been at his side through much of the journey from Springfield.

Earlier, Lincoln had heard from Boston supporter Thomas Cadwallerder, who, while traveling through Baltimore, had had his head shaved "merely for making the remark that I consider you a gentleman." Sadder but wiser, Cadwallerder warned Lincoln that "it will be madness for you to attempt to reach Washington at any time" via Baltimore.

Shortly before Lincoln left Springfield, this warning had been followed by an alarming letter from Henry C. Bowen, the editor of an antislavery newspaper in New York. Bowen forwarded a note he had received from an acquaintance named Charles Gould, warning of a plan "to kill Mr. Lincoln on his way to Washington," and claiming that it would not be possible for the president-elect "to go in safety to the Capital when his progress is known to the public." These statements, Gould insisted, "can be taken for truth without exaggeration."

As it happened, Gould's warning would not have satisfied Lincoln's desire for independent corroboration, as it had originated with none other than Samuel Felton, the very man who had sent Pinkerton to Baltimore. Even so, it is clear that Lincoln could not have been as unaware of the gathering threat as Pinkerton supposed. That he was content to keep his own counsel suggests a lawyerly effort to weigh the evidence, free of distraction, as he attempted to separate reasonable suspicion from hearsay. "The time comes upon every public man," he once had occasion to say, "when it is best for him to keep his lips closed."

In this situation, however, that time would be brief. The following day, Pinkerton would need a verdict.

CHAPTER TWENTY
THE ASSASSIN'S KNIFE

•

Tomorrow we enter slave territory. There may be trouble in Baltimore. If so,
we will not go to Washington, unless in long, narrow boxes.
—JOHN HAY, in a letter dated February 22, 1861

SHORTLY AFTER NOON ON THE FOLLOWING DAY, February 22, an
unusual train rolled into Baltimore's President Street Station, the southern terminus of Samuel Felton's Philadelphia, Wilmington and Baltimore
Railroad. A special sleeper car had been coupled to the regular passenger
train and darkened with drawn curtains, although the train was running
in broad daylight.

The atmosphere at the depot was charged. "The station was filled with
rough characters," according to one source, "and the temper of the crowd
was unmistakably hostile to the Union. There were oaths heard that 'no
damned abolitionist like Lincoln or Hamlin should enter the White House,'
and the mob seemed capable of carrying out its threats." As Felton's train
stood idling at the platform, a small contingent of "ruffians" pushed their
way aboard and swarmed through the carriages, apparently looking for
Lincoln. They made their way into the sleeper car at the back of the train
and made a noisy search, even pushing back the curtains, where a man
and his wife lay quietly on their berths. For a long moment, the intruders
glared down at the couple, who stared back with expressions of polite
confusion. Finally, finding themselves frustrated in their search, "the un-
cleanly creatures took themselves away, leaving an atmosphere of profanity and whiskey."

Left behind in their sleeping compartment, unrecognized by the hoo-
ligans, were Hannibal Hamlin and his wife, Ellen.

•

IN THE OFFICES OF THE *BALTIMORE SUN,* meanwhile, a special editorial was being prepared for the next day's paper. In a small masterpiece of benign contempt, the editors offered a plea for civility even as they thumbed their noses at the incoming president:

> Mr. Lincoln, President-elect of the United States, is expected, in fulfillment of the route programme, to arrive in Baltimore today. He will thus put his foot upon Southern soil, and enter that section of territory in which those institutions exist and are esteemed by the people against which he has declared an "irrepressible conflict." He comes into that territorial division of the country from which he received not one electoral vote, and in which but a meagre representation of his party and his views is to be found. To these few he might be very properly committed. But Mr. Lincoln, by virtue of the office to which he is elected, and the somewhat eccentric style, oratorical and otherwise, in which he approaches the capital, will be an object of curiosity to thousands, no doubt, consequently he may expect to meet a large multitude who, having nothing better to do, in this "artificial crisis," will avail themselves of a free ticket to have a look at him. With all this we have little concern, but we have for something else.
>
> It is of great concern to all who love and would honor the State of Maryland and the city of Baltimore that no demonstration whatsoever should be made, even by a single individual, inconsistent with our self-respect. We would a thousand times rather see the most elaborate exhibition of official courtesy, unbecoming as it would be in such a case, than that the slightest personal disrespect should mar the occasion, or blur the reputation of our well-ordered city.

Elsewhere in the city, an anonymous citizen was composing an urgent letter to be placed in the hands of Lincoln himself:

> *Dear Sir*
> *I think it my duty to inform you that I was assured last night by a*
> *gentleman that there existed in Baltimore a league of ten persons who*

had sworn that you should never pass through that city alive—This may be but one of the thousand threats against you that have emanated from some paltry Southerners, but you should know it that your friends may be watchful while you are in the place, as it was asserted positively to be the fact. God defend and bless you—The prayers of many go with you!

A Lady

In Philadelphia, Allan Pinkerton had been busy. With the help of Norman Judd, Samuel Felton, and others, the detective had worked through the night in an eleventh-hour effort to revise his plan for Lincoln's safe passage through Baltimore. There were now two extra difficulties to overcome. First, Lincoln's scheduled appearance in Baltimore was now only one day away. As the appointed hour drew closer, the chances of slipping through the city unnoticed became more remote. As Hamlin's unnerving experience at the President Street Station would demonstrate, the city's hostile elements were already on alert.

At the same time, Lincoln's insistence on making the time-consuming trip to Harrisburg had brought an extra dimension of difficulty to the planning. The state capital was roughly one hundred miles to the west of Philadelphia, adding an extra four hours of train travel in each direction. In order to accommodate this detour, Pinkerton would have to involve a second set of railroad men and telegraph operators, any one of whom could compromise the secrecy of the plan. Where possible, Pinkerton employed the latest word-substitution cipher from the Chicago office, in which the critical terms were replaced with the names of random foodstuffs. Over the wires, Pinkerton himself would be identified as "Plums," and—in a bizarrely inappropriate quirk of circumstance—Lincoln would be known as "Nuts."

The detective was also anxious to keep tabs on matters in Baltimore. For this, he turned to George Dunn, an agent of the local Harnden's Express Company, with whom he had worked on previous operations. Dunn was sent off to Baltimore with a key to the office on South Street, where he was to collect the reports Pinkerton's field agents had filed in the detective's absence. Kate Warne's report of that day, written while she was still in Philadelphia, offers a passing glimpse of Pinkerton's hectic efforts. She recorded that Pinkerton came to her room at three o'clock that morning—"sick, and tired out"—with a fresh set of instructions, pausing only a few moments before ducking back out into the night.

"Every possible contingency was discussed and re-discussed," said Norman Judd. Pinkerton crisscrossed the city, rousing railroad authorities from their beds and dispatching errand boys on secret missions. By the time he made his way back to the St. Louis for a quick change of clothes, swarms of people were converging on Independence Hall to witness Lincoln's flag-raising ceremony—"which," the detective noted wearily in his field report, "was announced for sun-rise."

Kate Warne would be on hand for the celebrations that morning, looking out from a crowd of some thirty thousand people as Lincoln's open carriage rolled slowly onto the plaza behind an honor guard of Mexican War veterans. Head uncovered, the president-elect climbed down and was led into the chamber where the Declaration of Independence had been signed, his features "betraying the emotion with which he stood in that historic room."

Speaking before the city council and other prominent citizens, Lincoln offered a moving tribute to the Founding Fathers. "He gave a most eloquent expression to the emotions and associations which were suggested by the day and by the historic old hall where he then stood," Pinkerton would remark, adding that a "tinge of sadness pervaded his remarks, never noticed before, and which were occasioned no doubt by the revelations of the preceding night." Elsewhere, Pinkerton would attempt to recall a particular line of the speech that hinted at Lincoln's uneasy state of mind. "I cannot quote it correctly," he admitted. "It was something like this: 'I will preserve the Union even if the assassin's knife is at my heart.'"

Lincoln's actual remarks, given in response to an introduction from Theodore Cuyler, an outspoken advocate of concession to the slaveholding states, were far more subtle, if no less dramatic. By this time, Lincoln had become a master at drawing urgent, timely lessons from the pages of history.

> I am filled with deep emotion at finding myself standing here,
> in this place, where were collected together the wisdom, the
> patriotism, the devotion to principle, from which sprang the
> institutions under which we live. You have kindly suggested to
> me that in my hands is the task of restoring peace to the present
> distracted condition of the country. I can say in return, Sir, that
> all the political sentiments I entertain have been drawn, so far as
> I have been able to draw them, from the sentiments which
> originated and were given to the world from this hall. I have

never had a feeling politically that did not spring from the sentiments embodied in the Declaration of Independence. I have often pondered over the dangers which were incurred by the men who assembled here, and framed and adopted that Declaration of Independence. I have pondered over the toils that were endured by the officers and soldiers of the army who achieved that Independence. I have often inquired of myself, what great principle or idea it was that kept this Confederacy so long together. It was not the mere matter of the separation of the Colonies from the motherland, but that sentiment in the Declaration of Independence which gave liberty, not alone to the people of this country, but, I hope, to the world, for all future time. It was that which gave promise that in due time the weight would be lifted from the shoulders of all men. This is a sentiment embodied in the Declaration of Independence. Now, my friends, can this country be saved upon that basis? If it can, I will consider myself one of the happiest men in the world if I can help to save it. If it cannot be saved upon that principle, it will be truly awful. But if this country cannot be saved without giving up that principle . . .

Lincoln paused here for a long moment, his head bowed before the portraits of Jefferson, Adams, and Madison. When he spoke again, having apparently struggled to find the proper words, his voice was firm and clear. "I was about to say," he declared, "I would rather be assassinated on this spot than surrender it."

Norman Judd would have been one of the few who understood the full significance of this extraordinary remark. In his mind, there was no doubt that the dramatic reference to "sacrificing himself for his country" sprang from Lincoln's meeting with Pinkerton the previous evening, and from thoughts of what lay ahead in Baltimore.

The somber moment passed quickly. As Lincoln brought his remarks to a close, he was led to a wooden platform outside the hall, where he looked down on the vast cheering crowd that had gathered for the flag raising. "They had come, many of them, from a distance," wrote Joseph Howard in the *New York Times,* "that they might witness the performance of a deed, the solemn beauty of which cannot well be overestimated." Stepping forward, Lincoln "threw off his overcoat in an offhand, easy manner" and took hold of the halyards. Pulling hand over hand, he ran the oversized American flag up the pole and watched as it unfurled overhead. The air filled with patriotic music as the soldiers below fired off a crisp salute. Lincoln's expression, according to more than one observer, was serene.

JUST AFTER 8:00 A.M., Pinkerton met again with Norman Judd at the Continental Hotel, where he learned that Lincoln had "signified his readiness to do whatever was required of him." Pinkerton remained secretive about the details of his plan—"No particulars were given and none were asked," he said—but it was understood that the broad strokes would remain the same, with Lincoln passing through Baltimore ahead of schedule. In this way, Pinkerton believed, he might yet catch the assassins off guard. "The common and accepted belief was that Mr. Lincoln would journey from Harrisburg to Baltimore over the Northern Central Railroad, and the plans of the conspirators were arranged accordingly," Pinkerton wrote. "It became a matter of the utmost importance, therefore, that no intimation of our movements should reach that city."

There were several channels by which this crucial information might reach Baltimore. Pinkerton had arranged to place friendly operators on the major telegraph lines to watch for suspicious messages, but he worried that this precaution would not be sufficient. If, as he believed, "agents of the conspirators" were shadowing the presidential party at all times, it was essential not to arouse suspicion. Any deviation from the official itinerary might signal an awareness of the plot. Toward that end, Pinkerton remained determined to withhold the details of his plan from all but the central participants. "I requested Mr. Lincoln that none but Mr. Judd and myself should know anything about this arrangement," Pinkerton recalled. "I said that secrecy was so necessary for our success that I deemed it best that as few as possible should know anything of our movements: that I knew all the men with whom it was necessary for me to instruct my movements and that my share of this secret should be safe, and that if it only was kept quiet I should answer for his safety with my life."

As Pinkerton reviewed the details that morning, Judd had grave misgivings. He admitted that the detective's plan appeared to be "the only feasible one under the circumstances," but he sorely regretted that it would "doubtless create a great deal of excitement throughout the country." Pinkerton saw no other option: "I assured Mr. Judd that I fully believed the course I had indicated was the only one to save the country from bloodshed at the present time."

Pinkerton now realized that he wasn't alone in this view. "I also learned that morning that General Scott and Mr. Seward had discovered some evidence of a plot to assassinate Mr. Lincoln," he reported, though he could not resist adding that the New York detectives had not illuminated the matter "as clearly as my own men." By the time Pinkerton learned of the parallel investigation, however, Frederick Seward had already been sent back to Washington "with just enough information" to prepare for Lincoln's surreptitious arrival. "I told Mr. Seward," Judd recalled, "that he could say to his father that all had been arranged, so far as human foresight could predict."

THE LINCOLN SPECIAL PULLED AWAY from the Pennsylvania Railroad's West Philadelphia depot at 9:30 that morning, bound for Harrisburg. John Hay, unaware of what was transpiring behind the scenes, took note of Lincoln's apparent distraction and reported him to be "so unwell he could hardly be persuaded to show himself." In fact, Lincoln spent a portion of the long journey sequestered with Judd, who briefed him on the latest report from Pinkerton. The detective himself stayed behind in Philadelphia to complete his arrangements. As the train pushed toward the state capital, Judd's secret knowledge weighed heavily on him. He told Lincoln that he "felt exceedingly the responsibility, as no member of the party had been informed of anything connected with the matter."

By this time, an atmosphere of foreboding had settled over the train. Ward Lamon and Colonel Ellsworth could see that "something was on foot," Judd recalled, "but very judiciously refrained from asking questions." John Nicolay could not muster the same restraint. "Judd," he said at one stage, "there is something *up*. What is it, if it is proper that I should know?" "There is no necessity for your knowing," Judd replied, "and one man can keep a matter better than two."

As the train neared Harrisburg, Judd's resolve crumbled. Though he had promised his silence to Pinkerton, he now told Lincoln that the matter was "so important that I felt that it should be communicated to the other gentlemen of the party." Lincoln concurred. "I reckon they will laugh at us, Judd," he said, "but you had better get them together."

Pinkerton would have been horrified at this development, but Judd was resolved. "It was therefore arranged," he said, "that after the reception at the State House had taken place, and before they sat down to dinner, the matter should be fully laid before the following gentlemen of the party: Judge David Davis, Colonel Sumner, Major David Hunter, Captain John Pope and Ward H. Lamon." Looking back on Judd's decision in later years, Pinkerton attempted to strike a diplomatic note. The full weight of the responsibility, he said, had been too much for one man.

Arriving in Harrisburg at 1:30 P.M., Lincoln made his way to the city's capitol building for an address to the Pennsylvania General Assembly. Of all present, only Judd and Lincoln himself knew that it would be the final speech of the long inaugural journey. Once again, Lincoln seized the moment, spinning a deceptively simple anecdote into a masterly statement of national unity and resolve:

> This morning I was, for the first time, allowed the privilege of standing in Old Independence Hall. Our friends had provided a magnificent flag of our country, and they had arranged it so that I was given the honor of raising it to the head of its staff, and when it went up I was pleased that it went to its place by the strength of my own feeble arm. When, according to the arrangement, the cord was pulled, and it flaunted gloriously to the wind, without an accident, in the bright glowing sunshine of the morning, I could not help hoping that there was, in the entire success of that beautiful ceremony, at least something of an omen of what is to come. Nor could I help feeling then, as I have often felt, that in the whole of that proceeding I was a very humble instrument. I had not provided the flag. I had not made the arrangement for elevating it to its place. I had applied a very small portion even of my feeble strength in raising it. In the whole transaction I was in the hands of the people who had arranged it. And if I can have the same generous cooperation of the people of this nation, I think the flag of our country may yet be kept flaunting gloriously.

Afterward, traveling to the Jones House hotel with his host, Governor Andrew Curtin, Lincoln made a surprising decision to take Curtin into his confidence, telling the governor that "a conspiracy had been discovered to assassinate him in Baltimore on his way through that city the next day." Curtin, a Republican who had forged a close alliance with Lincoln during the presidential campaign, pledged his full cooperation. He reported that Lincoln "seemed pained and surprised that a design to take his life existed." Nevertheless, he remained "very calm, and neither in his conversation or manner exhibited alarm or fear."

On reaching the Jones House, it was announced that Lincoln had allowed himself a period of rest before dinner. Instead, as the reporters and well-wishers dispersed, he withdrew into a private parlor for Norman Judd's emergency meeting. One by one, David Davis, Colonel Sumner, Major Hunter, Captain Pope, and Ward Lamon made their way into the room and found seats, all of them aware by this time that there was something very peculiar in the wind. Lincoln sat back and gave control of the meeting to Judd. He said little but listened attentively, as would become his habit in the White House, letting the others debate the matter before he entered the fray himself. "The facts were laid before them by me," Judd recalled, "together with the details of the proposed plan of action." Judd gave a tidy précis of the previous day's meeting with Pinkerton, and revealed that Lincoln had agreed to break away from the inaugural party in Harrisburg and travel through to Washington—ahead of schedule—under the detective's protection.

As Judd had expected, his fellow travelers were shocked by the revelation of a threat on Lincoln's life. As the discussion continued, however, they were perhaps even more unsettled by the extreme measures suggested by Pinkerton. "There was a diversity of opinion and some warm discussion," Judd allowed, "and I was subjected to a very rigid cross-examination."

As the debate over Pinkerton's proposal grew more and more heated, Colonel Sumner, the senior military officer in the room, offered a blunt appraisal. "That proceeding," he said, "will be a damned piece of cowardice."

Judd had expected this, and there was a note of weary impatience in his response: "I replied to this pointed hit by saying that that view of the case had already been presented to Mr. Lincoln." Sumner would not be placated. "I'll get a squad of cavalry, sir," he said heatedly, "and cut our way to Washington, sir."

In the circumstances, this struck Judd as empty posturing. Even if it were practical to exercise a military option, he explained with mounting irritation, it would be a time-consuming enterprise, and one that was likely to drag on past inauguration day. "It is important," he said drily, "that Mr. Lincoln should be in Washington that day."

As Judd and Sumner glared at each other, Judge Davis stepped in to take charge of the situation, displaying the instincts that would soon carry him to the Supreme Court. Judd would recall that Davis "expressed no opinion but contented himself with asking rather pointed questions," reviewing the facts in a cool, methodical manner that succeeded in lowering the temperature of the room. At length, when Judd had been made to reiterate all of the salient points, Davis turned to the president-elect and cut to the heart of the issue. "Well, Mr. Lincoln," he asked, "what is your judgment upon this matter?"

Lincoln sighed and gathered himself to speak for the first time. "I have thought over this matter considerably since I went over the ground with Pinkerton last night," he began. "The appearance of Mr. Frederick Seward, with warning from another source, confirms my belief in Mr. Pinkerton's statement. Unless there are some other reasons, besides fear of ridicule, I am disposed to carry out Judd's plan."

Davis turned to the others. "That settles the matter, gentlemen," he said. The room fell silent. There remained one final point to be decided. Pinkerton's plan allowed for one member of the suite to accompany Lincoln on the journey, along with the detective himself. "Now," said Judd, "the question was—who should go with him to Washington?" Tempers flared once again as each man present began arguing his own suitability. In Colonel Sumner's view, there could be no room for debate. Obviously, a military man would be the best choice, and he was the senior officer present.

Significantly, Col. Elmer Ellsworth was not in the room for these discussions. The young officer would undoubtedly have pressed hard for the position, being the only member of the party with any official designation as Lincoln's bodyguard. As it happened, Lincoln's train had been met in Harrisburg by a large delegation of Zouave soldiers, of the type made famous by Ellsworth's own drill team. "The corps of Zouaves elicited special attention," wrote Hay. "Colonel Ellsworth was in his glory." Ellsworth may well have been off reviewing the Zouave unit during the conference at the Jones House, or possibly he was fulfilling a second duty that had been pressed on him during the journey—entertaining Tad and Willie Lincoln. In any case, Ellsworth's fame would have made him a liability for the task ahead. He was nearly as recognizable as Lincoln himself. Captain Hazzard, who had been so prescient about the perils of Baltimore, was also absent from the discussions that afternoon. Although Major Hunter was present, and had spoken in favor of Pinkerton's plan, he would not have been seriously considered: His arm was still in a sling after the shoulder injury he had sustained in Buffalo.

Judd attempted to quiet the debate by proposing Ward Lamon as a compromise candidate. The others made to object, Judd said, but "Lincoln agreed with me, or I should have been kicked out of court." The burly, powerful Lamon, who had already done so much to protect Lincoln from the crush of unruly crowds along the way, never doubted that he would be chosen. There had already been discussions to that effect between Judd and Lincoln, he later reported, and "I had been selected as the proper person." In Lincoln's view, his wife would insist on Lamon, a man she knew and trusted.

Even now, Colonel Sumner would not be dissuaded. "It is against my judgment," he said of the planned subterfuge, "but I have undertaken to go to Washington with Mr. Lincoln, and I shall do it." The sixty-four-year-old Sumner, a veteran of the Black Hawk and Mexican-American wars, was perhaps not the most vigorous member of the party, but he was easily the most stubborn. His nickname of "Bullhead," according to legend, arose from the fact that a musket ball had once bounced off his head with little ill effect. Such men are not easily deterred. "I tried to convince him that any additional person added to the risk," Judd reported, "but the spirit of the gallant old soldier was up, and debate was useless." As the meeting came to a close, both Sumner and Lamon expected to travel with Lincoln to the capital.

AT FIVE O'CLOCK THAT EVENING, Lincoln sat down to dinner at the Jones House with Governor Curtin and several other prominent Pennsylvanians. Norman Judd was not at the table. He was said to be "giving personal attention to Mrs. Lincoln," who had now been notified of her husband's change of itinerary. Earlier, Lincoln had told Pinkerton that he would not be able to avoid bringing his wife in on the scheme. "This he said he could not avoid," Pinkerton reported, "as otherwise she would be very much excited at his absence." It appears that she was very much excited in any case. Though Judd and the other gentleman present that night declined to give any detail, it is clear that Mrs. Lincoln signaled her displeasure in no uncertain terms, and at such high volume that it threatened to give the game away. According to state senator Alexander K. McClure, one of the dinner guests that evening, "she narrowly escaped attracting attention to the movements which required utmost secrecy."

At about 5:45, having delivered the unhappy news to Mrs. Lincoln, Judd stepped into the dining room and tapped her husband on the shoulder. Lincoln had already shrugged off one or two similar signals, as if reluctant to acknowledge the necessity of his departure. McClure would later claim that Lincoln had expressed reservations at the table that night. He recalled, perhaps fancifully, that Lincoln spoke with "impressive earnestness" on the subject: "What would the nation think of its President stealing into the Capital like a thief in the night?" Be that as it may, Lincoln now rose from the table and excused himself, pleading fatigue for the benefit of any onlookers. Taking Governor Curtin by the arm, Lincoln strolled from the room without drawing any particular notice.

Upstairs in his room, Lincoln gathered a few articles of clothing for the journey. "In New York some friend had given me a new beaver hat in a box, and in it had placed a soft wool hat," he later commented. "I had never worn one of the latter in my life. I had this box in my room. Having informed a very few friends of the secret of my new movements, and the cause, I put on an old overcoat that I had with me, and putting the soft hat in my pocket, I walked out of the house at a back door, bareheaded, without exciting any special curiosity. Then I put on the soft hat and joined my friends without being recognized by strangers, for I was not the same man."

A "vast throng" had gathered at the front of the Jones House, perhaps hoping to hear one of Lincoln's balcony speeches. Governor Curtin, anxious to quiet any rumors if Lincoln were spotted leaving the hotel, called out orders to a carriage driver that the president-elect was to be taken to the Executive Mansion. If the departure drew any notice, he reasoned, it would be assumed that Lincoln was simply paying a visit to the governor's residence. As Curtin made his way back inside, he was joined by Ward Lamon and Colonel Sumner, the latter in full uniform, both waiting to depart with Lincoln. Drawing Lamon aside, Curtin asked if he was armed. Lamon "at once uncovered a small arsenal of deadly weapons, showing that he was literally armed to the teeth. In addition to a pair of heavy revolvers, he had a slung-shot and brass knuckles and a huge knife nestled under his vest." The slung-shot, a crude street weapon involving a weight tied to a wrist strap, was popular at that time among street gangs.

When Lincoln emerged, Judd would report, he carried a shawl draped over his arm. The shawl, according to Lamon, would help to mask Lincoln's features as he emerged from the hotel. Curtin led the group toward the side entrance of the hotel, where a carriage waited. As they made their way along the corridor, Judd whispered to Lamon, "As soon as Mr. Lincoln is in the carriage, drive off. The crowd must not be allowed to identify him."

Reaching the side door, Lamon climbed into the carriage first, then turned to help Lincoln and Curtin. At this, Judd stepped forward, steeling himself for the first of the evening's many deceits. "Colonel Sumner was following close after Mr. Lincoln," Judd recalled. "I put my hand gently on his shoulder. He turned round to see what was wanted, and before I had time to explain the carriage was off." Sumner, left behind on the pavement like a dim-witted schoolboy, was outraged. "A madder man you never saw," said Judd. One account has it that the old soldier wept with indignation.

Judd apologized in heartfelt terms. "When we get to Washington," he said, "Mr. Lincoln shall determine what apology is due you." Privately, Judd was relieved. The first phase of Pinkerton's scheme had gone according to plan.

TO THE END OF HIS LIFE, Pinkerton would enjoy telling a story concerning two newspapermen—possibly Joseph Howard of the *New York Times* and Simon Hanscom of the *New York Herald*—who were singled out for special treatment that evening. These two "knights of the quill," Pinkerton recalled, were preparing to attend a scheduled evening reception for Lincoln when "a gentlemanly individual, well-known to me" appeared at the door of their hotel room. "The visitor quickly informed the gentlemen that Mr. Lincoln had left the city and was now flying over the road in the direction of Washington," Pinkerton related. The reporters, startled by this unexpected news, "hastily arose, and, grasping their hats, started for the door," eager to get this bulletin onto the telegraph wires. "Their visitor, however, was too quick for them," Pinkerton noted with satisfaction, "and standing before the door with a revolver in each hand, he addressed them: 'You cannot leave this room, gentlemen, without my permission!'"

A heated exchange followed: "'What does this mean?' inquired one of the surprised gentlemen, blinking through his spectacles."

"'It means that you cannot leave this room until the safety of Mr. Lincoln justifies it,' calmly replied the other."

Before the journalists could protest further, the unnamed gentleman struck a deal. If they would bide their time until morning, he would "make matters interesting," with a full account of the "flank movement on the Baltimoreans."

"Their indignation and fright subsided at once," Pinkerton related, "and they quietly sat down. Refreshments were sent for, and soon the nimble pencils of the reporters were rapidly jotting down as much of the information as was advisable to be made public at that time."

Pinkerton's account bears the stamp of wishful thinking, but it is at least partially true. Years later, Joseph Howard of the *Times* would admit that he had been pulled aside that night and notified of what was transpiring. "The information had been given under an injunction of secrecy," he said. "We were bound by honor not to attempt to use it until the morning, and did not." Howard did, however, file a seemingly innocuous dispatch of earlier events in Harrisburg, which appeared the following morning. Seen in retrospect, the article appears freighted with secret knowledge of Lincoln's unexplained absence that evening: "Mr. Lincoln being physically prostrated by hard labor, did not give the anticipated reception, but like a prudent man went to bed early," Howard wrote. "We anticipate an exciting time today, and praying that it may prove an agreeable excitement, having a prosperous termination, I close."

Howard's next dispatch would be the most sensational of his career.

PART THREE

•

THE MARTYR and
THE SCAPEGOAT

Allan Pinkerton and Abraham Lincoln, with General John A. McClernand,
at Antietam, Maryland, October 3, 1862. *Courtesy of the Library of Congress*

CHAPTER TWENTY-ONE
THE FLIGHT OF ABRAHAM

•

Uncle Abe had gone to bed,
The night was dark and rainy
A laurelled night-cap on his head
Way down in Pennsylvany

They went and got a special train
At midnight's solemn hour,
And in a cloak and Scottish plaid shawl,
He dodged from the Slave-Power

Lanky Lincoln came to town
In night and wind, and rain, sir
Wrapped in a military cloak
Upon a special train, sir

—revised lyrics for "Yankee Doodle," which
appeared in several Democratic newspapers, February 1861

AT WILLARD'S HOTEL IN WASHINGTON the following morning—
Saturday, February 23—the ongoing Peace Convention was scheduled
to reconvene at 10:00 A.M. Lucius Chittenden, the Vermont delegate
whose midnight run to Baltimore one week earlier had left him convinced of a looming threat, noted an atmosphere of mounting excitement
among his colleagues. "There were a few Republicans whose faces shone
as they greeted each other," he reported, because they shared a momentous secret.

"Members were not particular about the position of their seats," Chittenden recalled, and that morning he happened to find himself squeezed between two outspoken Southerners: James A. Seddon, a former congressman from Virginia, and Missouri senator Waldo P. Johnson. Though Chittenden could not have known it at the time, both men would soon be serving the Confederacy—Johnson as an infantry colonel, and Seddon as secretary of war. That morning, however, both men had ostensibly gathered "to agree upon terms of compromise and peace." Moments after the morning session was gaveled to order, a note was handed to Seddon. "Mr. Seddon glanced at it," Chittenden wrote, "and passed it before me to Mr. Johnson, so near to my face that, without closing my eyes, I could not avoid reading it." The note confirmed what Chittenden and other Republicans already knew. "The words written upon it were: Lincoln is in this hotel!"

As Chittenden recalled the scene, Johnson "was startled as if by a shock of electricity" as he read the note. In the excitement, Johnson "must have forgotten himself completely," Chittenden continued. The Southern senator looked across at Seddon and blurted out, "How the devil did he get through Baltimore?"

With a look of "utter contempt" for the indiscretion, Seddon silenced his impulsive colleague with a sharp reply. "What," he growled, "would prevent his passing through Baltimore?"

"There was no reply," Chittenden noted, "but the occurrence left the impression on one mind that the preparations to receive Mr. Lincoln in Baltimore were known to some who were neither Italian assassins nor Baltimore Plug-Uglies." For the moment, Chittenden did not have time to ponder the implications of what he had overheard. As the news of Lincoln's unexpected arrival spread through the hall, the rising din of excited voices drowned out the repeated hammering of the speaker's gavel. It would be some time before the conference could resume.

IN BALTIMORE AT NEARLY THE SAME MOMENT, Otis K. Hillard fastened a palmetto cockade to his vest, a mark of the role he expected to play at the moment of Lincoln's arrival. Hillard had heard a rumor that Lincoln had already slipped through the city unannounced, but he did not believe it. He declared that he would carry through with his orders to be present at the Calvert Street Station at 12:30, when Lincoln's train was scheduled to arrive from Harrisburg. He asked his new friend Harry Davies to join him as he took up his assigned position.

As the two men made their way to Calvert Street, Davies noted that the streets were heaving with "some ten or fifteen thousand people," all of them pushing and jostling their way toward the depot. Hillard pointed out several members of the National Volunteers along the way, and stopped to speak with several of them. The excitement of the hour made Hillard far more talkative than he had been at any point since Davies's arrival in Baltimore. He swept his hand in the direction of a row of men standing in close formation. They were National Volunteers, too, he said, converging on the route that Lincoln was likely to take along Calvert Street. At Monument Square, site of a towering marble column commemorating the War of 1812's Battle of Baltimore, an especially large contingent had gathered. Hillard explained that "if by any mishap Lincoln should reach that point alive," having somehow emerged safely from the depot, he would get no farther than Monument Square, where the Volunteers would "rush en-mass" and strike him down. In the confusion, Hillard insisted, "it would be impossible for any outsider to tell who did the deed," and he boasted, "that from his position he would have the first shot."

The police, Hillard claimed, would present no obstacle. He told Davies that it was "so arranged, or was so understood by him, that the police were not to interfere." Instead, the officers would do just enough to give the appearance of doing their duty. Even if they did intervene, Hillard said, what could they do against a force of thousands? Besides, he noted with obvious satisfaction, their leader, Marshal Kane, was nowhere to be seen. "He knows his business," Hillard said.

By noon, as the rumors of Lincoln's safe arrival in Washington gathered force, cracks began to appear in Hillard's bravado. "Could it be true?" he asked Davies. If so, "how in hell had it leaked out that Lincoln was to be mobbed in Baltimore?" Lincoln must somehow have been warned, he told Davies, "or he would not have gone through as he did."

At 12:30, the scheduled arrival time of the Lincoln Special, Hillard began to panic. Had he and his colleagues been found out? Was he about to be arrested? Davies could not resist a gibe. "I told him he belonged to a damned nice set [if] seven thousand men could not keep track of one man." Hillard admitted that he could not explain how Lincoln could have given them the slip. He claimed that "they had men on the look out all the time," watching for any change of plan. Even now, Hillard clung to a hope that the rumors were false. The train was simply running late, he said. Lincoln would appear at any moment. But, he insisted, if "Lincoln got away" somehow, there would be a reckoning. It would be a signal that "the ball had commenced now for certain," and a direct attack on Washington would follow.

By 1:00 P.M., however, Hillard had spiraled into a state of despair. Special editions of the newspapers were now flowing into the streets. The rumors could no longer be denied: Lincoln was safe in Washington. William Louis Schley, one of the few Baltimore Republicans in the crowd that day, wrote to Lincoln to describe the scene: "[Y]ou may judge the disappointment at the announcement of your 'passage' through *unseen, unnoticed and unknown*—it fell like a thunder clap upon the Community." Schley went on to compliment Lincoln on a wise decision: "By your course you have saved *bloodshed and a mob.*"

Hillard still hoped the day was not lost. Leaving Davies at the depot, he went off in search of his fellow conspirators. By the time Davies caught up with him at his hotel later that afternoon, Hillard was much the worse for drink and "unusually noisy" as a result. "I told him to sit down, or lay down, and keep quiet," Davies said, but Hillard could not keep still. He paced back and forth, waving his hands in the air as he cautioned Davies to "be careful and not breathe a word." It was terrifying, Hillard admitted, to think that there might well be a spy in their midst. The Pinkerton man said nothing.

In spite of these fears, Hillard grew "quite merry" as the effects of the day's excitement and heavy drinking took hold. He insisted that a new plan was already being laid. Five thousand dollars had already been raised to buy arms, he told Davies, and soon there would be fifty men actively seeking a chance to kill Lincoln. "From what I could gather from him," Davies reported, "Washington City appeared now to be the principal point for action by those in the plot to take Lincoln's life."

Whatever happened next, Hillard claimed, at least one thing had been accomplished that day: Lincoln had disgraced himself in the eyes of both North and South. "It is a good thing that Lincoln passed through here as he did, because it will change the feeling of the Union men," Hillard declared. "They will think him a coward, and it will help our cause."

ON THIS LAST POINT, at least, Hillard appeared to have hit the mark. Though the details of Lincoln's "flanking movement" were not yet known—and would not be detailed at any length for some time—the obvious fact of his early arrival in Baltimore created an immediate sensation. In the absence of any official statement from Lincoln, rumors and half-truths churned through the newspapers. The previous day, an infuriated Colonel Sumner had blasted the Baltimore plan as "a damned piece of cowardice." Now, it appeared, much of the country agreed with him. "The telegraph brings astonishing news," ran a breathless dispatch in the *Cleveland Plain Dealer.* "Lincoln reached Washington this morning, twelve hours in advance of the appointed time. He runs through Maryland, traveling in a night train, and in cognito at that. He gives Baltimore the go by altogether." Having reported these few facts, the editors lost no time in passing judgment: "We fear he is wanting in pluck. If this flight cannot be reasonably accounted for, Maryland will take umbrage at this imputation upon her honor, and the public mind will be fired up and her secession will be inevitable."

Joseph Howard, breaking the story in the *New York Times*, attempted to characterize the action as a cunning piece of statesmanship. "Abraham Lincoln, the President Elect of the United States, is safe in the capital of the nation," he wrote, drawing on the advance warning he had almost certainly received in Harrisburg. "By the admirable arrangement of General Scott, the country has been spared the lasting disgrace, which would have been fastened indelibly upon it had Mr. Lincoln been murdered upon his journey thither, as he would have been had he followed the programme as announced."

The competing newspapers were unconvinced. "We don't believe it," exclaimed the *New York World.* "But even if it were true, how unfortunately was Mr. Lincoln advised. Had he known that there were murderers lying in wait for his life in Maryland, he should have refused the shelter of car or of carriage, and mounting a horse, like a man, have called his friends around him, and he would have ridden into Washington with an escort of thousands, and the conqueror of millions of loyal hearts." The *Herald,* unconsciously echoing a comment attributed to Lincoln himself, accused the president-elect of creeping into the city "like a thief in the night." The *New-York Tribune* appeared more conciliatory, stating that it seemed "probable" the decision had been wise, but there was scorn in a remark attributed to editor Horace Greeley: "Mr. Lincoln ought to have come through by daylight, if one-hundred guns had been pointed at him."

Even the members of Lincoln's own suite left behind in Harrisburg were reported to be dispirited. "The Republicans seem to feel the most chagrined at the sudden movement," wrote one observer. "Still, Mr. Lincoln is not blamed, but only his advisors. Others make a defense by saying that Mr. Lincoln can do as he pleases, that it is better to be prudent than rash, and that the matter was one of life and death."

Others were less forgiving. "I do not believe one word of the cock-and-bull story of the Italian assassins," declared the anonymous Washington insider known as "the Public Man." "When we have reached a point at which an elected President of the United States consents to be smuggled through by night to the capital of the country, lest he should be murdered in one of the chief cities of the Union, who can blame the rest of the world for believing that we are a failure?"

Perhaps the most striking perspective came from Frederick Douglass, whose memoir of life as a slave had sparked Allan Pinkerton's commitment to the abolitionist cause years earlier.

> The manner in which Mr. L entered the Capital was in keeping with the menacing and troubled state of the times. He reached the Capital as the poor, hunted fugitive slave reaches the North, in disguise, seeking concealment, evading pursuers, by the underground railroad, between two days, not during the sunlight, but crawling and dodging under the sable wing of night. He changed his programme, took another route, started at another hour, travelled in other company, and arrived at another time in Washington. We have no censure for the President at this point. He only did what braver men have done.

Douglass and many other writers drew particular attention to the fact that Lincoln was said to have made his journey in disguise. The matter of Lincoln's attire during the episode had by this time become a matter of furious debate, as well as a magnet for ridicule. Intentionally or not, Joseph Howard had touched off the controversy in his otherwise-sympathetic dispatch from Harrisburg, in which he gave a strangely elaborate description of Lincoln's traveling clothes. The president-elect, he noted, had set off for Washington in "a Scotch plaid cap and a very long military cloak, so that he was entirely unrecognizable." The words would haunt Lincoln for years to come. Though other witnesses reported him to be wearing perfectly ordinary clothing—"a soft, low-crowned hat," wrote one, "a muffler around his neck, and a short bob-tailed coat"—writers and illustrators across the country seized on Howard's description, transforming the plaid cap and long cloak into emblems of Lincoln's supposed cowardice. *Vanity Fair* published a giddy cartoon of Lincoln in a full Scottish kilt, complete with a coward's white feather protruding from a tartan cap, dancing a "Mac Lincoln Highland Fling" at the Harrisburg train station. *Harper's Weekly* chose to illustrate Howard's report with a sequence of drawings entitled "The Flight of Abraham," portraying Lincoln as a cringing milksop, ignoring the advice of his tearful advisers. Howard's description of the cap and cloak, quoted word for word, appeared beneath an image of a terrified Lincoln running at full speed toward the Capitol, with his coattails and the ribbons of his cap flying behind him. Another sketch, largely unknown until after the war, showed a wide-eyed Lincoln—again in a tartan cap—peering fretfully through the door of a freight car, alarmed at the hissing of a nearby cat.

One can only guess at Howard's motivation for describing Lincoln in these particular terms. Possibly he felt annoyance at his treatment in Harrisburg, or perhaps he intended a private dig at the Scottish-born Pinkerton, whose name he had been forbidden to include in his account. In any case, Howard's report had not been entirely without foundation, as Lincoln himself made reference to a "soft wool hat," and Lamon took note of a shawl that the president-elect used to disguise his features. Whatever Howard's intention, however, the resulting avalanche of scorn may well have come as a surprise even to him.

In years to come, the men who had been with Lincoln that night would attempt to blunt the edge of the derision. "The story of the Scotch cap I may as well at this time pronounce a falsehood made up out of the whole cloth," Pinkerton would write. "He wore an overcoat thrown loosely over his shoulders without his arms being in the sleeves, and a black Kossuth hat, which he told me somebody had presented to him." Ward Lamon, too, offered a pointed rebuttal. "As Mr. Lincoln's dress on this occasion has been much discussed," he would write, "it may be as well to state that he wore a soft, light felt hat, drawn down over his face when it seemed necessary or convenient, and a shawl thrown over his shoulders, and pulled up to assist in disguising his features when passing to and from the carriage. This was all there was of the 'Scotch cap and cloak' so widely celebrated in the political literature of the day." Lucius Chittenden, though not directly involved that night, would offer an alternate explanation, insisting that Lincoln, like other nocturnal travelers of the period, was provided with a "knitted woolen cap" to wear during the trip. "This he wore on his night-trip to Washington," Chittenden explained rather tepidly. "There was no necessity for disguise."

By this time, however, the damage had been done. Writing in the immediate aftermath, John Hay attempted to dispel the "picturesque illusion" of the unseemly disguise, but he conceded that it had now become "too dramatic to be squelched." The details would be greatly embellished as the story passed below the Mason-Dixon line. One Kentucky newspaper went so far as to suggest that Lincoln had exchanged clothes with his wife in Harrisburg and made his way through Baltimore in a dress. The story was typical of the reaction in the Southern press. "Everybody here is disgusted at this cowardly and undignified entry," reported the *Charleston Mercury.*

Not surprisingly, the most bitter words on the subject were to be found in the *Baltimore Sun,* where the news had been received as a wholesale slander:

> Had we any respect for Mr. Lincoln, official or personal, as a man, or as President elect of the United States, his career and speeches on his way to the seat of government would have cruelly impaired it; but the final escapade by which he reached the capital would have utterly demolished it, and overwhelmed us with mortification. As it is, no sentiment of respect of whatever sort with respect to the man suffers violence on our part, at anything he may do. He might have entered Willard's hotel with a "head-spring" and a "summersault," and the clown's merry greeting to General Scott, "Here we are!" and we should care nothing about it, personally. We do not believe the Presidency can ever be more degraded by any of his successors than it has been by him, even before his inauguration; and so, for aught we care, he may go to the full extent of his wretched comicalities. We have only too much cause to fear that such a man, and such advisers as he has, may prove capable of infinitely more mischief than folly when invested with power. A lunatic is only dangerous when armed and turned loose.

The editors went on to express outrage at the offense given to the honor and reputation of Baltimore. Not only were the accusations wholly without foundation, they insisted, but a large crowd had gathered to welcome Lincoln to the city, unaware that he considered them to be "a party of cutthroats, assassins and railway-accident makers." After several more columns of vitriol, the *Sun* called for proof of the "monstrous absurdities" that had been reported in the Northern press:

> If there were truth—one glimmer of truth in all this—the very first thing that truth itself would demand is the full exposition of the whole plot, and the trial and condemnation, on proof of

guilt, of every individual identified with it. And such, indeed, would be the course of procedure. It is, however, in the whole and in all its parts, a lie, a gross and shameless lie, concocted with a view to shield from the ignominy of his disgraceful flight the President elect of the United States, at the expense of the people of Baltimore.

The people of Baltimore were wholly justified in calling for this proof, but it would not be forthcoming. Both Lincoln and Judd had promised Pinkerton that the details of what had happened that night would be withheld so that the detective's work could continue in Baltimore and elsewhere. Honoring this pledge, however, resulted in a devastating blow to Lincoln's prestige at the worst-possible moment, adding fuel to the secessionist fervor sweeping through the Southern states. At a stroke, Lincoln appeared to have undone all the hard work of his inaugural journey and its carefully honed message of unity. In the days leading up to his all-important inaugural address, intended to "soothe the public mind," he would find himself fighting a rear-guard action to regain his political capital. "Public sentiment is everything," he later declared. "With public sentiment, nothing can fail; without it, nothing can succeed."

In the absence of a concrete, official account giving Lincoln's side of the story, the rumors and condemnations continued to mount. "The number of conjectures which have been hazarded would, if they were dollars, pay the national debt," wrote John Hay. "The stupid questions which have been expressed, the illogical explanations of the matter which have been offered, the amount, in brief, of vapor which has been conversationally emitted, may fairly be spoken of as the unknown quantity."

It would be many years before that vapor dispersed and a true account of "The Flight of Abraham" began to emerge.

CHAPTER TWENTY-TWO
THE HOUR OF PERIL

•

Hitherto I have kept silent upon this subject . . .
—ALLAN PINKERTON, January 8, 1868

"NOW THE RUMORS HITHERTO NEBULOUS began to take definite form," John Hay wrote two days after Lincoln's unscheduled arrival in Washington, "first whispered, then spoken, and finally bellowed from one end of the town to the other." The city of Washington, Hay reported, was rife with stories of oaths taken upon daggers, sharpshooters crouched in attic windows, torpedoes to be hurled beneath Lincoln's carriage, and plans to throw the presidential train off the track "for the gentle purpose of bayoneting any possible survivors." In fact, Hay insisted, if Lincoln had as many lives as a cat, he would have lost them all if even half the rumors were true. No arrests had been made, he continued, but there was no shortage of suspects: "An Italian barber wanders vaguely through this shadowy surmise; a leader of the Baltimore carbonari, probably, who wears a slouch hat and gives an easy shave for six cents." For all of that, Hay was at pains to say that Lincoln entertained no fears for his safety. His actions had been motivated by simple expedience, discretion being the greater part of valor. "There will, of course, be future disclosures concerning the matter," Hay concluded. "Even up to this time it is impossible to form an opinion which may not be controverted by the revelations of tomorrow."

As far as Pinkerton was concerned, there would be no future disclosures. He had sworn the main participants to secrecy, and arranged matters so that the minor players had no sense of the larger plan. In many cases, even those directly involved in carrying out crucial elements of the detective's design were ignorant of the roles they had played. Once again, secrecy had been the lever of his success. The entire operation, Pinkerton admitted with satisfaction, had gone off precisely as he had hoped.

AMONG THE CREW OF SAMUEL FELTON'S RAILROAD, it appeared that the most notable thing to occur on the evening of February 22 had been a set of special instructions concerning the eleven o'clock train from Philadelphia. Felton himself had directed the conductor to hold his train at the station to await the arrival of a special courier, who would hand off a vitally important parcel. Under no circumstance could the train depart without it, Felton warned, "as this package *must* go through to Washington on *tonight's* train."

In fact, the package was a decoy, part of an elaborate web of bluffs and blinds that Pinkerton had constructed to limit the number of people who knew what was actually happening that night. In order to make it convincing, Felton would recall, he and Pinkerton had assembled a formidable-looking parcel done up with an impressive wax seal. Inside was a stack of useless old railroad reports. "I marked it 'Very important—To be delivered, without fail, by eleven o'clock train,'" Felton recalled. The name on the package was Mr. E. J. Allen, care of Willard's Hotel, Washington, D.C. "E. J. Allen," as Pinkerton would later admit, "was the *nom-de-plume* I generally used when on detective operations."

Pinkerton realized that ruses of this type would be crucial if he expected to accomplish his task. Lincoln's original plans for traveling from Harrisburg to Washington had been admirably direct, a two-part run of just over one hundred miles, with a change of stations in Baltimore. Now, under Pinkerton's plan, Lincoln would instead set off on a three-part marathon, backtracking from Harrisburg to Philadelphia on the Pennsylvania Railroad, jumping from there to Baltimore on Felton's line, and finally connecting with a Baltimore and Ohio train into Washington. In all, Lincoln would have to cover some 250 miles in a single night—doubling the original distance—and running in darkness for most of the journey, with two changes of train. Though laborious and indirect, the revised scheme would accomplish Pinkerton's original goal of bringing Lincoln through Baltimore earlier than expected. In addition, Lincoln would make his approach to the city on a different rail line, and arrive at a different station, which might allow him to slip past any sentries acting on behalf of the conspirators, who expected him to arrive at the Calvert Street Station on the Northern Central line direct from Harrisburg.

The added mileage was only the first of many problems Pinkerton faced that night. Though Lincoln would be making the first leg of his trip in a private train, Pinkerton could not risk using special equipment for the remaining two segments of the journey, as it would draw attention to Lincoln's movements to have an unscheduled special train on the tracks that night. In order to travel anonymously, Lincoln would have to ride on regular passenger trains, gambling that the privacy of an ordinary sleeping compartment would be sufficient to conceal his presence.

Having charted this route, Pinkerton now confronted a scheduling problem. The train carrying Lincoln from Harrisburg on the first segment of his journey would likely not reach Philadelphia in time to connect with the second segment, the eleven o'clock train to Baltimore. Felton's decoy parcel, it was hoped, would hold the Baltimore-bound train at the depot, without drawing undue suspicion, until Lincoln could be smuggled aboard. If all went according to plan, Lincoln would arrive in Baltimore in the dead of night. His sleeper car would then be unhitched and drawn by horse to the Camden Street Station, where it would be coupled to a Washington train for the final leg of the journey.

Pinkerton had laid his plans "keenly, shrewdly and well," as Norman Judd would say, drawing on his long experience in railroad security to coordinate details across the three separate lines. So long as Lincoln's presence remained secret, Pinkerton assured Judd, there would be little danger of any of the three trains being attacked. It was essential, therefore, that Lincoln should not be recognized at any stage of the journey.

With that in mind, the task of getting Lincoln safely aboard the Baltimore-bound passenger train would be especially delicate, as it would have to be done in plain view of the passengers and crew. For this, Pinkerton needed a second decoy, and he counted on Kate Warne to supply it. In Philadelphia, Mrs. Warne made arrangements to reserve four double berths on the sleeper car at the back of the train. She had been instructed by Pinkerton to "get in the sleeping car and *keep* possession" until he arrived with Lincoln, but when the time came, the job proved difficult. "I found it almost impossible to save the berths together," she reported, because arriving passengers were permitted to take any available space. As the train began to fill up, Mrs. Warne grew anxious, fearing that only a few scattered places would remain by the time Pinkerton got there. In that case, he and Lincoln would be obliged to wedge themselves into whatever berths happened to be vacant, and any hope of concealing the president-elect's identity would be lost. As more and more passengers climbed aboard, rapidly filling the available berths, Mrs. Warne flagged down a conductor and pressed some money into his hand. She needed a special favor, she said, because she would be traveling with her "invalid brother," who would retire immediately to his compartment and remain there behind closed blinds. It was important, due to his fragile nature, that a group of spaces be held at the back of the train to ensure his comfort and privacy. The conductor, seeing the obvious concern in the young woman's face, nodded his head and took up a position at the rear door of the train.

IN HARRISBURG, SIMILAR ARRANGEMENTS were being carried out by a late addition to Pinkerton's network: George C. Franciscus, a superintendent of the Pennsylvania Railroad. Pinkerton had confided in Franciscus the previous day, since the last-minute revision of his plan required Lincoln to make the first leg of his journey on Franciscus's line. "I had no hesitation in telling him what I desired," Pinkerton reported, because he had worked with Franciscus previously and knew him to be "a true and loyal man." After spending much of Thursday night in conference with Pinkerton in Philadelphia, Franciscus had traveled to Harrisburg the following morning—catching a ride on the Lincoln Special—to make certain that the initial phase of the plan went smoothly.

Later that afternoon, when he got final word that Lincoln had consented to the plan, Franciscus put the wheels in motion. A Pennsylvania Railroad fireman named Daniel Garman recalled that Franciscus came hurrying up to him, "very much excited," with orders to get a special train charged and ready. "I quick went and oiled up the engine and lighted the head light and turned up my fire," Garman recalled. As he finished, he looked out and saw engineer Edward Black running along the track at full speed. Having been ordered by Franciscus to report for emergency duty, Black now hopped up into the cab and scrambled to make ready, apparently under the impression that a private train was needed to carry a group of railroad executives to Philadelphia. "I said everything was all ready," Garman recalled, and the two men backed the engine into the depot and coupled to an empty saloon car. This done, they ran the two-car special a mile south toward Front Street, as instructed, and idled at a track crossing to wait for their passengers. Franciscus, meanwhile, had circled back to the Jones House in a carriage, pulling up just as Governor Curtin, Ward Lamon, and Lincoln himself—his appearance masked by his unfamiliar hat and shawl—emerged from the side entrance of the hotel. As the door closed behind the passengers, Franciscus flicked his whip and started off in the direction of the railroad tracks, with the indignant cries of the abandoned Colonel Sumner trailing after him.

As the carriage clattered through the streets, Governor Curtin noted a crush of people gathering at his official residence on South Second Street. "The halls, stairways and pavement in front of the house were much crowded," he said, "and no doubt the impression prevailed that Mr. Lincoln was going to the Executive Mansion with me." Instead, the carriage thundered past and made directly for the waiting train.

At the Front Street crossing, engineer Black and fireman Garman had barely maneuvered their two-car special into position when the carriage rolled to a stop alongside. Garman looked on as a tall person quietly alighted, escorted by Franciscus, and made his way down the tracks to the saloon car, in the company of a group of local railroad men. Once he and the other travelers were on board, Garman said, "the gong rang and we did some lively running." Lincoln's 250-mile dash to Washington was under way.

Even as the train vanished into the darkness, Andrew Wynne of the American Telegraph Company was climbing a square-cut wooden utility pole two miles south of town. Under the direction of George Burns and others, Wynne carefully laid a copper ground wire across the cables at the top, cutting off all telegraph communication between Harrisburg and Baltimore. The wires that Wynne had cut, however, did not belong to the American Telegraph Company. Earlier that day, Wynne had been asked by his supervisor if he would object to "fixing the wires" of a rival company to prevent any communications from passing over them. "I answered I would not," he recalled, "in some cases." This, apparently, was one of those cases.

Governor Curtin, meanwhile, returned to the Executive Mansion and spent the rest of the evening turning away callers, so as to give the impression that Lincoln was resting inside. It was "eminently proper," Curtin said, "that it should not be generally known that Mr. Lincoln had left Harrisburg."

ON BOARD THE TRAIN, Edward Black and Daniel Garman were pushing their engine to the limit. "If ever I got a fast ride," Garman said, "I did that night." All other trains had been shunted off the main line to allow the special an unimpeded run. Black had been instructed to make no stops, apart from essential watering breaks, and to arrive at the West Philadelphia depot as speedily as could be managed without running off the tracks. Garman would recall shoveling coal at such a frantic pace that much of it wound up on the floor. At times, he said, he was literally rolling in it.

In the passenger coach, Lincoln and his fellow travelers sat in the dark, so as to reduce the chance that the president-elect would be spotted at a watering stop. The precaution wasn't entirely successful. At one of the stops, as Garman bent to connect a hose pipe, he caught sight of Lincoln in the moonlight streaming through the door of the coach. He ran forward to tell Black that "the rail-splitter was on the train," only to be muzzled by Franciscus, who warned him not to say a word. "You bet I kept quiet then," Garman recalled.

Climbing back into the cab alongside Black, Garman could not entirely contain his excitement. He cautiously asked his colleague if he had any idea what was going on in the saloon car. "I don't know," the engineer replied, "but just keep the engine hot." By this time, Black may well have had suspicions of his own. Earlier that day, he had driven the flag-draped special that brought Lincoln to Harrisburg to address the state legislature. "I was introduced to Lincoln," Black recalled, "and after a few words, he shook me by the hand, handed me a cigar, and passed into the train. Could I only have foreseen what was to occur in the next few years I think that cigar, instead of being smoked, would have been kept as a precious and hallowed remembrance."

Now, some nine hours later, there were no cigars or other pleasantries. Lincoln, exhausted from the labors of the previous days, sat in the darkened saloon car with his eyes closed as Garman and Black bent to their work in the cab. Compared to the luxurious trappings of the earlier trains in which Lincoln had ridden, the arrangements that night were notably spartan. As the train paused to take on more water in Downingtown, Lamon and the other passengers climbed down to find refreshments, leaving Lincoln huddled by himself in the dark train. "A cup of tea and a roll was taken to him in the car," recalled one of the railroad men.

Aside from watering stops, the train ran "mighty sharp" for the entire length of the line. "I have often wondered what people thought of that short train whizzing through the night," engineer Black would later say. "A case of life and death, perhaps, and so it was."

IN PHILADELPHIA, ALLAN PINKERTON had been in a state of suspense for two hours, awaiting word that Lincoln was safely under way. Though the telegraph wires between Harrisburg and Baltimore had been cut at the detective's instigation, communications into Philadelphia were operating normally under the watchful eye of a Pinkerton confidant. Eager for news, Pinkerton made the rounds of the telegraph and express offices to see if any reports had arrived. Finally, at 8:30 P.M., he fired off a message to George Burns, using the agreed-upon cipher: "Where is Nuts?" After forty-five agonizing minutes, the answer came: "Nuts left at six—Everything as you directed—all is right."

Greatly relieved, Pinkerton readied himself for the next phase of the operation. Hiring a closed carriage, he made his way to the Pennsylvania Railroad's West Philadelphia depot at Market and Thirty-Second streets. Pinkerton left the carriage waiting at the curb and took up a position near the main stairs, where he could keep an eye on the arriving trains. Soon, the detective was joined by H. F. Kenney, another of Samuel Felton's employees. Kenney reported that he had just come from the Philadelphia, Wilmington and Baltimore depot across town, where he had issued orders to hold the Baltimore-bound train for Felton's "important parcel." Pinkerton checked his watch. "Thus far," he noted, "everything had passed off admirably."

Just after ten o'clock, the squeal of brake blocks and the hiss of steam announced the arrival of the two-car special from Harrisburg, well ahead of schedule. As the train lurched to a halt, George Franciscus handed over two ten-dollar gold pieces to Black and Garman. Later, when Garman realized exactly what had happened that night, he commented on Franciscus's generosity: "So we can say that we got the first money in protecting the President," he declared proudly.

In fact, Garman's and Black's heroic efforts had created a problem for Pinkerton. As he stepped forward and exchanged hushed greetings with Lincoln, Pinkerton realized that the early arrival of the Harrisburg train left him with too much time on his hands. The Baltimore-bound train was not scheduled to leave for nearly an hour, and Felton's depot was only three miles away. It wouldn't do to linger at either train station, where Lincoln might be recognized, nor could he be seen on the streets. Pinkerton decided that Lincoln would be safest inside a moving carriage. To avoid arousing the carriage driver's suspicions, he told Kenney to distract him with a time-consuming set of directions, which included "driving northward in search of some imaginary person." Franciscus and the other Harrisburg railroad men took their leave of Lincoln at the depot and offered prayers for the remaining portion of the journey. "Mr. Lincoln thanked them for their kindness," Pinkerton reported, "and I promised to telegraph them in the morning." As Franciscus withdrew, Pinkerton, Lamon, and Lincoln, his features partly masked by his shawl, took their seats in the carriage. "I took mine alongside the driver," Kenney recalled, and gave a convoluted set of orders that sent them rolling in aimless circles through the streets.

ACROSS TOWN, STANDING BESIDE the Baltimore-bound train, George Dunn was growing anxious. Dunn, the Harnden's Express agent whom Pinkerton had sent to Baltimore earlier that day, had returned to Philadelphia in time to meet up with Kate Warne at the depot. He gave Mrs. Warne the reports he had collected at Pinkerton's South Street office, and assisted her in making the necessary arrangements for their "invalid friend," who was expected to appear at any moment. As the scheduled departure time neared, Dunn wished to satisfy himself that "everything was free, clear and safe." He decided to walk through the interior of the train to make sure he saw nothing suspicious. At the front of the sleeping car, he noticed "a small party of men, who from their quiet talk, vigilant appearance and watchfulness, seemed to be on the alert for somebody or something," Dunn reported. "This feature was not at all satisfactory to me. Knowing the public feeling, I felt very sure that it boded no good to my expected party."

As the suspicious characters clustered at the front door of the train, Dunn "quickly concluded" that Lincoln should enter at the back. Finding the rear door locked, Dunn sought out the porter of the sleeping car and asked for the key. "At first he declined," Dunn recalled, "but on explanation of the fact that it was for the accommodation of an invalid, who would arrive late, and did not desire to be carried through the narrow passageway of the crowded car, he consented to the arrangement." Dunn would recall this moment with pride to the end of his life. In a later conversation with Pinkerton, he reported, the detective "complimented me very highly on my forethought and complete arrangements."

For the moment, Dunn's greatest concern was letting Pinkerton know of his actions so that the detective could avoid the suspicious group at the front of the train. Dunn slipped quietly out the back of the sleeper, locked the door behind him, and kept an anxious eye on the front doors of the station.

LINCOLN, MEANWHILE, was clattering through the streets "as if on the lookout for someone," sandwiched between the small, wiry Pinkerton and the tall, stocky Ward Lamon. Lincoln used the time to brief the detective on what had occurred in Harrisburg. He admitted that he had shared the details of Pinkerton's plan with the members of his suite, as well as with Governor Curtin, explaining that he would have "found it impossible to get away from the crowd" without their help. Pinkerton was distressed by the ever-widening circle of people who were now in on the secret, but in his field report he expressed satisfaction with the way Lincoln had dismissed the objections of his closest advisers: "Mr. Lincoln said that he knew me, and had confidence in me and would trust himself and his life in my hands."

Lincoln also shared details of the visit from Frederick Seward the previous night at the Continental Hotel. The warning Seward brought had been "substantially the same" as Pinkerton's, Lincoln reported, but the details were "much stronger," suggesting a plot far greater in scope. According to Senator Seward and General Scott, there were "about fifteen thousand men" standing ready to prevent Lincoln's passage through Baltimore. In addition, Lincoln had been told, plans were laid to blow up the railroad tracks and set fire to the train. "Here," as Ward Lamon would write, "was a plot big enough to swallow up the little one."

Pinkerton had heard such claims many times in Baltimore, but it would have been unsettling to hear them repeated by Lincoln himself, on the authority of the highest-ranking military officer in the nation. The previous day, the detective had insisted to both Judd and Lincoln that only a small handful of men were in on the plot. Soon enough, he would claim that he had never wavered in this conviction, but at that moment, sitting in the darkened carriage beside Lincoln, Pinkerton must have experienced a ghastly moment of doubt. Whatever lay ahead in Baltimore—a dozen men or an army of thousands—the die was cast. Lincoln, at least, appeared perfectly content to press ahead. "Mr. Lincoln was cool, calm, and self possessed—firm and determined in his bearing," Pinkerton recalled. "He evinced no sign of fear or distrust."

Ward Lamon did not share Lincoln's confidence. Unsettled by what might lay ahead, and perhaps irritated at the manner in which Pinkerton had usurped his role, he now made an extravagant gesture to reclaim his ground as Lincoln's protector. Reaching into his pockets, Lamon pulled out a revolver and a bowie knife. As Pinkerton looked on in disbelief, he held them out to Lincoln, offering the president-elect a chance to arm himself. "I at once protested," Pinkerton wrote in his field report, "saying that I would not for the world have it said that Mr. Lincoln had to enter the National Capitol armed; that I anticipated no trouble; that if we went through at all we must do so by stratagem, but that if fighting had to be done, it must be done by others than Mr. Lincoln." The president-elect, Pinkerton later insisted, shared his views. "Mr. Lincoln said that he wanted no arms, that he had no fears and that he felt satisfied that all my plans would work right."

Pinkerton's reasoning was sound, but it is likely that the rebuff gave offense to Lamon. As Kate Warne would note, the detective was "sick, and tired out" from strain and lack of sleep. He had already expressed irritation with Lamon the previous evening upon being addressed by his proper name, rather than by his alias. In the carriage, having just learned of General Scott's estimation of the forces waiting in Baltimore, he likely interpreted Lamon's gesture as a lack of confidence in his plan. Even at the best of times, Pinkerton was not noted for his even disposition. One suspects, in these circumstances, that his response to Lamon had not been quite so measured as he reported, and that perhaps some colorful Scottish idioms were heard. In any case, Pinkerton would soon learn that Ward Lamon was a dangerous man to cross.

At last, the meandering drive through the outskirts of Philadelphia had consumed sufficient time. Pinkerton banged on the roof of the carriage and barked out an order to make straight for the PW&B depot. "Driving up to the sidewalk on Carpenter Street, and in the shadow of a tall fence, the carriage was stopped and the party alighted," Pinkerton wrote. Lamon kept watch from the rear as Pinkerton walked ahead, with Lincoln "leaning upon my arm and stooping a considerable [amount] for the purpose of disguising his height." As they approached the train, Pinkerton scanned for signs of anything that was out of place. Kate Warne came forward to lead them to the sleeper car, "familiarly greeting the President as her brother." In one rather colorful recounting of the scene, Lincoln responded in high style: "I believe it has not hitherto been one of the perquisites of the presidency to acquire in full bloom so charming and accomplished a female relation." It seems unlikely that this well-turned phrase was spoken that night, but even Ward Lamon had praise for Mrs. Warne's arrangements. "The business had been managed very adroitly by the female spy," he remarked.

As the travelers reached the train platform, George Dunn's great moment had at last arrived. "I quickly caught Mr. Pinkerton's eye," he reported. Dunn motioned toward the rear of the train, bent down to unlock the door, and stood aside as Pinkerton brought Lincoln aboard "without unnecessary delay, and without anyone being aware of the distinguished visitor who had arrived."

At the same moment, as the rear door closed behind the travelers, H. F. Kenney made his way to the front of the train to deliver Felton's decoy parcel. The package was placed in the hands of the unsuspecting conductor as the whistle sounded and the train lurched into motion. Pinkerton would claim that only two minutes elapsed between Lincoln's arrival at the depot and the departure of the train: "So carefully had all our movements been conducted, that no one in Philadelphia saw Mr. Lincoln enter the car, and no one on the train, except his own immediate party—not even the conductor—knew of his presence."

THE SECOND LEG OF THE JOURNEY, from Philadelphia to Baltimore, was expected to take four and a half hours. The accommodations in the sleeper were crude—George Pullman's luxurious "hotel" cars were not yet in use—and Lincoln's party had to make do with narrow padded benches. Kate Warne had managed to secure the rear half of the car, four pairs of berths in all, but there was little privacy. Only a curtain separated them from the strangers in the forward half, so the travelers were at pains to avoid drawing attention. Lincoln was shown to a berth and encouraged to remain out of sight behind hanging drapes, but he would not be getting much rest that night. As Mrs. Warne noted, he was "so very tall that he could not lay straight in his berth."

As the train cleared the Philadelphia city limits, Mrs. Warne handed over the reports George Dunn had collected in Baltimore. Pinkerton spent a few moments studying them, until a train conductor entered the car to collect their tickets. Pinkerton quickly intercepted him and produced Lincoln's ticket, explaining that the "sick man" had already retired for the evening. The conductor glanced briefly at the closed curtains but left without further scrutiny. Pinkerton noted with satisfaction that he "did not return again during the trip."

As the train pressed on toward Baltimore, Pinkerton, Lamon, and Mrs. Warne settled into their berths so as to appear to be ordinary travelers. Lamon recalled that Lincoln relieved the tension by indulging in a joke or two, "in an undertone," from behind his curtain. "He talked very friendly for some time," said Mrs. Warne. "The excitement seemed to keep us all awake." Apart from Lincoln's occasional comments, all was silent. "None of our party appeared to be sleepy," Pinkerton noted, "but we all lay quiet."

Pinkerton's nerves kept him from lying still for more than a few minutes at a time. At regular intervals, he would step through the rear door of the car and keep watch from the back platform, scanning the track for signs of trouble. "I had arranged with my men a series of signals along the road," he explained. It was still possible that "some reckless individuals" might be planning to destroy Felton's tracks, or that "a suspicion of our movements might be entertained by the conspirators, and therefore the utmost caution must be observed." As the train flashed past, each of Pinkerton's watchmen raised a lantern in turn, signaling that all was well.

The train slowed as it neared the Susquehanna River, where each car was to be uncoupled and ferried across the water by steamer to Havre de Grace. From the earliest days of the operation, even before he suspected a threat against Lincoln, Pinkerton had understood that this crossing marked the point of greatest danger to Felton's railroad. The ferry could be easily set ablaze, he realized, and if saboteurs had set their sights on the train itself, a night crossing would provide ideal cover. Timothy Webster and Hattie Lawton had been stationed in the area for weeks to ferret out and prevent hostile action, but if Lincoln had been spotted leaving Harrisburg—or if loose talk had filtered down to Baltimore—this would be the likely point of attack.

At last, as the crossing loomed, Pinkerton saw that his precautions had been effective. "I went to the rear platform of the car," he wrote, "and as the train passed on a bright light flashed suddenly upon my gaze and was as quickly extinguished, and then I knew that thus far all was well."

Lincoln, too, appeared conscious of the importance of the river crossing. "We are at Havre de Grace," he said when Pinkerton stepped back inside, "we are getting along very well. I think we are on time." Pinkerton marveled at his composure. "I cannot realize how any man situated as he was could have shown more calmness or firmness."

There would be several more points where danger might present itself that night, including the wooden bridge spanning the Gunpowder River, but Pinkerton was able to report that "nothing of importance transpired" for the remainder of the journey. Later, he would admit to a tremendous sense of relief at seeing the unbroken line of lantern signals each time he stepped out onto the rear platform. "From this point all the way to Baltimore, at every bridge-crossing, these lights flashed, and their rays carried the comforting assurance: 'All's Well!'"

◆

AT 3:30 A.M., SAMUEL FELTON'S "night line" train steamed into Balti-more's President Street depot on schedule. As the cars rolled to a halt, an "officer of the road" named William Stearns entered the rear compart-ment. Stearns, along with his brother George, had been assigned by Fel-ton to keep watch over the running of the train, in case further delaying tactics were needed on the final leg of the journey. As Pinkerton stepped forward, Stearns whispered that "all was right" in Baltimore.

Kate Warne took her leave of Lincoln while the train idled at the sta-tion, as she was no longer needed to pose as the sister of the "invalid trav-eler." She followed Pinkerton out of the car and set off for her hotel "for the purpose of ascertaining what the feelings of the people were in the city." Mrs. Warne likely carried instructions for Harry Davies and the oth-ers to watch for signs of fresh activity among the plotters once the news of Lincoln's "secret maneuver" became known. It has also been suggested that her departure was a nod to decorum, as it might be taken amiss if Lincoln were to arrive in Washington in the company of a woman who was not his wife. In any case, one hopes that Pinkerton permitted her an hour or two of sleep before resuming her duties.

As Mrs. Warne rode off in a carriage, Pinkerton climbed back up into the sleeper where Lincoln and Lamon lay quietly in their berths. Pinker-ton listened intently as rail workers uncoupled the sleeper and hitched it to a team of horses. With a sudden lurch, the car began its slow, creaking progress through the streets of Baltimore toward the Camden Street Sta-tion, just over a mile away. "The city was in profound repose as we passed through," Pinkerton remarked. "Darkness and silence reigned over all." Lamon would recall that Lincoln "lay close in his berth" during the trans-fer, while the other passengers, "tucked away on their narrow shelves, dozed on as peacefully as if Mr. Lincoln had never been born."

Pinkerton's thoughts raced as the sleeper rolled quietly through the streets he had come to know well. In particular, he brooded on his recent report from Harry Davies, which described the meeting where Cypriano Ferrandini had presided over the drawing of ballots to determine Lincoln's killer. "Perhaps, at this moment," he reflected, "the reckless conspirators were astir, perfecting their plans for a tragedy as infamous as any which has ever disgraced a free country—perhaps even now the holders of the *red* ballots were nerving themselves for their part in the dreadful work, or were tossing restlessly upon sleepless couches." If so, there was no sign of it along Pratt Street as the horses pulled the sleeper past the Light Street

Wharf. Apart from the gentle clatter of hooves and the faint squeal of the sleeper car's wheels, the night remained utterly still.

Pinkerton had calculated that Lincoln would spend only forty-five minutes in Baltimore if all went according to plan. Arriving at the Camden Street Station, however, he found that they would have to endure an unexpected delay, owing to a late-arriving train. For Pinkerton, who feared that even the smallest variable could upset his entire plan, the wait was agonizing. So far, there had been no sign of life in the "great slumbering city," but with the coming of dawn, the busy terminus would spring to life with the "usual bustle and activity." With every passing moment, discovery became more likely. Lincoln, at least, seemed perfectly sanguine about the situation. "Mr. Lincoln remained quietly in his berth," Pinkerton said, "joking with rare good humor."

After a time, Ward Lamon recalled, the silence was broken by a loud hammering noise, which proved to be the thump of a heavy club against a night watchman's wooden booth. "It was an Irishman," said Lamon, "trying to arouse a sleepy ticket-agent, comfortably ensconced within. For twenty minutes the Irishman pounded the box with ever-increasing vigor, and, at each report of his blows, shouted at the top of his voice, 'Captain! It's four o'clock! It's four o'clock!'" This went on for some time, according to Lamon, and even in the strained circumstances, he and Lincoln couldn't help but laugh. "The Irishman seemed to think that time had ceased to run at four o'clock," Lamon said, "and, making no allowance for the period consumed by his futile exercises, repeated to the last his original statement that it was four o'clock." Pinkerton added that Lincoln offered "several witty remarks" on the situation, "showing that he was as full of fun as ever."

As the wait dragged on, however, Lincoln's mood darkened briefly. Now and then, Pinkerton said, "snatches of rebel harmony" would reach their ears, sung by passengers waiting at the depot. At the sound of a drunken voice roaring through a chorus of "Dixie," Lincoln turned to Pinkerton and offered a somber reflection: "No doubt there will be a great time in Dixie by and by."

As the skies began to brighten with the coming of dawn, Pinkerton peered through the blinds for a sign of the late-arriving train that would carry them the rest of the way to Washington. Unless it came soon, all advantage would be swept away by the rising sun. If Lincoln were to be discovered now, pinned to the spot at Camden Street and cut off from any assistance or reinforcements, he would have only Lamon and Pinkerton to defend him. If a mob should assemble, Pinkerton realized, the prospects would be very bleak indeed.

As the detective weighed his limited options, he caught the sound of a familiar commotion outside. At last, a team of rail workers had arrived to couple the sleeper to a Baltimore and Ohio train for the third and final leg of the long journey. In his later writings about the episode, Pinkerton gave no indication of the relief he must have felt at that moment. "At length the train arrived and we proceeded on our way," he recorded stoically, perhaps not wishing to suggest that the outcome had ever been in doubt. Ward Lamon was only slightly less reserved: "In due time," he reported, "the train sped out of the suburbs of Baltimore, and the apprehensions of the President and his friends diminished with each welcome revolution of the wheels."

Whatever they found to say about the episode afterward, all three men would have been glad to put Baltimore behind them that morning. Washington was now only thirty-eight miles away.

CHAPTER TWENTY-THREE
SOME VERY TALL SWEARING

•

If the end brings me out wrong, ten angels swearing
I was right would make no difference.
—ABRAHAM LINCOLN

IT HAD BEEN AN ANXIOUS NIGHT for Elihu B. Washburne, of Capitol Hill's "independent committee of safety." The Illinois congressman was an old ally of Lincoln, bound to him by "the strongest ties of personal and political friendship." Earlier, Washburne had written to Lincoln, advising a course of "masterly inactivity"; now his concerns were fixed on a safe arrival in Washington. The previous week, Lucius Chittenden, on returning from his nocturnal meeting with the mysterious "Mr. H." in Baltimore, had roused Washburne from his bed in the middle of the night. After reporting the many threats and theories he had heard that night, the Vermont delegate was assured by Washburne that all was well, as Lincoln "had determined to follow the advice of his friends, and would reach Washington without risk."

As the date drew nearer, however, Washburne felt less assured of Lincoln's safety. The previous day, when it was thought that the president-elect would pass the night in Harrisburg, Washburne had shared his concerns with William Seward. The senator, who had already dispatched his son Frederick to warn Lincoln in Philadelphia, could offer little reassurance. Though he'd received a telegram to the effect that steps were being taken, he had been given no details. "Mr. Seward . . . told me he had no information from his son nor any one else in respect of Mr. Lincoln's movements," Washburne said, "and that he could have none, as the wires were all cut." Even so, Seward thought it probable that Lincoln would arrive in

Washington on an earlier train, as he had urged, perhaps on Friday evening's service from Philadelphia. Seeing the degree of Washburne's concern, Seward suggested that the two of them go to the station to meet the Philadelphia train. "We were promptly on hand; the train arrived in time, and with strained eyes we watched the descent of the passengers," Washburne reported. "But there was no Mr. Lincoln among them."

Both Seward and Washburne were "much disappointed," but they arranged to meet again the following morning to await the next likely train. "I was on hand in season," Washburne insisted, "but to my great disappointment Governor Seward did not appear." In fact, Seward had overslept, leaving Washburne to carry on alone. "I planted myself behind one of the great pillars in the old Washington and Baltimore depot, where I could see and not be observed," he reported. "Presently the train came rumbling in on time. It was a moment of great anxiety to me." Washburne looked on "with fear and trembling" as the train emptied and a steady line of passengers made its way past him. Lincoln was nowhere to be seen. In despair, Washburne started to turn away, when he saw three stragglers step down from the sleeping car at the rear of the train. Washburne at once recognized the "long, lank form" of his old friend, although he wore an unfamiliar "soft low-crowned hat" and a thick shawl, and looked more like "a well-to-do farmer" than the president-elect of the United States.

As Washburne recalled the scene, he stepped forward to offer a quick greeting—"How are you, Lincoln?"—while reaching out to grasp his old friend by the hand. Pinkerton, his nerves on edge after the long ordeal, reported the matter differently. "A gentleman looked very sharp at Mr. Lincoln who was on my right," the detective said, "and as we passed him he caught hold of Mr. Lincoln saying 'Abe, you can't play that on me.'" Pinkerton's instincts took over. "I hit the gentleman a punch with my elbow as he was close to me, staggering him back," he recalled. "I was beginning to think that we were discovered, and that we *might* have to fight, and drew back clenching my fist." Before Pinkerton could land another blow, Lincoln took hold of his arm. "Don't strike him, Allan!" Lincoln cried. "It is Washburne! Don't you know him?"

THIS WAS A PORTENT OF THINGS to come. At the very moment when Pinkerton should have basked in the satisfaction of a job well done, and received the thanks of a grateful Lincoln, he instead hauled off and sucker punched a sitting congressman. Lincoln had not yet emerged from the train station, and already Pinkerton's ham-fisted tactics had caused embarrassment. He watched as Lincoln helped Washburne to his feet and brushed him off, sensing that the operation was slipping out of his grasp. Here in Washington, Pinkerton would have a great deal of trouble telling his friends from his enemies.

It was in Lincoln's best interests, now that he was safe in Washington, to put the Baltimore plot behind him quickly and decisively. He had nine days remaining until the inauguration, and he would use the time to repair the damage done by his midnight flight, meeting the charges of cowardice with a forceful display of statesmanship. While the rest of the country picked over the events in Baltimore, as John Hay would write, Lincoln would go about his business in Washington, "leaving the town agog."

As far as Pinkerton was concerned, however, the operation in Baltimore was still running and his field operatives remained at risk. At the same time, he sincerely believed that Lincoln's evasive maneuver might spark a reprisal of some kind in Washington. Justified or not, these concerns put Pinkerton at odds with Lincoln, who simply wanted to close this chapter. Now, as Lincoln and Washburne walked arm in arm toward a waiting carriage, the detective could only trail behind, insisting that the congressman must not "do or say aught" to jeopardize matters. So far as Lincoln was concerned, the time for such warnings had passed.

At Willard's Hotel, the detective managed one last piece of subterfuge. As the carriage rolled along Fourteenth Street, Pinkerton climbed down with Lincoln and Washburne. He sent Lamon around the corner to the front entrance of the hotel to summon Henry Willard, the proprietor. On Pinkerton's instructions, Willard let the party in at the side door—the ladies' entrance—and ushered them into a small receiving room.

Willard, like everyone else in Washington, had not expected Lincoln to arrive until late afternoon, and the change of plan left him scrambling. A suite of five elegant rooms overlooking the White House had been set aside for Lincoln's use, but another guest occupied them at the moment, and it would be some time before the rooms could be cleared. Lincoln seemed untroubled by the delay, and he asked only to borrow a pair of slippers.

"We had not been in the hotel more than two minutes before Governor Seward hurriedly entered, much out of breath, and somewhat chagrined to think he had not been in season to be at the depot on the arrival of the train," recalled Washburne. Lincoln gave a brief summary of the night's events, whereupon he received Seward's assurance that both he and General Scott had approved of the step, though it would doubtless create an uproar. Seward insisted that he possessed "conclusive evidence showing that there was a large organization in Baltimore" intent on preventing Lincoln's safe passage through the city. He was in no doubt that the president-elect "could not have come through in any other manner without blood-shed." In fact, Seward maintained, General Scott was so thoroughly convinced of the danger that if Lincoln had not changed his route as advised, Scott would "in all probability" have sent troops to Baltimore to escort Lincoln through the city. Pinkerton was incredulous at the very suggestion of troops entering Baltimore. As he knew full well from the reports of Timothy Webster and others, a military provocation of this type would likely have triggered a disastrous response in Maryland, and perhaps open rebellion. For the moment, Pinkerton contented himself with questioning the accuracy of Seward's sources. "I informed Governor Seward of the nature of the information I had," he said, insisting frankly that he knew of no "large organization" posing a credible threat. Seward, swept up in the drama of Lincoln's arrival, would not be dissuaded. He firmly reiterated that he had conclusive evidence of a large-scale plot.

Pinkerton's insistence on this point must be counted as one of the most extraordinary features of the entire episode. Soon enough, his efforts as chief of Union intelligence under George B. McClellan would expose him to lasting criticism for his supposed inflations of the size and scope of enemy forces. That day at Willard's Hotel, however, Pinkerton insisted on calling Seward to account for exaggerating the number of "rebel spirits" in Baltimore. In political terms, Pinkerton would have done better simply to nod and be content with the successful outcome, but he brooked no argument where his detective operations were concerned, not even from the designated secretary of state.

In spite of the disagreement, Seward was eager to hear more about the events of the previous evening. While Lincoln withdrew for a brief rest, having "expressed himself rather tired," Seward invited Pinkerton and Lamon for a private chat at his residence on F Street, where they once again "talked over this danger of Mr. Lincoln's coming through Baltimore according to the published programe." Once Seward's curiosity had been satisfied, Pinkerton returned to the Willard and registered as "E. J. Allen of New York." Exhausted, but anxious to return to "the seat of danger" in Baltimore, the detective allowed himself a brief pause to bathe and have breakfast.

Downstairs in the lobby of Willard's Hotel, Seward soon reappeared to collect Lincoln, who was now refreshed after a short nap. Together, they began making the rounds of official Washington in the hope, as one congressman would remark, that the new president might "break through the prejudices created by the manner of his entry into the capital." Lincoln's first stop was an unannounced call at the White House, where outgoing President James Buchanan interrupted a cabinet meeting to greet his successor in "a very cordial manner." Buchanan led a brief tour of the premises, and he seemed especially pleased to hear that Lincoln had received "a satisfactory reception at Harrisburg," near Buchanan's Wheatland estate. Though friendly in tone, the surprise visit sent a strong mes-

Lincoln at Mathew Brady's studio in Washington on February 24, 1861, the day after his passage through Baltimore. *Courtesy of the Library of Congress*

sage that Lincoln was ready to serve—"a *coup d'état*," declared the *New York Herald*.

From the White House, Lincoln attempted to pay his respects at the headquarters of Winfield Scott, who had shared so fully in the concern for his safety. The general was not there to receive him, but he soon returned the call at Willard's Hotel, resplendent in his full dress uniform, including plumed hat and ceremonial sword. In spite of his advanced age and recent illness, General Scott made a point of greeting his new commander in chief with a deep, formal bow. "It would do the drawing room dudes of today good," wrote one observer, "to have witnessed the profound grace of the old hero's acknowledgment of the presence of the President-elect, as he swept his instep with the golden plumes of his chapeau." Like Seward, the general appeared keen to cast the best-possible light on Lincoln's decision to bypass Baltimore. "General Scott expressed his great gratification at Mr. Lincoln's safe arrival," reported the *Herald,* "and especially complimented him for choosing to travel from Harrisburg unattended by any display, but in a plain democratic way."

The notion that Lincoln had traveled as he did to avoid ostentation was easily the most peculiar of the many explanations advanced that day. Be that as it may, General Scott's public show of support was crucial, and it gave credence to newspaper reports that he, America's most revered military hero, had personally insisted that Lincoln avoid Baltimore. "Mr. Lincoln is in no way responsible for the change of route in coming to this city," ran one account. "He acted under official communication from General Scott." In addition, the press reported, the old soldier would remain vigilant throughout the inauguration, so that "no slip up, no stiletto, no revolver, no desperado can prevent the peaceful and actual installing of the man whom the people honor, in the place which Providence has ordained him to fill."

THOUGH WILLIAM SEWARD would be at Lincoln's elbow for most of the day, the future secretary of state detached himself for a few moments that afternoon to return to the train station and collect Mrs. Lincoln and her sons. The safety of his family had weighed heavily on Lincoln's mind throughout the night, and he had sent a telegram to Harrisburg that morning to reassure Mary of his own safe arrival. Even so, it would not escape the notice of the Southern press that Lincoln had consigned his family "to follow him in the very train in which he himself was to be blown up." The *Baltimore Sun* was especially outspoken on the subject, praising Mrs. Lincoln's sturdy resolve at the expense of her husband's timidity. The future first lady had "warmly opposed" the change of plan, the *Sun* reported, and determined "to disprove the whole story" by carrying out her husband's itinerary in his absence. "So there is to be some pluck in the White House," the account concluded, "if it is under a bodice."

In fact, the reports of how Mrs. Lincoln and her sons passed through

Baltimore are garbled and contradictory. By some accounts, Lincoln was advised that the simple fact of his absence from the train would protect his family from harm, with no further precautions needed. Others have suggested that he would not have left Harrisburg unless a plan had been set in motion for his family's safety. What is clear is that Mrs. Lincoln, her sons, and the remaining members of the suite departed from Harrisburg as scheduled at nine o'clock that morning, amid a climate of deep apprehension. Norman Judd would later tell Pinkerton that there had been "some very tall swearing" among the travelers who were not in on the secret. "All the party are on the train, though but few think we shall reach Washington without accidents," wrote one correspondent. "Colonel Ellsworth expects the train will be mobbed at Baltimore." Many on board were outraged by Lincoln's early departure, it was reported: "They call it cowardly, and draw a parallel between the conduct of Mr. Lincoln and the actions of the South Carolinians, very much to the disadvantage of the former." Robert Lincoln, at least, stood fast behind his father. A little before noon, as the train crossed into Maryland, he led his fellow passengers in a spirited rendition of "The Star-Spangled Banner."

Upon arrival in Baltimore, Pinkerton would relate, the travelers "met with anything but a cordial reception." Joseph Howard, apparently recovered from his brief incarceration the previous evening, gave a chilling account in the *Times*. "It was well that Mr. Lincoln went as he did—there is no doubt about it," he declared. "The scene that occurred when the car containing Mrs. Lincoln and her family reached the Baltimore depot showed plainly what undoubtedly would have happened had Mr. Lincoln been of the party. A vast crowd—a multitude, in fact—had gathered in and about the premises. It was evident that they considered the announcement of Mr. Lincoln's presence in Washington a mere ruse, for thrusting their heads in at the windows, they shouted 'Trot him out,' 'Let's have him, 'Come out, old Abe,' 'We'll give you hell'—and other equally polite but more profane ejaculations." A number of these "rude fellows" succeeded in forcing their way into Mrs. Lincoln's carriage, Howard continued, but John Hay managed to push them out and lock the door behind them. Meanwhile, the unseemly display on the platform continued: "Oaths, obscenity, disgusting epithets and unpleasant gesticulations were the order of the day."

For all its colorful detail, Howard's account may well have been a complete fabrication, part of the reporter's effort to demonstrate the wisdom of Lincoln's decision. Howard's story is directly contradicted by several sources that claimed Mrs. Lincoln was not on board the special when it arrived at the Calvert Street Station that day. The *Philadelphia Inquirer* was one of several newspapers to report that "the family of Mr. Lincoln left the train" at a track crossing at Charles Street, about a mile short of the station, to be spared any unpleasantness at the hands of the crowd. The story was given out that Mrs. Lincoln had accepted an invitation to lunch at the home of Col. John S. Gittings, the president of the Northern Central Railroad, to demonstrate that "no ill-feeling or suspicion towards him" had inspired her husband's change of plan. It was said that the family alighted at the city limits, along with Judge Davis and Colonel Sumner, and "took carriages that had been in readiness" to the Gittings mansion, located in the fashionable Mount Vernon district north of town. The remaining travelers, meanwhile, continued on to Calvert Street, then proceeded from there to a reception at the Eutaw House hotel, as previously announced in the press. In this version of events, Mrs. Lincoln was said to have rejoined the travelers later in the day to continue the journey from Camden Street.

If the details are murky, the role of Baltimore's marshal of police, George P. Kane, is nearly opaque. In the coming days, Kane would be accused of complicity in both extremes of the Baltimore plot: some would accuse him of active collusion with the conspirators, while others would claim that he engineered the change of plan for both the president-elect and his wife. Kane's own testimony did little to illuminate the matter. The day after Lincoln's arrival in Washington, he would issue a forceful statement, denying that any serious threat had been discovered. "It was thought possible that an offensive Republican display, said to have been contemplated by some of our citizens at the railroad station, might have provoked disorder," he admitted, but "ample measures were accordingly taken to prevent any disturbance of the peace." Elsewhere, Kane would deny any role in Lincoln's decision to alter his itinerary: "I did not recommend that the President-elect should avoid passing openly through Baltimore, nor did I, for one moment, contemplate such a contingency."

Later, when a *Harper's Weekly* article suggested that he had conspired against Lincoln, Kane wrote an angry response, elaborating on his role in the events. Kane now claimed not only that he had arranged for Mrs. Lincoln's reception at the home of Colonel Gittings but that he had intended for Lincoln himself to follow the same course, departing the train at the city limits. Kane had grown concerned, he said, that Lincoln would be annoyed by the "noise and confusion" at the depot, along with "candidates for office, and fanatics on the negro question." That being the case, he suggested to Colonel Gittings that "it would be a fit and graceful thing for him to meet Mr. Lincoln at the Maryland line, and invite him and his family to become his guests during their stay in Baltimore." In this telling of the events, Kane made it clear that he himself planned to escort Lincoln and his family to Mount Vernon Place. Even now, however, he maintained that the "intended debarkation" had nothing whatever to do with "apprehension or suspicion of intended violence or insult to Mr. Lincoln." To the contrary, he simply wished to show the city to its best advantage, and believed that the change of route afforded a view of "the most beautiful part of Baltimore."

Kane's statements must be treated with caution, as they encompass a fair number of evasions and inconsistencies. If the marshal had truly intended to give Lincoln a fitting reception, it seems curious that he did not inform Baltimore's mayor, George Brown, who was left waiting at Calvert Street that day, intending "to receive with due respect the incoming President." By some accounts, Kane himself was also at the station when the Lincoln Special arrived, directing the actions of a robust police presence. In spite of all the contradictions, there is strong evidence to suggest that Mrs. Lincoln did, in fact, accept Colonel Gittings's hospitality as a means of avoiding the scene at Calvert Street. Lincoln himself is said to have extended his thanks to Mrs. Gittings at a later meeting: "Madam, I owe you a debt. You took my family into your home in the midst of a hostile mob. You gave them succor, and helped them on their way."

If the story is true, and if Marshal Kane had a hand in the maneuver, it would perhaps place a different construction on Kane's actions in the days prior to the arrival. Pinkerton would dismiss Kane as a "rabid rebel," and was convinced that he would "detail but a small police force" as the conspirators did their sinister work at Calvert Street. The detective had been especially alarmed at the remark he overheard at Barnum's hotel, as Kane apparently told companions that he saw no need to provide a police escort during Lincoln's visit to the city. Pinkerton construed the remark as a sign of Kane's indifference to Lincoln's safety, or perhaps even his active participation in the plot. If, however, Kane had already hatched a design for removing Lincoln from the train, his attitude may be read as the confidence of a man who had already taken preventative measures. The wisdom of such a course would have been debatable at best, as violence would likely have erupted in any case, but there is reason to think that Kane would not have been greatly troubled if a brawl broke out at the station in these circumstances. He had already branded the probable victims—Lincoln's Republican supporters—as the "very scum of the city."

BACK IN WASHINGTON, Pinkerton reported Lincoln's safe arrival to Samuel Felton and others in a series of laconic telegrams. One of these, to Edward Sanford of the American Telegraph Company, declared:

"Plums arrived here with Nuts this morning—all right."

Ward Lamon would later grouse that Lincoln had been "reduced to the undignified title of 'Nuts'" in these messages, but as several of the recipients did not have the cipher key, most of Pinkerton's dispatches were sent in the clear. The telegram to Norman Judd, for instance, read simply "Arrived here all right."

Pinkerton remained convinced that the plotters in Baltimore still posed a threat, and he now made preparations to return to the city on the three o'clock train to resume his work as "John H. Hutchinson." So far as the detective was concerned, he was still on the job, and still operating under cover. Lincoln's safe passage, in Pinkerton's view, had been only one battle of a larger campaign. He knew full well that details of Lincoln's arrival were already appearing in newspapers across the country, but he still believed that his role in the matter must remain secret, especially while he and his agents remained at risk in Baltimore.

Lincoln himself had promised to treat the matter as confidential, but as Pinkerton now discovered, Ward Lamon had other ideas. "After sending the dispatches I met Mr. Lamon," Pinkerton recorded in his field report. "He was very much excited about the passage of Mr. Lincoln." In fact, Lamon was preparing to telegraph a reporter in Chicago with the full details. Now that Lincoln was safe in Washington, Lamon "was determined to make a 'splurge' and have his name figure largely in it."

Pinkerton was aghast. He had been annoyed ever since their paths crossed at the Continental Hotel two days earlier, when Lamon seemed to make a point of disregarding the detective's alias. His irritation deepened during the carriage ride between stations in Philadelphia, with Lamon's unseemly offer of weapons to Lincoln. Now, with this latest indiscretion, Lamon had gone too far. According to his field report, written later that day or the next, Pinkerton did his best to control his temper. "I endeavored to impress upon him that the arrival of Mr. Lincoln was yet considered secret," the detective wrote, "and that nothing should be done by anyone to make it public until it had been considered by Mr. Lincoln and his advisers what shape his sudden arrival should assume. . . . I also reminded Mr. Lamon that whatever light this movement might be placed in, he must remember that I held Mr. Lincoln's pledge that I should forever remain unknown as having anything whatever to do with it."

Lamon would not be dissuaded. In his view, the fact that General Scott and Senator Seward had endorsed the measures taken in Baltimore removed the matter from Pinkerton's sphere of influence. At this, Pinkerton's anger boiled over. "All I could say appeared to be futile," he recalled. "He talked so foolishly that I lost patience with him and set him down in my own mind as a brainless egotistical fool—and I still think so."

Turning his back on Lamon, Pinkerton set off for a walk along Pennsylvania Avenue, letting off steam before he departed for Baltimore. When he returned to Willard's Hotel about an hour later, however, he spotted Lamon deep in conversation with Simon Hanscom, a correspondent for the *New York Herald*. "I could plainly see that Lamon had been drinking," Pinkerton said. Worse yet, it seemed as if the two men were talking about him. "I observed Hanscom look very hard at me," the detective said, "and he kept his eye on me while I was around." Soon, Hanscom pulled Lamon into the hotel bar. Pinkerton watched with mounting agitation as the reporter ordered drinks, "repeating the dose" several times as he began jotting notes. The conclusion was obvious: "Hanscom was 'pumping' Lamon."

Finally, after watching for some moments, Pinkerton's temper flared again. He caught Lamon's eye and motioned him over. As Lamon approached, Pinkerton angrily tore into him for exposing his identity to the reporter. Lamon hedged, first telling Pinkerton that Hanscom already knew all there was to know, but finally acknowledging his indiscretion. "I got quite angry and swore some," Pinkerton admitted. He reproached Lamon for being so careless under the influence of alcohol, and threatened to take the matter directly to Lincoln. The president-elect had given him a "pledge of secrecy," the detective said, and would surely insist on "making Lamon hold his tongue." The threat had an immediate effect: "Mr. Lamon was very much excited, and begged that I should not do this." As a gesture of good faith, Lamon promised to speak with Hanscom at once to be certain that the detective's name would be held in confidence. Seemingly chastened, Lamon turned away and hurried back to his seat at the bar.

Pinkerton did, in fact, go directly to Lincoln after this heated encounter, but there is no evidence that Lamon's name was mentioned. "I sent a card signed 'E. J. Allen' to Mr. Lincoln, saying that I was about to leave for Baltimore and requesting to see him for a moment," Pinkerton recalled. "I received an immediate reply asking me to come to his room." Lincoln's suite was filled with callers, including Seward and a delegation of congressmen, but the president-elect led Pinkerton to a quiet room, where he offered "warm expressions of thankfulness for the part I had performed in securing his safety." Pinkerton told Lincoln that he would continue to monitor the situation in Baltimore, and that he expected to remain there until the inauguration. Lincoln asked to be kept informed of any fresh developments, and he promised once again that the detective's "connection with the affair should be kept secret." The two men shook hands as Pinkerton took his leave, setting off alone for Baltimore. So far as the president-elect was concerned, Pinkerton noted, "my object had been fully accomplished."

IN PINKERTON'S MIND, however, the job was far from over. He had not slept for more than a few hours for days on end, and no one would have begrudged him if he had waited until morning to leave Washington. But Pinkerton felt certain that the plotters would rise again, and that they might succeed this time unless he and his operatives resumed their efforts immediately.

The detective's first act on arriving in Baltimore was to seek out James Luckett, his neighbor at the office building on South Street, who informed him that Ferrandini and his conspirators "would yet make the attempt to assassinate Lincoln." There were no details as yet, Luckett continued, and there appeared to be a great deal of hard feeling among the plotters that they had been "cheated" by traitors in their midst. "[He] swore very hard against the damned spies who had betrayed them," Pinkerton said, "remarking that they would yet find them out, and when found they should meet the fate which Lincoln had for the present escaped."

Pinkerton felt relief that he and his agents were not suspected, but two of the New York detectives dispatched by Superintendent John Kennedy had not been so fortunate. As the events in Baltimore came to a boil, Thomas Sampson and Ely DeVoe found suddenly that they were under intense scrutiny. "It was no laughing matter," Sampson would recall. "The 'Volunteers' were loud in their threats against traitors. . . . There was even a detail whose duty it was to 'do away' with suspected persons." The two detectives took flight from the city in disguise, only managing to avoid discovery through the timely intervention of Timothy Webster. The Pinkerton operative had known Sampson years earlier in New York, and he became aware of his old friend's peril just as a group of pursuers was closing in. "I swear to you," Webster warned the New York officers, "there are twenty men after you this very instant." In the end, Sampson and DeVoe were forced to make a "jump for life" from a moving train to complete their escape. Pinkerton claimed that he and his men "laughed very heartily at the New York detectives being discovered," but the plight of Sampson and DeVoe underscored the dangers of exposure. In these circumstances, Ward Lamon's indiscretion continued to prey on Pinkerton's mind. On his return to Baltimore from Washington, Pinkerton's train had crossed the path of the Lincoln Special at a watering stop in Annapolis. Pinkerton had crossed the platform and sought out Norman Judd, bending his ear about "the foolish conduct of Mr. Lamon." Judd promised that he would "attend to the fool on his arrival in Washington."

Pinkerton hoped that would settle the matter, but there was worse to come. Two days later, an alarming dispatch in the *New York World* reported on the doings of a mysterious group of detectives who had spent several weeks in Baltimore, "discovering whether any peril menaced Mr. Lincoln in his passage through that city." This investigation, the *World* revealed, had been headed by "One Mr. Detective Pinkerton of Chicago—a gentleman of Vidocquean repute in the way of thief-taking—a very Napoleon in the respect of laying his hand upon the right man." When a copy of this flattering but all too explicit account reached Pinkerton in Baltimore, hand-delivered by George H. Burns of Harnden's Express, the detective sent the young messenger directly to Judd in Washington. "I directed Mr. Burns to say to Mr. Judd that Lamon and Judge Davis of Illinois were surely playing the Devil," Pinkerton fumed, "and unless they shut their heads about me, I would be obliged to leave."

In fact, though Pinkerton could not have known it at the time, the author of the account in the *World* was almost certainly John Hay, Lincoln's private secretary, who would have heard a great deal of talk about "Mr. Detective Pinkerton" while aboard the Lincoln Special. The misunderstanding served to deepen Pinkerton's ill feeling, and it would not be the last time he sought to make Ward Lamon shut his head.

FOR THE MOMENT, as the day of Lincoln's arrival in Washington drew to a close, Pinkerton had cause for satisfaction. Eighteen hours earlier, as the president-elect's darkened sleeper car passed unnoticed through the streets of Baltimore, Pinkerton looked out and saw a city in "profound repose." Now, he reported, there was more excitement than he had ever seen in his life. "Everybody appeared to be swearing mad," and there was "no end to the imprecations which were poured out on Lincoln and the unknown spies." Pinkerton spent about an hour mixing with a large gathering at the city's post office. He would later say that he had never seen so many people in "such a heated, excitable state." Walking back to his office to file a report, he allowed himself a moment of "quiet gratitude" that Lincoln had survived the day.

At the same moment, back at Willard's Hotel in Washington, Lincoln was also feeling the press of a heated and excitable crowd. The president-elect had agreed to meet with a large delegation from the continuing Peace Convention, the proceedings of which had been interrupted by his arrival that morning. For many of the delegates, especially those who favored compromise with the secessionists, it was distasteful even to acknowledge Lincoln's presence, much less extend an official greeting. "No delegate from a slave state had voted for him," wrote Vermont's Lucius Chittenden, "[and] many entertained for him sentiments of positive hatred. I heard him discussed as a curiosity by men as they would have spoken of a clown with whose ignorant vulgarity they were to be amused. They took him for an unlettered boor, with no fixed principles, whose nomination was an accident."

In many ways this gathering would mark the culmination of Lincoln's long journey from Springfield. He had set out with the intent of giving a nervous public the chance to see him in the flesh and hear something of his ideas. If the delegates were far from typical members of the electorate, being retired politicians and other men of influence, they represented a fair index of the strongly held opinions that had divided the country and brought Lincoln to Washington. As Chittenden noted, the circumstances of the meeting found Lincoln at a decided disadvantage. He was at the end of a long and grueling journey, and "had just escaped a conspiracy against his life." It would have been natural, as he faced this "contemptuously inimical audience," if he had seemed ill at ease. "But it was soon discovered," Chittenden wrote, that the new president "was able to take care of himself."

At nine o'clock that evening, Lincoln stood alone and unattended at the far end of one of the hotel's large drawing rooms. As the delegates began to file in, he extended a personal greeting to each man, addressing many of them by name. "The manner in which he adjusted his conversation to representatives of different sections and opinions was striking," said Chittenden. "He had some apt observation for each person ready the moment he heard his name." When the son of Kentucky's Henry Clay was presented to him, Lincoln was effusive: "Your name is all the endorsement I require. From my boyhood the name of Henry Clay has been an inspiration to me."

Every so often, as the conversation touched upon "the great controversy of the hour," a flash of icy resolve could be seen. At one stage, Virginia's William Cabell Rives stepped forward to urge compromise with the secessionists. "I can do little, you can do much," Rives intoned. "Everything now depends upon you."

"I cannot agree to that," Lincoln replied. "My course is as plain as a turnpike road. It is marked out by the Constitution. I am in no doubt which way to go. Suppose now we all stop discussing and try the experiment of obedience to the Constitution and the laws. Don't you think it would work?"

There would be several more thrusts and parries of this type over the course of the next hour as Lincoln met each challenge with a show of courtesy tempered by resolve. As he spoke, Chittenden observed, the Republican delegates appeared both surprised and gratified, while several of the more ardent Southerners slipped quietly from the room. At last, one of the New York delegates asked pointedly if the North should not offer whatever concessions were necessary to avoid war. Such a conflict, he insisted, would be ruinous, plunging the nation into bankruptcy—so that "grass shall grow in the streets of our commercial cities." Lincoln's reply was unequivocal: "I will, to the best of my ability, preserve, protect, and defend the Constitution of the United States," he insisted. "It is not the Constitution as I would like to have it, but as it *is*, that is to be defended. The Constitution will not be preserved and defended until it is enforced and obeyed in every part of every one of the United States. It must be so respected, obeyed, enforced, and defended, let the grass grow where it may."

These words, as well as the determined manner in which he spoke them, left a forceful impression. "He has been both misjudged and misunderstood by the Southern people," William Rives remarked as the reception concluded. "His will not be a weak administration."

IN THE DAYS TO COME, as Pinkerton and many others observed, the pace of national events quickened to a "high gallop." Soon enough, the Peace Convention would grind to an inconclusive halt, a compromise

Thirteenth Amendment to the Constitution having been proposed, an action that Nicolay and Hay would dismiss as "worthless as Dead Sea fruit." At the Capitol on March 4, in the shadow of General Scott's gun batteries, Lincoln delivered his carefully honed inaugural address in an earnest spirit of reconciliation. As he himself would later acknowledge, however, the scent of powder was already in the air. "All dreaded it, all sought to avert it," he would say at his second inaugural, four years later. "While the inaugural address was being delivered from this place, devoted altogether to *saving* the Union without war, insurgent agents were in the city seeking to *destroy* it without war—seeking to dissolve the Union and divide effects by negotiation. Both parties deprecated war, but one of them would *make* war rather than let the nation survive, and the other would *accept* war rather than let it perish. And the war came."

SOON AFTER THE BOMBARDMENT of Fort Sumter, in April, Timothy Webster arrived in Washington carrying several important dispatches— carefully sewn into his clothing by Kate Warne—for hand delivery to President Lincoln. One of these was a letter from Pinkerton:

> *Dear Sir*
> *When I saw you last I said that if the time should ever come that I could be of service to you I was ready—If that time has come I am on hand—*
>   *I have in my Force from Sixteen to Eighteen persons on whose courage, skill & devotion to their country I can rely. If they with myself at the head can be of service in the way of obtaining information of the movements of the traitors, or safely conveying your letters or dispatches, or that class of Secret Service which is the most dangerous, I am at your command.*
>   *In the present disturbed state of affairs I dare not trust this to the mail—so send by one of my force who was with me at Baltimore—You may safely trust him with any message for me—written or verbal—I fully guarantee his fidelity—He will act as you direct—and return here with your answer.*
>   *Secrecy is the great lever I propose to operate with—Hence the necessity of this movement (If you contemplate it) being kept <u>Strictly Private</u>, and that should you desire another interview with the Bearer that you should so arrange it as that he will not be noticed—The Bearer will hand you a copy of a Telegraphic Cipher which you may use if you desire to Telegraph me—*

*My Force comprises both Sexes—all of good character—and well
skilled in their business—*

> Respectfully yours
> Allan Pinkerton

At Lincoln's request, Webster returned the following morning to collect Lincoln's reply, which requested that Pinkerton make his way to Washington at once. Taking his leave of the president, Webster rolled the message into a tight cylinder and concealed it in a hollow compartment of his walking stick.

The case files marked "Operations in Baltimore" were now closed and filed away. A new operation had begun.

EPILOGUE
AN INFAMOUS LIE

•

He thinks too much: such men are dangerous. . . .
He is a great observer and he looks / Quite through the deeds of men . . .
Such men as he be never at heart's ease / Whiles they behold a greater
than themselves, / And therefore are they very dangerous.
—JULIUS CAESAR

FOR SEVERAL WEEKS IN MAY 1861, an enormous "Stars and Bars" could be seen clearly from the windows of the White House. The newly adopted flag of the Confederacy had been raised above the Marshall House hotel, directly across the Potomac River in Alexandria, Virginia. Though Virginia was still technically a state of the Union, with a vote on secession scheduled for May 23, the Confederate banner gave a clear indication of which way the wind was blowing. Newspapers carried reports of rebel troops massing in Alexandria and warned that an attack on Washington was imminent.

For Col. Elmer Ellsworth, a regular visitor to the Lincoln White House, the sight of the rebel flag was a particularly bitter affront. In the days following the inauguration, Ellsworth had been sidelined with a case of

"The Flight of Abraham," as depicted in *Harper's Weekly*.

measles contracted from Tad and Willie Lincoln, who so often had been under his care during the long journey from Springfield. On recovery, as the new president issued a proclamation calling up 75,000 militiamen, Ellsworth was eager to get into the fight. With Lincoln's help, he secured a commission and raised a regiment of battle-ready volunteers from among the "turbulent spirits" of the New York City Fire Department. "They are sleeping on a volcano in Washington," Ellsworth told a reporter, "and I want men who can go into a fight."

On the evening of May 23, as Virginia's secession became official, Ellsworth pulled strings to ensure that his "Fire Zouaves" would have the honor of being the first to march upon the Old Dominion state. Plans were laid to secure Alexandria the following morning. At midnight, alone in his tent on the banks of the Potomac, Ellsworth poured his feelings into a heartfelt letter to his fiancée:

> My own darling Kitty,
> My regiment is ordered to cross the river & move on Alexandria within six hours. We may meet with a warm reception & my darling among so many careless fellows one is somewhat likely to be hit.
> If anything should happen—Darling just accept this assurance, the only thing I can leave you—the highest happiness I looked for on earth was a union with you. . . . I love you with all the ardor I am capable of. . . . God bless you, as you deserve and grant you a happy & useful life & us a union hereafter.
>
> > Truly your own,
> > Elmer

At dawn, federal troop steamers ferried Ellsworth and his men across the Potomac toward Virginia. On his chest, the "gallant little Colonel" wore a gold medal inscribed with the Latin phrase *Non nobis, sed pro patria*, meaning "Not for ourselves, but for country." Setting down at an Alexandria wharf, Ellsworth's regiment met no resistance. A thin line of Virginia militiamen had pulled back an hour earlier. Advancing quickly, Ellsworth dispatched a company of men to secure the train station while he led a separate column toward the telegraph office. Heading up King Street, in the center of town, Ellsworth passed the Marshall House and caught sight of the Confederate flag that had "long swung insolently" in full view of the White House. "Boys," he said, "we must have that down before we return."

Ellsworth paused for a moment, torn between his objective of cutting the city's telegraph wires and his desire to pull down the offending flag. With a sudden resolve, he turned toward the Marshall House. Posting three guards on the ground floor, Ellsworth dashed up the stairs with a small detachment of men, trailed by reporter Edward House of the *New-York Tribune.* Scrambling up an attic ladder onto the roof, Ellsworth cut down the rebel banner and began rolling it up to carry back across the river. With Corp. Francis E. Brownell in the lead, Ellsworth climbed back down the ladder, still absorbed in gathering the flag as he made his way to the stairs. Edward House followed close behind, laying a balancing hand on Ellsworth's shoulder.

Suddenly, at the third-floor landing, a man leapt out from the shadows. James W. Jackson, the innkeeper, had sworn that the Stars and Bars would come down only over his dead body. Now, as he leveled a double-barreled shotgun, he intended to make good on the vow. Corporal Brownell batted at the weapon with his rifle, but Jackson pulled the trigger, firing one of its two barrels and striking Colonel Ellsworth square in the chest. "He seemed to fall almost from my grasp," the reporter Edward House said. "He was on the second or third step from the landing, and he dropped forward with that heavy, horrible, headlong weight which always comes of sudden death."

As Ellsworth fell, Jackson fired the second barrel, narrowly missing Corporal Brownell. At the same moment, the young soldier swung his rifle and returned fire. "The assassin staggered backward," House wrote. "He was hit exactly in the middle of the face." As Jackson crashed down the stairs, Brownell thrust his bayonet twice through the body.

"The sudden shock only for an instant paralyzed us," one of the soldiers would recall. Recovering, they turned their attention to Ellsworth, who lay facedown at the bottom of the stairs, "his life's blood perfectly saturating the secession flag." His men carried him to a bedroom and ran water over his face, attempting to revive him, but to no avail. Unbuttoning his coat, they discovered that the blast had driven Ellsworth's gold medal deep into his chest. "We saw that all hope must be resigned," wrote House. Ellsworth was dead at the age of twenty-four, the first Union officer to fall in the line of duty.

The news reached the White House later that morning. Lincoln, who stared in anguish across the Potomac to the spot where the flag had flown, found himself unable to speak. By that time, church bells were tolling across the city and flags were being lowered to half-mast. An honor guard brought the body to the East Room, where funeral ceremonies were held the following day. "My boy! My boy!" cried Lincoln at the sight of the body. "Was it necessary that this sacrifice should be made?" Ellsworth's men were so aggrieved that they had to be confined to a ship anchored in the middle of the Potomac, to be certain that they would not burn Alexandria to the ground. As the body lay in state at the White House, Lincoln composed a poignant letter to Ellsworth's parents. "In the untimely loss of your noble son, our affliction here is scarcely less than your own," he wrote. "In the hope that it may be no intrusion upon the sacredness of your sorrow, I have ventured to address you this tribute to the memory of my young friend, and your brave and early fallen child. May God give you that consolation which is beyond all earthly power." In the days to come, the phrase "Remember Ellsworth!" became the rallying cry of Union recruitment drives, and a regiment known as "Ellsworth's Avengers" was raised in his native New York. "We needed just such a sacrifice as this," declared one clergyman. "Let the war go on!"

The death of Colonel Ellsworth in Alexandria, Virginia. *Courtesy of the Library of Congress*

IN BALTIMORE, THE FIRST CASUALTIES of the war had already fallen. On the morning of April 19, a thirty-five-car military train had departed Philadelphia on Samuel Felton's railroad, answering President Lincoln's call for troops to reinforce the capital. On board were seven hundred well-equipped soldiers of the Sixth Massachusetts Regiment, as well as several companies of Pennsylvania infantrymen, who had not yet been issued arms or uniforms. In order to reach Washington, the troops would have to follow the same path through Baltimore that Lincoln had taken two months earlier, arriving at the President Street Station and passing through the center of town to Camden Street.

Trouble was expected. "You will undoubtedly be insulted, abused, and perhaps assaulted," the men were told. They were ordered to pay no attention, and to continue marching with their faces to the front, even if pelted with stones and bricks. Should they be fired upon, however, their officers would order them to return fire. If this should occur, the men were instructed to target any person seen with a weapon and "be sure you drop him."

On arrival at the President Street Station, it was decided that the troops would not march through the streets in columns, as expected. Instead, the train cars would be drawn through the city by horse while the soldiers remained inside, perhaps to avoid a provocative display of military force. For a time, all appeared well. The first few cars reached Camden Street, wrote Baltimore's mayor, George Brown, "being assailed only with jeers and hisses." As each successive car passed through the streets, however, the crowds of onlookers swelled, and "the feeling of indignation grew more intense." Soon, paving stones and bricks were thrown, breaking the windows of the train carriages and striking some of the soldiers inside. Elsewhere, a group of "intemperate spirits" dumped a cartload of sand in the path of one of the carriages, while others dragged heavy anchors into position from a nearby dock. The progress of the troop cars came to a halt.

When word of these obstructions reached the President Street Station, the remaining troops climbed down from their carriages and formed into columns, preparing to march through the center of town, come what may. By now, word of the movement of the soldiers had spread to every corner of the city. As the marchers advanced onto Pratt Street, an ever-growing mob of angry citizens threatened and pressed from both sides, "uttering cheers for Jefferson Davis and the Southern Confederacy, and groans for Lincoln and the north, with much abusive language." Soon, a Confederate flag appeared, spurring the crowd to greater extremes. As the columns of marchers skirted the docks, a shower of stones and bottles rained down, and two soldiers fell to the ground, seriously injured. Officers now ordered the men to a "double-quick" pace, in hopes of passing through the mob before the situation worsened. This action, according to one soldier's account, seemed to throw fuel on the crowd's rage.

Soon, shots rang out. The exact sequence of events remains a matter of dispute, but within minutes the troops were taking fire—some of it from street level, some from the upper stories of surrounding buildings—and at least one soldier fell dead. The order to return fire was promptly given, though some of the soldiers could barely raise their weapons under the press of the crowd. "It was impossible for the troops to discriminate between the rioters and the by-standers," wrote Mayor Brown. "The soldiers fired at will."

According to several accounts, Mayor Brown and Marshal Kane made a valiant effort to contain the violence. Brown boldly waded through the mob to extend his hand to a Massachusetts officer, "exerting all his influence to preserve peace." Kane also faced off with the rioters, placing himself in harm's way, just as he had years earlier in Annapolis. "Keep back, men," he shouted at the rioters, "or I shoot!" The maneuver "was gallantly executed," reported Brown. "The mob recoiled like water from a rock." In the end, however, these efforts proved futile. When the smoke cleared, as many as twenty-one people lay dead—both soldiers and civilians—with dozens of others badly injured. The death toll would likely have climbed higher if the troops had carried out a proposed counterattack from the Camden Street Station, but cooler heads prevailed. Instead, the soldiers departed as planned for Washington, where Lincoln himself was on hand to meet them. "Thank God you have come," the president declared.

"But peace even for the day had not come," Mayor Brown lamented. "It was manifest that no more troops, while the excitement lasted, could pass through without a bloody conflict. All citizens, no matter what were their political opinions, appeared to agree in this—the strongest friends of the Union as well as its foes." Accordingly, a telegram was sent to Lincoln at the White House, signed by both Brown and Governor Thomas Hicks. "A collision between the citizens and the northern troops has taken place in Baltimore," it read, "and the excitement is fearful. Send no more troops here. We will endeavor to prevent all bloodshed. A public meeting of citizens has been called, and the troops of the State and the city have been called out to preserve the peace. They will be enough."

Before Lincoln could respond, however, Brown received word that more troops were, in fact, coming by rail from both Harrisburg and Philadelphia. In the absence of guidance from Washington, he and other city authorities now made an extraordinary decision: "[I]t was necessary to burn or disable the bridges on both railroads so far as was required to prevent the ingress of troops," the mayor insisted. Later that night, two squads of men, including members of the police and the National Volunteers, set out from Baltimore armed with "picks, axes, crowbars and a good supply of turpentine." Several railroad bridges were set alight and badly damaged, though none would be entirely destroyed, perhaps owing in part to Samuel Felton's "nine-days wonder" of salt and alum whitewashing.

To the end of his life, Mayor Brown argued that this incendiary tactic had been calculated to preserve the peace—averting a second, perhaps even more violent confrontation by cutting off access to the city. It remains unclear whether Governor Hicks, who had become notorious for his vacillations and stalling tactics, approved the measure. Brown would attest that Hicks gave his assent under Brown's own roof before removing himself to the relative safety of Annapolis, where he subsequently denied any part in the action. In either case, the following day word came from Washington that President Lincoln would send no more troops through the city for the time being. Mayor Brown himself went to the White House on April 21—two days after the bloodshed—and learned that Lincoln was seeking alternate routes through Maryland, circumventing Baltimore to avoid sparking further trouble. The president insisted, however, on the "irresistible necessity" of having clear passage through the state. "Our men are not moles, and can't dig under the earth; they are not birds, and can't fly through the air," he told a subsequent delegation of Marylanders. "There is no way but to march across, and that they must do."

Despite these efforts, the situation in Baltimore remained tense, and the calls for secession grew louder by the day. Chief among the agitators was Marshal Kane, whose heroics in the early hours of the crisis were soon overshadowed by a call for armed resistance to the passage of any further troops. "We will fight them," Kane declared, "and whip them—or die." Mayor Brown conceded that Kane's pronouncement was "embarrassing in the highest degree to the city authorities," but he defended Kane as a valuable officer of the peace who had simply been "carried away by the frenzy of the hour."

Kane was not alone. "The war spirit raged throughout the city," reported the *Baltimore American,* "with an ardor which seemed to gather fresh force each hour." In the days to come, Lincoln would take a heavy hand in suppressing the secessionist element in order to keep Maryland in the Union and preserve the vital conduit to the North. By the end of the month, he would suspend the writ of habeas corpus along the route between Philadelphia and Washington, effectively allowing military authorities to make summary arrests of suspected Confederate sympathizers and detain them indefinitely. Critics judged the decision harshly, challenging it on both legal and moral grounds, but in some respects Lincoln had chosen a moderate path. At the time, Horace Greeley and others were calling for Baltimore to be put to the torch.

On the night of May 13, a violent thunderstorm rolled across the city, driving "all but the livestock" to shelter. When the city's residents emerged under clearing skies the following morning, they were astonished to find a battery of heavy artillery pointing down from the heights of Federal Hill, overlooking the harbor and business district, and fortified by some one thousand Union soldiers. Gen. Benjamin Butler, having been dispatched to repair the damaged railroad routes and reopen the lines of communication, had now concentrated his forces on Baltimore. For Butler, a Massachusetts man, the action was a direct response to the previous month's rioting. "I had promised my old comrades of the Sixth Regiment, with whom I had served for many years, that I would march them through Baltimore and revenge the cowardly attack made upon them," Butler wrote. Mayor Brown was outraged at Butler's audacity. "He immediately issued a proclamation," Brown complained, "as if he were in a conquered city subject to military law." In fact, Butler had acted without official sanction, and he was immediately stripped of command by an infuriated General Scott. Lincoln's view may be judged by Butler's subsequent elevation to the rank of major general, effective two days after the action on Federal Hill.

Authorized or not, Butler's show of force had a profound effect. "In the days to come," wrote Mayor Brown, "it became plain that no movement would be made towards secession." Many of the city's able-bodied men now went south to join the ranks of the Confederacy. For those who remained, the grip of martial law tightened. Within weeks, more than twenty members of Maryland's state legislature, along with several Baltimore newspaper editors, were placed under arrest.

Among those rounded up and shipped off to federal prison forts were Mayor Brown and Marshal Kane. The mayor's arrest came at the hands of a team of men led by none other than Allan Pinkerton, acting on orders from Secretary of War Simon Cameron. Brown recalled asking his accusers to produce a warrant, "but they had none." Marshal Kane was shipped off to New York's Fort Lafayette, where he protested to President Lincoln about the overcrowded conditions and "offensive and pestiferous" atmosphere. Kane had contracted a malarial fever en route to the prison, which added to the miseries of prison life. "Whilst suffering great agony from the promptings of nature and effects of my debility I am frequently kept for a long time at the door of my cell waiting for permission to go to the water-closet," he told Lincoln, "owing to the utter indifference of some of my keepers to the ordinary demands of humanity." Such treatment, he insisted, "cannot meet with the sanction of the President of the United States."

Mayor Brown would remain stoic about the hardships he endured as a prisoner at Boston's Fort Warren, but he had bitter words for the conduct of Governor Hicks, who managed to avoid arrest in spite of his "treasonable" actions in the previous months. The governor made a conspicuous, if belated, show of loyalty to the North, Brown wrote, so that he might "reap splendid rewards and high honors as the most patriotic and devoted Union man in Maryland."

Not surprisingly, Brown also had harsh words for Lincoln. In the mayor's view, much of this "dark and bitter" chapter of Baltimore's history might have been avoided if Lincoln had simply kept to schedule two months earlier and passed through the city "in the light of day." If Lincoln had set aside the advice of a certain "celebrated detective," Brown suggested, the tide of ill feeling might have been turned. "If Mr. Lincoln had arrived in Baltimore at the time expected, and had spoken a few words to the people who had gathered to hear him," Brown wrote, "he could not have failed to make a very different impression." Instead, Lincoln had demonstrated a "want of confidence and respect," thereby aggravating the city's grievances. "On such an occasion as this even trifles are of importance, and this incident was not a trifle," he insisted. "The emotional part of human nature is its strongest side and soonest leads to action. It was so with the people of Baltimore."

Others felt differently. Lincoln's allies and supporters saw the violence of April 19 as a forceful validation of his "midnight flight." In a letter to Allan Pinkerton, Norman Judd declared that Lincoln would have faced the "same spirit that slaughtered the Massachusetts soldiers" if he had appeared openly in Baltimore two months earlier. Pinkerton himself would speak of the riot as the "crowning act of disloyalty," and he decried the scenes of bloodshed as among the worst that had ever "blackened a page of American history."

Both Pinkerton and Mayor Brown had ample reason to be passionate in their views, but neither man could pretend to be objective. It is naïve to suggest that had Lincoln followed through with his public program on February 23, a few well-wrought phrases would have sufficed to quell the growing turbulence in the city. By the same token, it is too much to say with certainty that there would have been outright carnage if he had made the attempt. A great deal had transpired in the interim between Lincoln's passage and the fatal riot, not least of which was the bombardment of Fort Sumter. At the same time, many of Baltimore's most rabid secessionists had been at pains to say—even before Lincoln left Springfield—that the flash point of any violence would not be the president-elect himself, but a hostile intent signaled by the presence of a "military escort." As Otis K. Hillard had testified in Washington, he expected that Baltimore's residents would receive Lincoln with respect—"unless some military comes with him, which they look upon in the light of a threat." It is by no means clear that such reasoning would have withstood a trial by fire, but it is significant that so many in Baltimore had voiced objections to any display of armed force. Lincoln himself would likely have brushed aside such rationalizations and cut to the heart of the matter. "There is no grievance," he had declared years earlier in Springfield, "that is a fit object for redress by mob law."

Incredibly, while Mayor Brown and Marshal Kane were being rounded up, the "sinister Italian barber," Cypriano Ferrandini, escaped punishment entirely. There is no record to suggest that Ferrandini, Otis Hillard, or any of their fellow conspirators was ever arrested or even questioned in the matter. In his memoirs, Pinkerton would gloss over this peculiar lapse: "A general sentiment of rage and disappointment pervaded the entire circle of conspirators and secessionists," he wrote. "Finding that their plans had been discovered, and fearing that the vengeance of the government would overtake them, the leading conspirators had suddenly disappeared. All their courage and bravado was gone, and now, like the miserable cowards that they were, they had sought safety in flight."

It is probably true that Ferrandini and the others fled the scene in the immediate aftermath of the drama. Some of them undoubtedly joined the forces of the Confederacy, and others may have simply vanished into new lives to escape arrest. If Ferrandini was among those who bolted, his absence was brief. Soon enough, he could be seen back in his shop at Barnum's Hotel, razor and leather strop in hand, carrying on his work as Baltimore's "best-known hair-dresser." He remained there, a respected member of the community, for many years to come. The Baltimore Sun reported his death in December 1910, at the age of eighty-eight, under the headline ADORNED CITY'S FAIREST. Any involvement with the events of 1861 went unmentioned.

It has often been suggested that the absence of formal charges against

Ferrandini and his men absolves them of blame, but this ignores the state of political turbulence that existed in Baltimore in the early months of 1861. If the conspirators were known to have fled the scene, it is unlikely that authorities would have pursued a formal investigation, given the urgencies of the moment. Lincoln would not have wanted to draw any further attention to a matter that had made him an object of scorn, especially at a time when he was struggling to keep Maryland in the Union. Even so, it is striking that Ferrandini should have been able to return to his comfortable life at Barnum's without consequence, but he was not the only controversial figure to do so. Marshal Kane, who gave service to the Confederacy after his release from federal prison, would be elected mayor of Baltimore in 1877.

The riot of April 19 would cast a long shadow over the city, and foster lasting resentments. A Baltimore native named James Ryder Randall, who lost a close friend to the violence, gave voice to the divisive moment with a poem entitled "Maryland, My Maryland." Randall's sympathies were clear from the opening lines:

> *The despot's heel is on thy shore,*
> *Maryland!*
> *His torch is at thy temple door,*
> *Maryland!*
> *Avenge the patriotic gore*
> *That flecked the streets of Baltimore,*
> *And be the battle queen of yore,*
> *Maryland! My Maryland!*

The poem went on to revile Lincoln as a tyrant and a vandal, and exhorted Maryland to stand with her Confederate sisters: "Huzza! She spurns the Northern scum!" It became wildly popular in Maryland and throughout the South, and was soon set to music, achieving even greater acclaim as "the Marseillaise of the Confederacy." In time, "Maryland, My Maryland" would be adopted as the official state song, and it remains so to this day.

IN THE EARLIEST DAYS OF THE WAR, Allan Pinkerton believed that his service to the Union would be a natural extension of the work he had done in Baltimore. As he wrote in his letter to Lincoln, he had unbounded faith in the "courage, skill & devotion" of his operatives, and believed that they could supply vital information as to the "movements of the traitors." From the beginning, Pinkerton tied his fortunes to those of Gen. George B. McClellan, his dear friend and colleague from his days on the Illinois Central Railroad. As McClellan took command of the Army of the Potomac, Pinkerton signed on as his chief of intelligence. Operating as "Major E. J. Allen," Pinkerton attempted to adapt the skills he had pioneered in his civilian detective work to the gathering of military intelligence. Many of his undercover operatives, both male and female, now plied their trade behind enemy lines, sending back detailed reports on troop movements and artillery emplacements. In the capital, Pinkerton apprehended the notorious "Wild Rose of the Confederacy," Rose O'Neal Greenhow, a prominent society figure who had been passing along vital information to Southern officers. Pinkerton even conducted an unprecedented wartime aerial reconnaissance, sending his fifteen-year-old son, William, aloft in a hot-air balloon to scout enemy positions.

Not all of his efforts were successful, though his failures were perhaps not as absolute as commonly believed. For generations, Pinkerton has been the target of blame and ridicule for his "wildly inflated" estimates of enemy troop strength in the early years of the war. It is often claimed that Pinkerton's faulty intelligence was almost wholly responsible for the failures of McClellan's command. The "Young Napoleon," critics charge, hesitated at crucial moments and failed to press his advantages because he believed—on Pinkerton's information—that the forces arrayed against him were far greater than they actually were. If not for Pinkerton's blundering, it is suggested, the war would have ended much sooner, and with dramatically reduced casualties. In fact, though Pinkerton is far from blameless, a number of modern scholars have argued that his failures have been subject to their own form of exaggeration. McClellan's correspondence and official records make it clear that the general himself was prone to inflate the size of the forces arrayed against him, even before Pinkerton's operations were up and running. It is also apparent that Pinkerton's voice was only one in a chorus of advisers, whose information McClellan at times embroidered to advance his own agenda. It remains clear that Pinkerton's reports were flawed, but it is also evident on occasion that he exaggerated the Confederate numbers with McClellan's knowledge and approval, as fleetingly glimpsed in the detective's writings at the time. "The estimate was founded upon all information then in my possession," Pinkerton reported to McClellan in one instance, "and was made large, as intimated to you at the time, so as to be sure and cover the entire number of the enemy that our army was to meet." If Pinkerton cooked the numbers, he was not the only one stirring the pot.

In spite of his private admissions, Pinkerton never wavered in his public insistence that there had been "no serious mistake in the estimates" he presented to McClellan. "Self-constituted critics, whose avenues of information were limited and unreliable, have attempted to prove that the force opposed to General McClellan was much less than was really the case," he wrote near the end of his life, "and upon this hypothesis have been led into unjust and undeserved censure of the commanding general. From my own experience, I know to the contrary." History disputes him on this point—John Hay and John Nicolay would write of the general's "mutinous imbecility"—but Pinkererton's conviction is understandable. He was defending not only McClellan's honor—and, by extension, his own wartime service—but also the reputation of Timothy Webster, his "most capable and brilliant detective," who had met a horrifying death while helping to gather the disputed intelligence.

In the early months of the war, Webster had leveraged his undercover work in Perrymansville and Baltimore into a growing reputation as a Southern patriot. Soon he was working a perilous trade as a Confederate courier, carrying information back and forth to Richmond, where he won the confidence of no less a figure than Judah Benjamin, the Confederate secretary of war. Webster filled the role so successfully that he was once arrested by Union patrolmen and thrown into a federal prison, leaving Pinkerton with the delicate job of securing his release without arousing suspicion. From his base of operations at a Richmond hotel, Webster smuggled out reports to Pinkerton at McClellan's headquarters, detailing the placement of Confederate gun batteries and breastworks.

At the start of 1862, Webster fell mysteriously silent. "I heard nothing further from him directly, and for weeks was utterly ignorant of his movements or condition," Pinkerton reported. "I began to grow alarmed." Only later would Pinkerton learn that Webster had become seriously ill, the result of a plunge into icy waters to assist the passengers of a foundering boat. For weeks, Webster lay close to death in his Richmond hotel room, barely able to move.

"As the days and weeks passed, and brought no tidings from him, my apprehensions became so strong that I resolved to send one or two of my men to the rebel capital," Pinkerton recalled. It was a decision he would soon regret. Up to this point, Webster had carefully avoided any association with known Northern sympathizers, to avoid exposure as a federal agent. Pinkerton was well aware of the risks, and to avoid compromising his valuable operative, he selected two men—Pryce Lewis and John Scully—who had established themselves as "ardent secessionists" during the operations in Baltimore.

Lewis and Scully, having been made "fully conscious of the danger before them," set off on their delicate mission in February, promising to send word to Pinkerton as soon as they made contact with Webster. "Tortured by the uncertainty of their fate, I passed many an anxious hour," the detective wrote. It was not until April, as he paged through a captured Richmond newspaper, that he came across a chilling bulletin: Lewis and Scully had been arrested as Union spies and sentenced to death by hanging. Worse yet, their arrival in Richmond had also exposed Webster. "I cannot detail the effect which this announcement produced upon me," Pinkerton wrote. "For a moment I sat almost stupefied, and unable to move. My blood seemed to freeze in my veins—my heart stood still—I was speechless."

Pinkerton worked frantically to secure the release of his men, pleading with both McClellan and Lincoln to offer an exchange of prisoners under a flag of truce. A message was sent to Jefferson Davis, reminding him that the Union had thus far been "lenient and forbearing" toward captured Confederate spies. If the death sentences were carried out, the message implied, the North would "initiate a system of retaliation."

In the end, the efforts were to no avail. Lewis and Scully would eventually be released after a long and harrowing imprisonment, but not before Scully had provided his captors with damning evidence against Webster. Scully was widely denounced as a traitor, but Pinkerton refused to join in the recriminations: "Who can blame this man? Who, that has stood before the frowning scaffold, and with a free world before him, can utter words of censure? Only those who have suffered as he did, prostrated as he was, can know the terrible agony through which he passed ere the fatal words were forced from his trembling lips." Pinkerton was far less forgiving of his own actions. "For myself," he said bitterly, "I have no judgment to utter."

Weakened by illness and scarcely able to stand, Timothy Webster climbed the gallows at Richmond's Camp Lee on April 29, 1862. An inept executioner bungled the first attempt to hang him, leaving Webster horribly injured as he mounted the platform a second time. "I suffer a double death!" he cried as the noose tightened once again. "In a second the trap was again sprung," Pinkerton wrote. "Treason had done its worst, and the loyal spy was dead."

A heartsick Pinkerton appealed to have the body sent north across en-

emy lines, but Webster would instead be buried in a pauper's unmarked
grave in Richmond. This indignity drew a pained response from Pinkerton, who echoed the words of Sir Walter Scott in eulogizing his fallen colleague as "a martyr to the cause of the Union, who lies in unhallowed soil,
unwept, unhonored and unsung." After the war, Pinkerton would recover
Webster's body and erect a huge memorial at the Pinkerton family plot in
Chicago. The inscription praised the fallen operative as a "patriot and
martyr," and gave him a full measure of credit for his role in the Baltimore
episode:

> ON THE NIGHT OF FEBR. 22, 1861,
> ALLAN PINKERTON,
> TIMOTHY WEBSTER
> *and* KATE WARNE
> SAFELY ESCORTED
> ABRAHAM LINCOLN,
> A CONSPIRACY HAVING BEEN DISCOVERED
> FOR HIS ASSASSINATION, FROM
> PHILADELPHIA TO WASHINGTON,
> WHERE HE WAS INAUGURATED
> PRESIDENT OF THE U.S.
> *on*
> MARCH 4TH, 1861

Soon enough, Kate Warne would also have a memorial alongside Webster's. Mrs. Warne succumbed to a lingering illness in January 1868, at the
age of thirty-five, with Pinkerton himself at her bedside. In the coming
years, as Pinkerton collaborated on a series of books drawn from celebrated
cases, he repeatedly praised Mrs. Warne as "an intelligent, brilliant, and
accomplished lady." His high regard for her, together with the fact of her
internment in the Pinkerton family plot, has led some to suppose that relations between them had progressed beyond the confines of business. This
remains a matter of speculation. If Mrs. Warne's final resting place is to be
counted as suggestive, however, it should be mentioned that she is only
one of several Pinkerton employees who came to be buried there.

BY THE TIME TIMOTHY WEBSTER and Kate Warne were laid to rest
in Chicago's Graceland Cemetery, Pinkerton had resolved that their roles
in "sparing our President's life" would not be forgotten. Barely four years

after the drama in Baltimore, as Lincoln fell to an assassin's bullet at Ford's Theatre, the detective would be moved to a rare burst of emotion over the "great man who now sleeps in a martyr's grave." Pinkerton, his son William recalled, wept bitterly at the news of Lincoln's death. By that time, he had long since departed as chief of intelligence, following McClellan's dismissal, and had returned to Chicago to resume his detective operations. The unhappy bulletin from Washington reached him in New Orleans a full five days after the fact, in a newspaper account that detailed not only the events at Ford's Theatre but also the attack on Secretary of State Seward and his son Frederick, whose skull had been fractured as he struggled to defend his father. Based on the early, incomplete reporting, Pinkerton concluded that Seward was also dead.

Even now, Pinkerton could not seem to accept that his "Secret Service" days were over. Adopting his familiar wartime alias of "E. J. Allen," he dispatched a telegram to Secretary of War Edwin Stanton. His message, however well intentioned, carried a note of ill-timed posturing:

> This morning's papers contain the deplorable intelligence of the assassination of President Lincoln and Secretary Seward. Under the providence of God, in February 1861, I was enabled to save him from the fate he has now met. How I regret that I had not been near him previous to this fatal act. I might have been the means to arrest it. If I can be of any service please let me know. The service of my whole force, or life itself, is at your disposal, and I trust you will excuse me for impressing upon you the necessity of great personal caution on your part. At this time the nation cannot spare you.

By the time Pinkerton received Stanton's halfhearted reply, with advice to "watch the Western Rivers and you may get him," John Wilkes Booth was already dead.

Pinkerton mourned Lincoln as a friend and as a statesman. Though he had grown thoroughly disenchanted with Washington by this time, he continued to regard Lincoln as a man of noble principle. "If only I had been there to protect him," he declared wistfully, "as I had done before."

In the immediate aftermath of Lincoln's assassination, there would be a brief resurgence of interest in the Baltimore plot, amid rumors of a link between Booth and the earlier plotters. At least one memorial service for the fallen president forged a connection between Lincoln's assassin and those who had "organized a band of murderers to take [his] life while on his way to the seat of Government." On the surface, there were many provocative parallels. Booth was known to frequent Barnum's Hotel in Baltimore, where Cypriano Ferrandini plied his trade as a barber, and the actor even held meetings there with fellow conspirators Samuel Arnold and Michael O'Laughlen. There were also unverified accounts that placed Booth in Baltimore at the time of the rioting. Worthington Snethen, of Lincoln's "gallant little band" of supporters in Baltimore, accused the actor of heading one of the groups of "desperadoes" that had set fire to Maryland's railroad bridges after the April riot. "He escaped condign punishment," Snethen wrote, "through the mistaken leniency of the government." Snethen's account is almost certainly fanciful, one of many wild theories thrown up in the tumult that followed the assassination. No concrete link between the two events would ever be established.

Speculation about the Baltimore plot was only beginning, however. In the years to come, many of the men who had taken part in the events of 1861 would come forward with reminiscences and memoirs. Several would suggest that Lincoln had been advised poorly in the matter. Left to his own instincts, they claimed, the president-elect would have preferred to face the residents of Baltimore openly. This appeared to be consistent with views that Lincoln himself had expressed on the few occasions when he made reference to the episode. "I did not then, nor do I now believe I should have been assassinated had I gone through Baltimore as first contemplated," he had told an Illinois congressman, "but I thought it wise to run no risk where no risk was necessary." This would have been a politically expedient thing to say at the time, given the ridicule he had endured over the matter, but it stopped short of expressing regret for the course he had taken.

Others would claim that he had been greatly pained by the decision. "I have several times heard Lincoln refer to this journey, and always with regret," wrote the Pennsylvania Republican Alexander K. McClure. "Indeed, he seemed to regard it as one of the grave mistakes in his public career." James G. Blaine, a future secretary of state, would write that Lincoln took the night journey "much against his own will and to his subsequent chagrin and mortification." Blaine insisted that "to the end of his life he regretted that he had not, according to his own desire, gone through Baltimore in open day, trusting to the hospitality of the city, to the loyalty of its people, to the rightfulness of his cause and the righteousness of his aims and ends." Elihu B. Washburne, who had been the first to see Lincoln on his arrival in Washington, took issue with this interpretation. "I know he was neither 'mortified' nor 'chagrined' at the manner in which he reached Washington," the Illinois congressman wrote. "He expressed to me in the warmest terms his satisfaction at the complete success of his journey. . . . I do not believe that Mr. Lincoln ever expressed a regret that he had not, 'according to his own desire, gone through Baltimore in open day,' etc. It is safe to say he never had any such 'desire.'"

For a few years, Pinkerton kept his silence. In 1868, at the time of Kate Warne's death, however, he began to feel differently. As George Bangs, his right-hand man in Chicago, sadly noted, the "old group" had now dwindled to a proud few. Mindful of the passing years, Pinkerton decided to lift the veil on what had transpired in Baltimore. He began work on a pamphlet he would call *History and Evidence of the Passage of Abraham Lincoln from Harrisburg, Pa., to Washington, D.C., on the 22nd and 23rd of February, 1861.* In spite of the unwieldy title, the document was characteristically short and blunt. Pinkerton gave a businesslike summary of his role in the affair—addressed to "The People of the United States"—and attached several letters from witnesses and participants. Norman Judd, Samuel Felton, Governor Andrew Curtin of Pennsylvania, and the intrepid George Dunn of Harnden's Express—keeper of the key to the back door of the sleeper—all attested to Pinkerton's skill and prescience in delivering Lincoln safely to Washington. Even Andrew Wynne, who had cut the telegraph wires leading out of Harrisburg, produced what he called a "truthful statement of what passed."

Pinkerton insisted that he sought no glory for himself. "It would be egotistical on my part," he claimed, "to parade before the public my acts." Rather, he suggested, he had come forward merely to set the record straight, and to make history aware of the efforts of fallen comrades such as Timothy Webster. "He, amongst all the force who went with me, deserves the credit of saving the life of Mr. Lincoln," Pinkerton declared, "even more than I do."

For all his professed reluctance, Pinkerton had a transparent agenda. He had been goaded into writing the pamphlet by the actions of New York's police superintendent, John Kennedy, who at the time was noisily staking a claim to his share of the credit. The previous year, an article had appeared in the *New York Times* under the headline WHO SAVED MR. LINCOLN'S LIFE IN 1861? In it, Kennedy gave details of the work of his men in uncovering the plot, and expressed regret that there appeared to be confusion as "to whom the country is indebted" for the president-elect's safe passage. Kennedy stated confidently that "the assassination consummated in April, 1865, would have taken place in February of 1861" if not for the efforts of his men. He emphasized the role of David Bookstaver in carrying a timely warning to General Scott in Washington, which, Kennedy claimed, had been the clinching piece of evidence. "Mr. Lincoln has stated that it was this note which induced him to change his journey as he did," Kennedy wrote. He finished with a pointed swipe at the Chicago team: "I know nothing of any connection of Mr. Pinkerton with the matter."

"In this respect Mr. Kennedy spoke the truth," Pinkerton fired back, "[for] he did not know of my connection with the passage of Mr. Lincoln, nor was it my intention that he should know of it." The details of his secret plan for the night journey, he explained, had been imparted "only to those whom it was necessary should know it," and not to interlopers such as Kennedy. Pinkerton allowed that the superintendent had "done much service for the Union," but he gave damning evidence that Kennedy had not been a key figure in the Baltimore drama. During Lincoln's ride from Philadelphia to Baltimore, Pinkerton revealed, Kennedy had been "on the same train and occupied the third berth in the same sleeping car," although he remained oblivious of Lincoln's presence. Pinkerton's message was clear: Though Kennedy now claimed to have orchestrated the events, he had, in fact, been clueless as the plan unfolded under his nose.

Pinkerton's irritation with Kennedy was understandable, especially in light of the oddly conflicting statements the New York detective had made in the aftermath of the drama. Three days after Lincoln's arrival in Washington, Kennedy had written a cordial letter to Pinkerton. He expressed regret that he had not known of Pinkerton's presence in Baltimore, and offered his full cooperation now that the "field of operation" had transferred to the capital. Only two days later, however, Kennedy reversed course, sending a letter to Marshal Kane in Baltimore, in which he stated his belief that "there was no foundation in the story" of a plot to murder Lincoln. Moreover, Kennedy claimed that he had written to William Wood, Lincoln's "Superintendent of Arrangements," to assure him that the route to Washington was "perfectly safe." Given Kennedy's dismissal of the danger at the time, his later attempt to hog the credit would have been all the more exasperating to Pinkerton.

It would not be the last time Pinkerton felt the need to defend his record. Though the *History and Evidence* pamphlet included many impressive testimonials, one name was notably absent. Ward Lamon, who had traveled side by side with Lincoln and Pinkerton on the fateful journey, would not lend his voice to the chorus of praise.

Pinkerton realized that a statement from Lamon would carry considerable weight, and he tried earnestly to get one. Lamon had spent the war years as marshal of the District of Columbia, and he had often been found at Lincoln's side. He had continued to hold himself responsible for Lincoln's safety in the White House, often sleeping outside the door of the president's bedroom with his private arsenal at the ready, and he can be glimpsed in the only known photograph of Lincoln delivering the Gettysburg Address in November 1863. After Lincoln's death, Lamon often expressed his belief that he would have been able to save the president's life had he not been sent out of town at the time of the assassination. "I wanted him to promise me that he would not go out after night while I was gone," Lamon was quoted as saying, "particularly to the theatre."

On the very day that Superintendent Kennedy's comments appeared in the *New York Times,* Pinkerton composed a letter to Lamon, asking, "as a favor," for his recollections. Pinkerton knew that Lamon probably still harbored hard feelings over the unpleasant scene at Willard's Hotel, where Pinkerton had exploded over Lamon's drunken disclosures to the press. In addition, there had been Pinkerton's sharp rebuff in Philadelphia when Lamon offered a pistol and knife to Lincoln. Writing to him now, Pinkerton appealed to Lamon's sense of fair play. "If Mr. Kennedy or Mr. Seward is entitled to any credit in this, I beg of you to give it to them," Pinkerton wrote. "If I am entitled to any, I hope you will do the same by me."

No reply came. Pinkerton would try twice more, but Lamon maintained a stony silence. Lincoln's "particular friend," it seemed, was carrying a grudge.

Soon enough, Pinkerton would inadvertently hand him an instrument of revenge. For some time, Lincoln's former law partner William Herndon had been compiling research materials for the biography he intended to write. Learning of Pinkerton's detailed records of the Baltimore episode, Herndon wrote to the detective in 1866, asking permission to make use of them. Pinkerton readily agreed. Though Superintendent Kennedy had not yet come forward at that stage, Pinkerton was already eager for a chance to go on record with his side of the story. "Your book must be one of great interest to the American People," he told Herndon, "owing to your long and intimate acquaintance with Mr. Lincoln; and if I can add a mite to aid you it shall be done cheerfully."

Mindful of the sensitivity of the material, Pinkerton laid down a pair of conditions. First, Pinkerton asked Herndon to omit the name of James Luckett, who had occupied the neighboring office in Baltimore, and for whom he had feelings of genuine friendship. Luckett, the detective said, "was undoubtedly a rebel at heart, yet he is a man of not much means; he has lost considerable during the war, and the publication of his name might tend to his serious injury in business. I deprecate this in any publications coming from my records." Pinkerton's second condition addressed the more sensitive matter of his squabbles with Lamon. Even before his attempt to extract a testimonial, Pinkerton realized that the comments in his record books—especially his dismissal of Lamon as a "brainless egotistical fool"— would cause unnecessary embarrassment if they came to light. To avoid stirring up trouble, he told Herndon to "consider as confidential any remarks which are found therein concerning Ward H. Lamon, Esq."

Pinkerton might just as easily have blacked out the offending comments, but as he expected Herndon to make a copy of the record books and return the originals, it must have seemed sufficient to rely on Herndon's discretion without censoring his own materials. As it happened, Herndon would fail miserably in honoring Pinkerton's conditions. Within a few years, having suffered a number of financial reverses, Herndon would sell off his research archive, including the copies of Pinkerton's records, to another prospective Lincoln biographer, who also happened to be a former law partner of Lincoln's—none other than Ward H. Lamon, Esq.

Lamon soon came across Pinkerton's unflattering remarks, and his reaction is clearly recorded in the transcript itself: "A falsehood of Allen Pinkerton the Detective," he wrote on a scrap of paper jammed into the pages. In the margins of the text he scribbled an even more forceful denial: "This is an infamous lie from beginning to end. This detective, Allen Pinkerton was angry with me because I would not take sides with him—and make a publication in his favor when he and Kennedy—the New York detective—had the difficulty as to which of them the credit of saving Lincoln's life was due from the public—Ward H. Lamon."

Lamon's anger had apparently clouded his logic; Pinkerton's offending comments clearly date to February 1861, whereas the turf battle with Kennedy would not occur for another seven years. In any case, Lamon does not appear to have known that Pinkerton tried to suppress the remarks, nor is it likely that he would have been placated. Lamon's long-simmering resentments now came to a boil. In 1872, when Lamon's *The Life of Abraham Lincoln* appeared in print, it contained a bitter and prolonged attack on the detective. Lamon began with a claim that Lincoln "soon learned to regret the midnight ride" through Baltimore:

> His friends reproached him, his enemies taunted him. He was convinced that he had committed a grave mistake in yielding to the solicitations of a professional spy and of friends too easily alarmed. He saw that he had fled from a danger purely imaginary, and felt the shame and mortification natural to a brave man under such circumstances. But he was not disposed to take all the responsibility to himself, and frequently upbraided the writer for having aided and assisted him to demean himself at the very moment in all his life when his behavior should have exhibited the utmost dignity and composure.

Others had already suggested that Lincoln regretted the decision, but Lamon was not content to leave the matter there. He went on to accuse Pinkerton of having fabricated the entire episode to burnish his own reputation. The Baltimore plot, according to Lamon, had been a total fraud, "a mare's nest gotten up by a vainglorious detective." Pinkerton's motive, as Lamon explained it, had been a simple matter of advancing his own career:

> Being intensely ambitious to shine in the professional way, and something of a politician besides, it struck him that it would be a particularly fine thing to discover a dreadful plot to assassinate the President elect; and he discovered it accordingly. It was easy to get that far: to furnish tangible proofs of an imaginary conspiracy was a more difficult matter. But Baltimore was seething with political excitement. . . . It would seem like an easy thing to beguile a few individuals of this angry and excited multitude into the expression of some criminal desire; and the opportunity was not wholly lost, although the limited success of the detective under such favorable circumstances is absolutely wonderful.

In disparaging the "limited success" of Pinkerton's efforts, Lamon was referring to the fact that the detective had uncovered only a tiny cabal of potential assassins, in contrast to William Seward's claim that "about fifteen thousand men were organized" to prevent Lincoln's passage through Baltimore. "Here," Lamon claimed, "was a plot big enough to swallow up the little one." Pinkerton, in his view, had been blind to a more serious danger while focusing on a comparatively unimportant, if not wholly imaginary, threat.

The more serious charge, however, was that Pinkerton had set out for Baltimore with every intention of discovering an assassination conspiracy, whether one existed or not. "The process of investigation began," Lamon wrote, "with a strong bias in favor of the conclusion at which the detective had arrived." He went on to ridicule Pinkerton's methods, as well as his grammar, tearing apart the record books that had passed into his hands by way of Herndon. He complained that the daily reports were nothing more than accounts of "when the spies went to bed, when they rose, where they ate, what saloons and brothels they visited, and what blackguards they met and 'drinked' with." In these circumstances, Lamon insisted, there could be little wonder in the fact that several willing informants soon appeared to Pinkerton and his operatives. "One of them 'shadowed' a loud-mouthed, drinking fellow, named Luckett, and another, a poor scapegrace and braggart, named Hillard," he reported. "These wretches 'drinked' and talked a great deal, hung about bars, haunted disreputable houses, were constantly half-drunk, and easily excited to use big and threatening words by the faithless protestations and cunning management of the spies."

Lamon appeared to score a telling point in highlighting the fact that Cypriano Ferrandini, the supposed ringleader, was never brought to account for his role in the conspiracy. "If it had had any foundation in fact, we are inclined to believe that the sprightly and eloquent barber would have dangled at a rope's end long since," he wrote. "He would hardly have been left to shave and plot in peace, while the members of the Legislature, the police-marshal, and numerous private gentlemen, were locked up in Federal prisons."

Finally, having laid out his charges with lawyerly skill, Lamon delivered his summation:

> For ten years the author implicitly believed in the reality of
> the atrocious plot which these spies were supposed to have
> detected and thwarted; and for ten years he had pleased
> himself with the reflection that he also had done something to
> defeat the bloody purpose of the assassins. It was a conviction
> which could scarcely have been overthrown by evidence less
> powerful than the detective's weak and contradictory account
> of his own case. In that account there is literally nothing to
> sustain the accusation, and much to rebut it. It is perfectly

manifest that there was no conspiracy—no conspiracy of a hundred, of fifty, of twenty, of three; no definite purpose in the heart of even one man to murder Mr. Lincoln at Baltimore.

Lamon's indictment, all but glowing with righteous indignation, would take an enormous toll on Pinkerton and his reputation. Initially, however, Lamon's book was widely condemned for its portrait of Lincoln himself, which critics judged to be overly derogatory. "It is an oft repeated proverb that no man is a hero to his valet," said one reviewer. "It would seem from the character of this volume that no man is a hero to his law partner." Over time, however, the book would be reexamined for instances in which Lamon's long friendship with Lincoln gave him a unique perspective. The Baltimore episode appeared to be one such case. Lamon had, after all, been at Lincoln's side during the fateful journey, and perfectly positioned to take a clear and informed view of the matter.

Or so it seemed. In time, it became known that Lamon had not written the book himself; his "authentic biography of Mr. Lincoln" was, in fact, the product of a ghostwriter, who later asserted that "Lamon did not compose a line." His poor choice of a collaborator explained many of the book's shortcomings, but even so it remained evident that the personal venom directed at Pinkerton had originated with Lamon himself. Soon, the remarks concerning the Baltimore plot were seized upon and amplified by others. Mayor Brown of Baltimore was one of many who found vindication in Lamon's views, highlighting in his own memoir that Lamon had pronounced the conspiracy to be a "mere fiction." Maryland historian John Scharf, writing in 1879, quoted Lamon's account at length to show that there was "absolutely not a particle" of truth in Pinkerton's conspiracy. For generations to come, Lamon's "mingled disgust and astonishment," in Scharf's phrase, would fuel a lasting debate over Pinkerton's actions and motivations, and create an atmosphere of uncertainty as to whether any danger had ever existed in Baltimore.

PINKERTON HIMSELF WAS TAKEN ABACK when he read Lamon's denunciation. He fired off a letter demanding an explanation, but once again Lamon declined to reply. The best Pinkerton could do was to plan a book of his own, more detailed than his *History and Evidence* pamphlet, in which he could defend not only his actions in Baltimore but also his subsequent service to General McClellan. By providing a "truthful record," he claimed, he could "leave to the impartial reader, and historian, the question whether the course I pursued, and the General whom I loved and faithfully served, are deserving of censure, or are entitled to the praises of a free and enlightened people."

Pinkerton's memoir would be a long time in coming. Lamon's attack had been only the latest in a series of setbacks that would mark his declining years. "I feel no power on earth is able to check me," he had told George Bangs at the end of 1868, "no power in Heaven or Hell can influence me when I know I am right." It soon began to appear as if he had been tempting fate. A few months later, while dictating letters at his desk, Pinkerton suffered a devastating stroke, which left him partially paralyzed and unable to speak. Through sheer determination and an aggressive, radical course of treatment—including mud baths and painful leg braces—Pinkerton managed to drag himself out of his wheelchair and onto a pair of walking sticks. Over time, he slowly regained the use of his legs, forcing himself to take rigorous morning walks, and eventually covering distances of more than ten miles on a daily basis.

Further troubles lay ahead. The Chicago fire of 1871 destroyed Pinkerton's home office, taking his treasured case files and records with it, at a cost he estimated to be $250,000. Determined to battle back after this latest blow, Pinkerton found himself at odds with his sons William and Robert, who had assumed control of much of the business during his long convalescence. For some time, the agency had been contending with a new and more daring breed of train robbers, such as the Reno Brothers Gang, leading to violent clashes and increasingly heavy-handed tactics. An explosive standoff with the James-Younger Gang in 1875 resulted in the death of an eight-year-old boy—the half brother of Frank and Jesse James—and public opinion turned sour. Pinkerton's methods were now reviled as "needlessly barbarous," and he himself was branded a vigilante. Pinkerton was unrepentant, and he continued to claim, as he had done so often before, that "the ends justify the means, if the ends are for the accomplishment of Justice."

DURING THE SAME PERIOD, as the nation struggled with the effects of a crippling economic downturn, Pinkerton interceded in a vicious ongoing dispute between mine workers and local tycoons in the coal districts of eastern Pennsylvania, becoming entangled with a secretive society of Irish immigrants known as the "Molly Maguires," whose tactics were said to include arson, kidnapping, and murder. They were men without "an iota of moral principle," Pinkerton was told, and the entire region struggled in the "vise-like grip of this midnight, dark-lantern, murderous-minded fraternity." Pinkerton sent a rugged Ulster immigrant named James McParland, posing as a fugitive named James McKenna, whose Irish-Catholic background gave him the best chance of success in infiltrating the organization. In time, McParland gave dramatic testimony in a sensational murder trial that resulted in the execution of several alleged "Mollies," thereby sparking an enduring controversy. Pinkerton believed McParland's "noble effort" had brought a just and fitting verdict, but others saw the condemned men as martyrs to the cause of organized labor, and they dismissed Pinkerton as a tool of an emerging class of robber barons. The detective who had marched with the Chartists in his native Scotland, wrote one critic, now "preyed upon social freedom in America."

It was a charge that would stick. Pinkerton and his men came to be reviled as strikebreakers and skull-crackers, an image that would be cemented in years to come by the ghastly carnage during a strike at Andrew Carnegie's steel plant in Homestead, Pennsylvania, in which ten people died. This unhappy episode occurred during the tenure of his sons, several years after Pinkerton's death, but history has attached the blame to the agency's founder.

AMID THE TURMOIL OF HIS LATER YEARS, Pinkerton would have been especially sensitive to Ward Lamon's debunking of his efforts in Baltimore. He had come to regard the episode as the highlight of his career, and it would have been particularly galling to find himself accused of having stacked the cards in advance, determined to find an assassination plot upon arrival in Maryland. "From my reports you will see how accidentally I discovered the plot," he had candidly admitted when passing over his records to Herndon. "I was looking for nothing of the kind, and had certainly not the slightest idea of it." By the same token, in light of the tragedy at Ford's Theatre, he would have been shocked to find himself ridiculed for focusing his efforts on a small band of plotters, rather than on a rumored conspiracy of thousands. The "scapegrace" Otis Hillard, who likened his dilemma to that of Brutus, would not have been out of place in the company of John Wilkes Booth.

There is a measure of justice, however, in Lamon's criticism of Pinkerton's methods. As the detective admitted to Samuel Felton, he and his operatives were forced to cut corners due to limited time, and they adopted a course of action that amounted to entrapment, using alcohol and pledges of money to draw out revelations about the conspiracy. Pinkerton himself had written, in his agency's founding documents, that any confessions of guilt that relied on alcohol should not be trusted, as they tended to fall apart in court. It is fair to wonder how many of the statements made in the saloons of Baltimore would have held up to that scrutiny. By that standard, however, Pinkerton would have been in good company. Lincoln's own adherence to legal procedure had become a subject of debate by this time, following the summary arrests throughout the state of Maryland.

Lamon was also correct in pointing out that no one was ever arrested for having a direct connection to the plot. The fact that Cypriano Ferrandini returned to Barnum's Hotel and carried on with his barbering as if nothing had happened appears to weigh heavily against Pinkerton's accounting of the case, and remains one of the most bizarre features of the episode. Lamon described Ferrandini as an innocent, if foolishly outspoken, dupe, a "poor knight of the soap-pot," falsely accused and stitched up by Pinkerton to cover the weaknesses of the evidence. It is entirely possible that Pinkerton exaggerated and embellished Ferrandini's many operatic pronouncements, but it is disingenuous to suggest that the "noble Captain" was nothing more than Pinkerton's witless patsy. Nowhere did Lamon mention that Ferrandini's secessionist activities had already brought him before the select committee in Washington—before Pinkerton ever met him—or that a fiery Italian barber had featured in other, independent accounts of the drama. Similarly, when Lamon insisted that Ferrandini "would have dangled at a rope's end" if there had been any truth in the charges, he overlooked Lincoln's own agenda. Lincoln had been eager to put the matter behind him as he entered the White House, and soon enough the plot and its aftershocks would fade from the public mind, overtaken by the fast march of events on the battlefields of the Civil War. By the time the war had finished, when attention might have returned to the plot in Baltimore, Lincoln had fallen to an assassin's bullet. A photograph of the accused conspirators—including Mary Surratt—dangling at the ends of ropes soon became one of the indelible images of this dark chapter, amid lasting controversy. At a time when Washington was eager to move forward, there could not have been much political incentive to stir the ashes of a conspiracy that had failed.

Lamon intended to put the seal on his argument by charging that Pinkerton had fabricated the danger. There never was a threat, he insisted; the notion existed only in Pinkerton's mind, a product of ambition and an overheated imagination. Even if one sets aside Lamon's personal grudge, however, the conclusion is absurd. While the degree of the threat remains a legitimate subject for debate, the existence of a threat is beyond dispute, even by the measure of Lamon's own statements. Though Lamon admitted that Lincoln had made his decision based on independent warnings from William Seward and General Scott—and even acknowledged the vast scale of those warnings—he finally rejected the possibility of murderous intent, "in the heart of even one man," for fear that it might reflect credit on Pinkerton. This is nothing more than the expression of a small man's petty grudge. There is much to criticize about Pinkerton's efforts in Baltimore, and we can never know if Lincoln would have died had he attempted to pass through the city openly, but the coming years would bring a number of hard lessons on the subject of presidential security. By today's standards, it is hard to fault Pinkerton's conclusion that a small band of glory-seeking malcontents—men who vowed in the presence of witnesses that Lincoln would die in Baltimore—posed a viable threat. History has shown that such men are dangerous.

It was a point that Lamon appeared to reconsider in later life, though not without a characteristically oblique twist. A second volume of his collected writings about Lincoln appeared in 1895, assembled after Lamon's death by his daughter, who admitted that the result might appear "fragmentary and lacking in purpose." The new volume brought no fresh insight to the Baltimore plot, but Lamon touched on the matter briefly in his discussion of the journey from Springfield. In his manuscript, Lamon wrote, "There was never an hour from the time he entered Washington on the 23rd of February, 1861, to the 15th of April, 1865, that he was not in danger of his life from violence. . . ."

Dorothy Lamon, perhaps looking to dispel her father's old rancor, made a small but telling alteration: "It is now an acknowledged fact that there never was a moment from the day he crossed the Maryland line, up to the time of the assassination, that he was not in danger of death by violence. . . ."

PINKERTON DID NOT LIVE TO READ these words. He died more than a decade earlier, on July 1, 1884, a few days short of his sixty-fifth birthday. The man who had survived a pistol shot in the back at close range met his death through a bizarre and painful accident. On one of his customary morning walks, he tripped and fell to the ground, biting his tongue severely. He succumbed to infection three weeks later.

The previous year, Pinkerton had at last published his volume of wartime memoirs, *The Spy of the Rebellion,* a final attempt to put forward his version of his service to Lincoln and the Union. "Very often, as I sit in the twilight, my mind reverts back to those stirring scenes of by-gone days," he wrote, "and I recall with pleasure my own connection with the suppression of the rebellion, and in upholding the flag of our fathers. My task is done. In a few brief pages I have attempted to depict the work of years."

Pinkerton made no direct reference to his grievance with Lamon, saying only that he had attempted "a truthful narration" of what had occurred on that fateful night in Baltimore. "Exaggerated stories and unauthorized statements have been freely made with regard to this journey of Mr. Lincoln," he allowed. "The fact remains that Mr. Lincoln, as a gentleman, and in the company of gentlemen, successfully passed through the camp of the conspirators and reached in safety the capital of the county."

He closed on a note of quiet satisfaction: "I had informed Mr. Lincoln in Philadelphia that I would answer with my life for his safe arrival in Washington, and I had redeemed my pledge."

ACKNOWLEDGMENTS

This book would not have been possible without the assistance of the following institutions and their knowledgable research assistants: the Library of Congress, especially the Records of Pinkerton's National Detective Agency, as well as the Abraham Lincoln Papers and the John G. Nicolay papers; the John Hay Collection at Brown University; the Abraham Lincoln Presidential Library and Museum; the Baltimore Civil War Museum; the Baltimore B&O Railroad Museum; the Enoch Pratt Free Library of Baltimore; the Ford's Theatre Historic Site and Museum; the New York Public Library; the New York Historical Society; the Historical Society of Pennsylvania; the Free Library of Philadelphia; the Ward Hill Lamon Papers at the Huntington Library; the Maryland Historical Society; the National Archives; and the Willard Hotel.

In addition, I am grateful to the following individuals for lending their talents, assistance, and unflagging support: Charles Spicer, Andrew Martin, April Osborn, Hector DeJean, Larry Kirshbaum, Susanna Einstein, Steve Rothman, Jon Lellenberg, Harlan Coben, Jeff Abbott, Sonny Wareham, Gary Krist, Louis Bayard, Dennis Drabelle, the Allen Appels (père et fils), Larry Kahaner, Marc Smolonsky, John McKeon, and Professor John Corbett.

And finally, I owe a special debt of gratitude to my friends Marcia Talley, Elizabeth Foxwell, and Margaret Foxwell, who—over coffee one day in 1999—introduced me to Kate Warne.

SELECT BIBLIOGRAPHY

Books

American Annual Cyclopaedia and Register of Important Events of the Year 1861. New York: D. Appleton & Co., 1875.

Anonymous. *Diary of a Public Man.* Bullard, Lauriston F., ed. New Brunswick, NJ: Rutgers University Press, 1946.

Arnold, Isaac N. *The History of Abraham Lincoln and the Overthrow of Slavery.* Chicago: Clarke & Co., 1866.

Basler, Roy P., et al., eds. *The Collected Works of Abraham Lincoln.* 8 vols. New Brunswick, NJ: Rutgers University Press, 1955.

Beymer, William Gilmore. *On Hazardous Service: Scouts and Spies of the North and South.* New York: Harper and Brothers, 1912.

Brown, George William. *Baltimore & The Nineteenth of April, 1861.* Baltimore: Johns Hopkins University Press, 2001.

Brown, Thomas J. *Dorothea Dix, New England Reformer.* Cambridge: Harvard University Press, 1887.

Browne, Francis Fisher. *The Everyday Life of Abraham Lincoln.* Chicago: Brown & Howell Co., 1913.

Bryan, George S. *The Spy in America.* Philadelphia: J. B. Lippincott, 1943.

Burlingame, Michael. *Abraham Lincoln: A Life.* Baltimore: Johns Hopkins University Press, 2008.

———. ed. *Lincoln's Journalist: John Hay's Anonymous Writings for the Press.* Carbondale: Southern Illinois University Press, 1998.

———. ed. *An Oral History of Abraham Lincoln: John G. Nicolay's Interviews and Essays.* Carbondale: Southern Illinois University Press, 1996.

Burlingame, Michael, and Ettlinger, John R. Turner, eds. *Inside Lincoln's White House: The Complete Civil War Diary of John Hay.* Carbondale: Southern Illinois University Press, 1997.

Campbell, Tom. *Fighting Slavery in Chicago: Abolitionists, the Law of Slavery, and Lincoln.* Chicago: Ampersand, Inc., 2009.

Carton, Evan. *Patriotic Treason: John Brown and the Soul of America.* New York: Free Press, 2006.

Chittenden, Lucius Eugene. *Invisible Siege: The Journal of Lucius E. Chittenden, April 15, 1861–July 14, 1861.* San Diego: Americana Exchange Press, 1969.

———. *Recollections of Abraham Lincoln and His Administration.* New York: Harper and Brothers, 1891.

Cuthbert, Norma B. *Lincoln and the Baltimore Plot, 1861: From Pinkerton Records and Related Papers.* San Marino, CA: Huntington Library, 1949.

Donald, David Herbert. *"We Are Lincoln Men": Abraham Lincoln and His Friends.* New York: Simon & Schuster, 2003.

———. *Lincoln.* New York: Simon & Schuster, 1995.

Donald, David Herbert, and Harold Holzer, eds. *Lincoln in the Times: The Life of Abraham Lincoln as Originally Reported in the New York Times.* New York: St. Martin's Press, 2005.

Durie, Bruce, ed. *The Pinkerton Casebook: Adventures of the Original Private Eye.* Edinburgh: Mercat Press, 2007.

Epstein, Daniel Mark. *Lincoln's Men: The President and His Private Secretaries.* New York: HarperCollins, 2009.

———. *The Lincolns: Portrait of a Marriage.* New York: Ballantine Books, 2008.

Fishel, Edwin C. *The Secret War for the Union: The Untold Story of Military Intelligence in the Civil War.* Boston: Houghton Mifflin, 1996.

Foner, Philip S., and Yuval Taylor, eds. *Frederick Douglass: Selected Speeches and Writings.* Chicago: Lawrence Hill, 1999.

Forney, John W. *Anecdotes of Public Men.* New York: Harper and Brothers, 1873.

Goodwin, Doris Kearns. *Team of Rivals: The Political Genius of Abraham Lincoln.* New York: Simon & Schuster, 2005.

Greeley, Horace. *The American Conflict: A History of the Great Rebellion in the United States of America, 1860–'65.* Hartford: O. D. Case & Company, 1866.

Hall, Clayton Colman, ed. *Baltimore: Its History and People*. New York: Lewis Historical Publishing, 1912.

Hamlin, Charles Eugene. *The Life and Times of Hannibal Hamlin*. Cambridge: Riverside Press, 1899.

Hanchett, William. *The Lincoln Murder Conspiracies*. Urbana: University of Illinois Press, 1983.

Hay, Clara S. *The Life and Letters of John Hay*. New York: Harper and Brothers, 1915.

Herndon, William H., and Jesse W. Weik. *Herndon's Life of Lincoln*. Cleveland: World Publishing Co., 1942.

Herndon, William H., and Jesse W. Weik. *Abraham Lincoln: The True Story of a Great Life*. New York: D. Appleton & Co., 1930.

Holzer, Harold. *Lincoln President-Elect: Abraham Lincoln and the Great Secession Winter 1860–1861*. New York: Simon & Schuster, 2008.

———. ed. *Lincoln As I Knew Him*. Chapel Hill, NC: Algonquin Books, 1999.

———. ed. *Dear Mr. Lincoln: Letters to the President*. Reading, MA: Addison-Wesley, 1995.

Horan, James David. *The Pinkertons: The Detective Dynasty That Made History*. New York: Crown, 1967.

Horan, James D., and Swiggett, Howard. *The Pinkerton Story*. New York: G. P. Putnam's Sons, 1951.

Hynd, Alan. *Arrival: 12:30: The Baltimore Plot Against Lincoln*. Camden, NJ: Thomas Nelson & Sons, 1967.

Jeffreys-Jones, Rhodri. *Cloak and Dollar: A History of American Secret Intelligence*. New Haven: Yale University Press, 2002.

Jones, Thomas D. *Memories of Lincoln*. New York: Press of the Pioneers, 1934.

Kline, Michael J. *The Baltimore Plot*. Yardley, PA: Westholme Publishing, 2008.

Lamon, Ward Hill. *The Life of Abraham Lincoln from His Birth to His Inauguration as President*. Lincoln, NE: University of Nebraska Press, 1999.

———. *Recollections of Abraham Lincoln: 1847–1865*. Lincoln: University of Nebraska Press, 1994.

Lossing, Benson J. *The Pictorial History of the Civil War in the United States of America*. Philadelphia: G. W. Childs, 1868.

MacKay, James. *Allan Pinkerton: The First Private Eye*. New York: John Wiley & Sons, 1996.

McClure, Alexander K. *Abraham Lincoln and Men of War Times*. Lincoln: University of Nebraska Press, 1996.

McPherson, James M. *Battle Cry of Freedom: The Civil War Era*. New York: Oxford University Press, 1988.

Mansch, Larry D. *Abraham Lincoln, President-Elect*. Jefferson, NC: McFarland & Company, 2005.

Markle, Donald E. *Spies and Spymasters of the Civil War*. New York: Hypocrene Books, 2004.

Mearns, David C., ed. *The Lincoln Papers*. 2 vols. Garden City, NY: Doubleday & Co., 1948.

Miers, Earl Schenck, ed. *Lincoln Day by Day: A Chronology, 1809–1865*. 3 vols. Washington, DC: Lincoln Sesquicentennial Commission, 1960.

Miller, Edward A. *Lincoln's Abolitionist General: The Biography of David Hunter*. Columbia: University of South Carolina Press, 1997.

Morn, Frank. *The Eye That Never Sleeps: A History of the Pinkerton National Detective Agency*. Bloomington: Indiana University Press, 1982.

Muckenhoupt, Margaret. *Dorothea Dix: Advocate for Mental Health Care*. Oxford: Oxford University Press, 2003.

Nevins, Allan. *The Emergence of Lincoln*. 2 vols. New York: Charles Scribner's Sons, 1950.

Nicolay, Helen. *Lincoln's Secretary: A Biography of John G. Nicolay*. New York: Longmans, Green & Co., 1949.

Nicolay, John G., and Hay, John. *Abraham Lincoln, A History*. 10 vols. New York: Century Co., 1890.

Oates, Stephen B. *With Malice Toward None: The Life of Abraham Lincoln*. New York: Harper & Row, 1977.

Packard, Jerrold M. *The Lincolns in the White House*. New York: St. Martin's Press, 2005.

Pinkerton, Allan. *The Somnambulist and the Detective; The Murderer and the Fortune Teller*. New York: G. W. Dillingham Co., 1900.

———. *The Spy of the Rebellion*. New York: G. W. Carleton & Co., 1884.

———. *The Expressman and the Detective*. New York: G. W. Carleton & Co., 1880.

———. *Criminal Reminiscences and Detective Sketches*. New York: G. W. Carleton & Co., 1879.

———. *History and Evidence of the Passage of Abraham Lincoln from Harrisburg, PA, to Washington, D.C. on the 22d and 23d of February, 1861*. Chicago: Republican Print, 1868.

Potter, John Mason. *Thirteen Desperate Days*. New York: Ivan Obolensky 1964.

Radcliffe, George L. P. *Governor Thomas Hicks of Maryland and the Civil War*. Baltimore: Johns Hopkins University Press, 1965.

Randall, Ruth Painter. *Colonel Elmer Ellsworth: A Biography of Lincoln's Friend and First Hero of the Civil War*. Boston: Little, Brown and Company, 1960.

Robinson, Charles M., III, *American Frontier Lawmen 1850–1930*. Oxford: Osprey Publishing, 2005.

Rowan, Richard Wilmer. *The Pinkertons: A Detective Dynasty*. Boston: Little, Brown & Co., 1931.

Sandburg, Carl. *Lincoln Collector: The Story of Oliver R. Barrett's Great Private Collection*. New York: Bonanza Books, 1960.

———. *Abraham Lincoln: The Prairie Years and the War Years*. New York: Harcourt, Brace & Co., 1954.

Scharf, J. Thomas. *History of Baltimore City and Country*. Philadelphia: Louis H. Evarts, 1881.

———. *History of Maryland*. Baltimore: John B. Piet, 1879.

———. *The Chronicles of Baltimore: Being a Complete History of "Baltimore Town" and Baltimore City from the Earliest Period to the Present Time*. Baltimore: Turnbull Brothers, 1874.

Searcher, Victor. *Lincoln's Journey to Greatness: A Factual Account of the Twelve-Day Inaugural Trip*. Philadelphia: John C. Winston Co., 1960.

Seward, Frederick W. *Seward at Washington as Senator and Secretary of State*. New York: Derby and Miller, 1891.

Starr, John W., Jr. *Lincoln and the Railroads: A Biographical Study*. New York: Dodd, Mead, 1927.

Tiffany, Francis. *The Life of Dorothea Lynde Dix*. Boston: Houghton Mifflin, 1892.

Villard, Henry. *Lincoln on the Eve of '61: A Journalist's Story*. New York: Alfred A. Knopf, 1941.

Walling, George W. *Recollections of a New York City Chief of Police*. New Jersey: Patterson Smith Reprint Series, 1972.

Ward, William Hayes. *Abraham Lincoln: Tributes from His Associates; Reminiscences of Soldiers, Statesmen and Citizens*. New York: Thomas Y. Crowell, 1895.

Wilson, Dorothy Clark. *Stranger and Traveler: The Story of Dorothea Dix, American Reformer*. Boston: Little, Brown & Co., 1975.

Wilson, Douglas L., and Rodney O. Davis. *Herndon's Informants: Letters, Interviews, and Statements About Abraham Lincoln.* Urbana: University of Illinois Press, 1998.

Wilson, Rufus Rockwell. *Lincoln in Caricature.* New York: Horizon Press, 1953.

Periodicals and Newspapers

The Abraham Lincoln Quarterly; The Atlas & Argus; Baltimore Sun; Boston Commonwealth; Bulletin of the Abraham Lincoln Association; Century Magazine; Charleston Mercury; Civil War Times; Cleveland Plain Dealer; Douglass' Monthly; Frank Leslie's Illustrated Newspaper; Harper's New Monthly Magazine; Maryland Historical Magazine; McClure's Magazine; National Republic; New York Daily Graphic; New York Herald; New York Independent; New York Times; New-York Tribune: New York World; North American Review; Pennsylvania History: A Journal of Mid-Atlantic Studies; Pennsylvania Magazine of History and Biography; Philadelphia Inquirer; Transactions and Journal of the Illinois State Historical Society; True Magazine; Wisconsin Magazine of History.

Further information and source notes can be found at the author's Web site: www.stashower.com

INDEX

Abolitionist Party, 38
Adams, Charles Francis, 173
Adams Express Company, 50–58, 196, 234
  robbery, 50–51, 206
Albany, 200–202
alcohol
  during inaugural journey, 145–46
  in undercover work, 121, 328–29
Alexandria, troops in, 303
Allen, E. J., Pinkerton as, 270, 288–89, 318
American Anti-Slavery Society, 27
American Telegraph Company, 196, 207, 273
Anderson, Robert, 87
Anthony, Susan B., 49
Arnold, Samuel, 319
arrests
  federal, 310–11
  Maryland, 329
  Union spy, 316
artillery displays, during inaugural journey,
  173–74
assassination conspiracy, 77. *See also*
  Baltimore plan, for revised itinerary;
  Baltimore plot; Ferrandini, Cypriano
  backup plans for, 235–36, 261
  ballot selection of assassin, 189, 192, 281
  Booth's involvement in, 186, 318–19, 328
  Chittenden's Baltimore meeting revealing,
    183–86
  Hay's fear of, 1
  Hunter's letter of warning about, 84–85
  league of assassins, 186
  Lincoln's responses to, 2, 240
  Luckett's revelations to Pinkerton, 139–42
  parallel investigations of, 216, 249
  Pinkerton-Ferrandini meeting, 140–42
  Pinkerton's discovery of, 2, 105
  planned location for, 3
  plotters' response to Lincoln's secret
    maneuver, 281
  rewards for murder of president-elect,
    174–75
  Ruscelli's revelations, 185
  scale of, 277, 288
  secessionists and, 97
  Seward, W. H., and, 324–25
  suspects, 269
assassination of Ellsworth, 305
assassination of Lincoln, 305, 322
Astor House
  Lincoln dinner at, 213
  structure and exterior, 211
  Warne's meetings at, 204–8

Baker, Edward D., 15
Baltimore
  Buchanan in, 102
  close of operations in, 301
  editorial on Lincoln's imminent arrival,
    244
  Hamlins' stop in, 243
  house of prostitution in, 119, 120, 122

Baltimore (*continued*)
  Kane's police force in, 175–76
  Lincoln party train ride to, 279–83
  mob town image of, 101–2, 175
  Pinkerton detectives in, 103–4
  Pinkerton in, 100–101, 103, 118, 282–83, 296–97
  Pinkerton with Lincoln in, 282–83
  Pinkerton's arrival in, 100–101
  planning for dangers in, 115–18
  police support denied by Kane, 175–76, 177, 201
  Republican procession staged in, 176
  return to, 296–97
  rioting in, 306–8, 311, 312
  secessionists, 101, 104–5, 106, 312
  troops sent from Washington to, 306–8
  war spirit in, 309–10
  Washington access through, 101
Baltimore plan, for revised itinerary
  Baltimore leg of journey, 279–83
  boarding Baltimore-bound train, 278–79
  Camden Street Station, 282–83
  carriage ride to PW&B, 275–78
  as cowardice, 262–63
  danger points on PW&B, 280
  explanations advanced for, 290
  Harrisburg-Philadelphia railroad plans, 270–72
  Lincoln as invalid in, 272, 278, 281
  Lincoln's disguise, 254, 264–66
  Lincoln's Harrisburg departure, 262–63, 272–73
  Lincoln's prestige hurt by, 267
  Lincoln's wife informed of, 253
  perceptions of, 262–67, 319–20
  Philadelphia leg of journey, 273–74
  Pinkerton's, 4, 245–46, 281–83
  Pinkerton's Philadelphia phase in, 274–76
  Pinkerton's view of in later years, 328
  in press, 263, 266–67
  Washington itinerary, 89–90, 105, 124–25
Baltimore plot
  bridge-burning warning letter, 129, 130
  coded tracking system, 125
  controversy surrounding, 5–6
  dilemmas in assessing, 4–5
  discovery by operatives, 121–22
  for electoral vote count day, 122, 130–31

  Lincoln's arrival in Washington and, 287
  newspapers and, 225
  Pinkerton's pamphlet on, 320–22
  resurgence of interest in, 318–19
  select committee inquiry into, 126–27, 129–30, 131
  social class and, 260
  for Washington capture, 85, 92, 104–5, 122–31
Baltimore Plug-Uglies, 13, 260
Baltimore Railroad, 58
Baltimore Sun, 106, 266
  Washington departure announced in, 105
Bangs, George H. (Pinkerton detective), 44–45, 55, 163–64, 320
Barnum, P. T., 213
Barnum's Hotel, 319
barrel-making. *See* coopering trade
Barr's Saloon, 154–56
Bates House speech, 151
Bedell, Grace, 81, 174
Black, Edward, 272, 273–74
Black Laws, 62
Blaine, James G., 319
Bleeding Kansas crisis, 60
bodyguards, 113–14, 145, 252
Bogus Island, 29, 35
Bookstaver, David, 217, 238–39, 321
Booth, John Wilkes, 186, 318–19, 328
Border Ruffians, 60
border states, 139
Bosworth, Increase, 29, 30, 31, 32, 34
Bowen, Henry C., 241
Brady's studio in Washington, Lincoln in, *289*
Breckenridge, John C., 71, 167–68
bridges
  bridge keepers, 197
  warning letter about burning of, 129, 130
  whitewashed, 198–99, 309
Brown, George (Baltimore mayor), 307, 308–9, 326
  arrest of Kane and, 310–11
Brown, John, *60,* 229
  controversial figure of, 67–68
  execution of, 67
  fugitive status of, 61
  Pinkerton helping, 59–63

Buchanan, James ("The Old Public
  Functionary"), 86, 93
 in Baltimore, 102
 Brown, G., arrest ordered by, 61
 Fort Moultrie submission stance of, 87
 Lincoln and, 10–12, 14
 select committee authorized by, 126
Buffalo, New York, 182–83
Bulwer-Lytton, Edward, 27
Burns, George H., 208, 226, 275
 message to Judd sent through, 227–28
Burns, Robert, 74–75
Butler, Benjamin, 310

Cadwallerder, Thomas, 240
Cady, Elizabeth, 59
Calvert Street depot, 3
Camden Street Station, 282–83, 307–8
Cameron, Simon, 310
carpetbag incident, 152
carriage ride, to PW&B, 275–78
Cartwright, Peter, 37
Chartist movement, 17–19, 21, 22
Chase, Salmon P., 109, 110
Chicago
 1850s expansion of, 42
 fire of 1871, 327
 Pinkerton move to, 26
Chicago Judiciary Convention, 62
Chittenden, Lucius, 166–68, 216, 259–60
 Baltimore meeting with assassin suspect,
  183–86
 on Lincoln's disguise, 265
 on Peace Convention delegates, 298–99
 Pinkerton and, 187
 on sentiments towards Lincoln, 298
 Washburne informed by, 285
Church, William, 38
cigar gift, to Black, 274
Cincinnati stop, 162–65
Circular of Instructions, 111, 113
Cleveland, 173
Columbus, 169–71
Committee of Arrangements, 149
Confederacy, 137–39
 convention in Montgomery, 153
 flag of, 303, 304–5
 president of, 138, 181
Continental Hotel, 233, 238, 248–49

coopering trade, 20–21, 26, 28
Coopers' Union, 20
corruption, 43
counterfeiting, 42
counterfeiting gangs, 28–29
 Pinkerton and, 30–35
coup d'etat, Dix revealing planned, 92
Craig, John, 30–35
Curtin, Andrew, 250, 253, 254, 272, 273
Cuyler, Theodore, 246

Davies, Harry (Pinkerton detective), 99–100,
  119, 121–27, 139–40
 ballot drawn by, 192
 ballot plan revealed to, 189, 192
 on day of plan, 260, 261, 262
 Ferrandini band joined by, 190–93, 191
 Hillard paid by, 188–89
 Hillard's revelation to, 124–25
Davis, David, 71, 113–14, 249–52
Davis, Jefferson, 64, 137, 307
 as Confederacy president, 138, 181
 inaugural journey of, 181–82
 Lincoln and, 137–38, 182
 Union spies and, 316
Decatur incident, 147–48
Declaration of Independence, 245–47
decoy
 package, 270
 Warne's, 271–72
Democratic party, 21, 37
 split in, 71
Dennison, Theodore, 40–43
Dennison, William, Jr., 169
detective agency, 41–58, 46, 327
detective career, Pinkerton's start in, 25–35
detectives
 parallel tracks of Pinkerton and Kennedy,
  216, 249
 Washington, 215–17, 296–97
detectives, Pinkerton
 alcohol use by, 121
 in Baltimore, 103–4
 Baltimore plot discovered by, 121–22
 disguises of, 45–46, 98, 99–100
 female, 47–50
 government spies and, 189, 216
 Pinkerton's detectives as, 44–45
 Williams, Charles, 121–22

DeVoe, Ely, 215–17, 296–97
disguises. *See also specific detectives*
  alcohol and, 121, 328–29
  in Baltimore PW&B case, 103–4
  Lincoln's Washington trip, 254, 264–66
  Pinkerton's, 103, 270, 288–89, 294,
    318
  Pinkerton's anonymity concerns, 236
  Pinkerton's stockbroker, 103, 139, 154,
    164, 227–28, 236, 294
  Warne's Mrs. Barley, 104, 153, 195–96
Dix, Dorothea, 91–92
Douglas, Stephen A., 12, 15, 70
  debates between Lincoln and, 65–66,
    86
  New Jersey won by, 222
  as presidential candidate against Lincoln,
    71
  unity message of, 72
Douglass, Frederick, 16, 60
  on Baltimore revised plan, 264
  Pinkerton's admiration of, 27
Dred Scott v. Sanford, 16, 66
Dubois, Jesse, 153
Dundee, Illinois, 25–35
Dundee Baptist Church, 37–38
Dunn, George, 245, 276, 278–79
Dyer, Charles V., 27

electoral votes, 88–89, 108
  Baltimore plot for count day, 122,
    130–31
  Chittenden account of vote count day,
    166–68
  Lincoln's concerns about, 165
  results telegram, 170–71
  secessionists on vote count day, 167–68
  vote count safety and, 166
Ellsworth, Elmer, 134, 135, 252
  Confederate flag taken down by, 304–5
  crowd control by, 150, 227
  death of, 305–6, *306*
  duties of, 113
  illness of, 303
  Lamon and, 150
  letter to fiancée, 304
  as security point man, 111–13
  as Zouave, 111, 112, *112,* 135
Ellsworth's Avengers, 306

Engels, Friedrich, 21
Eugene Aram (Bulwer-Lytton), 27
express service, 50–51

Federal Bureau of Investigation (FBI),
  42
Felton, Samuel, 58, 91, 234. *See also*
  Philadelphia, Wilmington, and
  Baltimore Railroad
  attack plans on railroad of, 92, 95, 197–98,
    225
  bridge keepers of, 197
  Hamlin telegram to, 226
  leak to newspaper by, 225
  Philadelphia meeting with Judd and
    Pinkerton, 228–31
  Pinkerton hired by, 93, 142
  Pinkerton letter to, 98–99
  Pinkerton meeting in Philadelphia,
    224–25
  Pinkerton methods and, 328–29
  Pinkerton's safe arrival message to, 294
  Warne involvement in PW&B case, 98, 99,
    104
  whitewashed bridges of, 198–99, 309
Female Detective Bureau, 99
female detectives, 47–50, 99. *See also* Lawton,
  Hattie; Warne, Kate
Fergus, Robert, 21, 26, 41
Ferrandini, Cypriano, 185
  assassination intention of, 142, 179
  Davies's joining band of, 190–93, *191*
  government spies and, 189, 216
  Pinkerton and, 140–42, 153, 154–57,
    179
  punishment escaped by, 312
  reason for not arresting, 312–13
  return and death of, 312
  select committee summons of, 141
Fillmore, Millard, 182, 183
flagmen, 160
flag-raising ceremony, in Philadelphia, 109,
  247–48
Fort Moultrie, 87
Fort Sumter, 100, 312
Fort Warren prison, 311
Fountain Hotel, 216
Fox River, 28–29
Franciscus, George C., 272–73, 275

fugitives
    Brown, J., as, 61
    Underground Railroad name for, 28
Fugitive Slave Act, 5, 61

Garman, Daniel, 272, 273, 274
Gettysburg, 114
Gittings, John S., 293
Glasgow Universal Suffrage Association, 21
Gould, Charles, 241
Great Western Railroad time card, *116*
Greeley, Horace, 13, 16, 67, 203
    Lincoln's election reported by, 72
    Lincoln's safety concern of, 90
    pro-Lincoln influence of, 174
    threat to Lincoln's life reported by,
        174–75
    war spirit of, 310
    Washington route concerns of, 90
Greenhow, Rose O'Neal, 314
grenade rumor, 162–63

habeas corpus suspension, 309–10, 329
half horse half alligator, 52, 61
Hamlin, Hannibal, 14, 213
    Felton telegrammed by, 226
    on train through Baltimore, 243
Hammond, C. G., 63
Hanscom, Simon, 255, 295
Harper's Ferry raid, 67
Harper's Weekly, 303
Harrisburg
    arrangements made in, 272–73
    departure from, 262–63, 272–73
    detour, 245, 250–55
    itinerary, 248
    Judd's emergency meeting in, 249, 250–53
    speech in, 250
    Sumner left behind in, 254–55
Harrisburg-Philadelphia railroad plans,
    270–72
hate mail, 82–83, 86
Havre de Grace, 97, 100, 198
Hay, John Milton, 1, 5, 149, 249, 265, 267,
    297
    McClellan viewed by, 315
    Nicolay and, 136, *136*
Hazzard, George, 227, 240, 252
    Maryland plan of, 115–18

Herndon, William, 3, 66, 89, 112
    Lincoln's parting meeting with, 107–8
    Pinkerton and, 322–23
Hicks, Thomas H., 308
    bridge tactics and, 309
    partisan balancing dilemma of, 127–29,
        139, 202
    testifying before select committee, 129–30
    treason charges avoided by, 311
    warning letter received by, 129
Hillard, Otis K., 119–21, 122, 126, 229
    on Baltimore military escort issue, 177
    Davies in room with Hughes, A., and,
        123–24
    Davies payment to, 188–89
    government spies complaint of, 189, 216
    in Lamon's account, 325
    on Lincoln's route to Washington, 124–25
    Pinkerton on, 186–87
    response to Lincoln's change of plans,
        260–62
    vote count response of, 168
History and Evidence of the Passage of
    Abraham Lincoln from Harrisburg, Pa.,
    to Washington, D.C., on the 22nd and
    23rd of February, 1861 (Pinkerton),
    320–22, 326–27
House Divided speech, 66, 80
Howard, Joseph, 235–36, 255–56
Hunt, Henry, 25, 29–32, 34
Hunter, David, 113, 135, 202, 227, 251
    injuries in Buffalo, 182–83
    warning letter from, 84–85
Hutchinson, John H., Pinkerton as
    stockbroker named, 103, 139, 154, 164,
    227–28, 236, 294

Illinois Central Railroad, 47, 63, 64, 65,
    234–35
Illinois conventions, 69
inaugural address
    conclusion, 15–16
    war and, 300
    writing and deliberation of, 12–13
inaugural journey. *See also* Baltimore;
    Baltimore plan, for revised itinerary;
    itinerary, for inaugural journey; Lincoln
    Special; speeches
    Albany departure change, 202

inaugural journey (*continued*)
  alcohol drinking on, 145–46
  announced details of, 108
  artillery displays during, 173–74
  Astor House dinner, 213
  Buffalo pandemonium, 182–83
  carpetbag containing speech lost on, 152
  crowds at stops on, 114, *146,* 146–49, 150,
    202–3, 227
  dangers on, 152–53
  Decatur unexpected stop on, 147–48
  departure for Washington, 253–55
  grenade in hotel story, 162–63
  handshaking ordeals, 149, 162
  Harrisburg, 245, 248, 250–55, 262–63,
    272–73
  height contest with coal-heaver, 171
  Hillard on coded tracking system, 125
  Indianapolis stop and departure, 159–60
  Kentucky stop canceled, 161–62
  Lincoln's companions on, 135
  Lincoln's jokes during, 171, 279, 282
  Lincoln's ticket for, *1*
  Lincoln's wife traveling separately, 134–35
  Lincoln's young sons' behavior on, 160–61
  Maryland and, 115–18, 201–2
  military escort issue, 126–27, 177, 223–24,
    312
  New Jersey stop on, 221–23
  in New York City, 211–14
  planning, 108
  Springfield departure, 87–88, 133–37,
    146
  stops and invitations, 115
  time card for first day, *116*
  Washington arrival and first day, 286–92,
    297–98
  Washington companion, 252–53, 254
  Washington G., and, 109
  Wood's timetable, 110–11, 113, 114–15,
    135, 148–49, 199, 202
inaugural journey, of Davis, J., 181–82
inauguration
  cartoon on, 15
  ceremonies, *9*
  Inaugural Procession of 1861, *11*
  Lincoln's wait, 72–73
  press in days before, 11
  rumor and fears on, 13

secessionist plan to prevent, 104–5
secessionists and, 97
security, 9–10, 14
independent committee of safety, 285
Indianapolis, 159–60
Italian assassins, 263–64
itinerary, for inaugural journey, 109–11, 173
  early Albany departure, 202
  Harrisburg-Baltimore, 248
  Hazzard's plan for Maryland, 115–18
  need to change, 223, 230–31
  as publicized, 217–18
  superintendent of arrangements, 110–11,
    113, 135, 148–49, 199, 321
  Washington, G., birthday figured into,
    109
  Washington route, 89–90, 105, 124–25

Jackson, James W., 305
Johnson, Waldo P., 260
Jones, John, 62
Jones, Thomas D. (sculptor), 79–82
Juárez, Benito, 141
Judd, Norman, 113, 196, 297
  Burns, G. H., giving Pinkerton's message
    to, 227–28
  day before Baltimore stop, 246
  emergency disclosure meeting called by,
    249, 250–53
  Felton-Pinkerton meeting in Philadelphia,
    228–31
  Lincoln meeting with Pinkerton and,
    234–37
  Lincoln's response impressing, 240
  Pinkerton's messages to, 142–43, 161,
    163–65, 208–9, 214, 227–28
  Pinkerton's ten for one telegram to, 208–9,
    214
  Scott, William H., and, 163, 164–65
  Sumner and, 254–55
  telegrams to, 142–43, 208–9, 214
  train missed by, 202
  Warne and, 205–9

Kane, George P., *175,* 261
  arrest of Brown and, 310–11
  Baltimore riot and, 308
  danger denied by, 292
  debate over role of, 178, 293–94

elected mayor, 313
Kennedy letter to, 321
Kennedy's mistrust of, 215
Lincoln's family and, 292–93
Pinkerton's doubts about, 177–79, 187, 229
police support denied by, 175–76, 177, 201
as rabid rebel, 179
war spirit of, 309
Kansas, 60
Kansas-Nebraska Act, 66
Kennedy, John (police superintendent), 202–3, 213, 238–39
credit for saving president's life sought by, 320–21
Kane mistrusted by, 215
Lincoln's appreciation of, 214–15
suspected agents of, 296–97
Washington commission of, 214–15
Kenney, H. F., 275–76
Kentucky stop cancellation, 161–62

Lamon, Ward Hill (Lincoln's particular friend), 134, 152–53, 249, 277–78, 326
book written by, 323–24
crowds handled by, 114, *146*, 148, 150, 170
Harrisburg-Philadelphia leg of trip, 272
on Hillard, 325
indiscretion with reporter, 295
Lincoln assassination and, 322
as Lincoln's companion to Washington, 252–53, 254
Pinkerton indicted by, 294–96
Pinkerton's alias disregarded by, 236, 294
Pinkerton's memoirs and, 331
Pinkerton's secrecy compromised by, 297
whiskey and music provided by, 145–46
wife's altering of words in new volume of, 330
Lawton, Hattie (female detective), 99, 153
Webster and, 153, 280
Lee, Robert E., 67
letters, to Lincoln
advice to grow beard in, 81
Hunter's letter of warning, 84–85
threatening, 81–82
Lewis, Pryce, 45, 316

The Life of Abraham Lincoln (Lamon), 323–24
Lincoln, Abraham. *See also* assassination conspiracy; Baltimore plan, for revised itinerary; inaugural journey; inauguration; Lincoln, Robert; speeches
anonymous lady's letter of warning to, 244–45
assassination conspiracy and, 2, 240
assassination of, 318, 322
Baltimore plan hurting prestige of, 267
in Baltimore with Pinkerton, 282–83
beard of, 81
bodyguards, 113–14, 145, 252
in Brady's studio, *289*
Brown, G., viewed by, 60
Buchanan and, 10–12, 14
calm demeanor of, 280
calm response to news of conspiracy, 240
Cartwright and, 37
cash rewards for murder of, 174–75
children of, 160–61
cigar given to engineer Black by, 274
Davis, J., and, 137–38, 182
debates between Douglas and, 65–66, 86
disguise of, 254, 264–66
Douglas as opponent of, 71
electoral votes for, 165, 170–71
farewell remarks at Springfield, 137, 146
flight of, *303,* 319–20
Greeley and, 72, 90, 174–75
habeas corpus suspended by, 309–10
hate mail and threats received by, 82–83, 86
Herndon meeting with, 107–8
on Hicks's dilemma, 128–29
Hillard and, 124–25, 260–62
inaugural train ticket, *1*
inaugural trip toll on, 170
on Inauguration Day, 11, 13, 14, 72–73
inauguration wait of, 72–73
jokes of, 171, 182, 279, 282
in Judd's disclosure meeting, 250–53
Kane's arrangements for family in Baltimore, 292–93
Kennedy, J., and, 214–15
letter from Kane in prison, 310–11
McClellan and, 64–65
as Nature's orator, 67

Lincoln, Abraham (*continued*)
  nomination and election of, 69–72, 102
  Nuts code name for, 245, 275, 294
  particular friend of, 145–46
  Peace Convention delegates meeting,
    298–99
  personal secretary of, 1
  pig-tail whistle received by, 81–82
  Pinkerton, McClernand and, *257*
  Pinkerton meeting with over Lamon, 296
  Pinkerton summoned by, 301
  Pinkerton-Judd meeting, 234–37
  Pinkerton's carriage ride with, 275–78
  Pinkerton's offer of service to, 300–301
  posing for sculptor, 79–82
  as pressured to leave Springfield, 87–88
  as rail splitter, 11, 69, 71, 81, 136, 168,
    274
  railroad work of, 64–65, 71
  Scott, W., visited by, 289–90
  separate departure of wife, 134–35
  Seward, F., questioned by, 239–40
  Seward, W. H., and, 289
  slavery policy of, 86
  on Southern states and Republicans,
    66–67
  Southern votes for, 96
  Springfield departure of, 87–88, 133–37,
    146
  Springfield last days, 107–9
  State House policy of, 86
  on train to Baltimore, 279–83
  as Warne's invalid brother, 272, 278,
    281
  warnings received by, 238–40
  warnings received in Springfield, 240–41
  Washington arrival and first day, 286–92,
    297–98
  Washington departure of, 89–90, 105,
    124–25
  at Willard's Hotel, 10
Lincoln, Mary Todd, 134–35
  Baltimore trip, differing versions of,
    290–92
  itinerary change told to, 253
  on Lincoln Special, 147
Lincoln, Robert (son), 135–36, 159
  carpetbag incident, 152
  in Cincinnati, 165

Lincoln family in 1861, *161*
Lincoln Special. *See also* inaugural journey
  Albany arrival of, 200
  at Buffalo, New York, 182–83
  Cincinnati, 162–65
  in Cleveland, 173
  in Columbus, 169–71
  danger concerns and, 13
  Lincoln, M., on, 147
  Philadelphia arrival of, 226
  Philadelphia departure, 249
  Pittsburgh stop, 171–72
  southern route of, 201–2
  Westfield, New York, 174
Lincoln-Douglas debates, 65–66, 86
Louisville Journal, 151
Luckett, James, 139–42, 296, 323
Lyceum Theatre, 21

Mackintosh, James, 72
Marcy, Randolph, 63
Maroney, Mrs., 53
Maroney, Nathan, 50–58
Maroney case, 50–58
Marx, Karl, 21
Maryland, 309
  arrests made in, 329
  governor's dilemma over secession of,
    127–29, 139, 202
  Hazzard's plan for inaugural journey
    through, 115–18
  importance of, 96
  lack of welcome in, 115–18, 201–2
  state song, 6, 313
  struggle to keep, 313
  vote count response in, 168
A Masked Ball, 213–14
Mather, Thomas, 89
McAuley, William, 20
McClellan, George Brinton, 63, 288
  Lincoln and, 64–65
  Pinkerton's reports to, 314–15
McClernand, John A., *257*
McClure, Alexander K., 128–29, 253, 319
McKenna, James, 328
McParland, James, 328
military. *See also* security, inaugural journey
  Felton's bridge keepers, 196
  at inauguration, 9–10, 14

Palmetto Guard secret, 120, 124
  Webster's membership in local, 153–54
military escort, 126–27
  Baltimore, 177, 312
  Philadelphia, 223–24
Mississippi secession, 138
mob town image, of Baltimore, 101–2,
  175
Molly Maguires, 327–28
Montgomery stop, 182
Morgan, Edwin, 200, 201
Mount Vernon Place, 293
Mr. H., 184, 186, 285

Napoléon III, 156, 157
Narrative of the Life of Frederick Douglass,
  An American Slave (Douglass), 27
Nast, Thomas, 15
National Volunteers, 124, 126, 128, 141
  ballot lots and, 189
New Jersey, 221–23
New York, Buffalo, 182–83
New York City, 214
  ambivalent sentiments in, 203
  Astor House dinner in, 213
  Lincoln's City Hall speech, 211–13
  security and crowd control, 202–3
New York Herald, 12, 255
  on Lincoln's wife, 134
New York Times, 3, 14, 255
  assassination plans outlined in, 235–36
  Decatur incident revised in, 147
  Kennedy's article in, 320–21
  Maroney case and, 52
New York World, 10, 297
Newport Rising, 18–19
New-York Tribune, 13
Nicolay, John, 5, 84, 90, 115, 146, 170
  on crowds during journey, 150
  Hay and, 136, *136*
  McClellan viewed by, 315
  secret plan and, 249
North American, 225
Northern Democratic Association, 21
Nuts, Pinkerton's code name for Lincoln,
  245, 275, 294

O'Laughlen, Michael, 319
Old Independence Hall, 245–47

Operations in Baltimore, closing of, 301
operatives. *See* detectives, Pinkerton
Orsini, Felice, 141, 156, 157, 186
  Ruscelli's reference to, 185

Palmetto Guard, 120, 124
Peace Convention, in Washington, 138, 183,
  259–60
  Lincoln meeting with delegates of, 298–99
Pennsylvania Railroad, 272, 275
People's Charter of 1838, 17–18
Perrymansville, 197–98
personal secretary, 1
Philadelphia, 214
  arrival in, 226
  boarding Baltimore-bound train in,
    278–79
  departure from, 249
  flag-raising ceremony in, 109, 247–48
  Judd-Felton-Pinkerton meeting in, 228–31
  military escort, 223–24
  Pinkerton in, 223–31, 233–37, 245–46,
    274–76
  plans for Harrisburg to, 270–72
  security, 227
  speech in, 231, 247–48
  train ride to, 273–74
Philadelphia, Wilmington, and Baltimore
    Railroad (PW&B)
  Brown, G., orders to obstruct and burn,
    308–9
  carriage ride to, 275–78
  danger points on, 280
  decoys on, 270, 271–72
  Harrisbug-Philadelphia plan, 270–72
  letter from employee of, 129
  Pinkerton hired to protect, 95–99
  plan to destroy, 92, 95, 225
  protection for, 95–99
  Warne in Felton-PW&B case, 98, 99, 104
  Washington journey and, 90
pig-tail whistle, 81–82
pilot engines, 110
Pinkerton, Allan ("The Eye"), *7*, 16, 219, *257*
  agency opened by, 41–46
  as Allen, E. J., 270, 288–89, 318
  anger at Felton for news leak, 225
  assassination conspiracy discovered by, 2,
    105

Pinkerton, Allan (*continued*)
  as atheist, 37–38
  in Baltimore, 100–101, 103, 118, 296–97
  Baltimore episode viewed in later years by, 328
  Baltimore plan of, 4, 245–46, 281–83
  Baltimore return of, 296–97
  on Baltimore riot, 311
  in Baltimore with Lincoln, 282–83
  birth and childhood of, 19–20
  Brown, J., execution and, 67
  Brown, J., helped by, 59–63
  career turning point for, 29–30
  on carriage ride with Lincoln, 275–78
  character and habits of, 27
  in Chartist movement, 17–19, 21, 22
  in Chicago, 26
  as chief of intelligence, 314
  children of, 26, 39, 75
  Chittenden's account and, 187
  congressman punched by, 286–87
  contradictions and legacy of, 5–6
  as cooper (barrel maker), 20–21, 26, 28
  counterfeiting case taken by, 30–35
  courtship and wedding of, 21–23
  Craig case, 30–35
  criminals and, 74
  criticism of, 6
  on Davies in Baltimore, 119, 188
  death of Warne and Webster impact on, 317–18
  as deputy sheriff, 38–39
  detained reporter story of, 255–56
  detective career start, 25–35, 41–46
  detective role viewed by, 43
  detectives on PW&B protection case, 98, 99–100
  discussion with Felton on methods used by, 328–29
  disguises of, 103, 139, 154, 164, 227–28, 236, 270, 288–89, 294, 318
  on election campaign of 1860, 71
  employees of, 43–45
  enemy troop estimates of, 314–15
  ethical guidelines for employees, 43
  exhaustion and illness of, 245, 278
  Felton's hiring of, 93, 142
  female detectives hired by, 47–50
  Ferrandini and, 140–42, 153, 154–57, 179

  gunshot wound and recovery, 39–40
  Herndon and, 322–23
  Hillard targeted by, 120
  on Hillard's sentiments, 186–87
  home office destroyed in fire, 327
  investigations by Kennedy and, 216, 249
  Kane doubted by, 177–79, 187, 229
  Kennedy and, 321
  on labor unrest, 19
  Lamon and, 236, 277–78, 294–96, 297, 331
  Lamon's disregard for alias of, 236, 294
  Lamon's indictment of, 322–26
  letter to Felton, 98–99
  Lincoln's assassination news received by, 318
  Lincoln's code name used by, 245, 275, 295
  Lincoln's response impressing, 240
  Lincoln's summons of, 301
  Lincoln's verdict and, 241
  Luckett and, 139–42
  McClellan and, 63, 64
  meeting with Felton, 224–25
  meeting with Lincoln, 234–37
  memoirs published by, 330–31
  messages to Judd, 142–43, 161, 163–65, 208–9, 214, 227–28
  methods of, 6
  Molly Maguires and, 327–28
  money temptation moment, 34–35
  Northern Democratic Association started by, 21
  offer of service to Lincoln from, 300–301
  pamphlet written by, 320–22, 326–27
  in Philadelphia, 223–31, 233–37, 245–46, 274–76
  Philadelphia meeting with Judd and Felton, 228–31
  Plums and Nuts arrival message, 294
  postal robbery case solved by, 40
  PW&B railroad protection focus, 95–99
  reputation after Maroney case, 58
  safe arrival message to Felton, 294
  secrecy imperative, 206, 269–70, 297
  secret revised itinerary for Lincoln, 248–49
  Seward, W. H., disagreement with, 288
  social reform passion of, *20–21*
  stroke suffered by, 327

telegraph communication cipher system of,
163–64
ten for one telegram, 208–9, 214
undercover methods of, 40
Underground Railroad work of, 27–28,
59–63
violence viewed by, 68
work-home gulf, 73
Pinkerton, Joan, 21–23, 26–27
at Burns, R., celebration, 74–75
Cook County move and, 39
singing of, 74–75
Underground Railroad and, 61–62
Pinkerton's National Detective Agency
Chicago fire destroying home office, 327
logo of, *46*
Maroney case, 50–58
success of, 42, 47
Warne hired by, 47–49
year of opening, 41–42
Pittsburgh, 171–72
Plug-Uglies, 13, 260
police
Kane denial of support from, 175–76, 177,
201
Kennedy's New York City, 202–3, 213
Pope, John, 113, 227, 249, 251
postal robbery case, 40
Pottawatomie Massacre, 60
The President's Inaugural (cartoon), 15
presidents of road, 28
press. *See also specific newspapers*
Baltimore plan in, 263, 266–67
Baltimore plot and, 225
editorial prior to Lincoln's arrival in
Baltimore, 244
Prime, Irenaeus, 212–13
Prince of Rails, 136
prison, Fort Warren, 310–11
private eye, 2
prostitution, Baltimore house of, 119, 120, 122
PW&B. *See* Philadelphia, Wilmington, and
Baltimore Railroad

rail splitter, 11, 69, 71, 81, 136, 168, 274
railroad. *See also* Philadelphia, Wilmington,
and Baltimore Railroad
Baltimore, 58
Lincoln's work on, 64–65, 71

Pennsylvania, 272, 275
plan to attack Felton's, 92, 95, 197–98, 225
time card, *116*
Washington journey concerns about, 90
railway executives, 90, 91
Randall, James Ryder, 313
Ray, D. E., 86
Red River expedition, 63
reporters
Lamon's indiscretion with, 295
Pinkerton detained, 255–56
Republican National Committee, 200
Republican National Convention of 1860, 69
Republican State Convention, 102
Republicans
Baltimore procession staged by, 176
Lincoln's address to, 66–67
resignation, supporters asking for Lincoln's,
84
Rives, William Cabell, 299
robberies
Adams Express Company, 50–51, 206
postal, 40
train, 51, 96, 206
robber barons, 328
Ross, Thomas, 146, 148
Ruscelli (barber), Ferrandini as, 185

Sampson, Thomas, 215–17, 296–97
Sanford, Edward S., 50, 56, 196, 226
Warne and, 206–8
Sauganash Hotel, 32, 34, 70
Scharf, John Thomas, 6, 326
Scott, William H. (Pinkerton detective), 218,
249
Judd and, 163, 164–65
Scott, Winfield, 6, 14, 89, 92
Butler and, 310
electoral count safety overseen by, 166
Lincoln's visit to, 289–90
telegram to Lincoln's wife, 134
Scully, John, 45, 316
sculptor, Lincoln's posing for, 79–82
secession, 3
Felton's PW&B and, 96
Hicks's dilemma regarding Maryland,
127–29, 139, 202
Mississippi, 138
South Carolina, 86–87, 119

secessionists, 86
  assassination conspiracy and, 97
  Baltimore, 101, 104–5, 106, 312
  on electoral vote count day, 167–68
  Lewis and Scully as ardent, 316
  Lincoln inauguration and, 97
  military escort opposed by, 312
  plan to prevent inauguration, 104–5
security, inaugural journey. *See also* military;
    military escort
  artillery displays, 173–74
  bodyguards appointed for, 113–14, 145,
    252
  Ellsworth as point man for, 111–13, *112*
  flagmen, 160
  Kane refusing police support in Baltimore,
    175–76, 177, 201
  Kennedy's New York City police, 202–3,
    213
  military entourage, 113, 160
  Philadelphia, 227
  presidents of road, 28
Seddon, James A., 260
select committee
  Baltimore plot inquiry by, 126–27,
    129–30, 131
  Ferrandini summoned by, 141
  Hicks's testimony before, 129–30
  official report by, 131
Seward, Frederick, 238, 249, 252
  Lincoln's questions to, 239–40
  warning of, 277
Seward, William H., 13, 70, 87, 218–19
  assassination plot claims by, 324–25
  Lincoln and, 289
  Pinkerton disagreement with, 288
  Washburne and, 285–86, 287
Sherwood, Howell, 121–22
Shoemaker, Samuel, 234
slavery, 27
  Fugitive Slave Act, 5, 61
  Lincoln's policy on, 86
  McClellan's views on, 64
Snethen, Worthington G., 102, 201, 319
South Carolina secession, 86–87, 119
Southern Commercial Convention, 52
Southern Confederacy, 139
Southern patriots, Ferrandini's band of,
    190–93

southern route, of Lincoln Special, 201–2
southern states
  votes for Lincoln, 96
  Washington takeover by, 91–92, 128
Spafford, Carrie, 112
speeches
  artificial crisis, 199
  Bates House, 151
  in Cleveland, 173
  demands for, 200–201
  in Harrisburg, 250
  House Divided, 66, 80
  Lincoln's trick for avoiding, 199
  lost carpetbag containing, 152
  New Jersey, 222–23
  New York City Hall, 211–13
  at Old Independence Hall, 245–47
  in Philadelphia, 231, 247–48
  in Pittsburgh, 172
  relaxed manner during, 199–200
  Wood, F. W., moralizing, 212
spies, 296–97, 330–31
  arrest of Union, 316
  government, 189, 216
  parallel tracks of Pinkerton and
    government, 216, 249
Springfield
  Lincoln urged to leave early from, 87–88
  Lincoln's departure from, 133–37, 146
  Lincoln's last days in, 107–9
  warnings received by Lincoln in, 240–41
The Spy of the Rebellion (Pinkerton), 330–31
Stanton, Edwin, 318
State House policy, 86
Stearns, George, 129, 130
Stone, Charles P., 215, 217–18, 238–39
Sumner, Edwin Vose ("Bullhead"), 253, 262
  as left behind in Harrisburg, 254–55
Superintendent of Arrangements, 110–11,
    113, 135, 148–49, 199
  Kennedy letter to, 321
  timetable made by, 110–11, 113, 114–15,
    135, 148–49, 199, 202
Surratt, Mary, 329

Taney, Roger B., 16
telegraph communications, 134, 196, 207,
    226, 273
  electoral vote results sent through, 170–71

Pinkerton's telegrams to Judd, 142–43, 208–9, 214
word-substitution ciphers in, 163–64
Thirteenth Amendment, 300
time card, Great Western Railroad, *116*
Times, 13
timetable, Wood's, 110–11, 113, 114–15, 135, 148–49, 199, 202
train robberies, 51, 96, 206
Travis, Annette, 119, 120, 123
troops
in Alexandria, 303
Pinkerton's estimate of enemy, 314–15
sent to Baltimore, 306–8
Tyler, John, 138

undercover work, 153–54. *See also* disguises; *specific detectives*
alcohol in, 121, 328–29
Pinkerton's methods, 40
Walling's dispatch of detectives, 215
Underground Railroad
fugitives in, 28
name of, 27
Pinkerton's wife assisting, 61–62
Pinkerton's work on, 27–28, 59–63
terminology and positions in, 28
Union. *See also* Coopers' Union; secession
arrested spies of, 316
House Divided speech, 66, 80
Kansas entry debate, 60
sentiment toward maintaining, 3
United States Postal Service, 50

Verdi, Giuseppe, 213–14
Vidocq, Eugène-François, 44
Villard, Henry, 82, 86, 89, 110, 146, 160
on Lincoln's wife separate departure, 134–35
Vincent, Henry, 18
violence, 68
1856 election, 101–2
vote count. *See* electoral votes

Wallace, William S., 136
Walling, George, W., 214–15
war
Baltimore spirit of, 309–10
inaugural address and, 300

Warne, Kate
Astor House meetings of, 204–8
Baltimore plan for, 214
death of, 317
in Felton-PW&B case, 98, 99, 104
Judd and, 205–9
Judd and Sanford messages given to, 196
Lincoln as invalid brother of, 272, 278, 281
in Maroney case, 50–58
Mrs. Barley disguise of, 104, 153, 195–96
on Pinkerton's exhaustion, 245, 278
Pinkerton's hiring of, 47–49
PW&B decoy of, 271–72
Sanford and, 206–8
secrecy imperative for, 208
as superintendent, 50
Webster's message sewn in by, 300
Washburne, Elihu B., 72, 319–20
Pinkerton's punching of, 286–87
Seward, W., and, 285–86, 287
Washington. *See also* inaugural journey
Baltimore plot to capture, 85, 92, 104–5, 122–31
Brady studio in, *289*
departure for, 105, 253–55
detectives from, 215–17, 296–97
itinerary, 89–90, 105, 124–25
Kennedy commissioned by, 214–15
Lincoln's arrival and first day in, 286–92, 297–98
Lincoln's companion for trip to, 252–53, 254
Lincoln's departure from, 89–90, 105, 124–25
Peace Convention in, 138, 183, 259–60, 298–99
railroad concerns, 90
select committee in, 126–27, 129–30, 131, 141
southern takeover of, plan for, 91–92, 128
troops sent to Baltimore from, 306–8
Washington, George, 109
Webster, Timothy (Pinkerton detective)
death of, 315–17
Kennedy's agents aided by, 297
Lawton and, 153, 280
message from Pinkerton to Lincoln via, 300

Webster, Timothy (*continued*)
  in Perrymansville, 197–98
  Pinkerton's praise of, 320
  plot overheard by, 197–98
  undercover membership in local military,
    153–54
Weed, Thurlow, 70
Western Citizen, 37, 38
Westfield, New York, 174
whistle, pig-tail, 81–82
White, John H. (Pinkerton operative), 45,
  54–57
White House
  Confederate flag in view of, 303, 304–5
  unannounced call at, 289
whitewashed bridges, 198–99, 309
Whitman, Walt, 203–4

Whitney, Henry Clay, 82
Wide Awakes, 113
Wigwam, 70
Willard's Hotel, 10, 259, 270, 287
Williams, Charles, 121–22
Wisner, M. L. (pastor), 37–38
Wood, Fernando, 203, 211–12
Wood, William S. (Superintendent of
    Arrangements), 229
  Kennedy letter to, 321
  timetables of, 110–11, 113, 114–15, 135,
    148–49, 199, 202
Wynne, Andrew, 273, 320

Yates, Richard, 148

Zouave Cadets, 111, 112, *112,* 135

ROUTE *of* PRESIDENT-ELECT LINCOLN'S INAUGURAL TRAIN
1861

MICHIGAN

WISCONSIN

CLEVELAND, OH
February 15, 1861

ILLINOIS

INDIANA

COLUMBUS, OH
February 13, 1861

SPRINGFIELD, IL
February 11, 1861

OHIO

BEGIN

INDIANAPOLIS, IN
February 11, 1861

CINCINNATI, OH
February 12, 1861

MISSOURI

KENTUCKY

TENN.